CORVETTE V8
OWNERS HANDBOOK

1955-1962

Published by
FLOYD CLYMER PUBLICATIONS
*World's Largest Publisher of Books Relating to
Automobile, Motorcycles, Motor Racing, and Americana*
222 NO. VIRGIL AVENUE, LOS ANGELES , CALIF. 90004

INTRODUCTION

Welcome to the world of digital publishing ~ the book you now hold in your hand, while unchanged from the original edition, was printed using the latest state of the art digital technology. The advent of print-on-demand has forever changed the publishing process, never has information been so accessible and it is our hope that this book serves your informational needs for years to come. If this is your first exposure to digital publishing, we hope that you are pleased with the results. Many more titles of interest to the classic automobile and motorcycle enthusiast, collector and restorer are available via our website at www.VelocePress.com. We hope that you find this title as interesting as we do.

NOTE FROM THE PUBLISHER

The information presented is true and complete to the best of our knowledge. All recommendations are made without any guarantees on the part of the author or the publisher, who also disclaim all liability incurred with the use of this information.

TRADEMARKS

We recognize that some words, model names and designations, for example, mentioned herein are the property of the trademark holder. We use them for identification purposes only. This is not an official publication.

INFORMATION ON THE USE OF THIS PUBLICATION

This manual is an invaluable resource for those interested in performing their own maintenance. However, in today's information age we are constantly subject to changes in common practice, new technology, availability of improved materials and increased awareness of chemical toxicity. As such, it is advised that the user consult with an experienced professional prior to undertaking any procedure described herein. While every care has been taken to ensure correctness of information, it is obviously not possible to guarantee complete freedom from errors or omissions or to accept liability arising from such errors or omissions. Therefore, any individual that uses the information contained within, or elects to perform or participate in do-it-yourself repairs or modifications acknowledges that there is a risk factor involved and that the publisher or its associates cannot be held responsible for personal injury or property damage resulting from the use of the information or the outcome of such procedures.

WARNING!

One final word of advice, this publication is intended to be used as a reference guide, and when in doubt the reader should consult with a qualified technician.

Contents

Engine Tune Up	1
Trouble Shooting	53
Electrical Data	62
Wiring Diagram	63
Engine Repairs	64
Fuel Pump	108
Cooling System	109
Powerglide	114
Rear Axle	116
Brakes	119
Wheels & Tires	132
Body Service	139
Folding Top & Hard Top	151
Body Repairs & Painting	172
Paint Chart	191
Regular Production Options	192
Engines!	201
Four Speed Transmission	202
Positraction Rear Axle	225
Fuel Injection	237
Increasing Power & Performance	327

Engine Tune Up

Although the number of engine options and fuel induction arrangements to be encountered in Corvettes sometimes seems to cloak the car in a cloud of mystery, the tuneup procedures are straight forward and basically uncomplicated. The engines deliver peak performance for street and non-racing activities when the factory admonitions are heeded absolutely. This applies to both carbureted and fuel-injected models.

Experience has proven that if instruments are available the tune up and check-out processes can be made far more accurate and infinitely quicker. If they are not at hand, and, normally few enthusiasts will be in possession of a dwell-angle meter, for instance, the ordinary, time-honored mechanical methods are perfectly satisfactory. Try, of course, to strive for the most accurate measurements you can manage. The chassis dynamometer, which is now becoming a fixture in more and more shops, is the final authority. "Power-tuning" on one of these arbiters will get the last ounce of output from an engine and its dial is a far more sensitive indicator than the seat of one's pants.

It is felt that the average owner will leave major repairs in the hands of a capable mechanic—and preferably a Chevrolet-trained man—but it is also recognized that this same owner will often prefer to handle minor points of service and tuning himself, thus deriving greater pleasure and satisfaction from the ownership of his fine car. In addition, there are always emergency situations wherein a thorough knowledge of the vehicle can save hours of time, many dollars, or even the owner's life. One can never be too well acquainted with his automobile in this regard. Therefore we have prepared this handbook with one thought in mind: To give the Corvette owner as thorough a grasp of the most necessary details as possible without going into the step-by-step reconditioning techniques found in shop manuals.

In preparing this volume we have not hesitated to quote liberally and directly from Chevrolet's factory-supplied material utilized by Corvette mechanics all over the country. We have found it superior in every respect and knowing that it comes from such a complete facility for testing we have not failed to rely on it absolutely in the field. Using these factory-originated specifications and techniques will result in the best possible performance for the non-racing Corvette. The race-sharpened ideas and approaches recommended in the section Competition, are merely personal extensions and variations of these factory specs. They have been successful. Many other approaches have been tried, but in all cases the mechanics eventually return to factory-advised settings. So, beware the "expert" who can make your car go so much better than "stock."

Corvette has been close to the sports racing picture constantly and takes advantage of the field experimenting done by those in the **millieu**. A back-flow also takes place and it is not long before "speed secrets" are common knowledge. It may be over-stressing the point, but any far-out variation of the data supplied in this book is to be regarded with caution.

The pits . . . where proper tuning wins or loses races.

MECHANICAL CHECKS AND ADJUSTMENTS

The mechanical checks and adjustments described below are performed with the engine static. Except where noted, the engine may be at either room temperature or operating temperature.

1. REMOVE SPARK PLUGS

NOTE: On models equipped with radios, it will be necessary to remove the radio shielding for the tune-up procedure.

a. Remove any foreign matter from around spark plugs by blowing out with compressed air. Then loosen all plugs one turn.

b. Start engine and accelerate to 1000 RPM to blow out loosened carbon.

c. Stop engine and remove spark plugs. Clearing out carbon in this manner is important in preventing false compression readings due to chips of carbon being lodged under the valves.

TEST COMPRESSION

a. Remove air cleaner and block throttle (and choke on carburetor models) in wide open position. Several convenient tools are available to facilitate this operation.

b. Hook up starter remote control cable and insert compression gauge firmly in spark plug port, Fig. 1.

c/ Crank engine through at least four compression strokes to obtain highest possible reading.

d. Check and record compression of each cylinder. Compression should read as indicated below and variation between highest and lowest reading cylinders should be less than 20 pounds.
1956 All Std. Prod. Models—160 lbs. (min.)
1956 With Field Installed Heavy Duty Camshaft—140 lbs. (min.)
1957-60 With hydraulic lifters—160 lbs. (min.)
1957-60 With solid lifters—140 lbs. (min.)

NOTE: Unusually high compression pressures can result from carbon deposits.

e. If one or more cylinders read low or uneven, inject about a tablespoon of engine oil on top of pistons in low reading cylinders. Crank engine several times and recheck compression.

If compression comes up but does not necessarily reach normal, rings are stuck or worn.

If compression does not improve much, valves are sticking or seating poorly.

If two adjacent cylinders indicate low compression and injecting oil does not increase compression, the cause may be a head gasket leak between the cylinders. Engine coolant in cylinders and/or oil could result from this defect.

The compression check is important because an engine with low or uneven compression cannot be tuned successfully to give

Fig. 1—Testing Compression

maximum owner satisfaction. Therefore, it is essential that improper compression be corrected before proceeding with an engine tune-up. If a weak cylinder cannot be located with the compression check, see Cylinder Balance Test.

3. CLEAN, SERVICE AND INSTALL SPARK PLUGS

a. Inspect each plug individually for badly worn electrodes, glazed, broken or blistered porcelains and replace plugs where necessary. Refer to spark plug diagnosis information.

b. Clean serviceable spark plugs thoroughly using an abrasive-type cleaner such as sand blast. File the electrodes flat and clean, Fig. 2.

NOTE: This electrode filing operation is very important and should be very carefully performed.

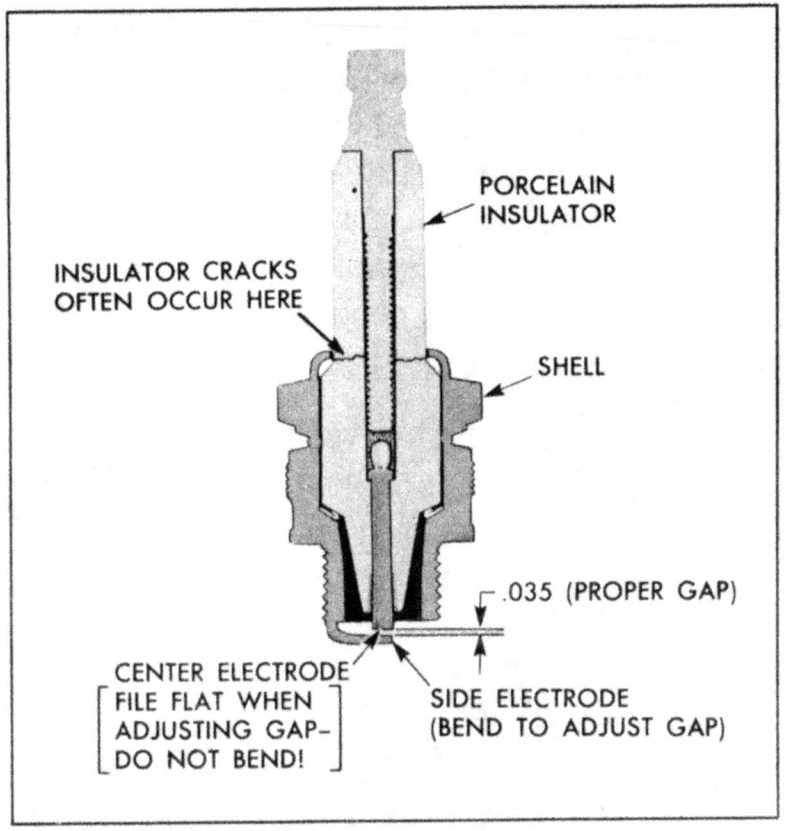

Fig. 2—Spark Plug Detail

c. Inspect each spark plug for make and heat range. See Spark Plug Recommendations. All plugs must be of the same make and number or heat range.

d. Adjust spark plug gaps to .035" using a round feeler gauge, Fig. 3.

CAUTION: Never bend the center electrode to adjust gap. Always adjust by bending ground or side electrode.

e. If available, test plugs with a spark plug tester.

f. Install spark plugs to the engine with new gaskets and tighten to 20-25 ft. lbs. torque, Fig. 4. Install ignition wires to proper plugs. Replace all brittle or damaged wires.

NOTE: Spark plug torque is extermely important on any engine used for extended high power output. If the spark plugs do not thread in easily by hand, the threads in the head should be cleaned out with a 14 MM x 1.25 SAE Spark Plug Tap. (Use grease on tap to catch chips.)

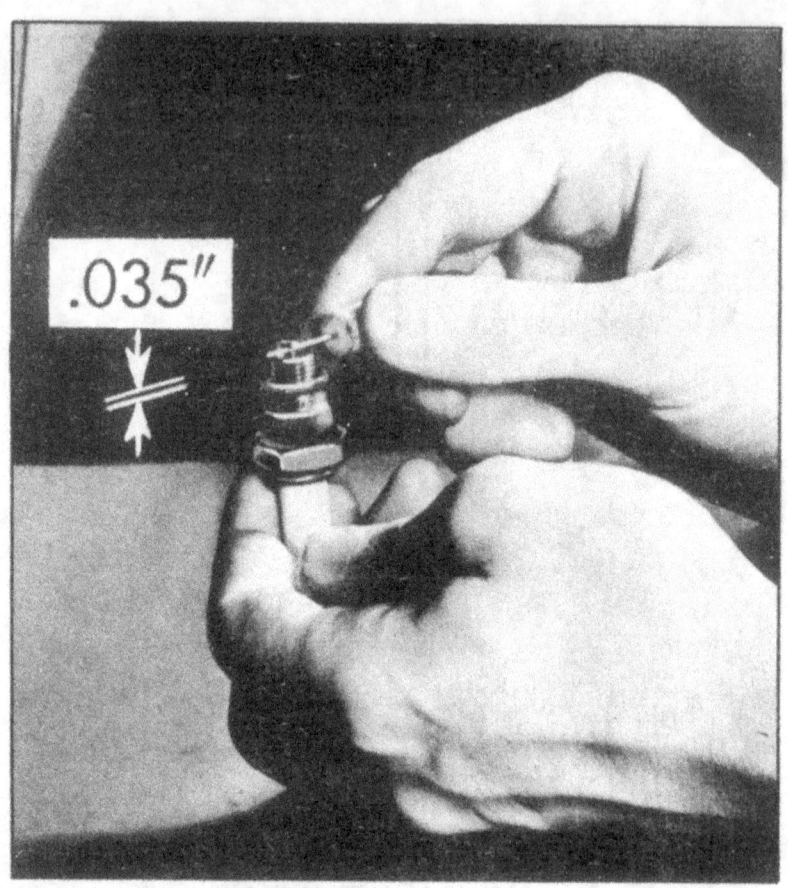

Spark Plug Diagnosis Summary

Spark plug life is governed to a large extent by operating conditions. To insure peak performance, spark plugs should be checked, cleaned and regapped every 5000 miles. Cleaning the plugs is especially important in high compression engines operating on high octane fuels. Cleaning and regapping will lower the voltage required to fire the plug.

Worn and dirty plugs may give satisfactory operation at idling speed, but under operating conditions they frequently fail. Faulty plugs are evident in a number of ways such as wasting gas, "missing," power loss, loss of speed, hard starting and general poor engine performance.

Spark plug failure, in addition to normal wear, may be due to dirty or leaded plugs, excessive gap or broken insulator.

Dirty or leaded plugs may be evidenced by black carbon deposits, or red, brown, yellow or blistered oxide deposits on the plugs. The black deposits are usually the result of slow speed driving and short runs where sufficent engine operating temperature is seldom reached. Worn pistons, rings, faulty ignition, excessive choking or over-rich carburetion and spark plugs which are too "cold" will also result in carbon deposits. Red, brown, and similar oxide deposits, a consequence of the use of leaded fuel, usually result in spark plug failure under severe operating conditions. The oxides have no adverse effect on plug operation as long as they remain in a powdery state. However, under high speed or hard pull, the powder oxide deposits melt and form a heavy glaze coating on the insulator which, when hot, acts as a good electrical conductor, allowing current to follow the deposits and short out the plug.

Excessive gap wear on plugs of low mileage or plugs with a grayish or white coating on the insulator or with insulators that have a blistered effect, usually indicates the engine is operating at speeds or loads that are consistently greater than normal or that a plug which is too "hot" is being used. In addition, electrode wear may be the result of plug overheating, caused by combustion gases

Fig. 4—Installing Spark Plug

leaking past the threads and gaskets, due to insufficient compression of the spark plug gaskets, or dirt under the gasket seat. Too lean carburetion will also result in excessive electrode wear.

The insulator of a normal operating plug of correct heat range will have a tan or very light brown color and be fairly smooth.

Broken insulators are usually the result of improper installation or carelessness when regapping the plug. Broken upper insulators usually result from a poor fitting wrench or an outside blow. The cracked insulator may not make itself evident immediately, but will as soon as oil or moisture penetrates the fracture. The fracture is usually just below the crimped part of the shell and may not be visible, see Fig. 2.

Broken lower insulators usually result from carelessness when regapping and generally are visible. In fairly rare instances, this type of a break may result from the plug operating too "hot" such as encountered in sustained periods of high speed operation or under extremely heavy loads. Spark plugs with broken insulators should always be replaced.

Improper installation is one of the greatest single causes of unsatisfactory spark plug performance. Improper installation is the result of one or more of the following practices:

Installation of plugs with insufficient torque to fully seat the gasket.

Installation of the plugs using excessive torque which changes gap settings.

Installation of plugs on used gaskets.

Installation of plugs on dirty gasket seats.

Failure to install plugs properly will cause them to operate at excessively high temperatures and result in reduced operating life under mild operation or complete destruction under severe operation where the intense heat cannot be dissipated rapidly enough.

Always use a new gasket and wipe seats in head clean: The gasket must be fully compressed on clean seats to complete heat transfer and provide a gas tight seal in the cylinder. For this reason as well as the necessity of maintaining correct plug gap, the use of correct troque is extremely important during installation.

1956-60 Corvette Engine Spark Plug Recommendations

1956-60 Corvette engines should not be equipped with AC-44-5 or 46-5 plugs due to spark plug boots not fitting these plugs properly.

In cases where units operating under city conditions continue to oil foul spark plugs, oil shedders should be installed on the valve stems. Shedders are recommended for all Corvette engines. Engines with hydraulic lifters must not be run in excess of 5000

**1956-60 Corvette Engine
Spark Plug Recommendations**

Cast Iron Cylinder Head	Driving	Aluminum Cylinder Head
AC-46	City Driving Only	AC44FF
AC-44	Town & Country	AC44FF
C-43 Comm.	Heavy Duty & High Output	AC42FF
C-42-1 Comm.	Extended & Extreme High Output	AC42FF

RPM. If shedders are to be installed on engines not so previously equipped, discard the 1/16" shim under each spring. Always use new valve stem seals.

4. SERVICE IGNITION SYSTEM

A. Replace brittle or damaged spark plug wires. Install all wires to proper spark plugs. Wire numbers formed on rubber support grommets indicate proper position.

NOTE: The location of the spark plug wires in their grommets is extremely important on these high output engines. Improperly located wiring can cause cross-fire on the plugs, particularly on over-run, and consequent major engine damage.

B. Tighten all ignition system connections.

C. Replace or repair any wires that are frayed, loose or damaged.

D. Remove distributor cap, clean cap and inspect for cracks, carbon tracks and burned or corroded terminals. Replace cap where necessary.

E. Clean rotor and inspect for damage or deterioration. Replace rotor where necessary.

F. Check the distributor centrifugal advance mechanism by turning the distributor cam in a clockwise direction as far as possible then releasing the cam to see if the springs return it to its retarded position. Fig. 5. If the cam does not return readily, the distributor must be disassembled and the trouble corrected.

G. Check to see that the vacuum spark control (if so equipped) operates freely by turning the breaker plate counterclockwise to see if the spring returns it to the retarded position. Any stiffness in the operation of the vacuum spark control will affect the ignition timing. Correct any interference or binding condition noted.

H. Examine distributor points and clean or replace if necessary.

Contact points with an overall gray color and only slight roughness or pitting need not be replaced.

Under normal operating conditions, distributor contact points will provide many thousands of miles of service. Points which have undergone several thousands of miles of operation will have a rough surface but this should not be interpreted as meaning that the points are worn out.

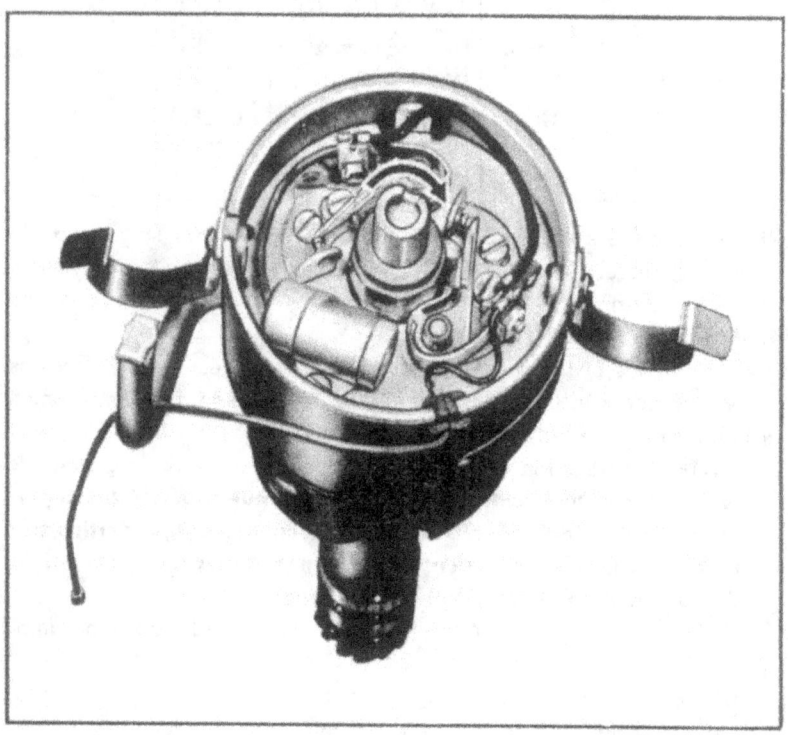

Fig. 5—Checking Centrifugal Advance

Dirty points should be cleaned with a clean point file.

Use only a few strokes of a clean, fine-cut contact point file. The file should not be used on other metals and should not be allowed to become greasy or dirty. Never use emery cloth or sandpaper to clean contact points since particles will embed and cause arcing and rapid burning of points. Do not attempt to remove all roughness nor dress the point surfaces down smooth. Merely remove scale or dirt.

Replace points that are burned or badly pitted.

NOTE: Where burned or badly pitted points are encountered, the ignition system and engine must be checked to determine

the cause of trouble so it can be eliminated. Unless the condition causing point burning or pitting is corrected, new points will provide no better service than the old points.

Contact point burning can result from high voltage, presence of oil or other foreign material, defective condenser or improper point adjustment. High voltage can cause an excessively high current flow through the contact points which burns them rapidly. High voltage can result from an improperly adjusted or inoperative voltage regulator.

Oil or crankcase vapors which work up into the distributor and deposit on the point surfaces will cause them to burn rapidly. This is easy to detect since the oil produces a smudgy line under the contact points. Clogged engine breather pipes permit crankcase pressure to force oil or vapors up into the distributor. Over-oiling the distributor will also produce the condition.

If the contact point opening is too small (cam angle too large), the points will be closed too large a part of the total operating time, Fig. 6. Average current flow through the points will be too high so

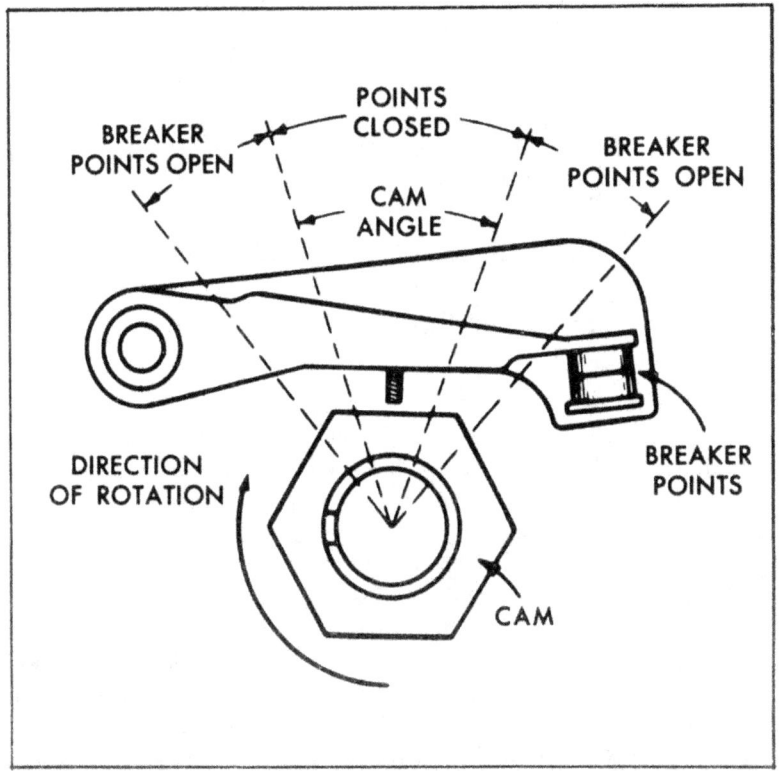

Fig. 6—Cam Angle

the points will burn rapidly and arcing will occur between the points resulting in low secondary voltage and engine miss.

Some Corvette engines are equipped with dual point distributors. This design permits the use of flatter cam lobes, reducing point-bounce at very high RPM. These dual points are wired in parallel, permitting a lower average current flow per set of points. One of the sets of points is used to close the primary circuit, and the other set is used to open the circuit. Through the geometry designed into the distributor, the two sets of points operating in parallel produce a longer dwell angle than either of the sets alone.

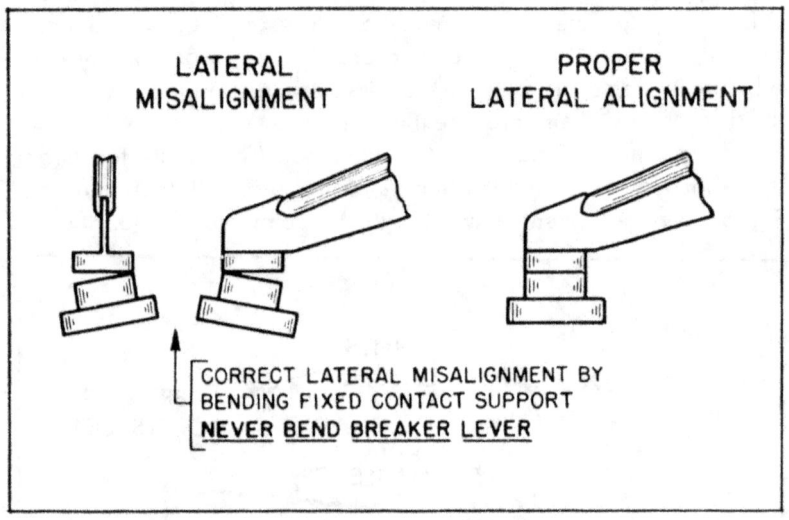

Fig. 7—Alignment of Points

High series resistance in the condenser circuit will prevent normal condenser action, causing the contact points to burn rapidly. This resistance may be caused by a loose condenser mounting or lead connection, or by poor connections inside the condenser.

Proper alignment of contact points is important to point life, Fig. 7. If the full faces of the points do not touch each other, the ability of the points to dissipate heat resulting from the primary current is reduced, causing excessive point burning.

Contact point pitting results from an out-of-balance condition in the ignition system which causes transfer of tungsten from one point to the other so that a tip builds up on one point while a pit forms in the other. The direction in which the tungsten transfers can be used as a basis for analysis and correction of pitting. For instance, if the material transfers from the negative to the positive point, Fig. 8, one or more of these corrections may be made: increase condenser capacity; shorten condenser lead; separate distributor-to-coil low-and high-tension leads; move these leads closer to ground.

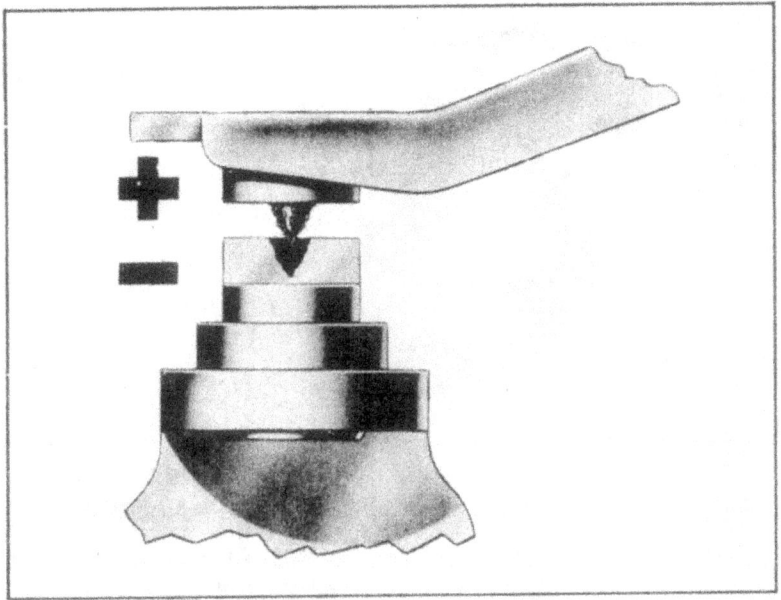

Fig. 8—Material Transfer, Negative to Positive Point

If the material transfers from the positive to the negative point, Fig. 9, reduce condenser capacity, move distributor-to-coil leads closer together, move these leads away from ground, or lengthen condenser lead.

NOTE: While condensers are supplied in only one value, production variations permit selection with a condenser checker.

1. Adjust distributor contact point gap to .019" (new points) or .016" (used points), using a feeler gauge, Fig. 10, or dial indicator. The specification on dual-point models is .018" for new points, and .014" for used points. Breaker arm rubbing block should be on extreme top of cam lobe during adjustment.

NOTE: Contact points should be cleaned before adjusting with a feeler gauge if they have been in service.

The use of a feeler gauge on rough or uncleaned points is not recommended since accurate gauging cannot be done on such points. The gauge measures between high spots on the points instead of the true point opening, Fig. 11.

New points must be set to a larger opening as the rubbing block will wear down slightly while seating to the cam.

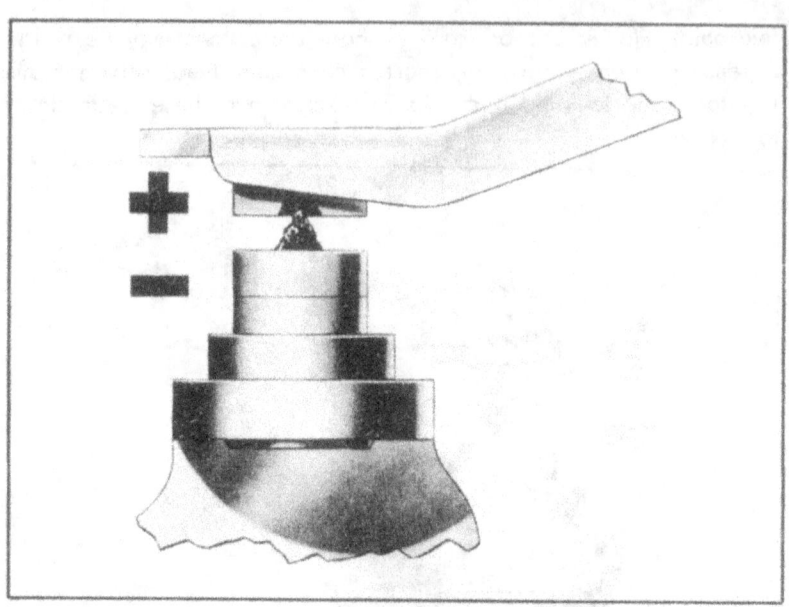

Fig. 9—Material Transfer, Positive to Negative Point

Correct contact point opening is important, especially during starting and low speed operation. If contact points are set too close, arcing and burning will occur, causing hard starting and poor low

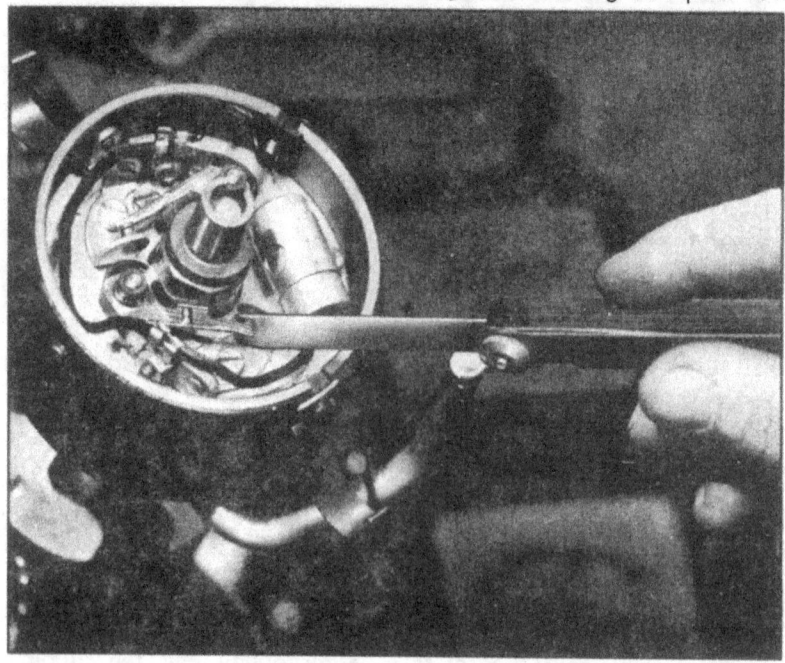

Fig. 10—Checking Distributor Point Gap

speed performance. If points are set too wide, the cam angle or dwell will be too small to allow saturation of the coil at high engine speeds, resulting in a weak spark.

Distributor point opening has a direct bearing on cam angle or dwell, which is the number of degrees that the breaker cam rotates from the time the points close until they open again. Fig. 6. The cam angle increases as point opening is decreased and vice versa. In view of the importance of point opening to low speed engine performance and cam angle to high speed engine performance, the cam angle should be checked after adjusting and aligning points. This will be performed during the instrument checkout later in this program.

J. Check alignment of distributor points with points closed, Fig. 7. Align new points where necessary, but do not attempt to align used points. Instead, replace used points where serious misalignment is observed.

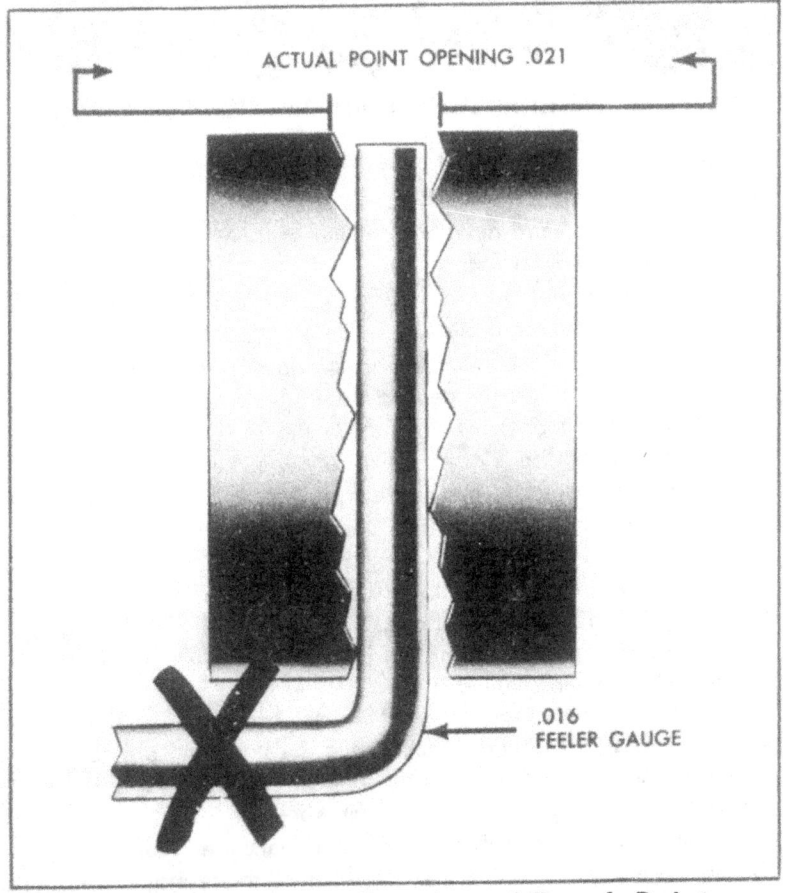

Fig. 11—Inaccurate Gauging of Rough Points

Fig. 12—Checking Distributor Point Spring Tension

Align points by bending fixed contact support as necessary, using an alignment tool if available.

NOTE: Do not bend movable breaker arm. After adjusting alignment, readjust point gap.

Inspect alignment of rubbing block with cam and check for a twisted arm or pivot pin if alignment is not correct.

K. Check the distributor point spring tension (contact point pressure) with a spring gauge hooked to breaker lever at the contact and pull exerted at 90 degrees to the breaker lever, Fig. 12. The points should be closed (cam follower between lobes) and the reading taken just as the points separate. Spring tension should be 19-23 ounces.

If the spring tension is not within limits loosen the primary lead retaining nut on the stationary point. Shift the spring (utilizing the elongated hole in the spring) to shorten its effective length to increase the tension. Lengthening the effective spring length will decrease the tension, Fig. 13.

Excessive point pressure will cause excessive wear on the points, cam and rubbing block while weak point pressure permits bouncing or chattering, resulting in arcing and burning of the points and an ignition miss at high speed.

L. Make sure all distributor wire terminals are clean and tight. On models equipped with a vacuum advance rotate moveable breaker plate to check for possible interference or bind.

M. Lubricate distributor. Fill hinge cap oiler with light engine oil, if so equipped.

Apply a thin film of Delco-Renny Cam and Ball Bearing Lubricant or other similar high melting point, non-bleeding grease to the cam, if the distributor is not equipped with a cam lubricator wick.

Apply 3 or 4 drops of light engine oil on the wick under the rotor.

Apply 1 or 2 drops of light engine oil on the breaker lever pivot.

Distributors equipped with cam lubricator should have the wick replaced at the same time contact point set is replaced. It is not necessary to lubricate the breaker cam when using a cam lubricator. Do not attempt to lubricate the wick.

When installing a new wick, adjust its position so the end of the wick just touches the lobe of the breaker cam.

N. Install rotor and distributor cap. Press all wires firmly into cap towers.

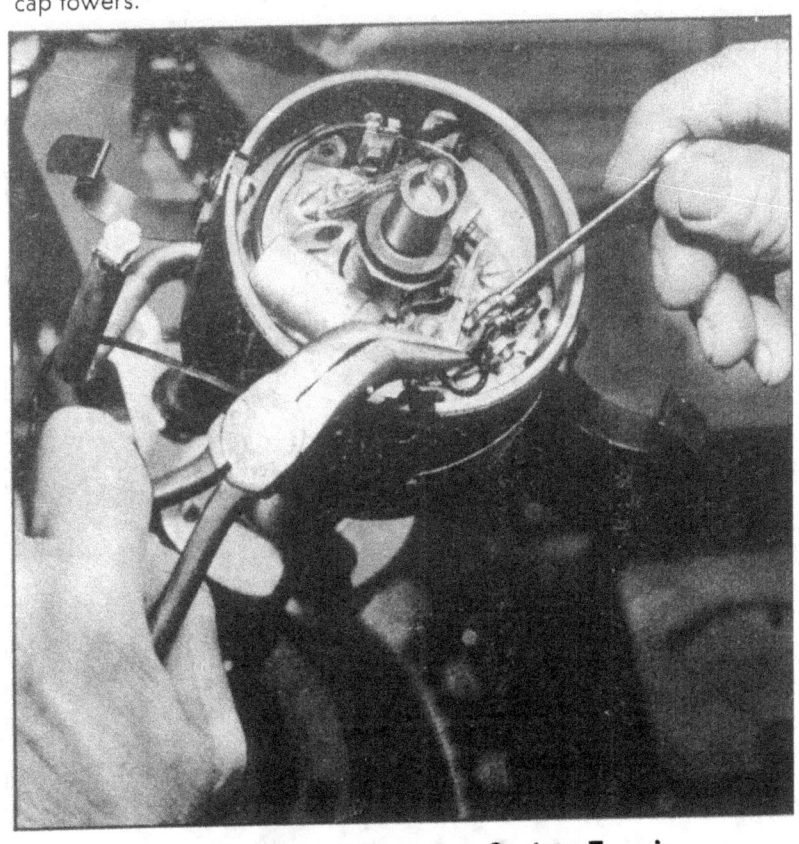

Fig. 13—Changing Point Spring Tension

5. SERVICE BATTERY AND BATTERY CABLES

Inspect battery and battery cables and perform necessary service on these components, see Fig. 14.

Inspect for signs of corrosion on battery, cables and surrounding area, loose or broken carriers, cracked or bulged cases, dirt and acid, electrolyt leakage and low electrolyte level. Fill cells to proper level with distilled water or water passed through a "demineralizer."

The top of the battery should be clean and the battery hold-down bolts properly tightened. Particular care should be taken to see that the tops of 12-volt batteries are kept clean of acid film and dirt because of high voltage between the battery terminals. For best results when cleaning batteries, wash first with a dilute ammonia or soda solution to neutralize any acid present and then flush off with clean water. Care must be taken to keep vent plugs tight so that the neutralizing solution does not enter the cell. The hold-down bolts should be kept tight enough to prevent the battery from shaking around in its holder, but they should not be tightened to the point where the battery case will be placed under a severe strain.

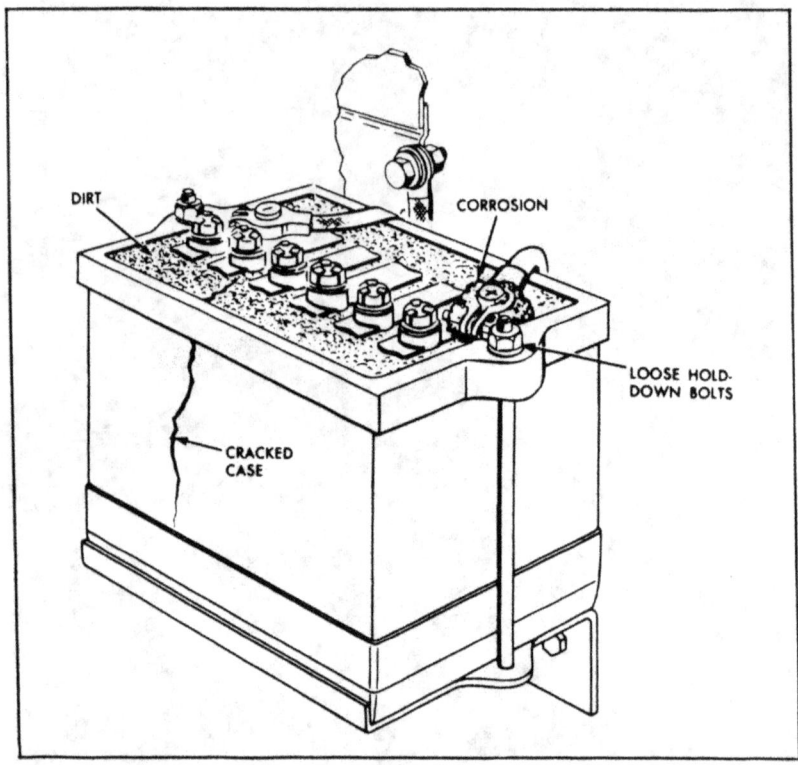

Fig. 14—Common Battery Ailments

To insure good contact, the battery cables should be tight on the battery posts. If the battery posts or cable terminals are corroded, the cables should be cleaned separately with a soda solution and a wire brush. After cleaning and before installing clamps, apply a thin coating of petrolatum to the posts and cable clamps to help retard corrosion.

If the battery has remained undercharged, check for loose genator belt, defective generator, high resistance in the charging circuit, oxidized regulator contact points, or a low voltage setting.

If the battery has been using too much water, the voltage regulator setting is too high.

6. SERVICE FAN BELT AN GENERATOR

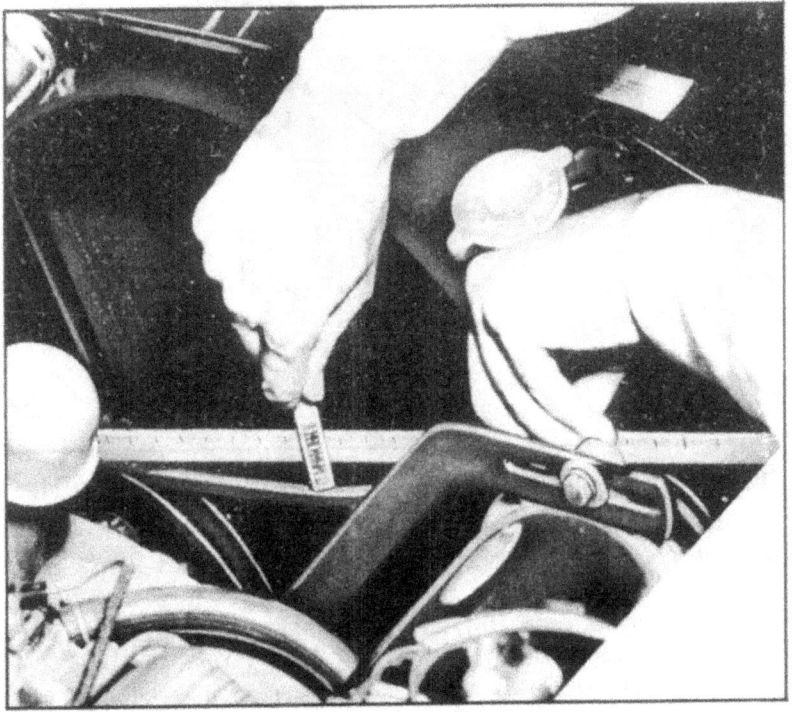

Fig. 15—Checking Belt Tension

A. Inspect fan belt condition and check adjustment. Adjust if necessary to give a 7/16" to 1/2" deflection of the belt when a light pressure (10#) is applied midway between water pump pulley and generator pulley, Fig. 15.

B. Inspect generator commutator and brushes for cleanliness and wear, Fig. 16. The commutator should be cleaned if dirty and the brushes should be replaced if worn down to less than half their original length.

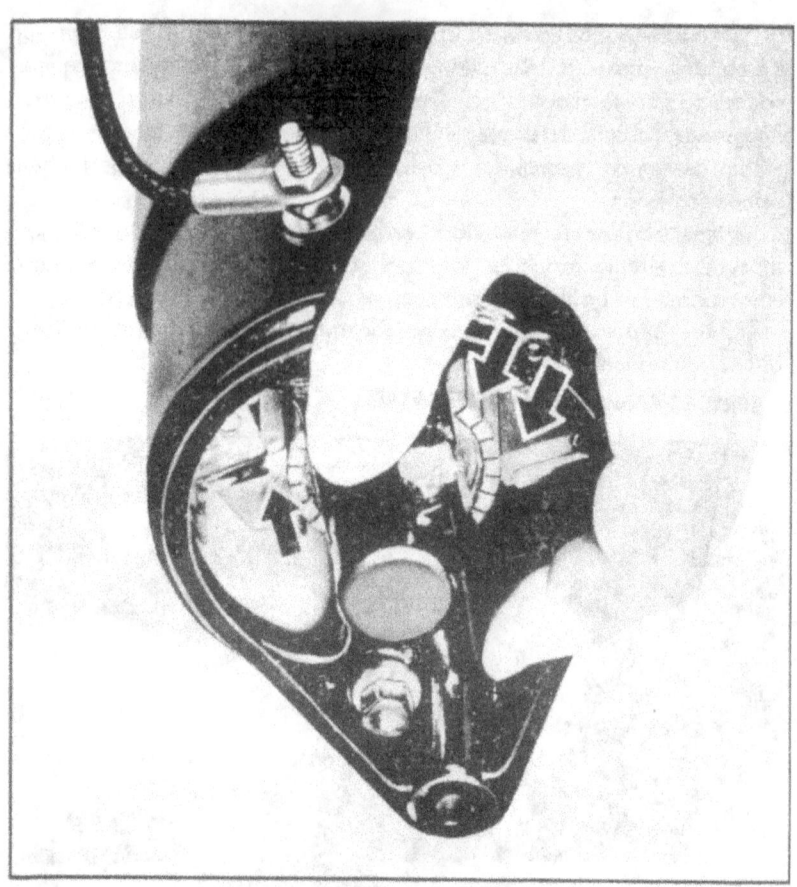

Fig. 16—Inspecting Generator Commutator and Brushes

The commutator may be cleaned by holding No. 00 sandpaper or a cleaning stone against it while the generator is operating at idle speed.

C. Replace or repair frayed or broken generator wires and tighten all wire connections.

D. Lubricate generator by filling hinge cap oilers with light engine oil, Fig. 17.

If oil reservoir in commutator end frame should become exhausted through failure to add oil during previous lubrication periods, the oil cup should be filled three times consecutively, allowing time between fillings for the oil to saturate the wick. Do not fill oiler on drive end frame more than once however.

7. CHECK OPERATION OF MANIFOLD HEAT VALVE

Check the manifold heat control valve on models so equipped, Fig. 18, for freedom of operation. If shaft is sticking, free it up with kerosene or alcohol containing a small amount of baking soda.

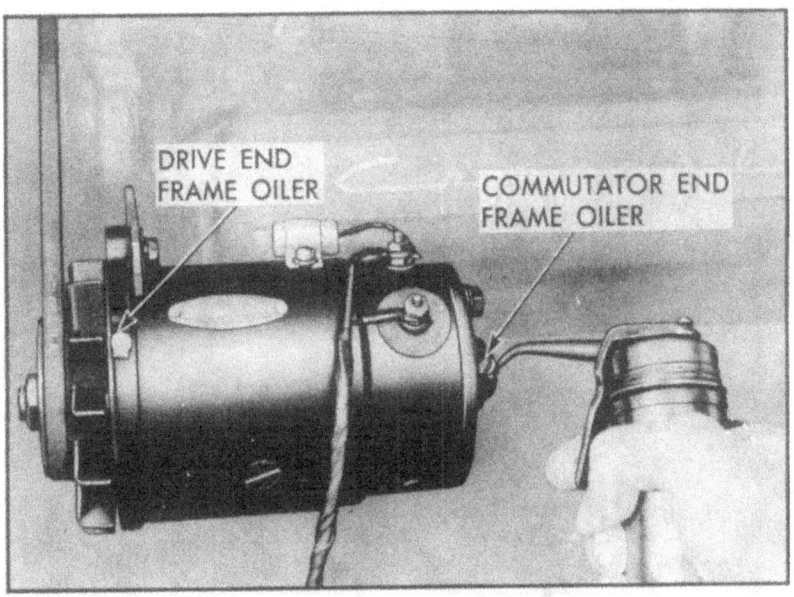

Fig. 17—Generator Lubrication

8. TIGHTEN MANIFOLD BOLTS

Tighten all intake manifold bolts to 25-36 ft. lbs. Tighten all exhaust manifold bolts to 18-22 ft. lbs.

A slight leak at the intake manifold destroys engine performance and economy.

NOTE: This is particularly important on Dual-Four-Barrel carburetion and Fuel Injection models.

9. CHECK FUEL LINES AND SERVICE FUEL FILTER

A. Inspect fuel lines for kinks, bends or leaks and correct any defects found.

B. If equipped with fuel filter, clean filter. On Fuel Injection models, the filter should be changed each spring and fall.

NOTE: If a complaint of poor high speed performance exists on the vehicle, fuel pump should be tested.

10. CHECK LINKAGE AND EXTERNAL ADJUSTMENTS

Perform the following adjustments in the sequence given for the particular unit involved.

NOTE: Float level and float drop checks and adjustments on carburetion models will not be covered in this course but may require checking in event of customer complaint.

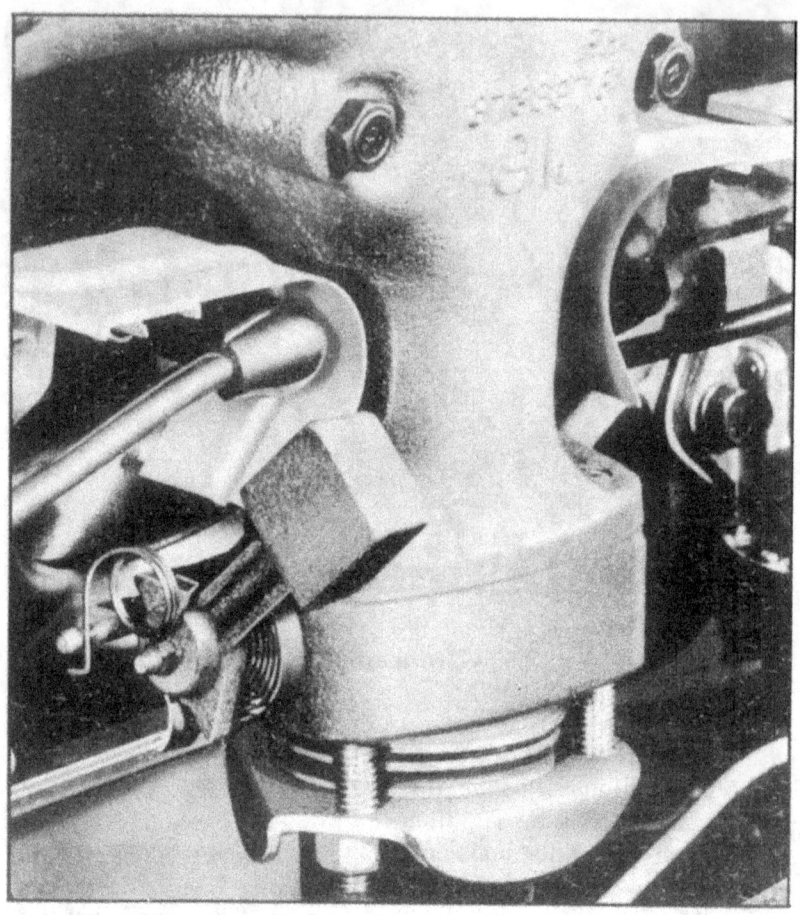

Fig. 18—Manifold Heat Control Valve

Four-Barrel Carburetor
(Carter WCFB)

   NOTE: The checks and adjustments below also apply to Carter dual four-barrel installation.

   A. Choke adjustment—Check alignment of scribe mark on choke cover and coil assembly with index mark on choke housing.

   Align marks, if necessary, by rotating cover. The single four-barrel carburetor for 1959 and 60 works the same as on previous models, but the adjustment works in the opposite direction. Always examine bakelite cover for proper direction of adjustment if richer or leaner settings are desired. Inspect choke for smooth operation.

   B. Intermediate Choke Rod Adjustment (Single Four Barrel Carburetor 1959 and 60).

   Remove three choke coil housing screws and remove retainer ring, and choke coil housing assembly.

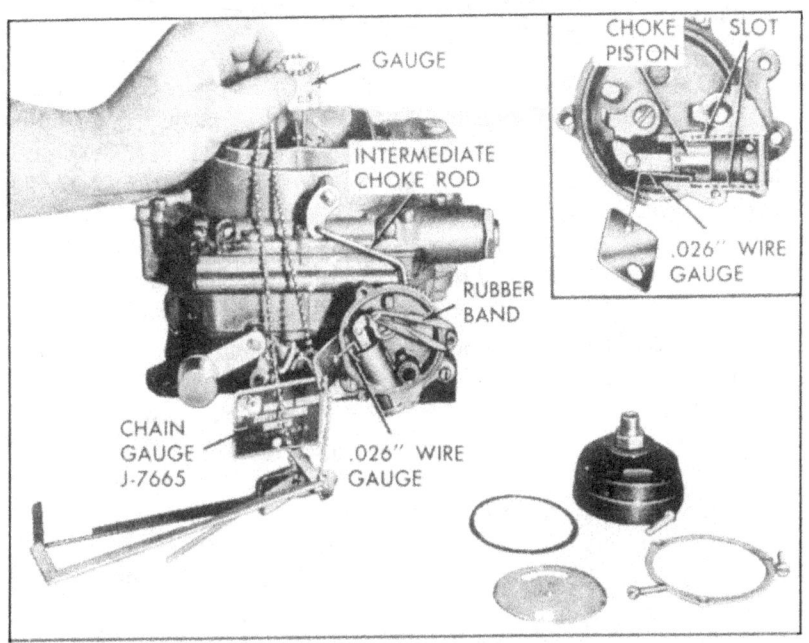

Fig. 20—Intermediate Choke Rod Adjustment

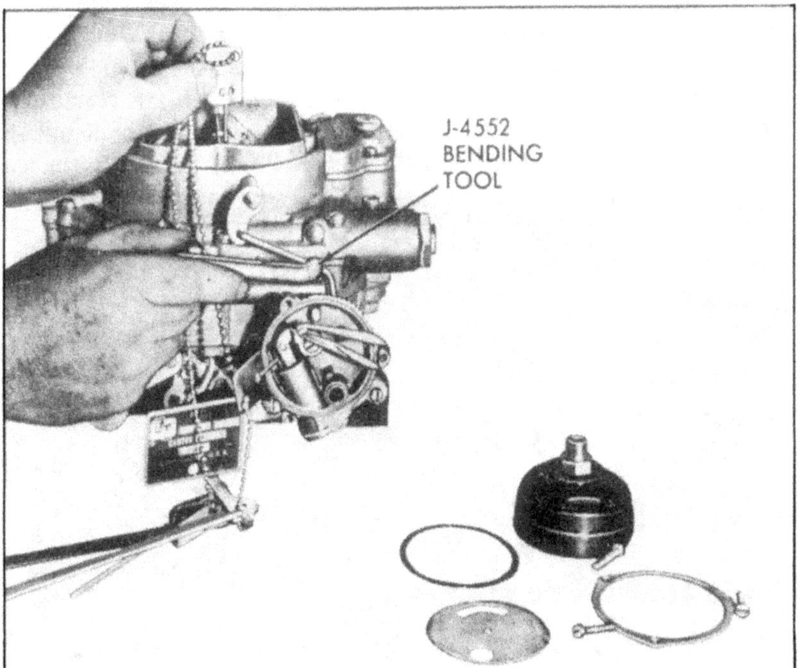

Fig. 21—Bending Intermediate Choke Rod

Remove coil housing gasket and baffle plate.

Open choke valve and insert .026" wire gauge, Tool J-7665, between bottom of slot in piston and top of slot in choke piston housing as shown in Figure 20. Close choke piston against this gauge (using a rubber band doubled will keep tension of piston against wire gauge leaving one hand free for adjustment while gauging choke valve Figure 21) and check clearance between top of choke valve and web of air horn casting (fig. 21). This dimension should be .096" on 283 V-8 engines. Wire gauge .096" is incorporated on Tool J-7665 chain gauge set.

If adjustment is required, bend intermediate choke rod using Bending Tool J-4552 as shown in Figure 21.

Remove gauges and rubber band from choke piston lever.

Install choke baffle plate, gasket and thermostatic coil housing assembly, retainer ring and screws.

C. Throttle Linkage Adjustment—On dual four barrel models, remove both throttle return springs. Disconnect front throttle rod from rear carburetor throttle lever, "C" Fig. 22. On all models, depress accelerator pedal to floor and check to see that throttle stop tang, Fig. 23, contacts throttle body (throttle valves wide open). If contact is not made, disconnect throttle rod from carburetor, depress accelerator pedal to floor and, while holding throttle valves wide open, adjust throttle rod swivel until pin enters throttle lever freely, then secure pin. On dual four barrel models, connect front throttle rod. With rear carburetor throttle wide open, front carburetor should also be wide open against stop. If not, shorten or lengthen the front carburetor throttle rod, "D" Fig. 22, as necessary. Install

Fig. 22—Dual Four-Barrel Carburetor Linkage

throttle return springs. The normal linkage arrangement is to have the linkage connected to the top hole in the rear carburetor throttle lever "C" Fig. 22, and to the bottom hole of the front carburetor throttle lever at "D" Fig. 22. This arrangement permits smooth accelerator pedal response. Some people prefer to mount the linkage in the top hole of each lever, "C" and "E", Fig. 22. This arrangement produces the fastest possible opening of the front carburetor, and makes the accelerator pedal very sensitive in the low speed range.

NOTE: Many 1956-57 dual four-barrel installations are equipped with large brass idle air by-pass screws, "A," Fig. 22. It is recommended that these screws, on both front and rear carburetors, be seated snugly, and an idle speed screw be installed on the rear carburetor, "B", Fig. 22.

D. Pump Adjustment—Back out throttle lever adjusting screw, remove dust cover and place gauge J818-3 on dust cover boss as illustrated in Fig. 24. Check relationship between top flat of pump arm and gauge. These surfaces should be parellel when properly

Fig. 23—Checking for Full Throttle

adjusted. If necessary, correct adjustment by bending pump rod with bending tool J-5496.

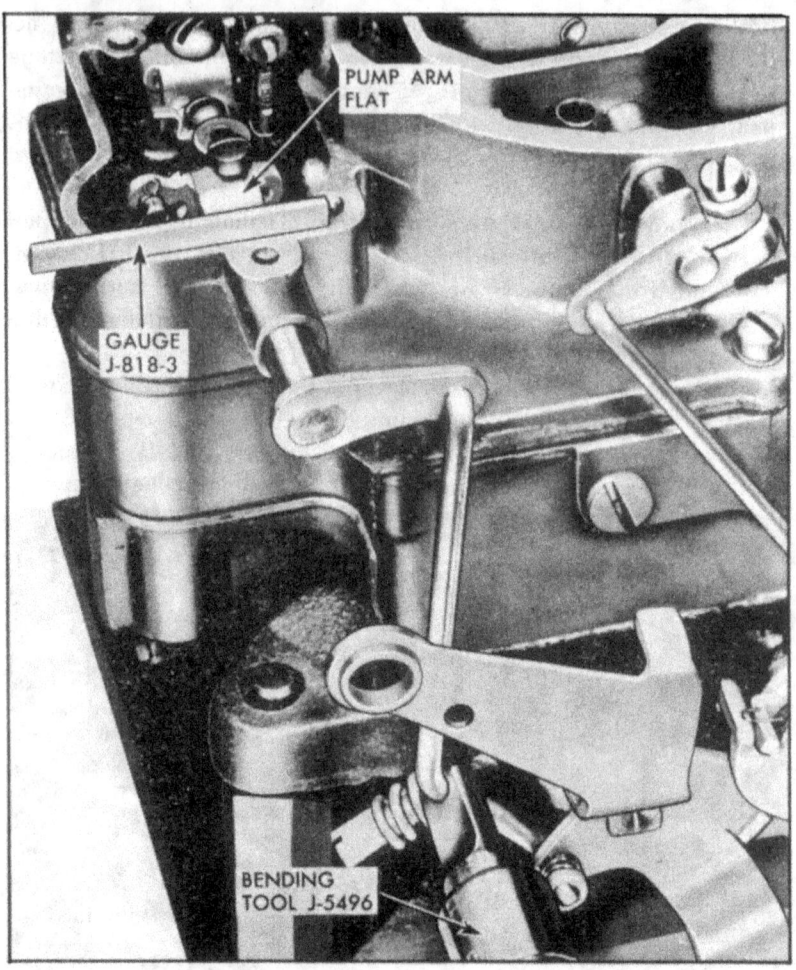

Fig. 24—Checking Pump Adjustment

E. Metering Rod Adjustment—Press down metering rod hanger, Fig. 25, until rods bottom. Metering rod arm should follow hanger. To adjust, loosen screw in metering rod arm and press down metering rod hanger until rods bottom. While holding metering rods down and with throttle valves seated (adjusting screw backed out) rotate metering rod arm upward until arm lightly contacts hanger, then tighten set screw to lock in position. Install dust cover using a new gasket.

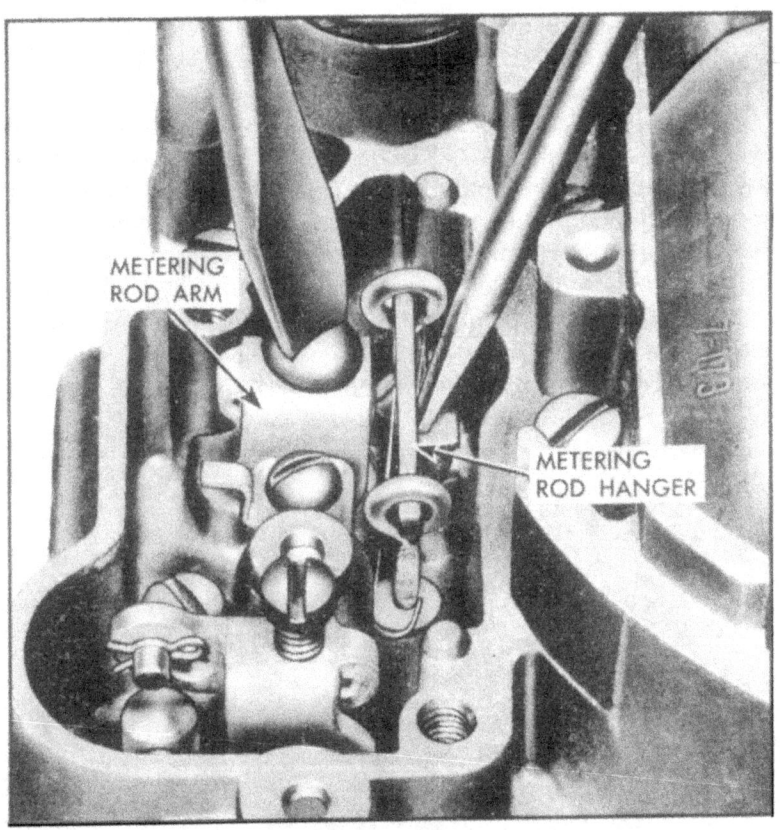

Fig. 25—Checking Metering Rod Adjustment

The dust cover gasket for 1959 and 1960 model "WCFB" Carter carburetors, shown in Figure 26 has been designed with tabs for better sealing of dust and foreign particles.

NOTE: 1959 and 1960 dust cover gaskets can be used on 1958 Carter WCFB carburetors. Do not use 1958 dust cover gaskets on 1959 or 1960 Carter carburetors.

Install a new dust cover gasket with tabs bent at 90°, on 1959 and 1960 single four barrel carburetors.

NOTE: For maximum low-speed economy, 1956 Dual-Four Barrel Carburetors should have Part No. 3742682 metering rods with .067", 063" and .054" steps, and Part No. 3721027 low speed jets with a .021" orfice.

F. Vapor Vent Adjustment—Insert gauge J-6039 between bottom of vapor vent and bottom of dust cover recess, Fig. 27. When properly adjusted, the gauge should just slip between bottom of vent and dust cover (1/16" clearance) with the throttle closed. To adjust, remove dust cover and bend vent arm tang (inset, Fig. 27), as required.

G. Fast Idle Cam and Choke Relationship—Loosen choke shaft lever screw and insert .020" gauge J-1388 between tang of fast idle cam and boss of throttle flange, Fig. 28. Holding choke valve closed tightly, pull choke shaft lever upward to eliminate all slack from linkage, then tighten screw in choke shaft lever.

H. Secondary Throttle Lockout Adjustment—Fully open choke valve, then open both primary and secondary throttle valves by fully depressing accelerator pedal to floor. Close choke valve and hold shut, then release accelerator pedal (closing throttle valves).

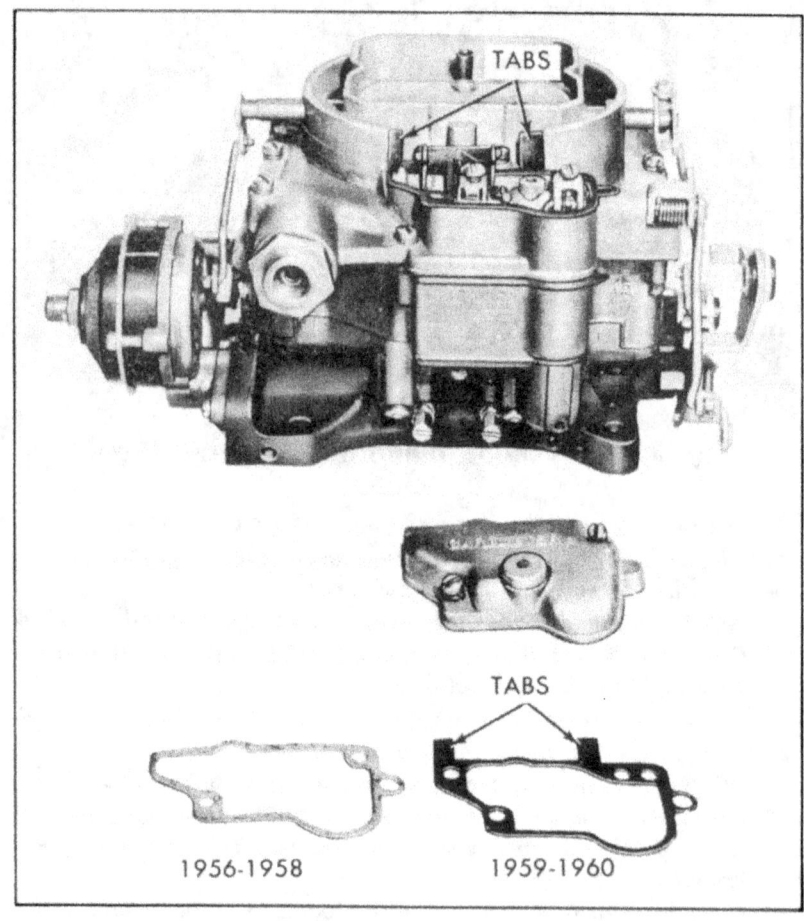

Fig. 26—Installation of Dust Cover Gasket

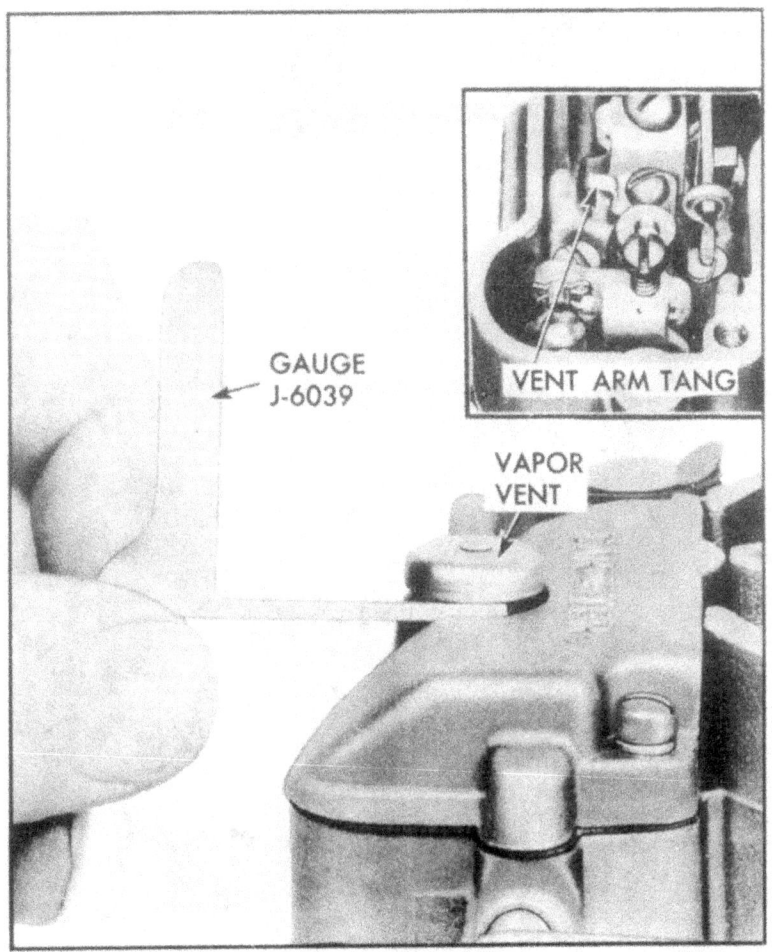

Fig. 27—Checking Vapor Vent Adjustment

Tang on secondary throttle shaft should freely engage notch in secondary lockout dog, Fig. 29. If necessary, bend tang to permit free engagement.

    I. Unloader Adjustment—Fully depress accelerator pedal (primary throttle valves wide open). Holding linkage in this position, insert 3/16" gauge J-818-3 between inboard edge of choke valve and center wall of bowl cover, Fig. 30. Gauge should just fit in this opening. If necessary, bend unloader tang with tool J-1137 as required to obtain proper adjustment.

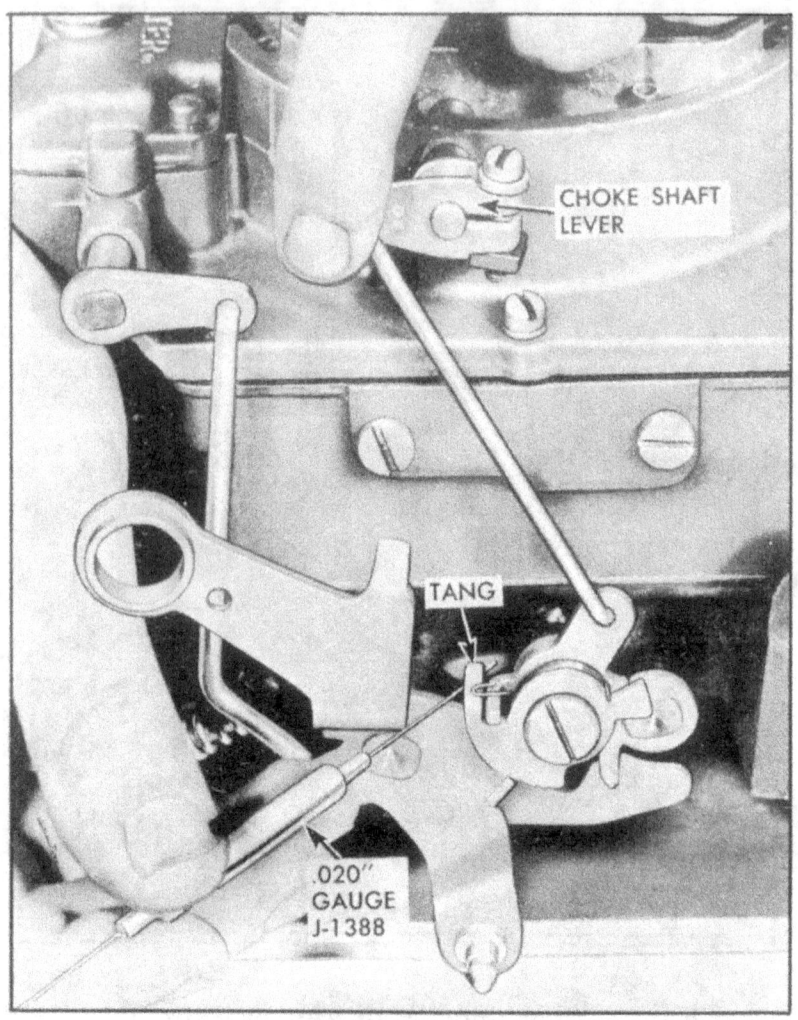

Fig. 28—Checking Choke Linkage for Fast Idle Adjustment

Fuel Injection

A. Cold Enrichment Coil Setting—Check the scribe marks on the cold enrichment housing and cover. The scribe mark on the cover should be set 1-1/2 notches rich from the scribe mark on the cold enrichment housing. The notches are the radial marks cast on the flange of the cover.

B. Cold Enrichment Rod Adjustment—This adjustment should be required only at the time of a complete Fuel Injection overhaul, but may be checked as part of the tune-up procedure. Refer to the Fuel Injection part of this manual for procedures.

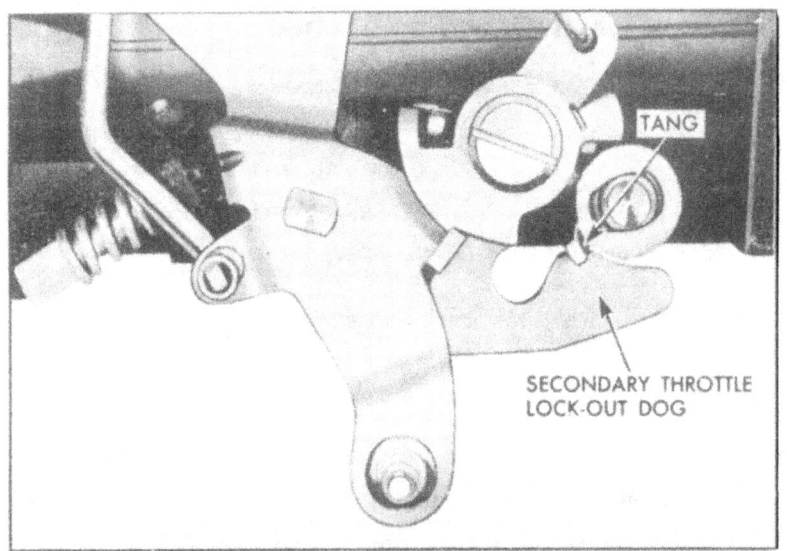

Fig. 29—Secondary Throttle Lockout Adjustment

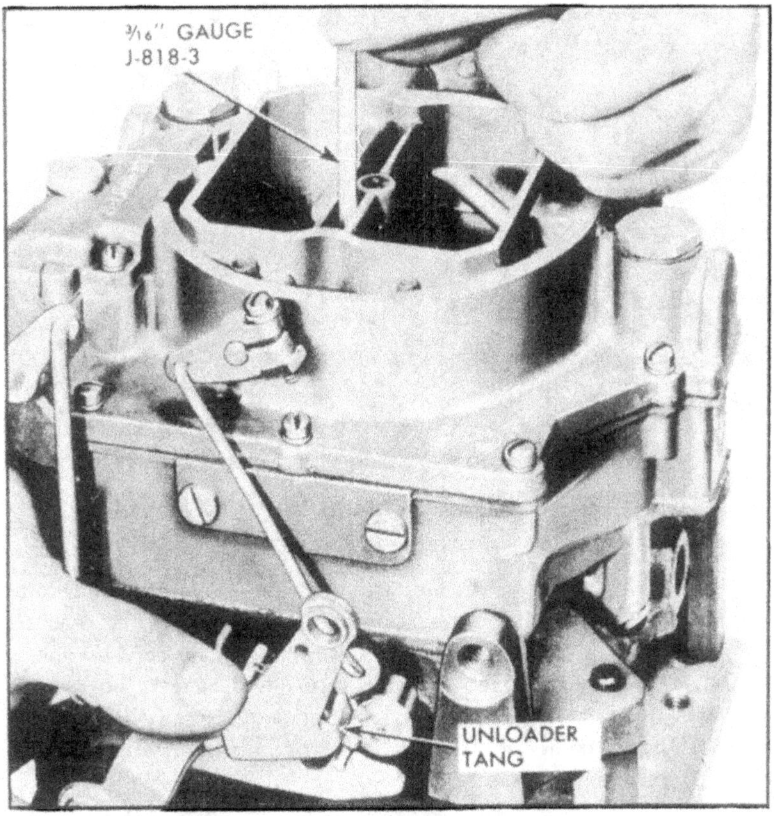

Fig. 30—Checking Unloader Adjustment

11. INSPECT AND SERVICE COOLING SYSTEM

Inspect cooling system for leaks, weak hoses, loose hose clamps and correct coolant level, and service as required.

NOTE: A cooling system pressure test may be performed to direct internal or external leaks within the cooling system.

12. CHECK LUBRICANT LEVEL AND INSPECT FOR LEAKS

13. TIGHTEN ENGINE MOUNTING BOLTS

Engine mounting bolt torque should be checked periodically, Fig. 31. The proper torque wrench specifications are:

Front Mounts	25-35 Ft. Lbs.
Rear Mounts	50-55 Ft. Lbs.
Front Mounting Beam and Water Pump to Engine Bolts	19-24 Ft. Lbs.

Fig. 31—Checking Front Engine Mounts

14. NORMALIZE ENGINE

Set parking brake and place transmission in Neutral, then start engine and run until normal operating temperature is reached. This should be approximately 10-15 minutes with a cold engine.

NOTE: If disturbed, throttle stop screw will have to be reset.

Warmup will insure that proper lubricant viscosity is provided at each engine component and that each component will be at operating temperature and size.

15. CLEANING AND CHECKING OPERATIONS

Perform these operations during warmup.

A. Clean air cleaner (on Fuel Injection models with paper-type air cleaner, use only a rapping operation. Do not use solvents).

B. Clean crankcase breather cap.

C. Check the following for proper operation: Windshield Wipers, Directional Signals, Headlights, Horns, Parking Lights, Instruments and Indicator Lights, Tail Lights, Brake and Cluch Pedal Adjustment, Stop Lights, Accessories.

16. TIGHTEN CYLINDER HEAD BOLTS

A. Stop engine and remove rocker arm covers.

B. Tighten head bolts to 60 to 70 ft. lbs., Fig. 32, using adaptor J-5860 wherever necessary.

C. Install rocker arm covers using new gaskets.

Fig. 32—Checking Cylinder Head Bolts

17. ADJUST VALVE LASH

On models equipped with mechanical lifters, adjust valve lash (Fig. 33) to: (engine hot)

	Cast Iron Cylinder Heads	Aluminum Cylinder Heads
Intake	.008"	.006"
Exhaust	.018"	.014"

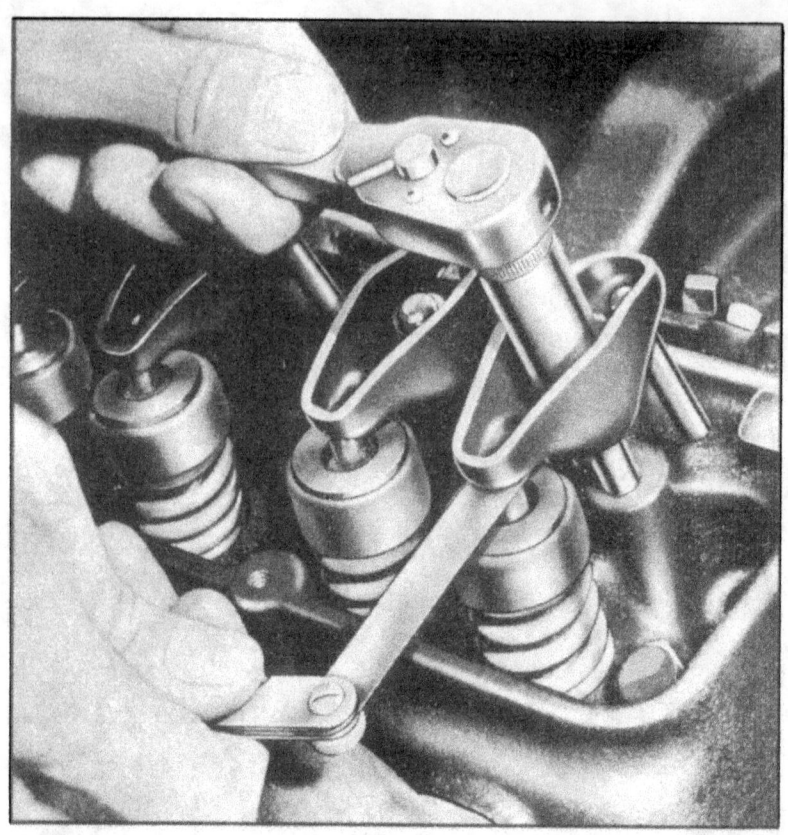

Fig. 33—Adjusting Valve Lash

INSTRUMENT CHECK-OUT

The instrument check-out may be performed with any one of several excellent pieces of equipment on the market. Although only one tester will be used in the following series of instrument checks, the same operations can be performed with other testers by following the specific operating instructions of the equipment manufacturer.

18. CALIBRATE METERS

A. Zero all meters (except vacuum and fuel pump gauge) to left side of scale, using adjustment on the face of each meter.

B. Make tach-dwell battery check by turning lobe switch to 1000 RPM, Fig. 34. If meter fails to read in black bar, replace battery in meter.

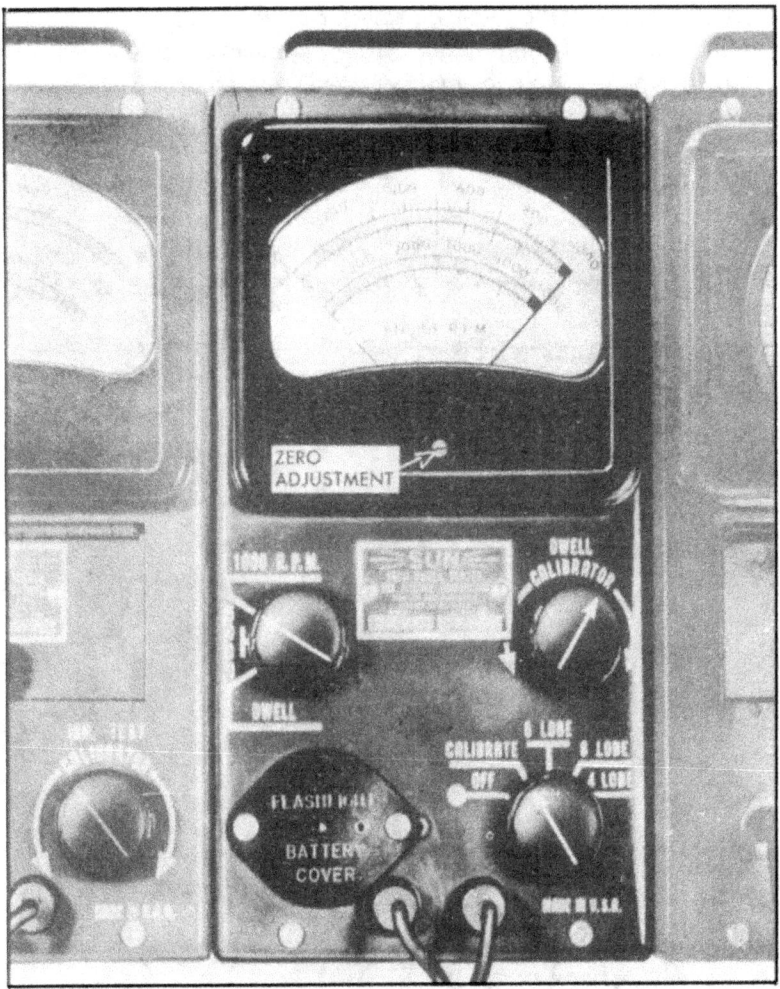

Fig. 34—Tach-Dwell Battery Check

C. Calibrate tach-dwell tester by setting knobs at CALIBRATE and DWELL positions, then turning CALIBRATOR knob until meter reads on SET LINE.

19. TEST CRANKING VOLTAGE

A. Remove high tension lead from distributor cap center terminal and connect to ground to prevent engine from firing during cranking.

B. Connect RED lead of volts-ignition tester to coil side of ignition resistor or to primary terminal on resistor side of coil. Connect BLACK lead to ground.

C. Set volts-ignition voltage selector switch to 16 volts.

D. Operate starting motor, using ignition-starter switch.

If voltage is 9 volts or more and cranking speed is satisfactory, the battery, starter, cables, starter switch and ignition circuit to coil (by-passing resistor) are in good condition.

If voltage is below 9 volts, check circuit until difficulty is located.

Meter reading below specification—Weak battery; defective cables, connections, switch or starter; defective ignition circuit to coil.

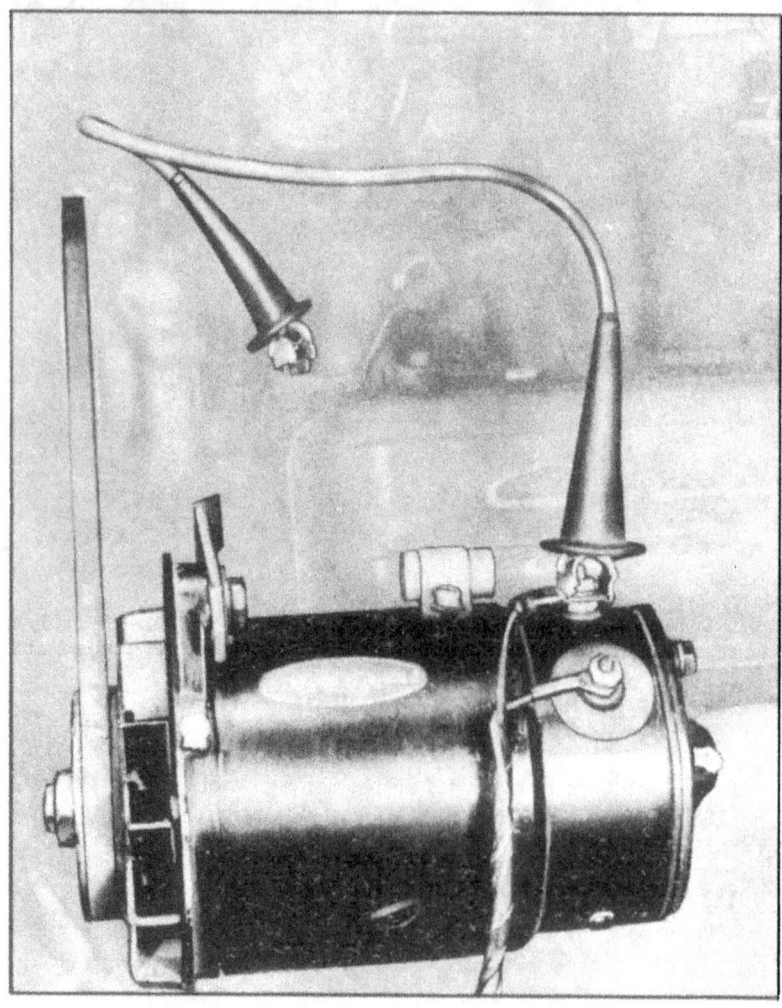

Fig. 35—Grounding Generator Armature Terminal
(L.H. Mounted Generator Shown)

Cranking speed below normal—Excessive resistance in cables or starting motor; excessive mechanical drag in engine.

Uneven cranking speed—Uneven compression, defective starter or starter drive.

20. TEST IGNITION SWITCH

A. With volts-ignition tester connected as described for the Cranking Voltage Test, turn ignition switch to ON. Voltage should drop to 5 to 7 volts as current is now passing through ignition resistor. If battery voltage of 12 volts is obtained, the ignition switch is by-passing the resistor and the ignition-starter switch must be replaced. (1956 thru 1960 Corvettes use a coil resistor by-pass circuit similar to that on the 1955 thru 1957 Chevrolet Passenger Cars.)

B. Reconnect high tension lead to distributor cap.

21. TEST DISTRIBUTOR RESISTANCE

A. Connect RED lead of tach-dwell unit to distributor primary terminal on coil and ground BLACK lead.

B. Remove jumper between coil terminal and ground.

C. Turn ignition switch ON.

If dwell meter reads in black band of lower scale, the ignition circuit from coil through distributor to ground is satisfactory.

If meter reads ZERO, distributor points are open—bump engine with starter until points close, then take reading.

If meter does not read within black bar, check for high resistance in primary circuit such as loose connections, dirty points or poor ground.

NOTE: Excessive resistance must be eliminated before continuing with test procedure.

22. TEST DWELL AND DWELL VARIATION

A. Connect jumper lead from ARMATURE terminal of generator to GROUND, Fig. 35.

This prevents generator from charging when engine is running, thus providing stable battery voltage to instruments for greater accuracy.

B. Turn Dwell Calibrator knob to readjust dwell meter to SET line, Fig. 36.

This will compensate for allowable primary circuit resistance.

C. Turn selector knob to 8 LOBE position.

D. Start engine, run at idle (not over 450 RPM) and read dwell.

On Single Point Models:

Dwell should be 26°-33° on single point models for satisfactory point gap and point dwell relationship (after points have been properly gapped).

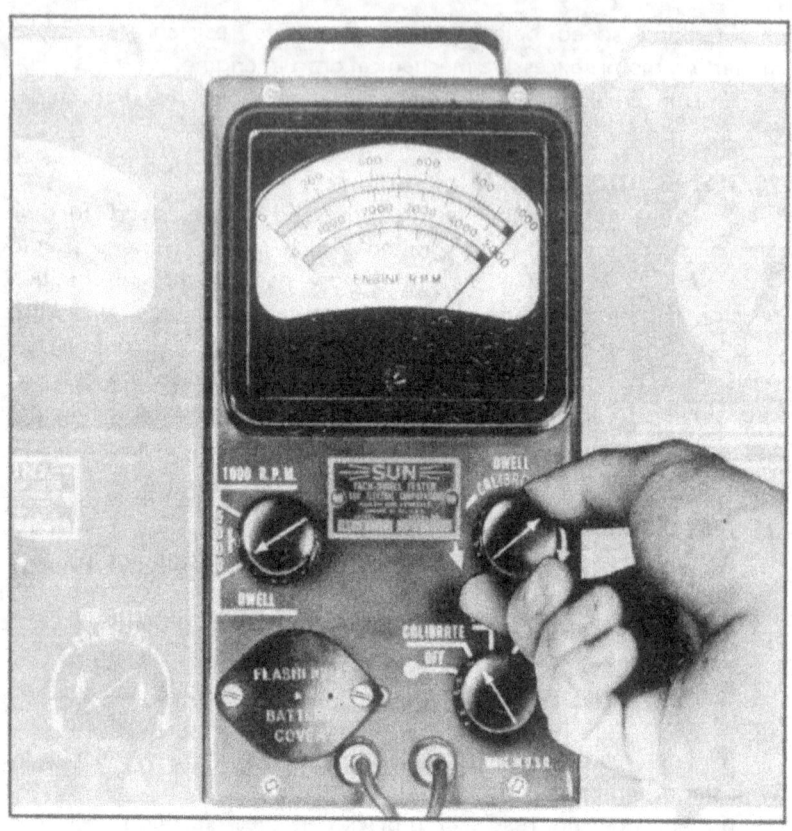

Fig. 36—Adjusting Dwell Meter

If dwell reading is not within specification recheck point gap, then check for wrong point assembly, defective or misaligned point rubbing block, or worn distributor cam.

On Dual Point Models:

Block one set of contact points by placing insulating material at least .025" thick between points, Fig. 37. Check dwell, and if necessary, adjust operating set of contact points to read 29 degrees.

Repeat operation for other set of contact points.

Check TOTAL DWELL ANGLE with both sets of points in operation. Dwell reading should be 34± 1 degree.

**NOTE: Adjusting dwell angle of each breaker individually to 29 degrees should give a point opening of .014"-.018."
Dwell angle with both breakers operating must be 34   1 degrees.**

E. Slowly accelerate engine to 1500 RPM and note dwell reading. Return engine to idle and note dwell reading. Dwell reading at no time should vary more than 3 degrees. If dwell reading varies more than 3 degrees, check for worn distributor shaft or bushings, and a loose breaker plate on models equipped with vacuum advance.

F. Stop engine.

The purpose of the dwell test is to verify that the cam angle is within specifications after point gap has been properly set. If not with specifications, then internal trouble within the distributor, such as worn cam or bearings or loose, bent or wrong breaker arm is responsible.

Cam angle is important in obtaining good ignition at high engine speeds, as the distributor points must remain closed long enough to allow the ignition coil to saturate during each interval. The dwell meter electrically measures the average number of degrees of cam rotation occurring in the intervals during which the points are closed in one complete revolution of the cam, Fig. 6. Thus with the distributor in operation, the dwell meter accurately measures the high speed performances of the cam and breaker contacts.

In view of the importance of cam angle to high speed engine performance and point opening to low speed engine performance, both the point opening and cam angle should be checked when testing a distributor.

The cam angle range allows differences between units caused by manufacturing tolerances on factors affecting cam angle, such as rubbing block shape, cam shape and shaft eccentricity.

Fig. 37—Checking Individual Point Dwell

23. TEST IGNITION TIMING AND ADVANCE

Ignition timing should be adjusted at idle with the distributor vacuum line disconnected, (if so equipped). The greatest accuracy is obtained by disconnecting the vacuum line and adjusting timing at slowest possible idle.

A. Disconnect vacuum line.

B. Install Pick-Up of distributor tester to No. 1 spark plug wire and connect No. 1 plug wire with adaptor to Pick-up, Fig. 38.

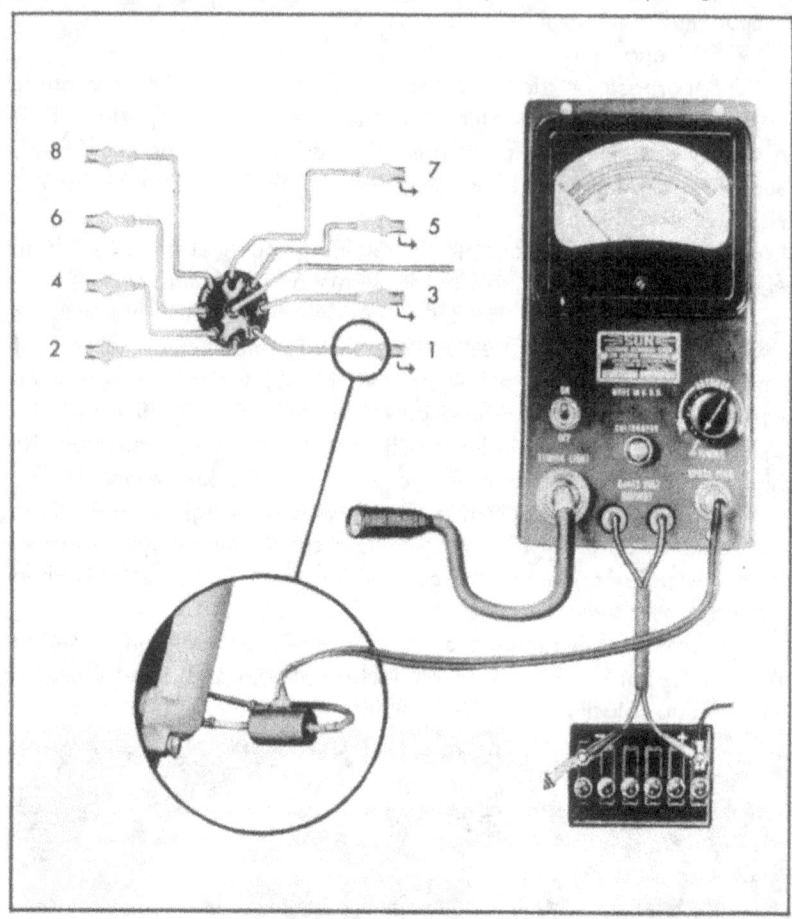

Fig. 38—Connections for Testing Ignition Timing and Advance

C. Connect distributor tester BATTERY leads to car battery.
D. Set distributor tester switches to ON and TIMING positions.
E. Start engine and run at slowest possible idle.
F. Point distributor tester timing light at the harmonic balancer, Fig. 39. Correct timing is indicated in table below.

Models	B. T. D. C. Timing
All Single Four-Barrel	4°
1956 Dual Four-Barrel	8°
1957-58-59 Dual Four-Barrel with Hydraulic Lifters	4°
1960 Dual Four-Barrel with Hydraulic Lifters	12°

1957-58 Dual Four-Barrel with Special Cam   4°
1959 Dual Four-Barrel with Epecial Cam   7°
1960 Dual Four-Barrel with Special Cam   12°
1957-58-59 Fuel Injection with Hydraulic Lifters 4°
1960 Fuel Injection with Hydraulic Lifters   8°
1957-58 Fuel Injection with Special Cam   14°
1959-60 Fuel Injection with Special Cam   18°

NOTE: Each mark equals 2 degrees.

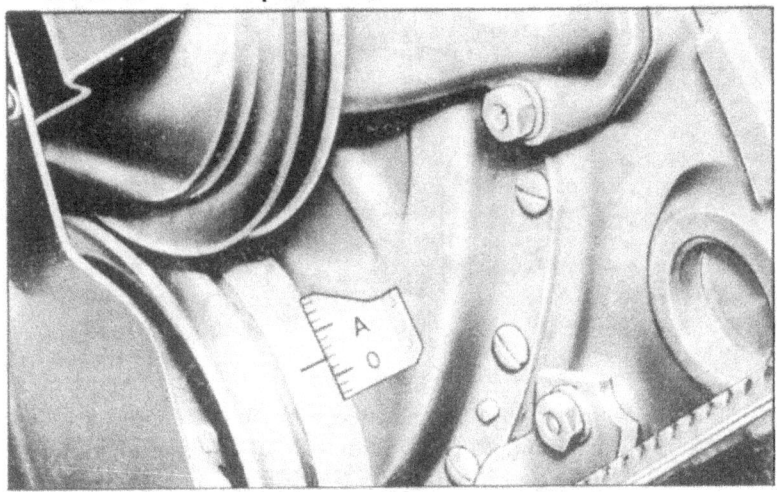

Fig. 39—Checking Ignition Timing

G. Adjust timing, as required, by loosening distributor clamp screws, "A" and "B", Fig. 40, on carburetor models, or clamp band "A" Fig. 41, on Fuel Injection Models, and rotating distributor body until mark on balancer lines up with correct advance (A) mark on timing tab. Tighten clamp screw or clamp band, and if disconnected, connect vacuum line to distributor.

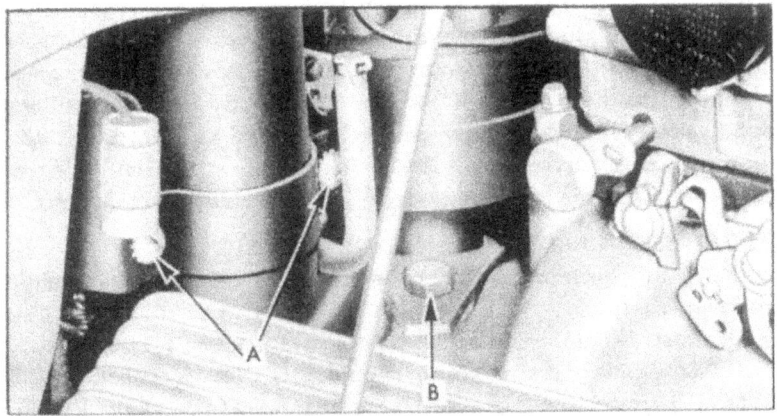

Fig. 40—Adjusting Timing-Carburetion Models

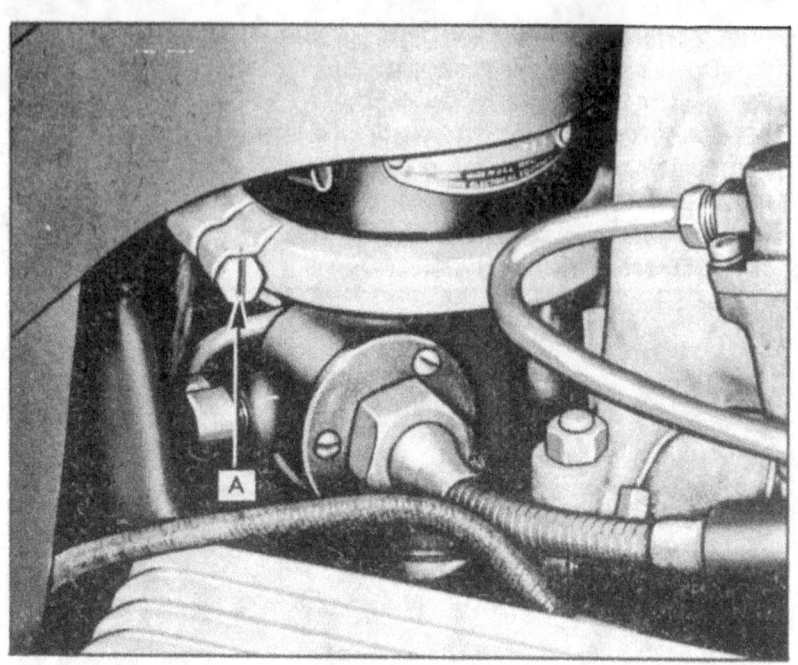

H. Note timing at idle, then increase engine speed to specified RPM to advance timing. Adjust tester ADVANCE control to return timing mark to idling position then read degrees of advance on the upper distributor degrees scale of the distributor tester, Fig. 42. On early 1956 models with 1110872 distributor, reading of 20 to 24 degrees at 2400 RPM indicates that the distributor centrifugal advance mechanism is operating satisfactorily. On all other 1956-60 models, a reading of 19-23 degrees at 2600 RPM is satisfactory. On models with vacuum advance distributor, vacuum advance should add 11 to 15 degrees.

If advance reading is not within limits, disconnect vacuum line from distributor if so equipped, and read advance. Spark advance due to the centrifugal mechanism only should be as specified above.

An unsteady position of the timing mark during either timing or advance test is generally caused by pitted or misaligned distributor points, improper distributor point spring tension, worn or loose vacuum breaker plate, worn distributor shaft or bushings.

24. TEST SECONDARY RESISTANCE AND POLARITY

A. With engine off, install extension clips between spark plugs and plug wires.

B. Start engine and adjust engine speed to 1500 RPM.

C. Set volts-ignition selector knob to SECONDARY RESISTANCE.

D. Disconnect volt-ignition leads from their previous location

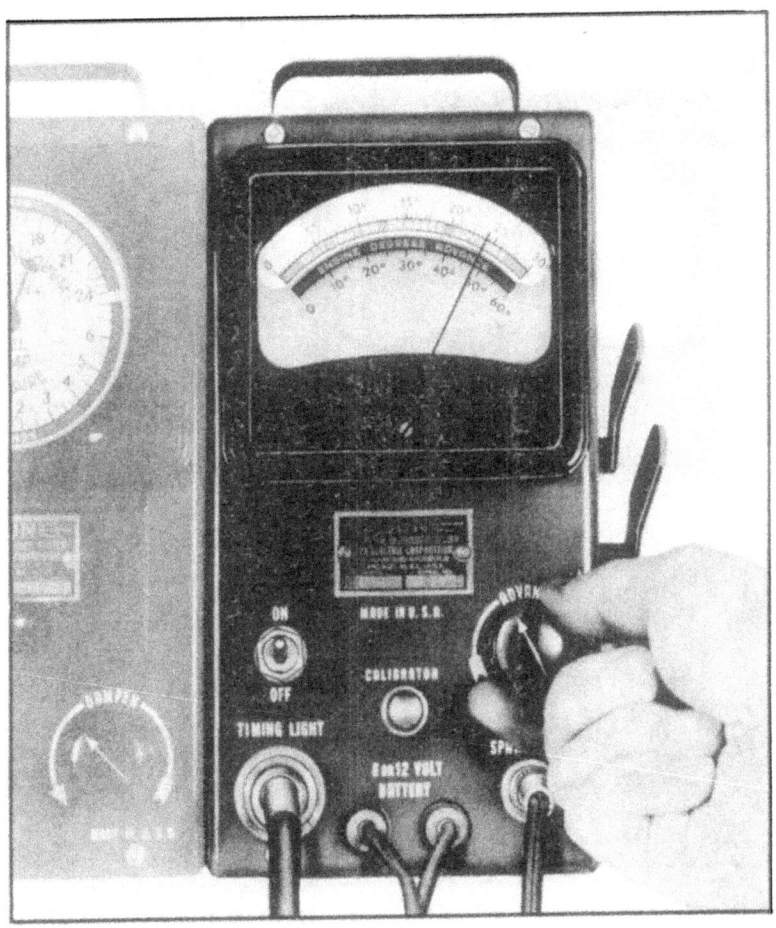

Fig. 42—Testing Distributor Advance

and connect RED lead to GROUND.

E. Touch BLACK volts-ignition lead to each spark plug clip in turn, Fig. 43.

Uniform readings at "3" on the SECONDARY RESISTANCE SCALE indicates all secondary circuit components are in good condition.

If all readings are below normal, check for corroded coil tower terminal, poorly connected or broken coil wire, center cap electrode or rotor tip burned, or an open secondary in coil.

If readings are higher than normal at two or more plugs adjacent in firing order, cross fire is occurring in distributor cap or between spark plug cables concerned.

If meter reads off scale to left with RED test clip grounded, the coil polarity is reversed. Check for reversed coil primary wires, wrong coil or reversed vehicle battery connections.

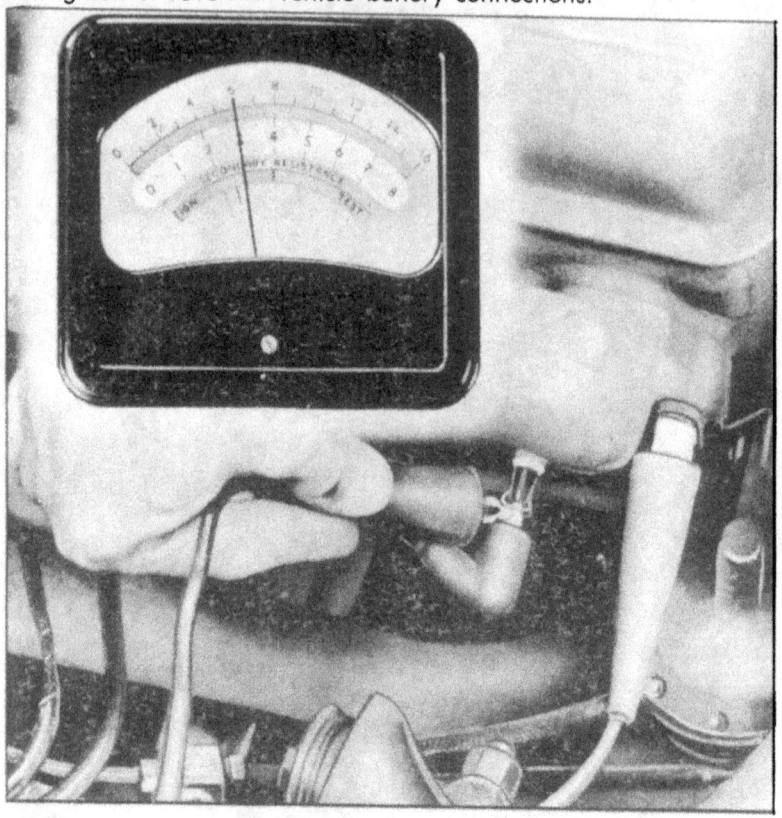

Fig. 43—Testing Secondary Resistance and Polarity

25. TEST IGNITION OUTPUT AND SECONDARY LEAKAGE

A. Set volts-ignition selector knob to IGNITION TEST.

B. Connect volts-ignition leads to coil primary terminals (BLACK lead to distributor side of coil).

C. Adjust engine speed to 1500 RPM.

D. Adjust CALIBRATOR knob until meter reads on 8-CYLINDER SET LINE, Fig. 44.

E. Using insulated pliers, remove a spark plug wire, Fig. 45. Meter should read in GOOD band. Replace wire and repeat check at each plug.

GOOD readings indicate both ignition output and secondary insulation are good. If all readings are BAD or if ignition test calibrator cannot be adjusted to Set Line, check for high resistance in primary circuit, defective distributor points, coil or condenser.

If readings are BAD only when certain plug wires are lifted off,

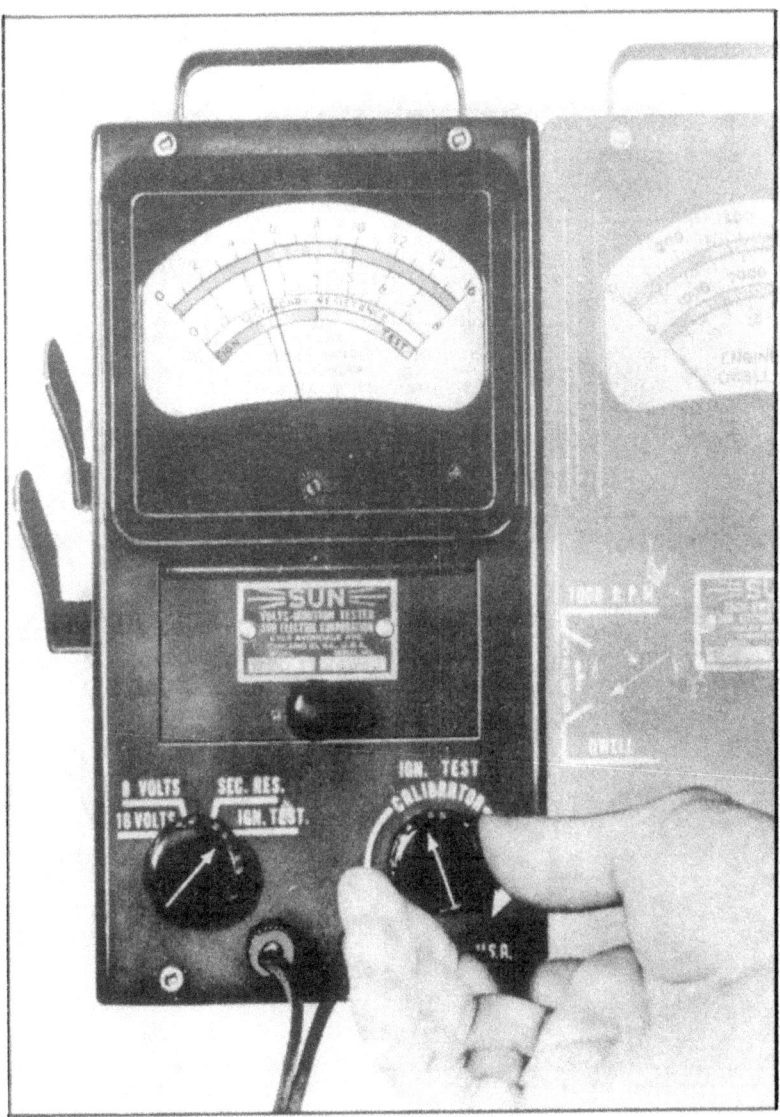

Fig. 44—Adjusting Ignition Test Meter

check for cracks or carbon tracks in distributor cap or defective insulation on those plug wires being lifted off. Errors in testing may be introduced if:

    coil is not at operating temperature, improper engine speed or SET LINE are used, or

    distributor point setting is not within specified limits.

26. TEST CHARGING VOLTAGE

    A. With engine remaining set at 1500 RPM, remove jumper wire from generator.

Do not remove jumper wire at a greater engine speed than 1500 RPM.

B. Connect RED volts-ignition lead to "battery" side of ballast resistor (BROWN wire terminal) and BLACK lead to GROUND.

C. Turn selector knob to the 16 volts position.

D. When voltage stablizes at 1500 RPM, read charging voltage on voltmeter.

A reading of 14-15 volts indicates the charging system and voltage regulator are operating satisfactorily.

A charging voltage below 14-15 volts may be the result of a defective generator or generator drive, defective or misadjusted voltage regulator or high resistance in circuits.

A charging voltage above 14-15 volts may be the result of a defective or misadjusted voltage regulator, high resistance in regulator ground circuit or defective field circuit.

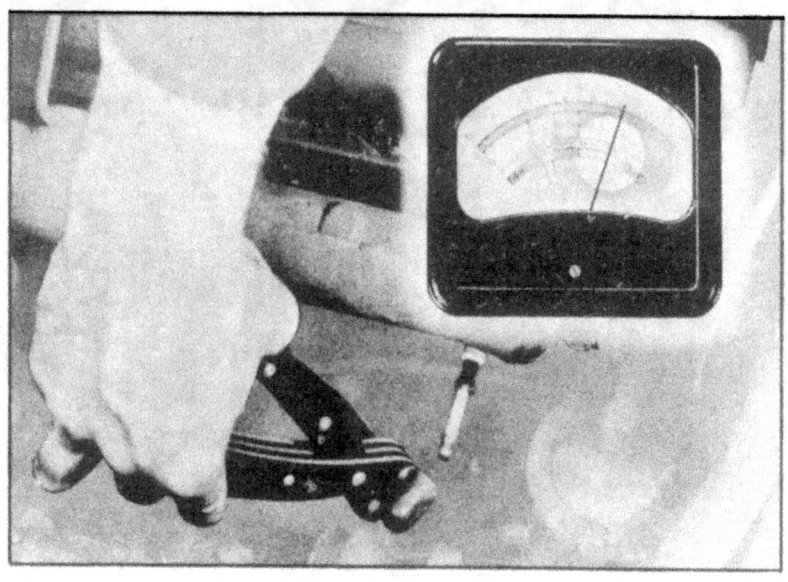

Fig. 45—Testing Ignition Output and Secondary Insulation

27. ADJUST IDLE SPEED AND MIXTURE

A. Connect hose from vacuum-pressure unit to vacuum port on carburetor or intake manifold on Fuel Injection models.

B. Install air cleaner.

C. With engine operating and choke fully "off" adjust idle speed and mixture as described below for the various types of installations.

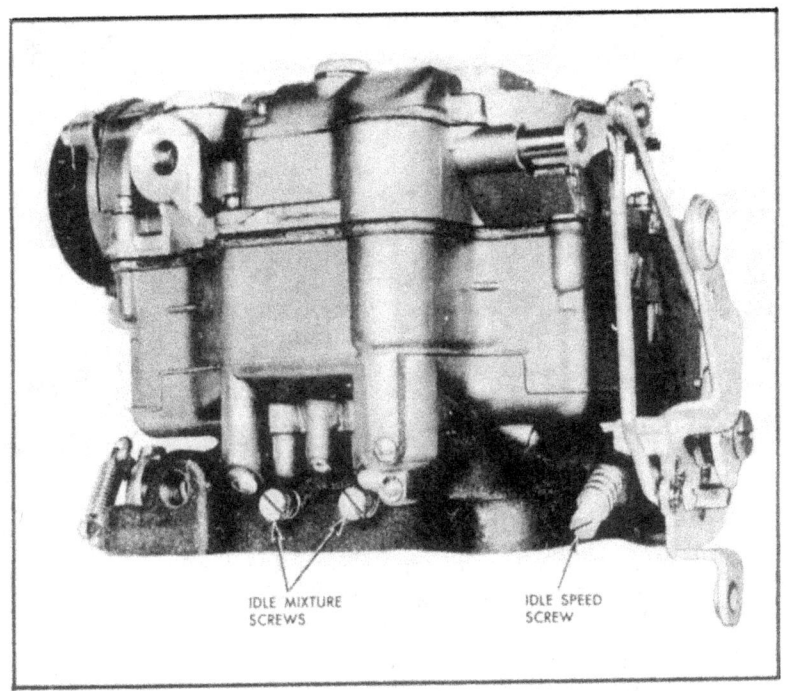

**Fig. 46—Idle Speed and Mixture Adjustment
Single Four-Barrel—Typical**

Carter WCFB
(Single Four-Barrel)

1. Adjust throttle lever screw, Fig. 46, to obtain the following idle speeds:

With standard transmission —475 RPM
With automatic transmission —450 RPM (in Drive)

2. Adjust each idle mixture screw, Fig. 46, separately to give highest steady vacuum reading.

3. If necessary, readjust engine idle to prescribed RPM, then make a "fine" adjustment of each mixture needle to obtain maximum smoothness and vacuum.

Carter WCFB
(Dual Four-Barrel)

1. Adjust the four idle mixture screws one (1) turn off of seat to obtain initial adjustment, Fig. 47.

2. Start engine and adjust idle speed screw to obtain 600 RPM in Drive on Automatic Transmission) for all 1956 models with conventional camshaft and 1957-60 models with rydraulic lifters, 800-850 RPM on 1956 models with heavy-duty field-installed camshaft

**Fig. 47—Idle Mixture Adjustment
Dual Four-Barrel**

and 1957-60 models with solid valve lifters.

3. Adjust mixture screws on rear carburetor until highest steady vacuum reading is obtained.

4. Repeat operation on front carburetor mixture screws.

5. Readjust idle speed screw to set speed at specifiecd idle.

6. After obtaining smooth idle, turn mixture screws clockwise one to two flats of screw to lean out the idle mixture. This will produce slight roughness on a shop idle, but will give maximum smoothness to a road idle.

Fuel Injection

To adjust idle speed and fuel mixture on Fuel Injection equipped engines, proceed as follows:

1. Turn both the idle air adjustment screw and idle fuel adjustment screw (2) turns off their seats. Fig. 48.

2. Start and warm-up engine, then adjust idle air screw to provide highest engine idle speed.

3. Adjust idle fuel adjustment screw to smooth out engine operation.

4. Readjust idle air adjustment screw to bring idle speed to approximately 500 RPM on engines with hydraulic valve lifters or to 700 RPM on engines equipped with mechanical valve lifters.

5. Finally adjust the idle fuel adjustment screw for possible further smoothness.

If engine runs smoothly at specified RPM and at a steady and satisfactory vacuum reading, the engine, ignition and fuel system are operating normally.

If vacuum reading is steady but lower than normal, check for late ignition timing, low compression, valves improperly adjusted or excessive mechanical drag in engine.

If vacuum reading is abnormally unsteady, check idle mixture, distributor point spacing, spark plug gapping, choke adjustment, valve adjustment, poor plug or carburetor condition, manifold air leaks, defective valves or uneven compression. If trouble with the Fuel Injection system is suspected, see the Fuel Injection portion of this manual for Trouble Shooting.

Fig. 48—Idle Adjustments—Fuel Injection

ADDITIONAL CHECKS AND ADJUSTMENTS

The following tests are included for use as required where either an abnormal condition requiring further checking has been detected during Tune-Up or a specific customer complaint exists:

Cylinder Balance Test
Fuel Pump Test
Cooling System Pressure Test

Additional checks and adjustments on items such as the battery, starting circuit, charging circuit and ignition circuit are fully presented in the Chevrolet Passenger Car Shop Manuals. Reference should be made to that publication, as these items are basically the same on the Chevrolet Passenger Car and the Corvette.

CYLINDER BALANCE TEST

It is often difficult to locate a weak cylinder, especially in an eight cylinder engine. A compression test for example, will not locate a leaky intake manifold, a valve not opening properly due to a worn camshaft, or a defective spark plug.

With the cylinder balance test, the power output of one cylinder may be checked against another, using a set of grounding leads. When the power output of each cylinder is not equal, the engine will lose power and run roughly.

Perform a cylinder balance test as follows, See Fig. 49.

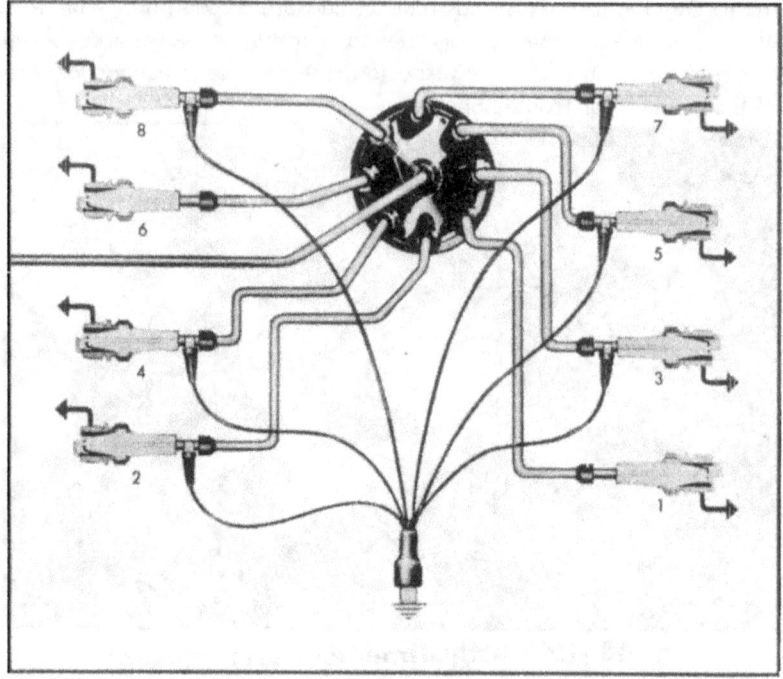

Fig. 49—Cylinder Balance Test Connections

A. Connect the tachometer and vacuum gauge.

B. Start engine and run at 1500 RPM.

C. Ground large clip of grounding leads and connect individual leads to all spark plugs EXCEPT the pair being tested.

Divide the firing order in half and arrange one half over the other. The cylinders to be tested together appear one over the other: i.e.

FIRING ORDER
    1-8-4-3-6-5-7-2 = 1-8-4-3 =
                         6-5-7-2
    1-6, 8-5, 4-7, 3-2.

D. Operate engine on each pair of cylinders in turn and note engine RPM and mainifold vacuum for each pair.

A variation of more than 1 inch of vacuum or 40 RPM between pairs of cylinders being tested indicates that the cylinders are off balance.

E. To isolate one weak cylinder, short out one bank of cylinders at a time.

The bank giving the lower readings will include the weak cylinder.

FUEL PUMP TEST

If the owner has complained of poor high speed performance, the fuel pump may be at fault. Too low a pump pressure or volume will cause a high speed miss because of lack of fuel delivered to the carburetor, while too high a pressure will cause carburetor flooding.

Pump Volume Test

1. Disconnect fuel line at carburetor and direct it into a container, preferably one indicating the PINT level.
2. Start engine and run at idle speed on fuel in carburetor bowl.
3. Measure the time required to deliver one pint of fuel then shut off engine. The pump should deliver one pint of fuel in 45 seconds or less.

If no gasoline or only a small amount flows from open end of pipe, then the fuel line is clogged, filter clogged or the pump is inoperative. Before removing pump, remove gas cap, disconnect both both inlet and outlet pipes and blow through them with an air hose to make sure they are clear. Reconnect pipes to pump and retest flow.

If capacity is within limits, proceed with Pump Pressure Test below.

Pump Pressure Test

1. Attach vacuum-pressure gauge hose to fuel line.
2. Operate engine at idle RPM and observe reading on gauge. Pressure should be 4-5 pounds on 1956 models, 4¾-5½ pounds on 1957-60 models and should remain constant at all speeds between 450 and 1000 RPM.

If pressure is to low or too high or varies materially at different speeds, the pump should be removed for repairs or replacement.

If the fuel pump checks out correctly on a high speed complaint, overhaul the carburetor or check out the Fuel Injection system on models so equipped.

3. Remove gauge and reconnect fuel line to carburetor. Inspect fuel lines for kinks and bends, and check all connections for leaks.

COOLING SYSTEM PRESSURE TEST

The following test may be performed with pressure testing equipment available commercially for this purpose. This test provides an excellent means of detecting internal or external leaks within the cooling system.

2. Apply a test pressure 3 pounds higher than the setting of the radiator cap, i.e. 10½ pounds for a 7½ pound cap or 12 pounds for a 9 pound cap.

3. If the pressure will not hold, there is either an internal or external leak within the system.

There's more than one way to beat a hot summer sun.

TROUBLES AND REMEDIES
ALL ENGINES

| Symptom and Probable Cause | Probable Remedy |

Lack of Power

1. **Poor Compression**
   a. Incorrect valve lash
   b. Leaky valves
   c. Valve stems or lifters sticking
   d. Valve springs weak or broken
   e. Valve timing incorrect
   f. Leaking cylinder head gasket
   g. Piston rings broken
   h. Poor fits between pistons, rings and cylinders

   a. Adjust valve lash according to instructions under "Valve Adjustment"
   b. Remove cylinder head and grind valves
   c. Free up or replace
   d. Replace springs
   e. Correct valve timing
   f. Replace gasket
   g. Replace rings
   h. Overhaul engine

2. **Ignition System Improperly Adjusted**
   a. Ignition not properly timed
   b. Spark plugs faulty
   c. Distributor points not set correctly

   a. Set ignition according to instructions under "Engine Tune-Up"
   b. Replace or clean, adjust and test spark plugs
   c. Set distributor points and time engine

3. **Lack of Fuel**
   a. Dirt or water in carburetor
   b. Gas lines partly plugged
   c. Dirt in gas tank
   d. Air leaks in gas line
   e. Fuel pump not functioning properly

   a. Clean carburetor and fuel pump
   b. Clean gas lines
   c. Clean gas tank
   d. Tighten and check gas lines
   e. Replace or repair fuel pump

4. **Carburetor Air Inlet Restricted**
   a. Air cleaner dirty
   b. Carburetor choke partly closed

   a. Clean air cleaner
   b. Adjust or replace choke mechanism

5. **Overheating**
   a. Lack of water
   b. Fan belt loose
   c. Fan belt worn or oil soaked
   d. Thermostat sticking closed
   e. Water pump inoperative
   f. Cooling system clogged
   g. Incorrect ignition or valve timing
   h. Brakes dragging
   i. Improper grade and viscosity oil being used
   j. Fuel mixture too lean
   k. Valves improperly adjusted
   l. Defective ignition system
   m. Exhaust system partly restricted

   a. Refill system
   b. Adjust or replace
   c. Replace belt
   d. Replace thermostat
   e. Replace water pump
   f. Clean and reverse flush
   g. Retime engine
   h. Adjust brakes
   i. Change to correct oil
   j. Overhaul or adjust carburetor
   k. Adjust valves
   l. See "Engine Tune-Up"
   m. Clean or replace

6. **Overcooling**
   a. Thermostat holding open

   a. Replace thermostat

Excessive Oil Consumption

1. **Leaking Oil**
   a. Oil pan drain plug loose
   b. Oil pan retainer bolts loose
   c. Oil pan gaskets damaged
   d. Timing gear cover loose or gasket damaged
   e. Oil return from timing gear case to block restricted, causing leak at crankshaft fan pulley hub on six cylinder models
   f. Rocker arm cover gaskets or, on six cylinder models, push rod cover damaged or loose
   g. Fuel pump loose or gasket damaged
   h. Rear main bearing leaking oil into clutch housing or flywheel housing
   i. Oil drain slots in intake manifold splash guard closed

   a. Tighten drain plug
   b. Tighten oil pan bolts
   c. Replace pan gaskets
   d. Tighten cover bolts or replace gasket
   e. Remove oil pan and clean oil return passages

   f. Tighten covers or replace gaskets

   g. Tighten fuel pump or replace gasket
   h. Adjust or replace main bearing or main bearing oil seal
   i. Remove intake manifold and open slots to .100"

2. Burning Oil

- a. Broken piston rings
- b. Rings not correctly seated to cylinder walls
- c. Piston rings worn excessively or stuck in ring grooves
- d. Piston ring oil return holes clogged with carbon
- e. Excessive clearance between piston and cylinder wall due to wear or improper fitting
- f. Cylinder walls, scored, tapered or out-of-round

- a. Replace rings
- b. Give sufficient time for rings to seat. Replace if necessary
- c. Replace rings
- d. Replace rings
- e. Fit new pistons
- f. Recondition cylinders and fit new pistons

Hard Starting

1. Slow Cranking

- a. Heavy engine oil
- b. Partially discharged battery
- c. Faulty or undercapacity battery
- d. Poor battery connections
- e. Faulty starter switch
- f. Faulty starting motor or drive

- a. Change to lighter oil
- b. Charge battery
- c. Replace battery
- d. Clean and tighten or replace connections
- e. Replace switch
- f. Overhaul starting motor

2. Ignition Trouble

- a. Distributor points burned or corroded
- b. Points improperly adjusted
- c. Spark plugs improperly gapped
- d. Spark plug wires loose and corroded in distributor cap
- e. Loose connections in primary circuit
- f. Series resistance in condenser circuit
- g. Low capacity condenser
- h. Ballast resister faulty or out of circuit

- a. Clean or replace points
- b. Readjust points
- c. Set plug gap at .035"
- d. Clean wire and cap terminals
- e. Tighten all connections in primary circuit
- f. Clean all connections in condenser circuit
- g. Install proper condenser
- h. Inspect and correct

3. Engine Condition

- a. Valves holding open
- b. Valves burned
- c. Leaking manifold gasket
- d. Loose carburetor mounting
- e. Faulty pistons, rings or cylinders

- a. Adjust valves
- b. Grind valves
- c. Tighten manifold bolts or replace gasket
- d. Tighten carburetor
- e. See "Poor Compression"

4. Carburetion

- a. Choke not operating properly
- b. Throttle not set properly
- c. Carburetor dirty and passages restricted

- a. Adjust or repair choke mechanism
- b. Set throttle
- c. Overhaul carburetor

Popping, Spitting and Detonation

1. Overheated Intake Manifold

- a. Manifold heat control spring not properly installed
- b. Manifold heat control valve sticking

- a. Check operation under "Engine Tune-Up"
- b. Free up heat control valve

2. Ignition Trouble

- a. Loose wiring connections
- b. Faulty wiring
- c. Faulty spark plugs

- a. Tighten all wire connections
- b. Replace faulty wiring
- c. Clean or replace and adjust plugs

3. Carburetion

- a. Lean combustion mixture
- b. Dirt in carburetor
- c. Restricted gas supply to carburetor
- d. Leaking carburetor or intake manifold gaskets

- a. Clean and adjust carburetor
- b. Clean carburetor
- c. Clean gas lines and check for restrictions
- d. Tighten carburetor to manifold and manifold to head bolts or replace gaskets

4. Valves

- a. Valves adjusted too tight
- b. Valves sticking

- a. Adjust valve lash
- b. Lubricate and free up. Grind valves if necessary

c. Exhaust valves thin and heads overheating
d. Weak valve springs
e. Valves timed early

c. Replace valves
d. Replace valve springs
e. Retime

5. Cylinder Head

a. Excessive carbon deposits in combustion chamber
b. Cylinder head water passages partly clogged causing hot spot in combustion chamber
c. Partly restricted exhaust ports in cylinder head
d. Cylinder head gasket blown between cylinders

a. Remove head and clean carbon
b. Remove cylinder head and clean water passages
c. Remove cylinder head and clean exhaust ports
d. Replace cylinder head gasket

6. Spark Plugs

a. Spark plugs glazed
b. Wrong heat range plug being used

a. Clean or replace spark plugs
b. Change to correct spark plugs

7. Exhaust System

a. Exhaust manifold or muffler restricted causing back pressure

a. Clean or replace manifold and muffler

Rough Engine Idle

1. Carburetor

a. Improper idling adjustment
b. Carburetor float needle valve not seating

a. Adjust according to instructions
b. Clean or replace

2. Air Leaks

a. Carburetor to manifold heat insulator or gasket leaks
b. Manifold to head gasket leaks
c. Air leaks in windshield wiper vacuum line

a. Tighten carburetor to manifold bolts or replace heat insulator or gasket
b. Tighten manifold to head bolts or replace gaskets
c. Check for leaks and repair

3. Valves

a. Improper lash adjustment
b. Valves not seating properly
c. Valves loose in guides or bores

a. Check and adjust valves
b. Grind valves
c. Condition valves

4. Cylinder Head

a. Cracks in exhaust ports
b. Head gasket leaks

a. Replace cylinder head
b. Replace cylinder head gasket

Engine Misses On Acceleration

1. Carburetion

a. Accelerating pump jet misadjusted plugged or vapor vent ball in pump plunger not working
b. Lean fuel mixture

a. Overhaul carburetor or, on eight cylinder models, adjust pump travel
b. Overhaul carburetor

2. Ignition Trouble

a. Faulty spark plugs
b. Faulty ignition wiring
c. Improperly adjusted or faulty distributor points
d. Weak coil

a. Clean, adjust or replace plugs
b. Replace faulty wiring
c. Adjust or replace distributor points
d. Replace coil

3. Engine

a. Burned or improperly adjusted valves
b. Leaky manifold gaskets
c. Poor compression due to cylinder, piston or ring condition
d. Leaky cylinder head gasket

a. Adjust, replace or grind valves
b. Tighten manifold or replace gaskets
c. Overhaul engine
d. Replace gasket

| Symptom and Probable Cause | Probable Remedy |

Engine Noise

1. Crankshaft Bearings Loose

a. Bearings improperly fitted
b. Crankshaft journals out-of-round
c. Crankshaft journals rough
d. Oil passages in block restricted
e. Insufficient oil
f. Improper grade and viscosity oil being used
g. Oil pump failure

h. Contaminated oil

a. Readjust main bearings
b. Replace or recondition crankshaft
c. Replace or recondition crankshaft
d. Clean passages
e. Adjust or replace bearings. Replenish oil
f. Adjust bearings and change to correct oil
g. Replace oil pump, adjust or replace bearings and damaged parts
h. Wash motor thoroughly. Adjust or replace bearings and other damaged parts

2. Connecting Rod Bearings Loose

a. Worn bearings
b. Crankpins rough

c. Insufficient oil
d. Oil pump failure

e. Improper grade and viscosity of oil used

a. Replace bearings
b. Polish or replace shaft. Adjust or replace bearings
c. Adjust or replace bearings and replenish oil
d. Replace oil pump. Replace or adjust rod bearings
e. Replace rod bearings and change to proper oil

3. Pistons or Pins Loose

a. Excessive cylinder wear

b. Improperly fitted pistons or pins
c. Contaminated Oil

d. Faulty fuel or ignition system causing unburned fuel to flush the oil from cylinder walls
e. Piston pin or bore wear

a. Hone cylinders and fit new pistons and rings. Make sure all abrasive that would cause cylinder wear is removed
b. Replace pistons or pins
c. Make necessary replacements, flush oiling system and use new oil
d. Make necessary repairs to fuel or ignition system, replace worn parts and change oil
e. Ream pin bore and install oversize piston pins on six cylinder models. Replace pistons and pins on eight cylinder models

4. Engine Noise—General

a. Bent connecting rod
b. Excessive end play in camshaft on six cylinder models
c. Excessive crankshaft end play
d. Broken piston ring

e. Loose timing gears or chain
f. Dry push rod sockets
g. Bent oil gauge rod
h. Improperly adjusted valve lash
i. Sticking valves

a. Replace rod
b. Replace camshaft thrust plate, or correct end play by pressing gear on further
c. Replace main bearings
d. Replace broken ring and check condition of cylinder wall
e. Replace timing gears or chain
f. Polish and lubricate push rod sockets
g. Replace oil gauge rod
h. Adjust valve lash
i. Free sticking valves or grind valves

COOLING SYSTEM

| Symptom and Probable Cause | Probable Remedy |

Overheating

a. Lack of Coolant
b. Fan belt loose
c. Fan belt oil soaked
d. Thermostat sticks closed
e. Water pump inoperative
f. Cooling system inoperative
g. Incorrect ignition timing
h. Brakes dragging severely

a. Refill system and check for leaks
b. Adjust
c. Replace fan belt
d. Replace thermostat
e. Repair or replace water pump
f. Clean system and reverse flush
g. Retime engine
h. Adjust brakes

Overcooling

a. Thermostat remains open
b. Extremely cold climate

a. Replace thermostat
b. Cover part of radiator area

Symptom and Probable Cause	Probable Remedy
Loss of Coolant a. Leaking radiator b. Loose or damaged hose connection c. Leaking water pump d. Loose or damaged heater hose e. Leaking heater unit f. Leak at cylinder head gasket g. Cracked cylinder head h. Cracker cylinder or block expansion plug loose i. Engine operating at too high temperature	a. Replace or repair b. Tighten or replace hose connections c. Repair water pump d. Tighten or replace hose e. Replace or repair heater core f. Replace gasket and tighten bolts securely and evenly g. Replace cylinder head h. Make necessary repairs or replacements i. See overheating causes
Circulation System Noisy a. Pump bearing rough b. Fan blades loose or bent c. Fan blades noisy in pulley d. Fan belt inner plies loose e. Improper fan to shroud clearance	a. Replace pump b. Tighten or replace fan blades c. Dress with belt dressing or soap and adjust d. Replace fan belt e. Adjust clearance, ⅝" to ¾"

RADIATOR REPLACEMENT

Removal

1. Remove drain plug and drain radiator.
2. Remove six bottom bolts (3 on each side) holding shroud and radiator on vehicles equipped with V-8 engines.

   NOTE: Leave two bolts holding radiator and shroud until radiator and shroud is ready to be removed.

   NOTE: Vehicles equipped with six cylinder engines use no shroud. Fan blade to radiator core clearance should be ½" minimum.

3. Remove radiator inlet and outlet hoses.
4. Remove transmission oil cooler lines, if so equipped.
5. Remove remaining two bolts and move shroud back onto fan. Remove radiator.

Installation

1. Slide radiator core into position.
2. Support radiator and install attaching bolts for shroud and radiator.
3. Install radiator hoses and radiator drain plug.
4. Install oil cooler lines on automatic transmission models.
5. Fill cooling system and check for leaks.

FUEL PUMP

Symptom and Probable Cause	Probable Remedy
Fuel Pump Leaks—Fuel a. Loose housing screws. b. Ruptured or torn diaphragm. c. Loose fittings. d. Stripped thread on inlet and outlet fittings.	a. Tighten housing screws. b. Install new diaphragm. c. Tighten fittings. d. Replace fittings.
Fuel Pump Leaks—Oil a. Hole in diaphragm. b. Leak at mounting flange. c. Damaged oil seal.	a. Install new diaphragm. b. Install new mounting gasket and tighten fuel pump mounting bolts. c. Replace oil seal.
Insufficient Fuel Delivery a. Loose fuel line fittings. b. Damaged diaphragm. c. Cracked or broken fuel line.	a. Tighten fittings. b. Install new diaphragm. c. Replace line.
Fuel Pump Noise a. Pump loose at mounting. b. Worn rocker arm. c. Broken or weak rocker arm spring.	a. Tighten fuel pump mounting bolt. b. Replace. c. Install new rocker arm spring.

BATTERY AND STARTING CIRCUIT

Slow Engine Cranking Speed Partially discharged battery Low capacity battery Faulty battery cell Loose or corroded terminals Under capacity cables Burned starter solenoid switch contacts Internal starting motor trouble Heavy oil or other engine trouble causing undue load	Charge or change battery and determine cause of battery condition Cycle battery to improve capacity or replace it Replace battery Clean and tighten terminals Replace battery cables Replace solenoid Overhaul starting motor Make necessary repairs to engine

Starter Engages but Will Not Crank Engine

Partially discharged battery	Charge or change battery
Faulty battery cells	Replace battery
Bent armature shaft or damaged drive mechanism	Overhaul starter
Faulty armature or fields	Overhaul starter

Starter Will Not Run

Battery fully discharged	Replace or charge battery
Disconnected battery cables	Replace faulty cables
Shorted or open starter circuit	Make necessary repairs

GENERATING CIRCUIT

Low Charging Rate

Fully charged battery and low charging rate	This is a normal condition with a fully charged battery
Fan belt slipping	Replace or adjust belt
Generator commutator dirty	Clean commutator
High resistance in charging circuit	Check charging circuit progressively and make necessary repairs to remove high resistance
Too low voltage setting of voltage regulator unit	Adjust voltage regulator
Oxidized voltage regulator points	Clean and adjust points
Partially shorted field coils	Overhaul generator

High Charging Rate With Fully Charged Battery

Voltage regulator setting too high	Adjust voltage regulator
Voltage regulator points stuck	Clean and adjust points and readjust regulator
Regulator unit improperly grounded	Remove regulator and clean connections. Readjust regulator
Generator field circuit to regulator short circuited	Test to locate short circuit and make necessary repairs
Shunt field circuit short circuited within regulator	Replace regulator

Low Battery and No Charging Rate

Fan belt broken or loose	Replace or tighten fan belt
Charging circuit open between regulator and battery	Locate open circuit and make necessary repairs
Cut-out voltage winding open circuited	Replace regulator unit
Corroded points in current and voltage regulator	Clean points and readjust regulator
Open circuit between generator and regulator	Locate open circuit and make necessary repairs to wiring
Internal trouble in generator	Overhaul generator

IGNITION CIRCUIT

Engine Will Not Start
(See Starting and Fuel System Troubles)

Weak battery	Charge battery
Excessive moisture on high tension wiring or spark plugs	Dry parts
Cracked distributor cap	Replace cap
Faulty coil or condenser	Replace faulty unit
Coil to distributor high tension wire not in place	Properly install wire
Loose connections or broken wire in low tension circuit	Tighten or replace wires
Improperly adjusted or faulty distributor points	Clean and adjust or replace points

Hard Starting
(See Starting and Fuel System Troubles)

Faulty or improperly set spark plugs	Clean and adjust or replace spark plugs
Improperly adjusted or faulty distributor points	Clean or replace and adjust points
Loose connections in primary circuit	Tighten loose connections
Worn or oil soaked high tension wires	Replace high tension wires
Low capacity condenser	Replace condenser
Low capacity coil	Replace coil
Faulty distributor cap or rotor	Replace faulty part

Engine Misfires

Dirty or worn spark plugs	Clean or replace plugs
Damaged insulation on high tension wires or wires disconnected	Connect or replace wires
Distributor cap cracked	Replace cap
Poor cylinder compression	See Engine Troubles
Improper distributor point adjustment	Adjust distributor points

SPARK PLUG DIAGNOSIS

Plug Conditions	Factors Causing This Condition	Corrective Action
Plug "Flash Over" (Firing from upper terminal to base of plug)	Dirty insulator tops—oil dirt and moisture on insulator will shunt current to base of plug. The above condition can be caused by failure of spark plug boot.	Keep plugs wiped clean with cloth moistened with cleaning solvent. Check spark plug boot and replace if necessary.
Oil or Carbon Fouling	Wet, black deposits on firing end of plug indicate oil pumping condition. This is usually caused by worn piston rings, pistons, cylinders or sticky valves.	Correct engine condition. In most cases plugs in this condition will be serviceable after proper cleaning and regapping.
	Soft, fluffy, dry black carbon deposits usually indicate a rich mixture operation, excessive idling, improper operation of automatic choke or faulty adjustment of carburetor.	If troubles are not eliminated, use "hotter" type plug.
	Hard baked-on, black carbon deposits result from use of too cold a plug.	Use "hotter" type plug.
Lead Fouling (Light & powdery or shiny glazed coating on firing end)	By-products of combustion and fuel additives, deposited as a powder which may later melt and glaze on insulator tip.	Remove deposits by blast cleaning. If this is not possible, plugs should be replaced.
Normal Electrode Wear	Due to intense heat, pressure and corrosive gases together with spark discharge, the electrode wears and gap widens.	Plugs should be regapped every 5000 miles.
Rapid Electrode Wear	Condition may be caused by (1) burned valves, (2) gas leakage past threads and seat gaskets, due to insufficient installation torque or damaged gasket, (3) too lean a mixture or (4) plug too "hot" for operating speeds and loads.	Correct engine condition. Install plugs to specified torque. Use a new spark plug seat gasket each time a new or cleaned spark plug is installed. Use "colder" type plug if condition continues to exist.
Broken Upper Insulator (Firing around shell crimp under load conditions)	Careless removal or installation of spark plug.	Replace with a new spark plug.
Broken Lower Insulator (Firing Tip)	The cause is usually carelessness in regapping by either bending of centerwire to adjust the gap or permitting the gapping tool to exert pressure against the tip of the center electrode or insulator when bending the side electrode to adjust the gap.	Replace with a new spark plug.
	Fracture or breakage of lower insulator may also occasionally occur if the engine has been operated under conditions causing severe and prolonged detonation or preignition.	Use "colder" type plug for the particular type of operation.
Damaged Shell	Very seldom occurs but cause is almost always due to mishandling by applying excessive torque during installation. This failure is usually in the form of a crack in the Vee of the thread next to the seat gasket or at the groove below the hex.	Replace with a new spark plug.

Symptom and Probable Cause	Probable Remedy

HEADLAMP AND CIRCUIT

Headlights Dim (engine idling or shut off)

Partly discharged battery — Charge battery
Defective cells in battery — Replace battery
High resistance in light circuit — Check headlight circuit including ground connection. Make necessary repairs
Faulty sealed beam units — Replace sealed beam units

Headlights Dim (engine running above idle)

High resistance in lighting circuit — Check lighting circuit including ground connection. Make necessary repairs
Faulty sealed beam units — Replace sealed beam units
Faulty voltage control unit — Test voltage control and generator Make necessary repairs

Lights Flicker

Loose connections or damaged wires in lighting circuit — Tighten connections and check for damaged wiring
Light wiring insulation damaged producing momentary short — Check light wiring and replace or tape damaged wires

Lights Burn Out Frequently

High voltage regulator setting	Adjust voltage regulator
Loose connections in lighting circuit	Check circuit for loose connections

Lights Will Not Light

Discharged battery	Recharge battery and correct cause
Loose connections in lighting circuit	Tighten connections
Burned out bulbs	Replace bulbs or sealed beam unit
Open or corroded contacts in lighting switch	Replace lighting switch
Open or corroded contacts in dimmer switch	Replace dimmer switch

Thermal Circuit Breaker Causing Current Interruption

Short in headlamp wiring	Check wiring of circuits in use for short circuits and make necessary repairs
Short within some light or instrument in use	Check lights or instruments for short. Headlamps are on separate circuit breaker from remainder of lighting units. Instruments are fused.

GASOLINE GAUGE

Gauge Shows Empty at All Times

Tank unit shorted	Replace unit
Wire from dash unit to tank unit shorted	Replace wire or repair short
Float stuck in empty position	Replace tank unit
Dash unit improperly grounded on instrument panel	Properly ground dash unit

Gauge Shows Full at All Times

Tank unit burned out	Replace tank unit
Wire between units disconnected or broken	Connect or replace wire
High resistance in wire between units	Clean connections and terminals
Float stuck in full position	Replace tank unit

Gauge Does Not Register Accurately (within normal limits)

Bent hand on dash unit	Replace unit or straighten hand
High resistance in circuit	Check and correct circuit
Partial short in circuit	Correct cause of short
Loose electrical connections	Tighten connections at dash unit and tank unit

STOPLIGHT AND CIRCUIT

Will Not Light

Switch faulty	Replace switch
Wires broken, disconnected or loose	Make necessary repairs
Bulb burned out	Replace bulb
Loose connection or poorly grounded lamp body	Tighten loose connections or properly ground lamp body
Burned out fuse	Check for shorts and replace fuse

HORNS

Will Not Blow

Loose connections or broken wire	Tighten loose connections or replace broken wire
Horn button not making contact	Adjust horn button contact
Faulty horn	Replace horn
Defective horn relay	Replace horn relay

Horn Tone Poor

Faulty horn	Replace horn

Horn Operates Intermittently

Loose connections or intermittent connections in horn relay or horn circuit	Check connections and repair as required
Horn switch out of adjustment	Adjust horn button contact
Defective horn relay	Replace horn relay
Defects within the horn	Replace horn

Horn Operates Continuously

Relay sticking	Replace relay
Horn button sticking	Adjust horn button contact

GENERATOR TELLTALE LIGHT

Ignition on, Engine Not Running, Telltale Off

Indicator bulb burned out	Replace bulb
Open circuit or loose connection in telltale circuit	Locate open circuit or loose connection and correct

Telltale Light Stays On After Engine is Started

If on at idle only, improper idle speed
Low generator output

Adjust idle speed and check for loose fan belt
Check generator output

OIL PRESSURE INDICATOR

Telltale Light On, Engine Running

Circuit grounded betwen telltale light and pressure switch
Oil pressure switch not functioning properly
Oil pressure switch calibration wrong
Oil pressure low

Locate and correct grounded condition
Replace switch
Replace switch
Correct as necessary

Ignition On, Engine Not Running, Telltale Off

Telltale light burned out
Open circuit between light and ignition switch or light and pressure switch
Pressure switch stuck
Pressure switch not grounded

Replace bulb
Find and correct open circuit
Replace switch
Check threads of switch for foreign material

LAMP BULB DATA

Location	Candle Power	Number
Headlamp—Outer–high	37½ (Watts)	5¾"
Outer–low	50 (Watts)	
Inner–high	37½ (Watts)	Sealed Beam
Headlamp Beam Indicator	1	53
Parking and Direction Signal	4-32	1034
Tail and Stop-Direction Signal	4-32	1034
Ignition Switch	1	53
Tachometer	2	57
License Plate Lamp	3	67
Instrument Panel	2	57
Electric Clock	2	57
Courtesy Lamp (Optional Eqpt.)	6	90
Radio Dial (Optional Eqpt.)	2	GE 1891
Cigarette Lighter (Optional Eqpt.)	1	53
Parking Brake Alarm Lamp (Optional Eqpt.)	6	90

FUSE AND CIRCUIT BREAKER DATA

Circuit	Ampere Rating	Circuit Breaker or Fuse
Headlamp, Headlamp Beam Indicator, and Parking Light.	15 amp.	Circuit Breaker
Tail, Stop, License, and Courtesy Lamp	3AG/AGC 10 Amp.	Fuse
Instrument and Clock Lights	3AG/AGC 3 Amp.	Fuse
Radio (Optional Eqpt.)	3AG/AGC 7½ Amp.	Fuse
Parking Brake Alarm (Optional Eqpt.)	3AG/AGC 10 Amp.	Fuse
Heater (Optional Eqpt.)	3AG/AGC 10 Amp.	Fuse

Junction Block—Fuses for the Radio, Parking Brake Alarm and Heater (All Optional equipment) are on the junction block located on the fire wall just above the dimmer switch.

Wiring Diagram

Engine Repairs

CRANKCASE VENTILATION—STANDARD

The breather filter should be cleaned with a solvent every 2000 miles. After cleaning, oil the mesh with light engine oil.

The road-draft tube seldom requires service.

CRANKCASE VENTILATION—POSITIVE

The positive crankcase ventilation system will operate effectively as long as normal maintenance is applied. Due to the nature of the materials carried by the ventilating system, the valve and pipe are subject to fouling with sludge and carbon formation.

At regular intervals of 10,000 miles or less, depending on operating conditions, the metering valve, the pipe running from the valve to the intake manifold and manifold fitting should be removed from the engine, disassembled and cleaned thoroughly.

> **NOTE:** Under cold weather operating conditions, when vehicles are operated at slow speeds with low engine temperatures, more rapid accumulations of harmful fumes may be present in the

engine. Under these conditions of operation the valve and tube must be cleaned more frequently than specified above. However, no specific mileage recommendation can be made under these conditions. Frequency of cleaning must be dictated by experience.

VALVE LASH ADJUSTMENT—ENGINE RUNNING

The following procedure, performed with the engine running, supplements the valve lash adjustment as instructed under Service Operations—Valve Lash Adjustment.

1. After the engine has been normalized, remove valve covers and install a reworked valve cover (cut the top out of a used valve cover) and gasket, on cylinder heads to prevent oil from running out.
2. With the engine running at idle, back off valve rocker arm nuts (one at a time) until the valve rocker arm starts to clatter.
3. Turn rocker arm nut down until the clatter just stops; continue to turn nut down exactly 1 turn.
   NOTE: The engine will run rough for a few seconds until the lifter plunger adjusts to its normal operating position. Noisy lifters should be replaced.
4. Remove reworked covers, install new gaskets and valve covers.

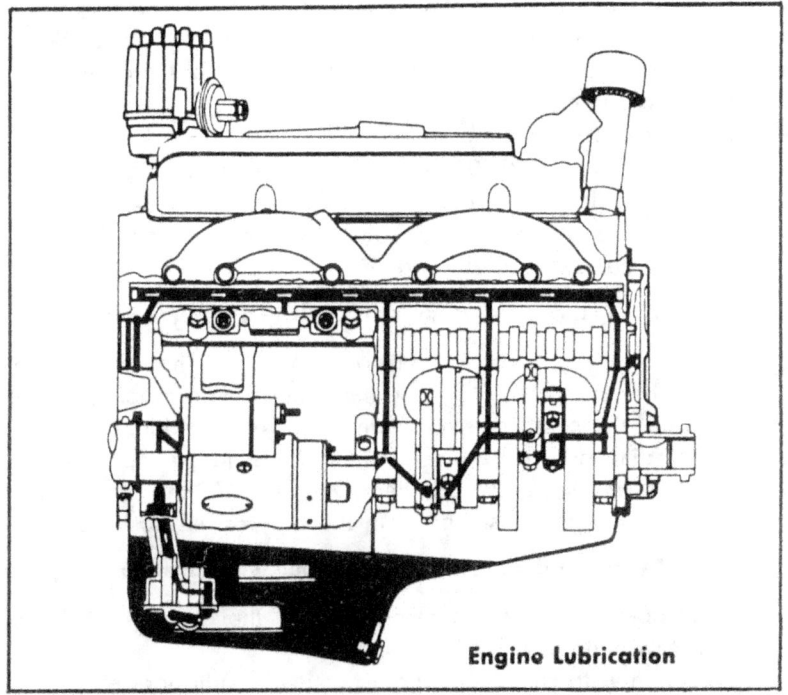

Engine Lubrication

Fig. 58—Checking Camshaft Lobe Lift

CHECKING CAMSHAFT LOBE LIFT

NOTE: Procedure is similar to that used for checking valve timing. If improper valve operation is indicated, check the lift of each lobe in consecutive order and record the readings.

1. Remove valve rocker covers and gaskets.
2. Remove rocker arms and balls.
3. Attach Tool J-8520 to stud as shown in Figure 58.
4. Position clamp on Tool J-8520 as shown in Figure 58.
5. Position indicator with ball socket adapter on Tool J-8520 to push rod as shown in Figure 58.

NOTE: Make sure push rod is in the lifter socket.

6. Rotate the crankshaft balancer slowly in the direction of rotation until the lifter is on the heel of the cam lobe. At this point, the push rod will be in its lowest position.
7. Set dial indicator on zero, then rotate the damper slowly, or attach an auxiliary starter switch and "bump" the engine over, until the push rod is in the fully raised position.

NOTE: Ground primary wire on coil, when cranking engine.

8. Compare the total lift recorded from the dial indicator Tool J-8520 with specifications.
9. Continue to rotate the engine until the indicator reads zero.

This will be a check on the accuracy of the original indicator reading.
10. If camshaft readings for all lobes are within specifications, remove dial indicator assembly Tool J-8520 from cylinder head stud.
11. Install all push rods and valve rocker arms and balls. Adjust valves as outlined in this section.
12. Replace valve rocker covers and gaskets.

CAMSHAFT—WEAR LIMIT

1961 283 Engine	Turbo-Fire	Super Turbo-Fire
	Inlet and Exhaust	Inlet and Exhaust
New	.222" ± .002"	.266" ± .002"
Worn	.217" ± .003"/.002"	.261" ± .003"/.002"

INTAKE MANIFOLD

Removal
1. Drain radiator, remove air cleaner, crankcase ventilator and by-pass cooling hose to water pump.
2. Disconect carburetor linkage, fuel and vacuum lines, temperature sending unit and coil primary wires. Disconnect coil to distributor secondary wire. Remove distributor clamp and remove distributor.
3. Remove bolts attaching intake manifold to cylinder heads. Remove manifold and discard gaskets.

Installation
1. Clean gasket faces of manifold and cylinder heads.
2. Install intake manifold end gaskets on cylinder block. Coat ends of intake manifold side gaskets around water passages with a good gasket sealing compound and install on cylinder heads.
3. Install intake manifold and bolts and check for misalignment of manifold and gaskets, reposition if necessary. Tighten bolts a little at a time according to the sequence shown in Figure 59. Final torque should be 25-35 ft. lbs.
4. Install distributor and distributor holding clamp. Connect coil to distributor secondary wire and coil primary wire. Con-

Fig. 59—Intake Manifold Bolt Torque Sequence

nect temperature sending unit wire, fuel and vacuum lines.
5. Connect all carburetor linkage and adjust as outlined in Section 10. Install carburetor air cleaner and crankcase ventilator.
6. Connect all radiator hoses and by-pass hose to thermostat housing.
7. Fill radiator, start engine and check for leaks.

HYDRAULIC VALVE LIFTERS

Hydraulic valve lifters very seldom require attention. The lifters are extremely simple in design, readjustments are not necessary, and servicing of the lifters require only that care and cleanliness be exercised in the handling of parts.

The easiest method for locating a noisy valve lifter is by use of a piece of garden hose approximately four feet in length. Place one end of the hose near the end of each intake and exhaust valve with the other end of the hose to the ear.

In this manner, the sound is localized making it easy to determine which lifter is at fault.

Another method is to place a finger on the face of the valve spring retainer. If the lifter is not functioning properly, a distinct shock will be felt when the valve returns to its seat.

The general types of valve lifter noise are as follows:
 1. **Hard Rapping Noise**—Usually caused by the plunger becoming tight in the bore of the lifter body to such an extent that

the return spring can no longer push the plunger back up to working position. Probable causes are:

a. Excessive varnish or carbon deposit causing abnormal stickiness.

b. Galling or "pick-up" between plunger and bore of lifter body, usually caused by an abrasive piece of dirt or metal wedging between plunger and lifter body.

2. **Moderate Rapping Noise**—Probable causes are:
   a. Excessive high leakdown rate.
   b. Leaky check valve seat.
   c. Improper lash adjustment.

3. **General Noise Throughout the Valve Train**—This will, in almost all cases, be a definte indication of insufficent oil supply, or improper lash adjustment.

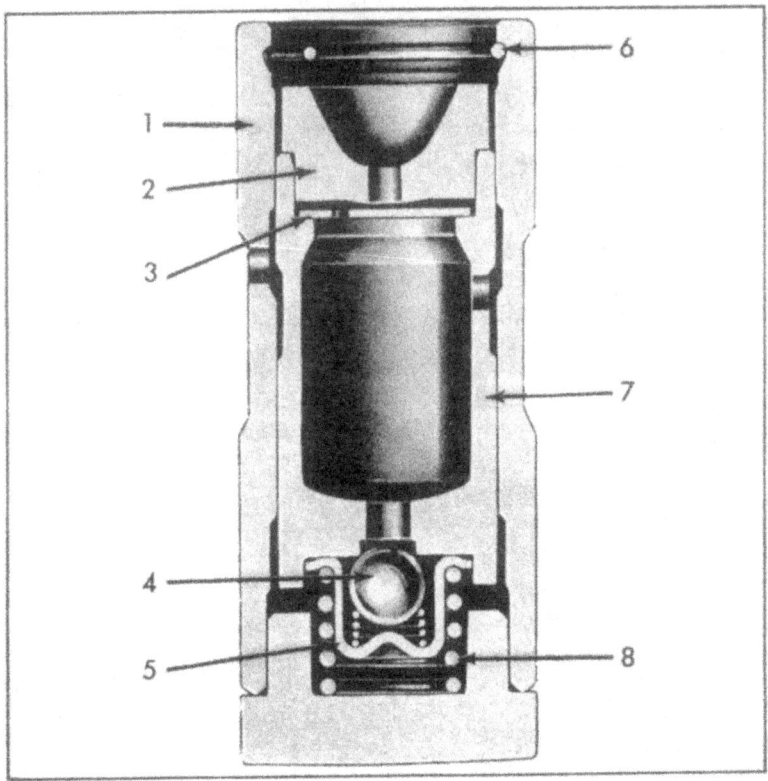

Fig. 60—Hydraulic Valve Lifter

1. Lifter Body
2. Push Rod Seat
3. Metering Valve
4. Check Ball
5. Ball Retainer
6. Push Rod Seat Retainer
7. Plunger
8. Plunger Spring

4. **Intermittent Clicking**—Probable causes are:
   a. A microspocic piece of dirt momentarily caught between ball seat and check valve ball.
   b. In rare cases, the ball itself may be out-of-round or have a flat spot.
   c. Improper Lash adjustment.

In most cases where noise exists in one or more lifters, all lifter units should be removed, cleaned in a solvent, reassembled, and reinstalled in the engine. If dirt, varnish, carbon, etc. is shown to exist in one unit, it more than likely exists in all the units, thus it would only be a matter of time before all lifters caused trouble.

In instances where parts are damaged, particularly the plunger or lifter body, the complete lifter unit should be replaced. However, in rare or emergency cases an Arkansas hard stone may be used to remove metal scratches or humps; and if after correcting, the plunger will operate freely in the lifter body, the parts may be thoroughly cleaned and the unit assembled and installed.

A few precautions to follow when servicing the valve lifter are:
1. Plungers are not interchangeable, they are a selective fit at the factory. Should a plunger or lifter body become damaged, it is necessary to replace the whole unit.
2. The plunger must be free in the lifter body. A simple test for this is to be sure the plunger will drop of its own weight in the body.
3. There must be no excessive leakdown and there must be no ball check valve leakage.

VALVE LIFTER
Removal
1. Remove rocker arm cover attaching screws with reinforcements and remove covers and gaskets.
2. Remove intake manifold as described in previous outline.
3. Back off rocker arm nuts until arms may be pivoted away from push rods. Remove push rods.
4. Remove hydraulic valve lifters.

NOTE: Valve lifters should be placed in a rack in their proper sequence so they can be installed in their same positions in the cylinder block.

Disassembly and Assembly
1. Hold plunger down with a push rod and, using a small screwdriver or awl, remove push rod seat retainer.
2. Remove push rod seat and metering valve, plunger and spring from lifter body.
3. Pull check valve ball retainer from plunger and remove ball

and spring.
4. Thoroughly clean all parts in cleaning solvent, and inspect them carefully. If any parts are damaged, the entire lifter assembly should be replaced.
5. To reassemble the lifter:
   a. Place check ball on small hole in bottom of plunger.
   b. Insert check ball spring on seat in ball retainer and place retiner over ball so spring rests on ball. Carefully squeeze retainer and press into position in plunger.
   c. Place plunger spring over ball retainer and slide lifter body over spring and plunger.
   d. Install push rod seat and metering valve in open end of plunger, push plunger into body and install retainer.
6. Compress plunger to open oil holes and fill plunger with SAE 10 oil. Work plunger up and down and refill.

Installation
1. Install valve lifters.
2. Install intake manifold as described in this section.
3. Install push rods.
4. Pivot rocker arms to engage push rods and adjust valve lash.

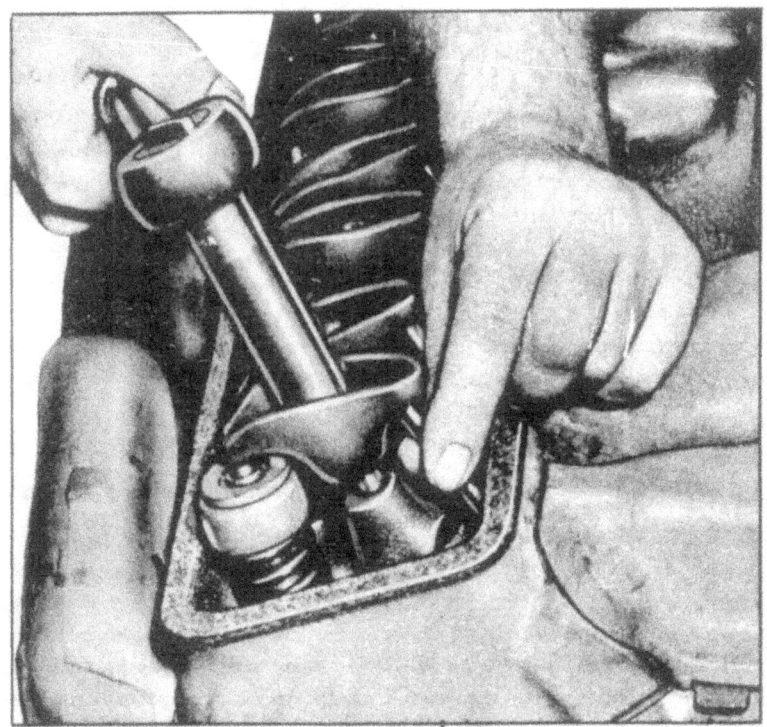

Fig. 61—Adjusting Valve Lash

VALVE LASH ADJUSTMENT

1. Adjust valve as follows:

    a. Crank engine until mark on harmonic balancer lines up with center or "0" mark on the timing tab fastened to the timing chain cover, with the engine in the Number 1 firing position. This may be determined by placing fingers on the number 1 cylinder valve as the mark on the balancer comes near the "O" mark on the front end cover. If the valves are not moving, the engine is in the number 1 firing position. If the valves move as the mark comes up to the timing tab, the engine is in number 6 firing position and should be turned over one more time to reach the number 1 position.

    b. Valve adjustment is made by backing off the adjusting nut (rocker arm stud nut) until there is play in the valve push rod and then tightened to just remove all push rod to rocker arm clearance. This may be determined by rotating push rod with fingers as the nut is tightened (fig. 61). When rod does not readily move in relation to the rocker arm, the clearance has been elimiated. The adjusting nut should then be tightened an additional 1 turn to place the hydraulic lifter plunger in the center of its travel. No other adjustment is required.

    c. With the engine in the number 1 firing position as determined above, the following valves may be adjusted.

    Exhaust—1,3,4,8
    Intake—1,2,5,7

    d. Crank the engine one revolution until the pointer "0" mark and harmonic balancer mark are again in alignment. This is number 6 firing position. With the engine in this position, the following valves may be adjusted.

    Exhaust—2,5,6,7
    Intake—3,4,6,8

2. Install rocker arm covers using new gaskets, and tighten screws to 2½ ft. lbs., after determining that cover hole reinforcements are in place.

Start engine and check for oil leaks at rocker arm covers.

NOTE: If noisy, refer to valve lash adjustment—engine running.

CYLINDER HEAD AND VALVE CONDITIONING

The condition of the cylinder heads and valve mechanism, more than anything else, determines the power, performance and economy of a valve-in-head engine. Extreme care should be exercised when conditioning the cylinder heads and valves to maintain correct valve stem to guide clearance, correctly ground valves, valve seats of correct width and correct valve adjustment.

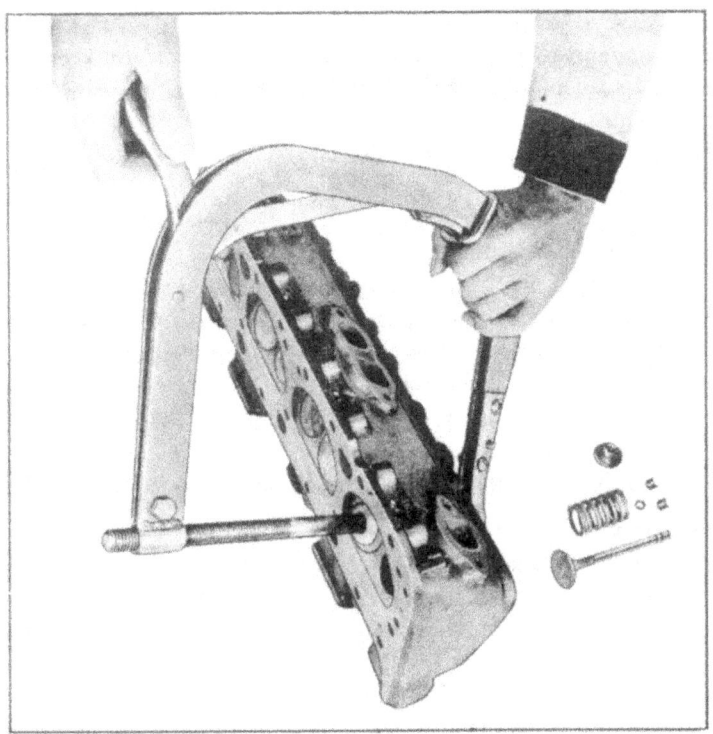

Fig. 62—Removing Valves

Removal
1. Drain radiator, engine block, remove air cleaner wing nut and remove air cleaner.
2. Disconnect throttle rod from carburetor. On Powerglide or Turboglide models, disconnect lower transmission throttle lever rod.
3. Disconect fuel, vacuum and automatic choke lines from carburetor.
4. Disconnect coil primary wires. Disconnect coil to distributor secondary wire. Remove distributor clamp and remove distributor.
5. On over-drive equipped models, disconnect kick-down switch wires from switch.
6. Remove spark plug wires from spark plugs and remove plugs.
7. Remove water outlet hose and heater hose, if so equipped, from intake manifold.
8. Remove temperature indicator unit from intake manifold.
9. Remove bolts attaching intake manifold to cylinder heads. Remove manifold.
10. Remove fan belt.

11. Remove exhaust manifold to exhaust cross-over pipe stud nuts and allow cross-over pipe to drop for clearance. Remove exhaust manifold heat control valve from right bank exhaust manifold.
12. Disconnect generator field and armature wires from generator.
13. Remove exhaust manifold to cylinder head bolts and remove exhaust manifolds.
14. Remove choke heat tube and remove rocker arm covers.
15. Back off rocker arm nuts, pivot rocker arms to clear push rods and remove push rods. Be certain that push rod seats on solid lifters do not come out of lifters with push rods. Snap push rod lower end to one side before lifting, to break the push rod loose from the seat.
16. Remove cylinder head bolts, cylinder heads and gaskets.

Disassembly

1. Place cylinder head assembly on its side on a bench and, using Tool J-8062, compress valve spring and remove valve locks. Release tool and remove spring retainer, valve shield, spring and dampener and seal from stem. Repeat this operation on each valve (fig. 62).
2. Remove valves from bottom of cylinder head and keep them in their proper sequence for inspection and assembly.
3. Remove rocker arm nuts, lift rocker arms off studs and remove pivots from rocker arms.

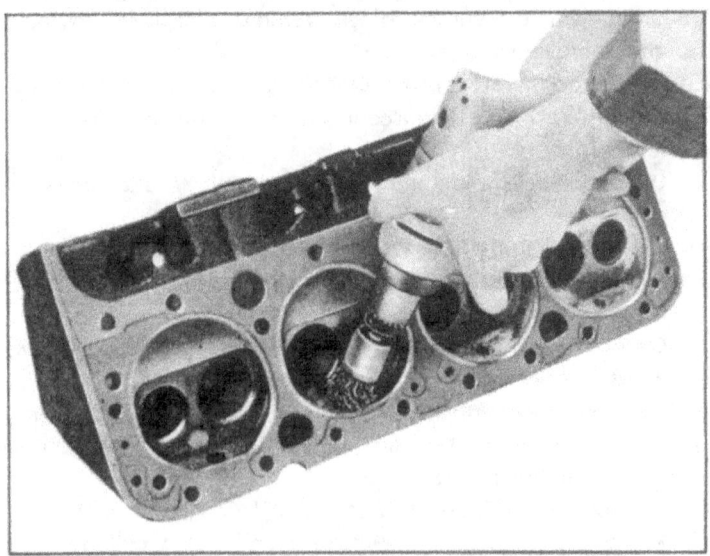

Fig. 63—Removing Carbon from Combustion Chambers

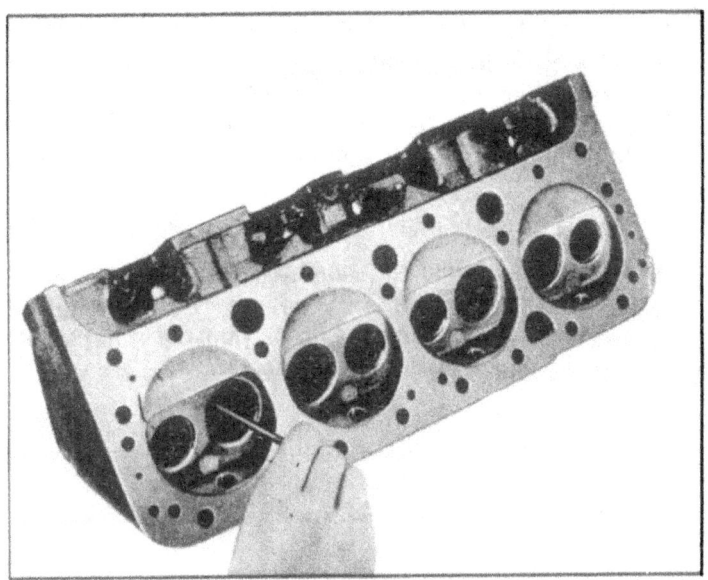

Fig. 64—Cleaning Valve Bores

Cleaning
1. Clean all carbon from combustion chambers and valve ports using Tool J-8089 (fig. 63).
2. Thoroughly clean the valve bores, using Tool J-8101 (fig. 64).
3. Clean all deposits from hollow push rods, inside and outside; disassemble, clean and reassemble all valve lifters.
4. Clean valve stems and heads on a buffing wheel.
5. Clean carbon deposits from pistons and cylinders.
6. Wash all parts in cleaning solvent and dry them thoroughly.

Inspection
1. Inspect the cylinder heads for cracks in the exhaust ports, combustion chambers, or external cracks to the water chamber.
2. Inspect the valves for burned heads, cracked faces or damaged stems.
3. Check fit of valve stems in their respective bores.

NOTE: Excessive valve to bore clearance may cause lack of power, oil consumption, rough idling and noisy valves. Insufficient clearance will result in noisy and sticky functioning of the valve and disturb engine smoothness of operation.

Intake valve stem to bore clearance should be .001" to .003" while exhaust stem clearance should be .002" to .004". Valve stem clearance may be accurately determined by using a micrometer and a suitable telescope hole gauge. Check the diameter of the valve stem in three places; top, center and bottom. Insert telescope hole gauge in valve guide bore, measuring at the center. Subtract highest reading of valve stem diameter from valve guide bore center diameter to obtain valve to guide clearance. If clearance is not within .002" of above limits, use next oversize valve and ream valve bore to fit.

4. Check valve spring tension with Tool J-8056 (fig. 65).

NOTE: Spring should be compressed to 1 45/64" at which height it should check 74.5 pounds. Weak springs affect power and economy and should be replaced if not within 10 lbs. of the above load without dampers.

5. Check valve lifters for free fit in block. The end that contacts the camshaft should be smooth. If this surface is worn or rough, the lifter should be replaced.

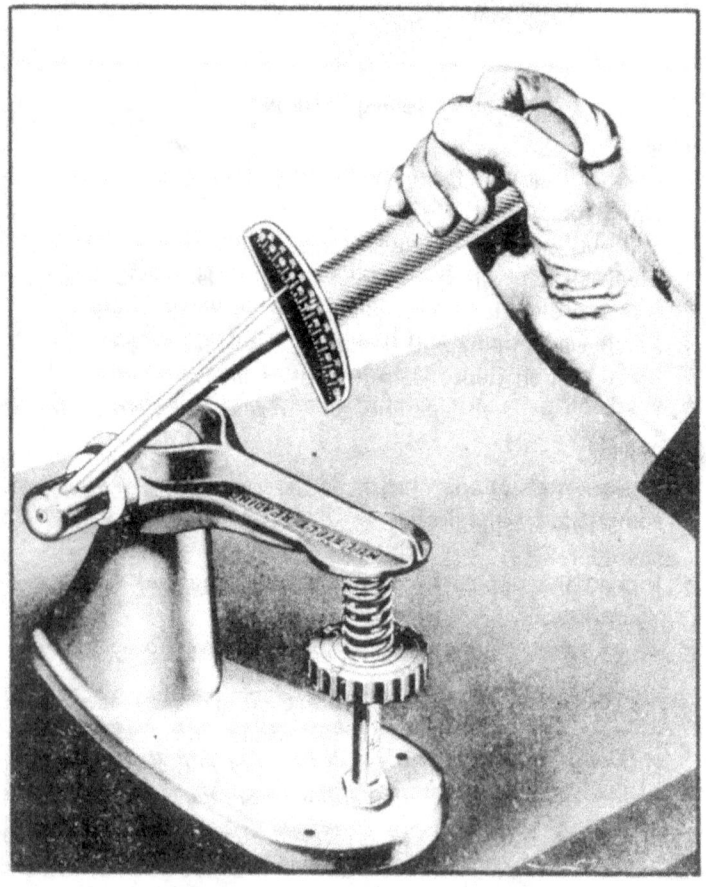

Fig. 65— Checking Valve Spring Tension

VALVE SPRING INSTALLED HEIGHT

Check the installed height of the valve springs, using a narrow, thin scale to measure from the top of the shim, or spring seat, in the head to the top of the valve spring shield. If this is found in excess of 1 23/32", install a valve spring seat shim, approximately 1/16" thick. At no time should the spring be shimmed to give an installed height of less than 1 21/32".

Installation

1. Thoroughly clean out cylinder head bolt holes in the block and clean cylinder bolt threads. Then place new cylinder head gaskets in position on cylinder block. Use a good head gasket paste with these steel gaskets.
2. Place the cylinder head in position over the two dowel pins in the block.
3. Coat threads of all cylinder head bolts with a suitable oil and water thread sealing compound such as G. M. Perfect Seal or its equivalent.
4. Install bolts finger tight.

NOTE: Two intermediate length bolts are used: one at No. 17 position and one at No. 14 position (fig. 73).

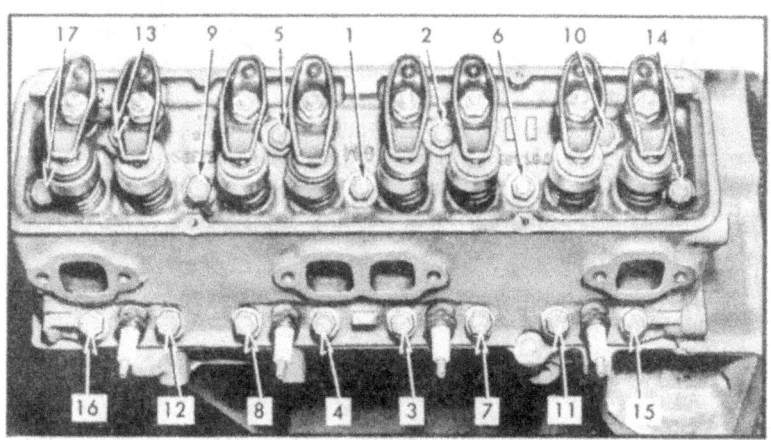

Fig. 73—Head Bolt Torque Sequence

5. Tighten the cylinder head bolts a little at a time in the order shown (fig. 73). The final tightening torque should be 60-70 ft. lbs.
6. Install 16 valve lifters and 16 push rods in their respective bores.
7. Insert pivots in valve rocker arms, install rocker arms over studs, and install nuts. Adjust valves, as outlined under "Valve Lash Adjustment."

8. Clean gasket faces of manifolds and cylinder heads.
9. Install intake manifold end gaskets on cylinder block. Coat ends of intake manifold side gaskets around water passage with a good gasket sealing compound and install on cylinder heads.
10. Install intake manifold bolts and check for misalignment of manifold and gaskets, reposition if necessary. Tighten finger tight. Tighten bolts a little at a time according to the sequence shown in Figure 59. Final torque should be 25-35 ft. lbs.
11. Install temperature indicator element in intake manifold.
12. Install radiator core to intake manifold hose.
13. Install exhaust manifolds and bolts. Tighten center bolts 25 to 35 ft. lbs. and install french locks under end bolts and tighten to 15-20 ft. lbs. torque.
14. Clean mating surfaces and install exhaust manifold heat control valve and exhaust cross-over pipe, using new gaskets and seals.
15. Clean all spark plugs with abrasive type cleaner, inspect for damage and set gap at .035" using a round feeler gauge.
16. Place new gaskets on plugs and install. Tighten to 20-25 ft. lbs.
17. Install distributor, distributor clamp and distributor and coil wiring. Roughly set timing, by adjusting for points just breaking with engine in number 1 firing position.
18. Connect spark plug wires to their respective terminals and install generator field and armature wires.
19. Connect throttle linkage.
20. Connect gasoline and vacuum lines to carburetor.
21. Clean and install air cleaner and crankcase ventilator.
22. Fill cooling system and check for leaks.
23. Normalize engine and re-torque cylinder head bolts (Refer to Figure 73).
24. Install rocker arm covers.
25. Check ignition timing

HARMONIC BALANCER

Removal
1. Drain radiator and disconnect radiator hoses, and necessary oil cooler lines.
2. Remove fan belt, fan and pulley.
3. Remove bolts from fan shroud and radiator.
4. Remove radiator core and shroud assembly.
5. Remove harmonic balancer pulley bolts and remove pulley or dual pulley (fig. 74).

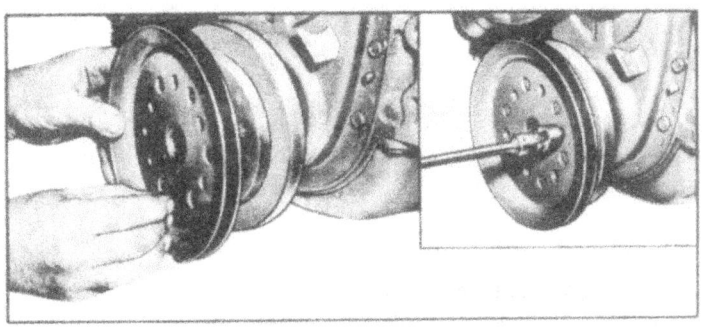

Fig. 74—Remove Crankshaft Pulley

Fig. 75—Removing Balancer

NOTE: The puller used (if Chevrolet Tool J6978 is not available) must be one which bolts into the fan pulley holes. A puller which fits the outside diameter will destroy the harmonic balancer.

    6. Install Tool J-6978 to harmonic balancer and turn puller screw to remove balancer from crankshaft (fig. 75).
    7. Remove tool from balancer.

Installation
    1. Coat front cover seal contact on balancer with engine oil.
    2. Position balancer on crankshaft aligning the key on the crankshaft with the keyway balancer.
    3. Using Tool J-5590, drive balancer on crankshaft until the hub bottoms on the crankshaft timing sprocket (fig. 76).
    4. Install crankshaft pulley on dual pulley (fig. 74).
    5. Install fan pulley, spacer and fan to water pump fan hub and tighten bolts securely.

6. Lay fan shroud over fan blade and lower radiator into place. Install radiator and shroud-to-radiator, retaining bolts.
7. Install fan belt and adjust
8. Install radiator hoses and oil cooler lines.
9. Fill cooling system, start engine and check for leaks.

CRANKCASE FRONT-END COVER

Removal
1. Remove harmonic balancer and radiator.
2. Remove oil pan.
3. Remove heater hose from water pump if so equipped. Remove water pump from cylinder block.
4. Remove crankcase front end cover attaching screws and remove front end cover and gaskets.

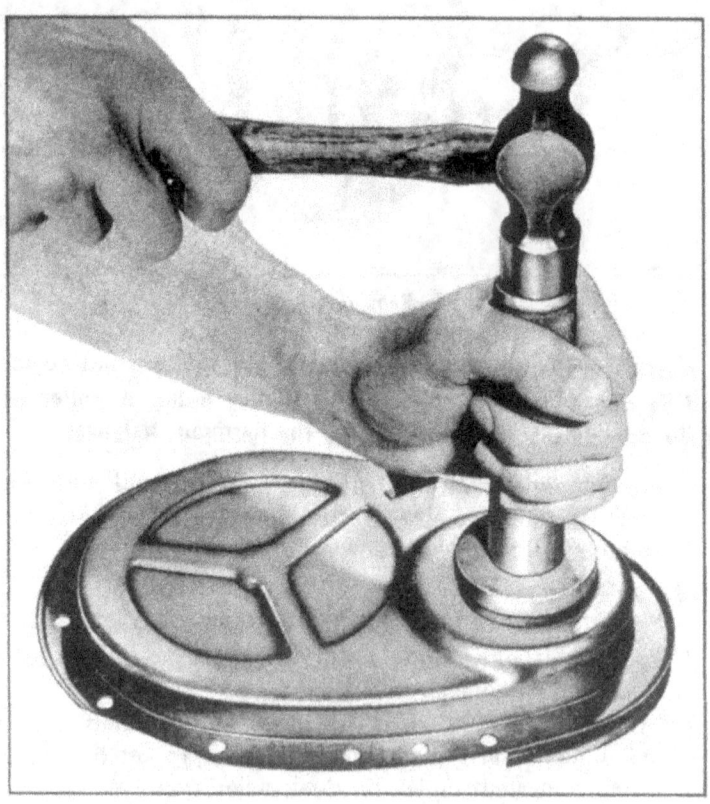

Fig. 77—Installing Oil Seal

REPAIRS

Crankcase Front End Cover Oil Seal Replacement
1. Pry old seal out of cover from the front with a large screwdriver.
2. Install new seal so that open end of the seal is toward the inside of cover and drive it into position with Tool J-996 (fig. 77).

CAUTION: Support cover at sealing area.

Installation
1. Make certain that cover mounting face and cylinder block front end plate face are clean and flat.
2. Make certain oil slinger is in place against crankshaft timing sprocket.
3. Coat the oil seal with light grease and, using a new cover gasket, install cover and gasket over dowel pins in cylinder block.
4. Install cover screws and tighten to 6-8 ft. lbs. torque.

NOTE: The preferred method for timing gear cover seal replacement, is to remove the cover and replace seal with Tool J-0995 as outlined above; however, an alternate method as outlined below may be used.

Fig. 78—Timing Sprocket "O" Marks

Fig. 79—Installation of Timing Chain

5. Remove harmonic balancer with Tool J-6978.

   a. Pry old seal out of cover from the front with a large screwdriver, being careful not to damage the seal surface on the crankshaft.

   b. Install new seal so that open end of seal is toward the inside of cover and drive it into position with a hollow piece of pipe.

TIMING CHAIN OR SPROCKET REPLACEMENT
1. Remove harmonic balancer and crankcase front end cover as previously described. Remove crankshaft oil slinger.
2. Crank engine until "0" marks on camshaft and crankshaft sprockets are in alignment (fig. 78).
3. Remove three camshaft sprocket to camshaft bolts.
4. Remove camshaft sprocket and timing chain together. Sprocket is a light press fit on camshaft for approximately 1/8".

If sprocket does not come off easily, a light blow with a plastic-faced hammer on the lower edge of the camshaft sprocket should dislodge the sprocket.
5. If crankshaft sprocket is to be replaced, remove, using Tool J-5825. Install new sprocket, aligning key and keyway, using Tool J-5590.
6. Install timing chain on camshaft sprocket. Hold the sprocket vertical with the chain hanging below, and orient to align "0" marks on camshaft and crankshaft sprockets.
7. Align dowel in camshaft with dowel hole in camshaft sprocket and install sprocket on camshaft (fig. 79).

NOTE: Do not attempt to drive cam sprocket on shaft as welsh plug at rear of engine can be dislodged.

8. Draw camshaft sprocket onto camshaft, using the three mounting bolts. Tighten to 15-20 ft. lbs. torque.
9. Lubricate timing chain with engine oil.
10. Install crankcase front end cover and harmonic balancer as previously described.

Fig. 80—Removing Camshaft

CAMSHAFT

Removal

1. Remove valve lifters.
2. Remove fuel pump and fuel pump push rod
3. Remove grille assembly.
4. Remove timing chain and camshaft sprocket as previously described.
5. Install two bolts, 5/16"-18 x 4" in two of camshaft bolt holes. Remove camshaft from engine (fig. 80).

CAUTION: All camshaft journals are the same diameter and caution must be used in removing cramshaft to avoid damage to bearing.

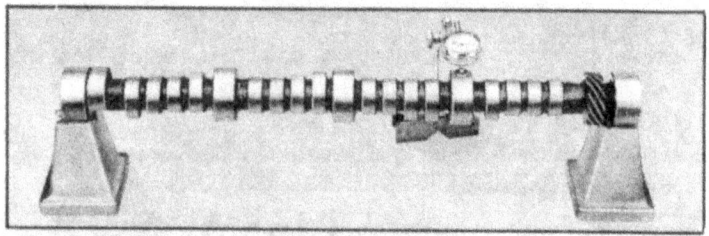

Fig. 81—Checking Camshaft Alignment

Inspection

The camshaft bearing journals are 1.8682"-1.8692" in diameter. The journals should be checked with a micrometer for an out-round condition. If the journals exceed .001" out-of-round, the camshaft should be replaced.

The camshaft should also be checked for alignment. The best method is by use of "V" blocks and a dial indicator (fig. 81). The dial indicator will indicate the exact amount the camshaft is out of true. If it is out more than .002" dial indicator reading, the camshaft should be straightened. Examine the camshaft bearings and if any bearing needs replacement, replace all bearings.

Installation

1. Install two bolts in camshaft, lubricate camshaft and install camshaft in engine. Remove bolts.
2. Install timing sprocket and chain as previously described.
3. Install crankcase front and cover and harmonic balancer as previously described.
4. Install grille assembly.
5. Install valve lifters, valve mechanism, intake manifold and distributor.
6. Install fuel pump push rod, mounting plate and pump.

OIL PAN
Removal
1. Raise front of vehicle and place on stand jacks or raise vehicle on a hoist.
2. Remove oil pan drain plug and drain crankcase oil.
3. Drain water and disconnect the radiator hoses at radiator.
4. Disconnect battery ground strap at engine.
5. Disconnect the clutch pedal push rod at clutch pedal control, intermediate lever and shaft (refer to Section 11).
6. Remove clutch pedal control, intermediate lever and shaft assembly at frame mounting bracket leaving shaft assembly attached to engine.
7. Remove carburetor fuel feed pipe at fuel pump. Remove fuel pump from engine.

NOTE: Hose connected from fuel pump to fuel tank feed pipe, need not be removed.

8. Remove accelerator control rod from accelerator control rod lever.
9. If power brake equipped, remove power brake vacuum hose at check valve on engine manifold.
10. If power steering equipped, move power steering pump to clear.
11. Remove transmission lower control rods at transmission shift levers.
12. Remove exhaust pipe flange to exhaust manifold nuts and gasket. Lower exhaust pipe and muffler assembly.
13. Remove oil filter.
14. Loosen transmission mounting bolts.
15. Remove nut, washer and long bolt from each front mounting.

NOTE: Turn crankshaft so that harmonic balancer key-way slot is at bottom of engine. This will index crankshaft counterweights so baffle in oil pan will clear.

16. Engine may be raised from below at harmonic balancer.

NOTE: Engine will have to be raised approximately 3" to clear frame crossmember for oil pan removal. Raise engine until transmission housing comes in contact with underbody toe pan. Note clearance at fan blade and shroud while lifting engine and adjust for clearance as required.

17. Remove oil pan bolts using a universal socket and long extension handle. Tilt oil pan, while removing.

NOTE: Removal of the oil pan with Turboglide transmission

installed, is identical to the proceude above with one exception. Remove the transmission control lever cross-shaft at transmission shifter lever and shaft assembly.

Installation
1. Thoroughly clean all gasket sealing surfaces.
2. Install side gaskets on pan rails, using grease as a retainer. Rear end of side gaskets lap rear end gasket. Tuck front ends of side gaskets into gap between front end cover seal groove and cylinder block.
3. Install rear oil pan seal in groove in rear main bearing cap. Tuck ends into groove openings in cylinder block.
4. Install oil pan front seal in groove in front end cover, with ends butting side gaskets.
5. Install oil pan and pan to cylinder block bolts. Tighten bolts to 12-15 ft. lbs. torque.

Piston Rings

All compression rings in the V-8 engines are the deep section twist type.

This type compression ring takes its name, twist type, from its installed position which is cocked or twisted. It assumes and maintains this position for life because the I.D. is chamfered or stepped, making the ring unbalanced in cross section.

Fig. 93—Checking Ring Gap

Fig. 95—Checking Groove Clearance

Compression ring for the upper ring has the chamfer, or step, at the upper edge. The second ring has the step at the lower edge.

All compression rings are marked with the letters "G.M.." cast in the upper side of the ring. When installing compression rings, make sure the marked side is toward the top of the piston. The top ring is chromed for maximum life.

The oil control rings used are of the three piece type, consisting of two segments (rails) and a spacer.

Chevrolet piston rings are furnished in standard sizes as well as .020", .030" and .040" oversizes.

Piston Ring Installation
1. Select rings comparable in size to the piston being used.
2. Slip the ring in the cylinder bore; then using the head of a piston, press the ring down into the cylinder bore about two inches.

    NOTE: Using a piston in this way will place the ring square with the cylinder walls.

3. Check the space or gap between the ends of the ring with a feeler gauge (fig. 93).
4. If the gap between the ends of the ring is below specifications, remove the ring and try another for fit.

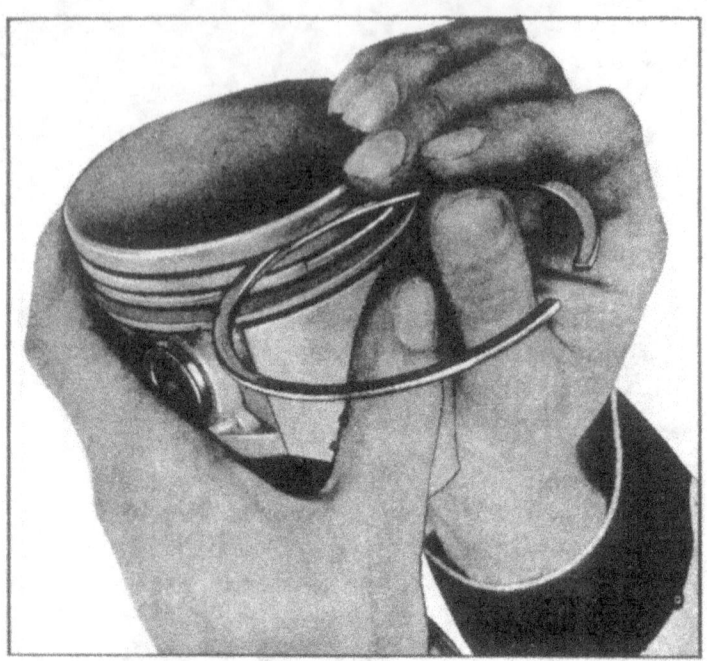

Fig. 94—Rolling Ring in Groove

5. Fit each ring separately to the cylinder in which it is going to be used.
6. New pistons, rings and cylinder bores wear considerably during seating and gaps widen quickly; however, engine operation will not become seriously affected if ring gaps do not become greater than 1/32".
1. Starting with the rear main bearing, remove bearing cap and grooves in the piston and inspect the grooves carefully for burrs or nicks that might cause the rings to hang up.
8. Slip the outer surface of the compression ring into the piston ring groove and roll the ring entirely around the groove to make sure that the ring is free and does not bind in the groove at any point (fig. 94). If binding occurs, the cause should be determined and removed by carefully dressing with a fine cut file. However, if the binding is caused by a distorted ring, install a new ring.
9. Install the oil ring spacer in the oil ring groove and position gap in line with piston hole. Hold spacer ends butted and install steel rail on top side of spacer. Position gap at least 1" to left of spacer gap, then install second rail on lower side of spacer. Position gap at least 1" to right of spacer gap.

10. Flex the oil ring assembly in its groove to make sure ring is free and does not bind in the groove at any point. If binding occurs, the cause should be determined and removed by carefully dressing with a fine cut file. However, if the binding is caused by a distorted ring, install a new ring.
11. Proper clearance of the piston ring in its piston ring groove is very important in maintaining engine perofrmance and in preventing excessive oil consumption. Therefore, when fitting new rings, the clearances between the top and bottom surfaces of the ring grooves should be inspected (fig. 95). Refer to **Engine Specifications** for correct clearances.

Piston and Connecting Rod Installation

NOTE: Be sure to install the pistons in the same cylinders from which they were fitted. Each connecting rod and bearing cap should be marked either 1, 3, 5 and 7 in the left bank and 2, 4, 6 and 8 in the right bank, beginning at the front of the engine. The numbers on the connecting rod and bearing cap must be on the same side when installed in the cylinder bore. If a connecting rod is ever transposed from one block or cylinder to another, new bearings should be fitted and the connecting rod should be numbered to correspond with the new cylinder number.

Fig. 96—Installing Piston Assemblies

Fig. 97—Plastigage on Crankpin

1. Lightly coat pistons, rings and cylinder walls with light engine oil.
2. With bearing caps removed, install Tool J-6305 on bearing cap bolts.
3. Install each piston in its respective bore, using Tool J-6305 on each assembly. The side of the piston with the cast depression in the head should be to the front of the cylinder block. Use Tool J-8037 (fig. 96) to compress the rings for installation.

    Guide the connecting rod bearing into place on the crankshaft journals with the long detail of Tool J-6305 Connecting Rod Guide Set.
4. Install the bearing caps and check the bearing clearance as described below.

Connecting Rod Bearing Clearance

Connecting rod bearing inserts are available in standard sizes and undersizes of .001", .002", .010" and .020". These bearings are not shimmed and when clearances become excessive the next undersize bearing insert should be used. DO NOT FILE ROD OR ROD CAPS.

1. Remove the connecting rod bearing cap.

2. Wipe bearing insert shell and crankpin clean of oil.
3. Place a piece of Plastigage the full width of the bearing or crankpin (parallel to the crankshaft) (fig. 97).
4. Reinstall the bearing cap and evenly tighten the retaining bolts to 30-35 ft. lbs. torque.
   CAUTION: Do not turn crankshaft with the Plastigage installed.
5. Remove the bearing cap and without removing the Plastigage check its width at the widest point with Plastigage scale (fig. 98).
   NOTE: If the crankpin is out-of-round be sure to fit the bearing to the maximum diameter of the crankpin. If the flattened plastic is not uniform from end to end in its width, the crankpin or bearing is tapered, has a low spot or some other irregularity. Check the crankpin with a micrometer for taper if the flattened Plastigage indicates more than a .001" difference.
6. If the reading is not over .004" (worn), or .003" (new) or not less than .001" the fit is satisfactory. If, however, the clearances are not within these limits, replace the bearing with the proper undersize bearing.

Fig. 98—Measuring Plastigage

Fig. 99—Connecting Rod Side Clearance

NOTE: The insert bearing shells are not adjustable and no attempt should be made to adjust by filing the bearing caps.

7. Rotate the crankshaft after bearing adjustment to be sure the bearings are not too tight.
8. Check connecting rod clearance between upper half of connecting rod and side of crankpin. This clearance should be .008" to .014" with two rods on each crankpin of crankshaft (fig. 99).

CRANKSHAFT AND MAIN BEARINGS

CRANKSHAFT

Removal
1. Drain the cooling system and the crankcase. Disconnect all radiator hoses.
2. Remove fan shroud, radiator, fan blade, spacer and pulley.
3. Remove engine from chassis and install on engine stand. If Tool J-5856 Stand is to be used, J-5831 Bracket set Adapter Kit will allow engine to be mounted securely.
4. Remove water pump, underpan, flywheel housing and flywheel.
5. Remove harmonic balancer and crankcase front end cover.

6. Remove camshaft sprocket and timing chain. Remove crankshaft oil slinger.
7. Remove crankshaft sprocket using Tool J-5825 (fig. 100).
8. Remove oil pan and oil pump.
9. Make sure all bearing caps (main and connecting rods) are marked so they can be installed in their original locations. Remove connecting rod bearing caps, then push the piston and rod assemblies towards the heads.
10. Remove main bearing caps and carefully lift the crankshaft out of the cylinder block. Remove rear main bearing oil seal from cylinder block and rear main bearing cap following procedures outlined under **Rear Main Bearing Oil Seal.**
11. If new main and/or connecting rod bearings are to be installed, remove the main bearing inserts from the cylinder block and bearing caps, and/or connecting rod bearing inserts from the connecting rod and caps. Install new bearings following procedures outlined in this section.

Installation

   NOTE: Be sure that all bearings and crankshaft journals are clean.

1. Install a new rear main bearing oil seal in cylinder block

Fig. 100—Removing Crankshaft Sprocket

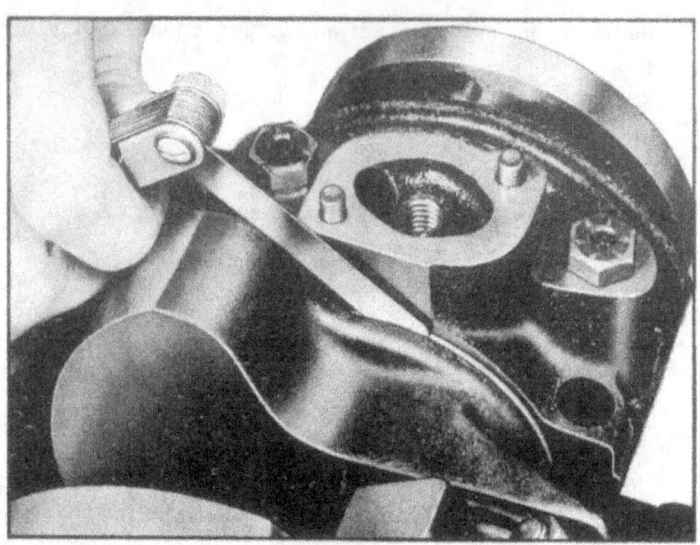

Fig. 101—Checking Crankshaft End Play

and rear main bearing cap.
2. Carefully lower the crankshaft into place. BE CAREFUL NOT TO DAMAGE THE BEARING SURFACES.
3. Check clearance of each main bearing following procedure outlined under **Main Bearing Clearance** in this section. If the bearing clearances are satisfactory, apply a light coat of engine oil to the journals and bearings.
4. Install all bearing caps and bolts. Torque all main bearing cap bolts, except the rear main bearing 60 to 70 ft. lbs. When tightening rear main bearing cap, torque bolts 10 to 12 ft. lbs. first, then tap end of crankshaft rearward with a lead hammer (this will locate bearing cap and bearing). Then tap crankshaft forward (this will line up both upper and lower crankshaft bearing thrust surfaces). Proceed with final tightening of all main bearing cap bolts—60 to 70 ft. lbs. torque.
5. Check crankshaft end play for forcing the crankshaft to its extreme front position. Check at the front end of the rear main bearing with a feeler gauge (fig. 101). Clearance should be from .002" to .006" with a new bearing. If greater than a maximum .009" clearance, the rear main bearing must be replaced.

MAIN BEARINGS

Crankshaft main bearing service may be performed with the engine inverter and oil plan, spark plugs, oil pump and timing chain removed. The Plastigage method of measuring bearing clearance is recommended on both main and connecting rod bearings.

Bearing and Journal Inspection

In general, the lower half of the bearing shows a greater wear and the most distress from fatigue. If upon inspection the lower half is suitable for use, it can safely be assumed that the upper half is also satisfactory. If the lower half shows evidence of fatigue, distress, abrasion, erosion, scoring or the like, both upper and lower halves should be replaced. Never should one half be replaced without replacing the other half.

If the running clearance of a bearing is too great with the used inserts, it will be necessary to install both upper and lower bearing halves. Should this become necesary, the crankshaft journals should be checked with a micrometer for out-of-round, taper or undersize. If out-of-round more than .001" or tapered, the shaft should be replaced or reconditioned. Check the crankshaft thrust faces at the rear main bearing for scoring or excessive wear. Experience has shown that clearance increase from wear in main bearings is not only due to bearing wear, but is also due in part to crankshaft journal wear.

Main Bearing Clearance

Plastigage consists of a wax-like plastic material which will compress evenly between the bearing and journal surfaces without damaging either surface. To obtain the most accurate results with

Fig. 102—Plastigage on Journal

Fig. 103—Measuring Plastigage

Plastigage, certain precautions should be observed. If the engine is out of the chassis and upside down, the crankshaft will rest on the upper bearings and it can be assumed that the total clearance can be measured between the cap bearing and journal.

> **NOTE:** To assure the proper seating of the crankshaft, the rear main bearing oil seal should be removed and all bearing cap bolts should be at their specified torque. In addition, preparatory to checking fit of bearings, the surface of the crankshaft journal and bearing should be wiped clean of oil.

1. Starting with the rear main bearing, remove bearing cap and wipe oil from journal and bearing cap.
   wipe oil from pournal and bearing cap.
2. Place a piece of Plastigage the full width of the bearing (parallel to the crankshaft) on the journal (fig. 102).

   > **CAUTION:** Do not rotate the crankshaft while the Plastigage is between the bearing and journal.

3. Install the bearing cap and evenly tighten the retaining bolts to 60-70 lb. ft. torque.
4. Remove bearing cap. The flattened Plastigage will be found adhering to either the bearing shell or journal. On the edge of Plastigage packing envelope there is a graduated scale which is correlated in thousandths of an inch.
5. Without removing the Plastigage, check its compressed width (at the widest point) with the graduations on the Plastigage envelope (fig. 103).

NOTE: Normally, main bearing journals wear evenly and are not out-of-round. However, if a bearing is being fitted to an out-of-round journal be sure to fit to the maximum diameter of the journal. If the bearing is fitted to the minimum diameter of the journal and the journal is out-of-round .001" or more, interference between the bearing and journal will result in rapid bearing failure. If the flattened Plastigage tapers toward the middle or ends, there is a difference in clearance indicating a taper, low spot or other irregularity of the bearing or journal. Be sure to check the journal with a micrometer if the flattened Plastigage indicates more than wipe oil from journal and bearing cap.

6. If the bearing clearance is not over .004" (worn) or .003" (new) or less than .001" the bearing insert is satisfactory. If the clearance is not within these limits replace the insert.

NOTE: If a new bearing cap is being installed and clearance is less than .001", check for burrs or nicks; if none are found then install shims as required.

7. A .002" undersize bearing may produce the proper clearance. If not, it will be necesary to regrind the crankshaft journal for use with the next undersize bearing.
NOTE: Bearings are available in standard sizes and .002", .010", .020" and .030" undersize.
8. Proceed to the next bearing. After all bearings have been checked rotate the crankshaft to see that there is no excessive drag.
9. Check the end play by forcing the crankshaft to its extreme front position. Check at the front end of the rear main bearing with a feeler gauge (fig. 101). This clearance should be from .002" to .006".
10. Install a new rear main bearing oil seal in the cylinder block and main bearing cap.

Main Bearings — Replace

The main bearings used as service replacement are of high quality with close tolerances of fit and will not require line reaming on installations. The close dimensional tolerances assure an equalized bearing surface at all points on the crankshaft when replaced in sets.
1. Remove main bearing caps and connecting rod caps and lift crankshaft out of cylinder block. Push pistons to top of bores.
2. Inspect the crankshaft. All main bearings are ground to 2.2978"-2.2988", and crankpin journals to 1.999"-2.000".

These dimensions should be checked with a micrometer for out-of-round, taper or undersize. If the journals exceed .001" out-of-round or taper the crankshaft should be replaced or reconditioned to an undersize figure that will enable the installation of undersize precision type bearings.

The crankshaft should also be checked for runout. To perform this operation, support the crankshaft at the front and rear main bearing journals in "V" blocks and indicate the runout of both the rear intermediate and front intermediate journals, using a dial indicator. The runout limit of each of these journals is .002". If the runout exceeds .002" the crankshaft must be repaired or replaced.

3. Remove old bearing shells from cylinder block and caps.
4. Remove rear main bearing oil seal.
5. Install new bearing shells in the cylinder block and caps.

NOTE: Main bearing shells with oil holes are the upper halves of the bearing shells and are inserted between the crankshaft and cylinder block.

6. Carefully place the crankshaft in the bearings.
7. Install the bearing caps as previously outlined under **Crankshaft Installation.**

NOTE: The caps are marked with an arrow for identification purposes. The caps are to be installed with the arrows pointing to the front of the engine.

8. Check crankshaft end clearance as previously outlined.
9. Check main bearing clearance as previously outlined.
10. Install new rear bearing oil seal.
11. Install connecting rod bearings and caps.

REAR MAIN BEARING OIL SEAL

Removal and Installation

The rear main bearing oil seal, shown in Figure 104, can be removed (both halves) without removal of the crankshaft.

1. Drain crankcase and remove oil pan.
2. Remove rear bearing cap.
3. Remove oil seal from groove, prying from bottom, using a small screwdriver as shown in Figure 105.

NOTE: Always clean crankshaft surface before installing a new seal.

4. Insert new seal well lubricated on lip only (keep oil off of parting line surface, this is treated with glue) with engine oil (lip facing toward the front of engine) with finger and

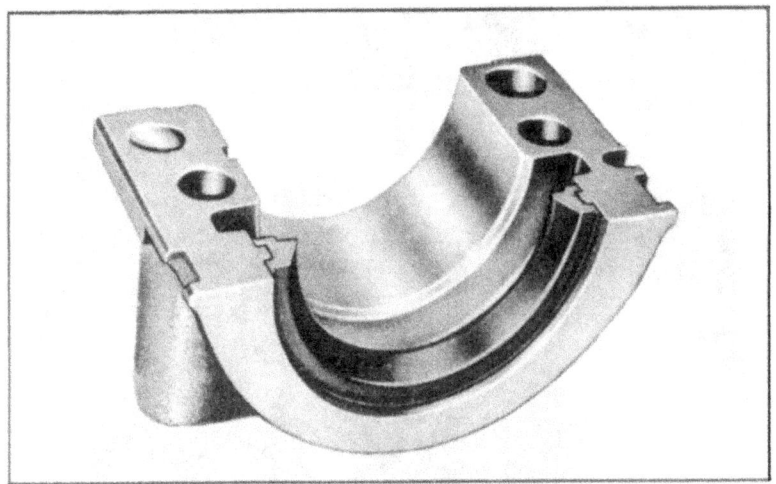

Fig. 104—Rear Main Bearing Seal

thumb, roll seal in place, being careful not to cut bead on back of seal with seal tangs at parting line.

NOTE: Always replace upper and lower seal as a unit.

5. To replace the upper half of the seal, use a small hammer and tap a brass pin punch on one end of seal (fig. 106) until it protrudes far enough to be removed with pliers as shown in Figure 106.

NOTE: Be careful of seal retainer tang while inserting a new seal so that it doesn't cut the seal.

6. Insert a new seal well lubricated with engine oil in groove (keep oil off of parting line surface, this surface is treated

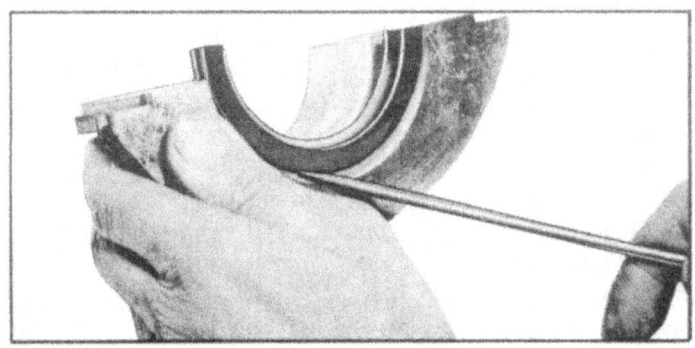

Fig. 105—Removing Seal from Cap

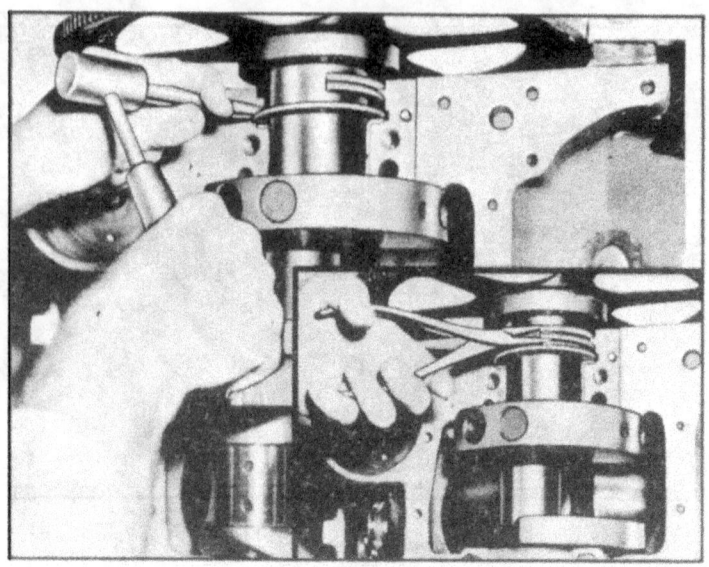

Fig. 106—Removing and Installing Oil Seal

with glue) gradually push with a hammer handle until seal is rolled into place. Install bearing cap and torque bearing cap bolts 60-70 ft. lbs.

CLUTCH HOUSING INSTALLATION, AND ALIGNMENT
(Standard Transmissions)
1. Install clutch housing to cylinder block over dowel pins, install attaching bolts and tighten to 25 to 35 ft. lbs.
2. Install Tool J-2494 in one of the crankshaft flange bolt holes.
3. Install Dial Indicator and position to read bore runout of the housing (fig. 109). Check runout by rotating crankshaft. This runout should not exceed .008".
4. Reposition the dial indicator to read face runout and rotate crankshaft. The maximum allowable runout is .010".
5. If more runout is in excess of .008" or if housing face parallelism exceeds .010", remove indicator and the housing from engine block.
6. Remove the cylinder block to housing dowel pins.
7. Clean mating faces of housing and engine block and make certain there are no burrs or metal extrusion around dowel or bolt holes.
8. Install flywheel housing and tighten attaching bolts evenly to 25-35 ft. lbs. torque.
9. Mount indicator on indicator post and indicate flywheel

housing face. Set indicator at zero at the six o'clock position and carefully check indicator readings at the 9, 12 and 2 o'clock positions. The runout limit is .010".

NOTE: Care should be exercised so that the indicator button is not on the edge of a bolt hole when readings are taken.

10. If the face runout exceeds .010", shim as necessary, using shim stock between the housing and block at the attaching bolt locations.
11. After the housing face has been brought within tne .010" limit with bolts tightened to 25-35 ft. lb. torque, reset indicator to read zero at the six o'clock position on the machined inside diameter of the flywheel housing bore.

NOTE: Be careful that the indicator button is centered on the narrow machined flange and does not touch flange step.

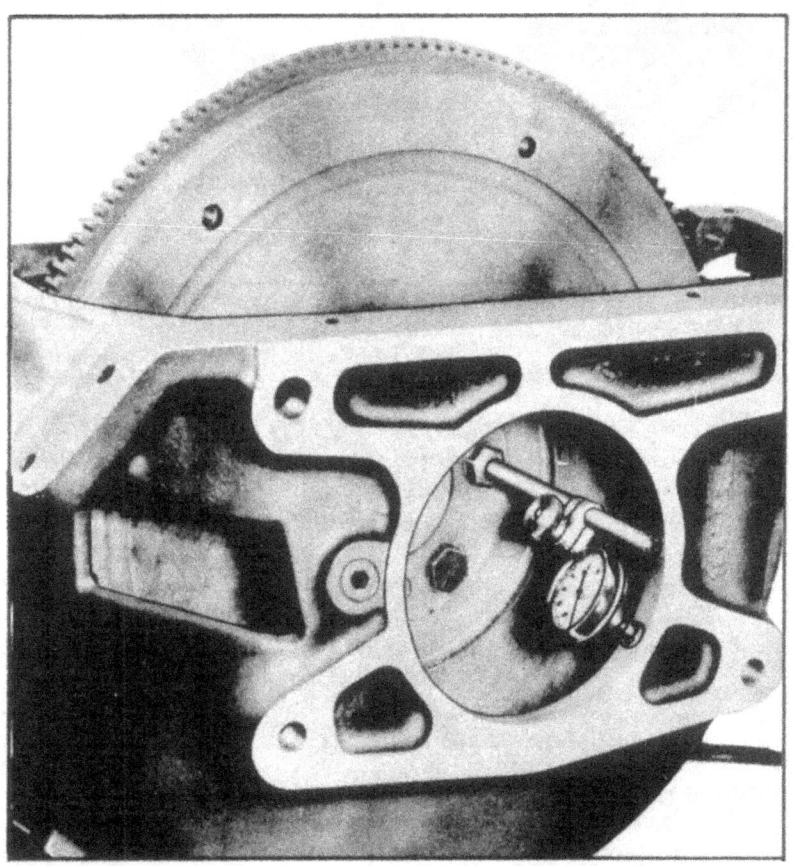

Fig. 109—Checking Bore Runout

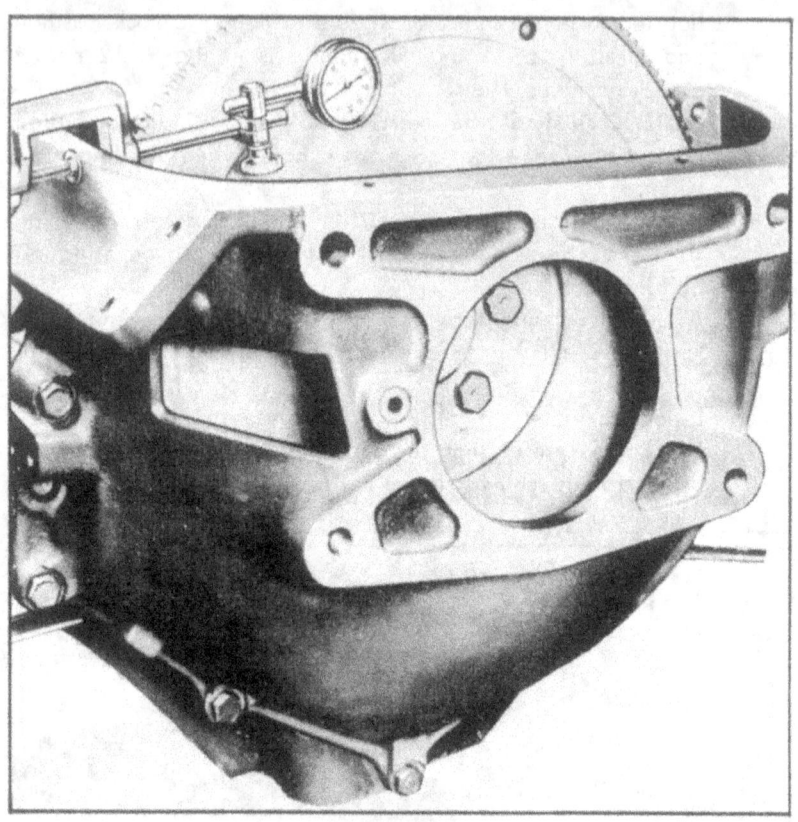

12. Check indicator readings at the 9, 12 and 3 o'clock positions and, if the readings exceed the .008" runout limits, loosen bolts slightly and tap housing with a soft hammer in required direction until runout is within limits. Tighten attaching bolts evenly to 25-35 ft. lbs. torque and recheck.
13. With housing in proper alignment, carefully ream dowel holes, using a 21/32" expansion reamer.
14. Blow out holes and then install special oversize dowels.
15. Recheck flywheel housing bore and the face to make sure they still are within proper limits.
16. Remove indicator and attachments.

FLYWHEEL INSTALLATION
1. Clean the mating flanges of flywheel and crankshaft carefully and make sure there are no burrs on either mounting face.
2. Place the flywheel in the clutch housing and position it so

that the dowel in crankshaft flange will enter the hole in the flywheel.
3. Install the six bolts and lock washers.
4. Tighten bolts to 55-65 foot-pounds with a torque wrench.
5. Mount a dial indicator on the clutch or flywheel housing so that the button of the indicator will contact the machined surface of flywheel (fig. 110), and check the flywheel runout.
6. Runout should not exceed .008" on conventional, .005" on automatic. If excessive, remove flywheel and recheck for burrs or replace flywheel.

FLYWHEEL BALANCE MARKINGS

Balance markings are incorporated on Engines and Automatic Transmissions to provide closer indexing of these components and improve Engine-transmission balance conditions.

Flywheel assemblies used with the Powerglide transmission have been changed to provide six transmission attaching holes instead of three.

The three holes have been added to permit more accurate indexing of the converter to flywheel. The actual attachment, however, will remain the same three bolt type.

All flywheels used with automatic transmissions will have a "white" paint mark on the outer rim on the transmission side to indicate "heavy" side of engine.

All automatic transmissions will have ¼ to ½" stripe of "Dykem Blue" across the ends of both converter cover and housing to denote the "light" side of the transmission.

These paint markings are to be aligned as closely as possible during assembly of transmission to engine to obtain best balance conditions.

ENGINE ASSEMBLY

The following engine assembly is to be performed after the crankshaft, connecting rods and pistons, clutch or flywheel housing and flywheel have been installed.
1. Install three new oil gallerys plugs in front of cylinder block.
2. Assemble oil pump and extension shaft assembly to rear main bearing cap, aligning slot on top end of extension shaft with drive tang on lower end of distributor drive shaft.
3. Install oil pump to rear main bearing cap bolt and tighten to 45 to 50 ft. lbs.
4. Install two 5/16-18 x 4" bolts in camshaft, lubricate camshaft and install camshaft in engine. Remove bolts.
5. Install crankshaft timing sprocket on crankshaft, aligning keyway with key installed in crankshaft. Drive in place,

using a hammer and Tool J-5590.
6. Rotate crankshaft until "0" mark on crankshaft is up toward camshaft.
7. Install timing chain on camshaft sprocket. Hold the sprocket vertical with the chain hanging below, and orient to align "0" marks on camshaft and crankshaft sprockets.
8. Align dowel in camshaft with dowel hole in camshaft sprocke and install sprocket on camshaft.
9. Draw camshaft sprocket onto camshaft, using the three mounting bolts. Do not drive sprocket, as camshaft bore rear plug can be driven out of block. Tighten to 15-20 ft. lbs. torque.
10. Lubricate timing chain with engine oil.
11. Install crankshaft oil slinger on crankshaft.
12. Make certain that cover mounting face and cylinder block front end plate face are clean.
13. Coat the oil seal with light grease and, using a new cover gasket, install cover and gasket over dowel pins in cylinder block.
14. Install cover screws and tighten to 6-7½ ft. lb. torque.
15. Install harmonic balancer on crankshaft with a light coating of oil. Position harmonic balancer on crankshaft, aligning the key on the crankshaft with the keyway in the balancer.
16. Using Transmission Front Bearing Installer J-5590, drive balancer on crankshaft until the hub bottoms on the crankshaft timing sprocket.
17. Remove two capscrews from balancer.
18. Thoroughly clean all oil pan gasket sealing surfaces.
19. Install rear oil pan seal in groove, in rear main bearing cap. Tuck ends into groove openings in cylinder block.
20. Install side gaskets on pan rails, using grease as a retainer. Rear ends lap end gasket. Tuck front ends of side gaskets into gap between front end cover seal groove and cylinder block.
21. Install oil pan front seal in groove in front end cover, with ends butting side gaskets.
22. Install oil pan to cylinder block bolts. Tighten front and rear 5/16" bolts to 12 to 15 ft. lbs., intermediate ¼" bolts should be tightened to 6-9 ft. lbs.
23. Install oil pan drain plug.
24. Install inner crankcase ventilator body to crankcase and install retaining screw. Use caution to avoid damage to vent body.
25. Install the valve lifters in same bores as removed.
26. Thoroughly clean out cylinder head bolt holes in the block and clean cylinder bolt threads. Then place new cylinder head

gaskets in position on cylinder block. Use a good head gasket paste such as G. M. Perfect Seal Compound or its equivalent with these steel gaskets.
27. Place the cylinder heads in position over the two dowel pins in the block.
28. Coat threads of all cylinder head bolts with a suitable water and oil thread sealing compound such as G. M. Perfect Seal. These bolts protrude into the water passages and require compound to prevent rusting.
29. Install bolts finger tight.
30. Tighten the cylinder head bolts a little at a time in the order shown (fig. 73). The final tightening should be 60-70 ft. lbs.
31. Install 16 push rods in their respective bores.
32. Insert pivots in valve rocker arms, rocker arms over studs, and install nuts.
33. Clean gasket faces of intake manifold and cylinder heads.
34. Install intake manifold end gaskets on cylinder block. Coat ends of intake manifold side gaskets around water passages with a good gasket sealing compound such as G. M. Perfect Seal and install on cylinder heads.
35. Install intake manifold and bolts with pipe clips and plug wire supports in place. Tighten finger tight. Tighten bolts a little at a time according to the sequence shown in Figure 59. Final torque should be 25-35 ft. lbs.
36. Install thermostat, water outlet gasket and thermostat housing and tighten bolts to 18 to 23 ft. lbs. Install water pump. Tighten bolts to 25-35 ft. lbs.
37. Mount coil and install distributor. (See Section 9 "Engine-Electrical" for installation procedure.)
38. Attach coil wires to distributor.
39. Install rocker arm cover gaskets, covers and screws with reinforcements.
40. Clean all spark plugs with abrasive type cleaner, inspect for damage and set gap at .035" using a round feeler gauge.
41. Place new gaskets on plugs and install. Tighten to 20-25 ft. lbs.
42. Install plug wiring harness.
CAUTION: Plug wire location is extremely important. Numbers formed in rubber support grommets show sequence.
43. Install carburetor. On Powerglide or Turboglide models, install transmission throttle control upper rod to carburetor.
44. Install automatic choke heat tube.
45. Install push rod, fuel pump mounting plate gasket, mounting plate, fuel pump. Mounting plate bolts should be tightened to 6 to 9 ft. lbs. Install fuel pump to carburetor feed

pipe.
46. Install lift Tool J-4536. Engine may have to be removed from stand for following steps, depending on stand used.
47. Install exhaust manifolds and bolts. Tighten center bolts 25-35 ft. lbs. torque. Install French locks under end bolts and torque to 15-20 ft. lbs.
48. Install generator on left band of exhaust manifold.
49. On all STANDARD TRANSMISSION MODELS:
   a. Lubricate the clutch pilot bearing with a small amount of high melting point grease. Place the clutch disc and clutch cover assembly in position and install Tool J-5284.
   b. Turn the clutch cover until the "X" on the cover lines up with the "X" on the flywheel. Install the attaching bolts loosely and then tighten them a turn at a time to take up the spring pressure evenly and prevent clutch distortion. Tighten bolts to 25-30 ft. lbs. torque with a torque wrench and then remove pilot tool.
   c. Pack the clutch fork ball seat with a small amount of high melting point grease and snap the fork onto the ball with the end extending through opening in clutch housing.
   d. Install clutch throw-out bearing.
   e. Install transmission and tighten attaching bolts securely.
   f. Install flywheel underpan and extension.
50. On all POWERGLIDE TRANSMISSION MODELS:
   a. Remove Tool J-5384.
   b. Install transmission on flywheel housing and tighten attaching bolts securely.
   c. Install converter to flywheel bolts and tighten to 25 to 30 ft. lbs.
   d. Install flywheel housing cover and starting motor.
   e. Install crankcase breather road draft tube.

ENGINE INSTALLATION TO VEHICLE
1. Install lift Tool J-4536-A.
2. Tilt and lower engine and transmission assembly into the chassis as a unit, guiding engine to align supports with frame.
3. Install front mounts, and tighten nuts.
4. Remove lifting attachments. Tighten transmission mounting bolts.
5. Install propeller shaft.
6. On all STANDARD TRANSMISSION MODELS:
   a. Install clutch bell crank, connect clutch pedal adjusting link to clutch fork and adjust.
   b. Connect speedometer cable to speedometer driven gear.

- c. Connect transmission control rods to shifter levers on transmission side cover. Adjust control rods.
- d. Check transmission lubricant level.
- e. If equipped with overdrive, connect associated wires and cables.
7. On all POWERGLIDE MODELS:
   - a. Connect speedometer cable to speedometer driven gear.
   - b. Connect transmission control rod to transmission control rod bell crank and adjust rod.
   - c. Install transmission filler tube and dip stick.
   - d. Install transmission throttle control rod.
8. Install exhaust manifold heat control valve and gaskets and install exhaust cross-over pipe and packing.
9. Replace exhaust pipe to cross-over pipe and tighten attaching bolts securely.
10. Connect vacuum lines.
11. Connect wire to oil pressure sending unit and temperature sending unit on intake manifold.
12. Install air cleaner.

   NOTE: If oil bath cleaner is used, disassemble, clean, and refill before installing.
13. Attach generator and field wires to generator.
14. Attach gasoline line to fuel pump.
15. Install battery. Attach battery cable and voltage regulator wire to large terminal. Install wire to solenoid and install starter switch wire to small terminal and connect coil wire to coil.
16. Install fan pulley and fan blade. Install radiator core and fan shroud.
17. Install oil cooler lines on powerglide model and connect radiator hoses.
18. Refill radiator and crankcase.
19. Install and adjust fan belt.
20. Start engine and allow to run until properly normalized and check for leaks.
21. Fill transmission.
22. On Powerglide equipped cars, place selector lever in reverse and check linkage adjustment.
23. Replace hood assembly, aligning previously scribed marks.

Fuel Pump

MAINTENANCE AND ADJUSTMENTS

The fuel pump should be checked regularly to make sure that the mounting bolts, cover to body bolts, pulsator diaphragm cover screws and inlet and outlet connections are tight.

FUEL PUMP INSPECTION AND TEST

Always check pump while it is mounted on the engine and be sure there is gasoline in the tank.

The line from the tank to the pump is the suction side of the system and the line from the pump to the carburetor is the pressure side of the system. A leak on the pressure side, therefore, would be made apparent by dripping fuel, but a leak on the suction would not be apparent except for its effect of reducing volume of fuel on the pressure side.

1. Tighten any loose line connections and look for bends or kinks in lines which would reduce fuel flow.
2. Tighten diaphragm flange screws.
3. Disconnect fuel pipe at carburetor. Disconnect distributor to coil primary wire so that engine can be cranked without firing. Place suitable container at end of pipe and crank engine a few revolutions. If little or no gasoline flows from open end of pipe then fuel pipe is clogged or pump is inoperative. Before removing pump disconnect fuel pipe at gas tank and outlet pipe and blow through them with an air hose to make sure they are clear. Reconnect pipes to pump and retest while cranking engine.
4. If fuel flows from pump in good volume from pipe at carburetor, check fuel delivery pressure to be certain that pump is operating within specified limits as follows:
a. Attach a fuel pump pressure test gauge to disconnected end of pump to carburetor pipe.
b. Run engine at approximately 450 and 1,000 rpm on gasoline in carburetor bowl and note reading on pressure gauge.
c. If pump is operating properly the pressure will be 5¼ to 6½ psi for V-8 Engine and will remain constant at speeds between 450 and 1,000 rpm. If pressure is too low or too high, or varies materially at different speeds, the pump should be removed for repair.

Cooling System

The cooling system is designed with two purposes in mind; first, to carry off a certain amount of heat created in the engine so it will not operate at too high a temperature; and second, to maintain the engine heat at the temperature which will produce the most efficient and economical operation of the engine.

The cooling system consists of radiator, (an optional aluminum radiator is available) fan, water pump, thermostat, water passages in cylinder block and cylinder head, and the necessary connections and fittings.

The standard equipment 17⅛ inch fan is driven by a V-type belt at 9/10ths engine speed. This assures a constant flow of air through the radiator and around the engine to aid in cooling the water. An optional thermo-modulated fan reduces fan noise by limiting fan speed to approximately 3200 rpm. In addition, the fan partially "freewheels" until the radiator core temperature reaches about 130°-150° F. The permanently lubricated centrifugal type water pump keeps the water circulating thereby constantly bringing cooler water to the areas around the combustion and exhaust chambers where most heat is generated. The thermostat restricts the flow of water to the radiator until the engine warms up to normal operating temperature.

CARE AND MAINTENANCE

The cooling system must be kept in good condition if it is to cool the engine properly under all operating conditions. The cooling system should be kept clean. Use only rust-inhibiting anti-freeze solutions, following the manufacturer's specification. When plain water is used as a coolant, it is recommended that G.M. Rust Inhibitor be added to the coolant. Since the action of the cooling system controls the operating temperature of the engine, it is essential that systematic inspection of units in the system be made periodically to maintain the efficiency of the system. See the special instructions at end of this section pertaining to the optional aluminum radiator.

The radiator cap should be removed and the coolant level checked frequently. If the coolant level is low, water or anti-freeze should be added.

NOTE: Since the volume of solution in the cooling system expands when heated, the cooling system should be left from one pint to one quart low if filled cold, especially when anti-freeze is used, to prevent loss of solution through the radiator overflow pipe and to prevent pressure build-up.

The system should be thoroughly checked for leaks and all hose clamps tightened occasionally.

Twice a year the radiator and cylinder block drain cocks should be opened, all coolant removed and the system thoroughly flushed.

The front of the radiator core should be checked occasionally for bugs, leaves, etc., which would restrict air circulation. These can be flushed out from the back side of the radiator with an ordinary water hose and city water pressure.

The fan belt tension should be checked occasionally and if necessary, adjusted.

The cooling system should be checked during periods of sub-freezing temperatures to determine if the system contains adequate amounts of anti-freeze.

CLEANING THE COOLING SYSTEM

Unless water in the cooling system is treated with a corrosion preventative, rust and scale may eventually clog water passages in the radiator and water jackets. This rust accumulation will result in inefficient optation of the cooling system, vitally affecting engine performance and economy of operation. Two common causes of corrosion are:
1. Air Suction—Air may be drawn into the system due to low liquid level in the radiator, leaky water pump, or loose hose connections.
2. Exhaust Gas Leakage—exhaust gas may be blown into the cooling system past the cylinder head gasket or through cracks in the cylinder head and block.

Scale and deposits in the cooling system which will not flush out can generally be removed by using G.M. Cooling System Cleaning Compound (Pt. No. 987418). When using a cleaning compound in the cooling system it is advisable to follow the instructions furnished with the compound.

If cooling system cleaning compound will not thoroughly clean the system, it is advisable to reverse-flush the system. See your Chevrolet dealer regarding reverse-flushing of your Corvette cooling system.

FAN BELT ADJUSTMENT
1. Loosen bolt at generator slotted bracket.
2. Pull generator away from engine until desired belt tension is obtained. With correct adjustment a light pressure on the belt at a point midway between pulleys should cause a 7/16" to ½" deflection.
3. Tighten all generator bolts securely.

THERMOSTAT

The thermostat consists of a restriction valve actuated by a

thermostatic element. This unit is mounted in the housing at the cylinder head water outlet above the water pump. Thermostats are designed to open and close at predetermined temperatures and if not operating properly may cause abnormally high or abnormally low engine temperatures. If the condition of the thermostat is questioned, it can be removed and tested as follows:
1. Open radiator drain cock and drain out about half the coolant to bring the coolant level below the thermostat, then close the drain cock.
2. Remove the two cap screws that attach the water outlet to the thermostat housing, and lift water outlet (with hose attached), gasket, and thermostat from housing.
3. Heat a container of water to a temperature 25° above the temperature stamped on the thermostat and place thermostat in the water and see if it opens fully. If it does not fully open, it should be replaced.
4. Place thermostat in water 10° below the temperature stamped on the thermostat and see if thermostat fully closes. If it does not fully close, it should be replaced.
5. Place thermostat in housing, then using a new gasket, install water outlet and cap screws. Tighten screws evenly and securely.
6. Fill cooling system and check for leaks.

CHANGING TO ANTI-FREEZE

In determining the anti-freeze solution for winter operation, the local conditions and the type of service must be considered. To be certain that the solution will not leak out and be lost entirely, the following procedure should be followed in conditioning the system:
1. Drain the entire cooling system including the cylinder block. If considerable rust, scale, oil, or grease is present in the water drained out, it is advisable to flush and clean the system.
   NOTE: For complete draining, the drain cock at left side of radiator should be opened and the drain plug at each side of the V-8 block should be removed.
2. Tighten all cylinder head bolts in sequence. Anti-freeze or water, mixed with engine oil may form sludge which will interfere with lubrication and in some cases may form varnish-like deposits which will cause gumming and sticking of the moving parts.
   NOTE: Tightening cylinder head bolts may decrease valve clearance. Check and adjust valves if necessary.
3. Inspect the fan belt and adjust or replace if necessary.

4. Inspect all hoses including heater hoses. If hoses are collapsed, cracked or in any way indicate a rotted condition on the inside, replacement should be made. Carefully check and tighten all hose clamps.
5. Check the thermostat. Make sure it does not stick open or closed. A 181° thermostat should be used when permanent anti-freeze is used.
6. Fill the cooling system with the proper quantity of G.M. anti-freeze and water allowing 2" between fluid level and top of radiator. Allow additional amount of anti-freeze for car heater.
7. Warm up engine and check radiator, water pump, hoses and hose connections for leaks with engine hot.

TESTING ANTI-FREEZE SOLUTION

A hydrometer test is used to indicate whether anti-freeze, or water or both should be added to bring the solution to the proper level and to maintain the desired freezing point. Some devices used for testing anti-freeze solutions will indicate the correct freezing point only when the test is made at a specific temperature. Other testers provided with thermometers and tables, indicate the freezing points corresponding to readings made at various temperatures. Disregarding the temperature of the solution when tested may cause an error as large as 30°F. Some testing devices are made to test only one kind of anti-freezing solution. Others have several scales and may be used for the corresponding kinds of anti-freeze.

SPECIAL INSTRUCTIONS FOR ALUMINUM RADIATORS

Aluminum radiators have been designed to combine heavy-duty structure with high performance cooling. However, due to the physical properties of aluminum these radiators will require special maintenance and repair procedures. Recommended servicing for a standard brass and copper radiator may actually destroy an aluminum radiator.

Additives—In general, aluminum is easily destroyed by caustic solutions. No cooling system compound should be added to this system unless it is specifically recommended for use with aluminum by a reliable manufacturer.

Anti-freezes—Most well-known brand commercially available anti-freezes are acceptable. However, general rules for the selection of anti-freeze are: **Avoid** the use of salt base inhibited anti-freezes and **use** an anti-freeze with a soluble oil inhibitor.

Inhibitors—When no anti-freeze is in the system, a soluble oil inhibitor is recommended to prevent corrosion of the cooling system.

Cleaners—Use an acid-base cleaner recommended by its manufacturer for use in aluminum radiators. If such a cleaner is not available pressure flushing is the only cleaning procedure recommended. **Do not use the common caustic base cleaners generally available.**

Stop Leak Preparations—Soap leak preparations should not be required with aluminum radiators but may be used if desired to seal other points in the system.

Liquid Level—It is recommended that the liquid level be checked with the cooling system completely cooled. With a cold system, coolant should be added if more than three plate edges are visible above the liquid level. When the system is hot, the radiator will probably be completely full and there may be water in the supply tank (which is standard operating condition). If so, the water in the supply tank may flow back into the radiator and flow out over the filler neck when the filler cap is removed to check the liquid level. If water is lost in checking the hot radiator, either due to such overflow loss or due to boiling, the radiator will not be full when it cools down. This will be true even when the radiator is refilled while hot. If the system is refilled (when hot) it will perform satisfactorily until it cools to air temperature. Then refill when cool.

An exception to the above occurs when the system has been completely drained and is to be refilled. Due to the blocking action of the thermostat, the engine must be operated while coolant is being added. The operation of the engine will heat the coolant, open the thermostat and eliminate air pockets. However, it will be impossible to completely fill the system once it is hot. Therefore, it will be necessary to add additional coolant after the system has cooled to air temperature.

Filler Neck—It is necessary that the inside top of the pressure cap make an air tight seal to the top of the filler neck. Care must be used to avoid nicking or denting the sealing surface of the top of the filler neck.

Filler Cap—An aluminum drop-valve filler cap with a special gasket is furnished with this radiator. A conventional steel filler cap may be used as a temporary substitute provided that a gasket is used to seal the inside top of the cap to the top of the filler neck. This steel cap will cause increased wear of the aluminum filler neck and some loss of efficiency in the gravity vacuum return system.

Drain Cock—Either an all aluminum or an aluminum-plastic drain cock must be used with this radiator. In the event of loss or damage, a conventional brass drain cock must not be used. A cast iron ⅛ NFT plug may be used temporarily. If used for an extended period this plug will cause serious corrosion of the aluminum threads.

Powerglide Transmission

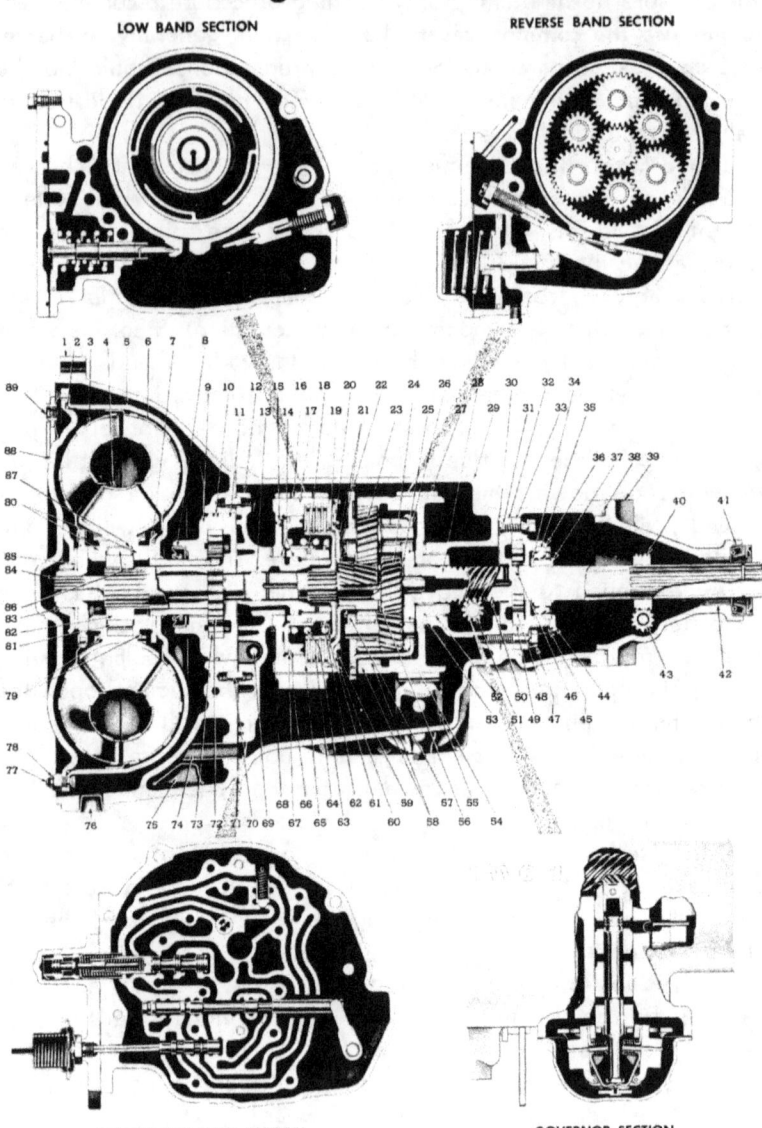

The Powerglide transmission installed in the Corvette is the same as used in Chevrolet passenger cars. It is a sturdy and reliable piece of equipment which seldom calls for adjustment or repair. However, when such attention is required it is best to leave it in the hands of a specialist. The average owner is not likely to have either the tools or knowledge required to carry out successful repair operations. The accompanying cutaway will give a rudimentary picture of the Powerglide's components.

1. Transmission Housing
2. Converter Cover "O" Ring Seal
3. Turbine Assembly
4. Stator Assembly
5. Converter Housing & Pump Assembly
6. Converter Pump
7. Converter Pump Thrust Washer
8. Front Oil Pump Body Oil Seal
9. Front Oil Pump Body
10. Front Oil Pump Body "O" Ring Seal
11. Stator Support
12. Transmission Valve Body
13. Input Shaft Oil Seal Ring
14. Clutch Drum Oil Seal Rings
15. Clutch Relief Valve Ball
16. Low Brake Band
17. Clutch Drum
18. Clutch Piston Inner Seal
19. Clutch Hub
20. Clutch Hub Thrust Washer
21. Low Sun Gear & Clutch Flange Assembly
22. Parking Lock Gear
23. Planet Short Pinion
24. Planet Input Sun Gear
25. Planet Input Sun Gear Thrust Washer
26. Planet Carrier
27. Reverse Brake Band
28. Output Shaft
29. Transmission Case
30. Rear Oil Pump Gasket
31. Rear Oil Pump Cover to Body Attaching Screw
32. Rear Oil Pump Cover
33. Rear Oil Pump Body
34. Rear Bearing Locating Front Snap Ring
35. Transmission Rear Bearing Assembly
36. Transmission Rear Bearing Retainer
37. Rear Bearing Locating Rear Snap Ring
38. Transmission Extension "O" Ring Seal
39. Transmission Extension
40. Speedometer Drive Gear
41. Extension Rear Oil Seal
42. Extension Bushing
43. Speedometer Drive Gear
44. Transmission Rear Bearing Retainer Screw
45. Transmission Rear Bearing Retainer Screw Lockwasher
46. Rear Oil Pump Drive Gear Drive Pin
47. Rear Oil Pump Assembly Attaching Screw
48. Rear Oil Pump Drive Gear
49. Rear Oil Pump Driven Gear
50. Governor Drive Gear
51. Governor Driven Gear
52. Transmission Case Bushing
53. Reverse Drum Thrust Washer
54. Planet Long Pinion
55. Reverse Band Lever & Link Assembly
56. Low Sun Gear Thrust Washer
57. Planet Pinion Shaft Lock Plate
58. Reverse Drum & Ring Gear
59. Clutch Flange Retainer
60. Clutch Flange Retainer Ring
61. Clutch Spring Seat
62. Clutch Spring Snap Ring
63. Clutch Spring
64. Clutch Drive Plates
65. Clutch Driven Plates
66. Clutch Piston
67. Clutch Piston Outer Seal
68. Clutch Drum Thrust Washer (Selective)
69. Manual Valve
70. Converter Housing Dowel Pin
71. Converter Housing to Case Gasket
72. Front Oil Pump Drive Gear
73. Front Oil Pump Driven Gear
74. Sump Baffle
75. Oil Pickup and Suction Screen
76. Access Hole Plug
77. Converter Pump Housing Bolt
78. Converter Pump Housing Nut
79. Stator Retaining Rings
80. Stator Thrust Washers
81. Over-Run Cam Roller
82. Stator Race
83. Converter Cover Hub Bushing
84. Input Shaft
85. Turbine Thrust Washer
86. Over-Run Cam Roller Spring
87. Over-Run Cam
88. Converter Cover Assembly
89. Flywheel to Transmission Anchor Nut Assy.

115

Rear Axle
Maintenance And Adjustments

LUBRICANT

Built-in oil baffle ledges, above the point of contact between the ring and pinion gears, insure adequate lubrication and reduced gear wear at this vital point. The ring and pinion gear sets are manganese phosphate coated to insure a more efficient break-in. This necessitates draining the rear axle after the first 1000 miles of operation and refilling with a High Grade Multi-Purpose Lubricant as recommended in the lubrication section. A drain plug is located in the bottom of the axle housing to facilitate this draining procedure.

Thereafter, the lubricant level should be periodically checked and maintained at the level of the filler plug with a warm axle. It is also recommended that the rear axle be drained and refilled seasonally or at a maximum of every 10,000 miles.

Lubricant Leaks

Lubricant leaks should be checked for at the companion flange or rear universal joint rear yoke oil seal, differential carrier to axle housing gasket, lubricant filler and rain plugs, and at axle shaft bearings. Correction of these leaks consists of replacing the defective seals or gaskets involved as described in this section.

HUB NUTS

For continued safe operation, wheel hub nuts should be periodically inspected for secure installation.

REAR AXLE NOISE DIAGNOSIS

Mechanical failures of the rear axle are relatively simple to locate and correct. Noise in a rear axle is a little more difficult to diagnose and repair. One of the most essential parts of rear axle service is proper diagnosis.

One of the cardinal points of axle noise diagnosis is the fact that all rear axles are noisy to a certain degree. The action of transmitting the high engine torque through a 90° turn and reducing propeller shaft speed produces noise in rear axles. This point establishes the need for a line between normal and abnormal or unacceptable axle noises.

Slight axle noise heard only at a certain speed or under remote conditions must be considered normal. Axle noise tends to "peak" at varying speeds and the noise is in no way indicative of trouble in the axle.

If noise is present in an objectionable form, loud or at all speeds, an effort should be made to isolate the noise as being in one particular unit of the vehicle. Axle noise is often confused with other noises such as tire noise, transmission noise, propeller shaft vibration and universal joint noise. Isolation of the noise as in any one unit requires skill and experience. An attempt to eliminate a slight noise may baffle even the best of diagnosticians. Such practices as raising tire pressure to eliminate tire noise, listening for the noise at varying speeds and on drive, float and coast, and under proper highway conditions, turning the steering wheel from left to right to detect wheel bearing noise, will aid even the beginner in detecting alleged axle noises. Axle noises fall into two categories, gear noise and bearing noise.

Gear Noise

Abnormal gear noise can be recognized since it produces a cycling pitch and will be very pronounced in the speed range at which it occurs, appearing under either "drive," "float" or "coast" conditions. Gear noise tends to peak in a narrow speed range or ranges, while bearing noise will tend to remain constant in pitch. Abnormal gear noise is rare and usually originates from the scoring of the ring gear and pinion teeth as a result of insufficient or improper lubricant in new assemblies. Side gears rarely give trouble as they are used only when the rear wheels travel at different speeds.

Bearing Noise

Defective bearings will always produce a rough whine that is constant in pitch and usually most noticeable under "drive" conditions. This fact will allow you to distinguish between bearing noise and gear noise.
1. Pinion bearing noise resulting from a bearing failure can be identified by a constant rough sound. Pinion bearings are rotating at a higher speed than differential side bearings or axle shaft bearings. This particular noise can be picked up best by testing the car on a smooth road (black top). However, care should be taken not to confuse tire noise with bearing or gear noise. If any doubt exists, tire treads should be examined for irregularities that would produce such noise.
2. Wheel bearing noise may be confused with rear axle noise. To differentiate between wheel bearings and rear axle, drive the vehicle on a smooth road at medium-low speed. With traffic permitting, turn the vehicle sharply right and left. If noise is caused by wheel bearings, it will increase, in the turns because of the side loading. If noise cannot be isolated to front or rear wheel bearings, inspection will be necessary.

3. Side bearings will produce a constant rough noise of a slower nature than pinion bearings. Side bearing noise will not fluctuate in the above wheel bearing test.

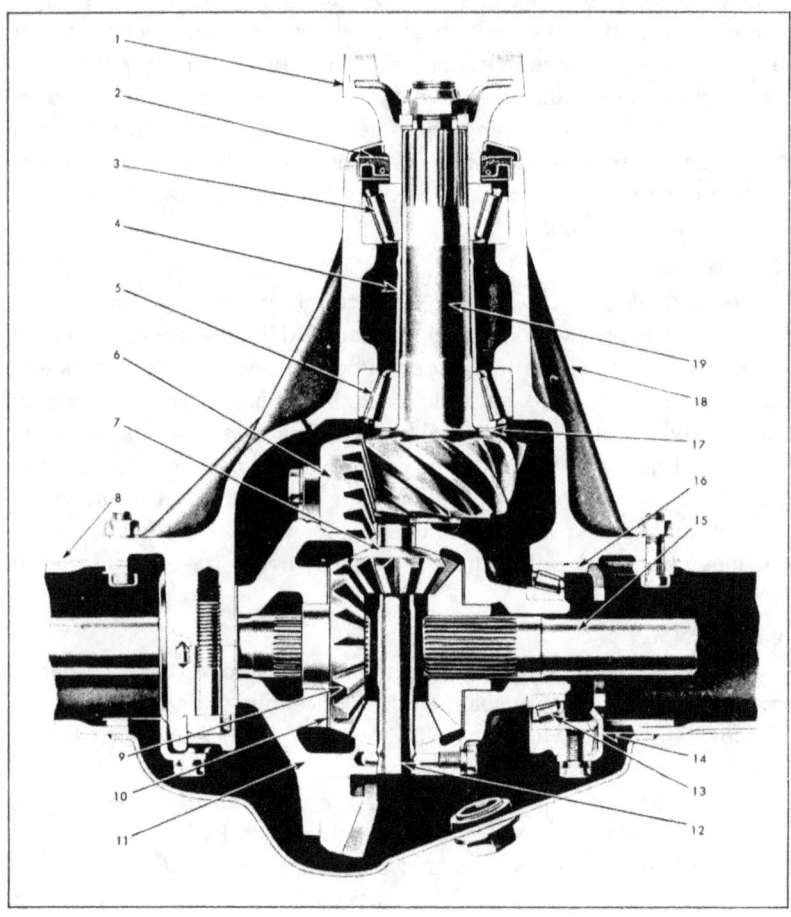

1. Pinion Drive Flange
2. Oil Seal
3. Front Pinion Bearing
4. Pinion Bearing Spacer
5. Rear Pinion Bearing
6. Ring Gear
7. Differential Pinion
8. Axle Housing
9. Differential Side Gear
10. Differential Side Gear Thrust Washer
11. Differential Case
12. Differential Pinion
13. Differential Side Bearing
14. Adjusting Sleeve Lock
15. Axle Shaft
16. Adjusting Sleeve
17. Pinion Shim
18. Carrier
19. Drive Pinion

BRAKES

General Description

The brakes used on both front and rear of all models are the Duo-Servo single anchor type which utilize the momentum of the vehicle to assist in the brake application. This self-energizing of self-actuating force is applied to both brake shoes at each wheel in both forward or reverse motion.

Wheel cylinders are the double piston type permitting even distribution of pressure to each brake shoe. To keep out dust and moisture and to prevent gumming of the brake fluid, both ends of each wheel cylinder are sealed with a rubber boot. The wheel cylinders have no external adjustments.

The main cylinder consists of a piston which receives mechanical pressure from the push rod and exerts pressure on the fluid in the lines, building up the hydraulic pressure, which moves the wheel cylinder pistons.

Maintenance and Adjustments

In any service operation it is extremely important that absolute cleanliness be observed. Any foreign matter in the system will tend to clog the lines, ruin the rubber cups of the main and wheel cylinders and cause inefficient operation or even failure of the braking system. Dirt or grease on a brake lining will cause that brake to grab first on brake application and fade out on heavy brake application.

HYDRAULIC BRAKE FLUID

Only G.M. Hydraulic Brake Fluid Super No. 11 should be used when bleeding brakes. This brake fluid is satisfactory for any atmospheric temperature hot or cold and has all the qualities necessary for satisfactory operation, such as a high boiling point to prevent evaporation and tendency to vapor lock and remains fluid at low temperatures.

In the event that improper fluid has entered the system, it will be necessary to—
1. Drain the entire system.
2. Thoroughly and vigorously flush the system with clean alcohol, 188 proof, or a hydraulic brake system cleaning fluid such as "Declene."

HYDRAULIC BRAKE ADJUSTMENT

To compensate for lining wear, which is evidenced by excessive pedal travel, a minor adjustment can be made to reduce the clearance between the brake lining and brake drum. All hydraulic

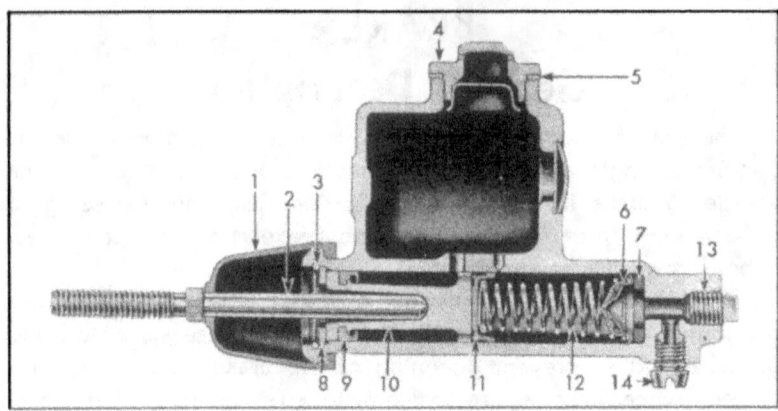

Fig. 3—Main Cylinder

1. Rubber Boot
2. Push Rod
3. Lock Ring
4. Filler Plug
5. Filler Plug Gasket
6. Valve Assembly
7. Valve Seat
8. Flat Washer
9. Secondary Cup
10. Piston
11. Primary Cup
12. Spring
13. End Plug
14. Outlet Fitting

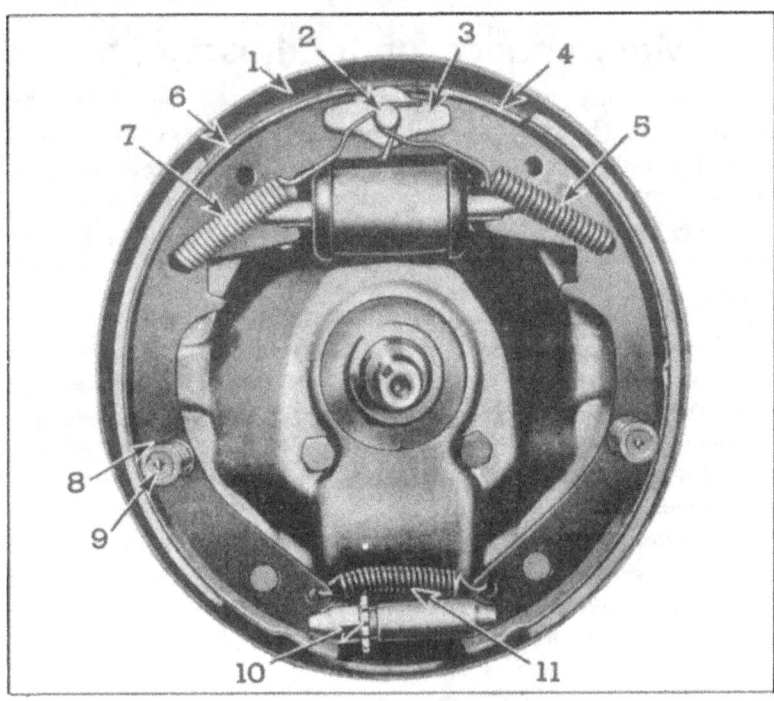

Fig. 1—Duo-Servo Brake

1. Backing Plate
2. Anchor Pin
3. Guide Plate
4. Secondary Shoe
5. Pull Back Spring
6. Primary Shoe
7. Pull Back Spring
8. Hold Down Spring
9. Hold Down Pin
10. Adjusting Screw
11. Adjusting Screw Spring

brakes can be adjusted without removal of the wheels as all brake flange plates have openings with removable spring snap covers. As brakes are self-energizing through energizing links, only one service adjustment at each wheel cylinder is needed.
1. Jack up wheel and remove adjusting hole cover from flange plate.
2. Through hole in flange plate, insert screw driver or similar tool and engage it in teeth of adjusting wheel.
3. To expand shoes, move outer end of tool toward center of wheel until shoes drag slightly.
4. Turn adjusting wheel in opposite direction 7 notches (12 notches if equipped with metallic lining) to insure running clearance and check to see that wheel turns freely without drag. It may be necessary to tap backing plate to permit shoes to centralize before brake will be free.
5. Repeat this operation on each brake and replace hole covers.

PARKING BRAKE ADJUSTMENT

The parking brake adjustment should be checked each time the hydraulic brakes are adjusted. When making a parking brake adjustment, the service brakes must be properly adjusted first as a base for the parking brake adjustment.
1. Jack up both rear wheels.
2. Pull out hand brake handle for 7 clicks of pawls (not 7 notches).
3. Loosen check nuts at cable ends. Turn the forward check nuts against the clevis plates to draw up each brake cable until a moderate drag is felt when rotating drum.
4. Tighten check nuts securely.
5. Set parking brake lever back to 2 clicks from full release position, at which point no brake shoe drag should be felt.

BLEEDING HYDRAULIC SYSTEM

Air in the hydraulic system must be removed by a bleeding operation after the system has been opened at any point, or when air has entered the system in any manner. Air in the system is usually indicated by:
1. A "spongy" or "springy" feeling of the brake pedal when the brakes are applied.
2. Too much travel of the brake pedal (when the brake shoe adjustment is known to be correct).

Bleeding should be done on the longest line first to remove effectively all air from the system. The proper sequence to follow is left rear, right rear, right front and left front. In the bleeding operation it is extremely important that absolute cleanliness be observed. Any foreign matter in the system will tend to clog the lines, ruin the rubber cups of the main and wheel cylinders and cause inefficient operation or even failure of the braking system.

The manual method of bleeding the brake lines is described below. It is recommended that a helper be used to assist in performing this operation.

1. Raise hood, clean all dirt from top of main cylinder mounted on the dash panel, and remove filler plug.
2. Fill the reservoir with brake fluid. The reservoir must be kept full, or nearly full, of brake fluid while bleeding the brake system.
3. Remove bleeder valve screw from end of bleeder valve near the brake fluid pipe or hose connection at wheel.
4. Attach a bleeder hose to the bleeder valve at this point and place the free end of the bleeder hose in a clean container having sufficient fluid at all times during this operation.
5. With a wrench, open bleeder valve by turning ¾ turn in.
6. Slowly depress the brake pedal by hand to approximately the halfway point, then let the pedal return slowly to the release position. Repeat this procedure several times, keeping the end of the hose submerged in brake fluid until the fluid expelled from the bleeder hose is free of air bubbles.
7. Close bleeder valve tightly by turning clockwise with wrench as soon as bubbles stop and fluid flows in a solid stream.
8. Remove bleeder hose and install bleeder valve screw in bleeder valve.
9. Add new fluid to the main cylinder, and repeat the operation on the other wheels in turn.

CLUTCH AND BRAKE PEDAL

Removal

1. Remove cotter pin and clevis pin from brake pedal arm.
2. Push clutch pedal to floor and remove over-center spring from dash panel brace and clutch pedal arm.
3. Remove lock bolt nut and remove bolt from over-center spring lever (on brake pedal side of panel brace) and remove lever from shaft.
4. Remove clutch pedal push rod by removing retainer clip and washer and pushing rod out of clutch pedal arm.
5. Slide the clutch pedal arm assembly to the left and remove from panel brace. Brake pedal arm tension spring will then fall free.
6. Withdraw brake pedal.
7. Remove nylon bushings from brake pedal side of panel

brace and from pivot shaft on upper end of clutch pedal arm.

Inspection
1. Clean all metal parts with a good cleaning solvent.
2. Wipe the nylon bushings clean with a clean cloth.

   CAUTION: Nylon bushings should not be treated with cleansing agents of any nature.
3. Inspect all nylon bushings for wear or damage. Replace if necessary.
4. Inspect all mating surfaces of bushings for wear or damage. Replace any parts if necessary.

Installation
1. Install nylon bushing on clutch pedal pivot and one through panel brace on opposite side.
2. Set brake pedal arm and spring in place and install clutch pedal arm and pivot shaft. Make certain that spring indexes on panel brace (in stamped notch) and on brake pedal arm.
3. Align over-center spring lever lock bolt passage with notch in pivot shaft and slide lever onto shaft, then install lock bolt and nut in lever and shaft and install over-center spring.
4. Attach clutch pedal push rod and secure with washer and retainer clip.
5. Install main cylinder push rod clevis pin and cotter pin.

   NOTE: Check stop light switch position and adjust if necessary so that electrical contact is made when the pedal is depressed ⅝ inch.

BRAKE SHOE REPLACEMENT

In all cases of brake complaints denoting actual brake lining or shoe failure, the brake drums should be removed and before disassembly of the shoes from the flange plate, all linings should be inspected for wear, improper alignment causing uneven wear and oil and grease on the linings. If any of these conditions exist, it will be necessary to replace the shoes. If, in checking the linings, it is noticed that they have the appearance of being glazed, this is a normal condition with the hard type lining used. **Do not use a wire brush or an abrasive on the lining to destroy this glazed surface as it is essential for proper operation.** When brake lining replacement is necessary, all shoes and linings should be replaced. In no case should a single lining and shoe be replaced; however, in exceptional cases, it may be satisfactory to replace the shoes and linings on both front or both rear wheels.

Removal
1. Raise vehicle and place on stand jacks.
2. Loosen check nuts at forward end of parking brake cable sufficently to remove all tension from brake cable.
3. Remove rear brake drums and front hub and drums assemblies.

   NOTE: Since boots are recessed in grooves on wheel cylinders to prevent pistons from leaving cylinders, it is not necessary to install wheel cylinder clamps when brake shoes are removed; however, brake pedal must not be depressed while drums are removed.

4. Unhook brake shoe pull back springs from anchor pin using Tool J-8049 (fig. 115).

   NOTE: Be certain that the primary and secondary springs are kept separate as they have unequal tension. The secondary spring which is colored black has a spring rate of 50 lbs. The primary spring which is colored grey, has a spring rate of 40 lbs.

5. Remove brake shoe hold down pins and springs using a pair of needle nosed pliers (fig. 16).
6. Spread shoes to clear wheel cylinder connecting links and remove shoes from backing plate (fig. 17).

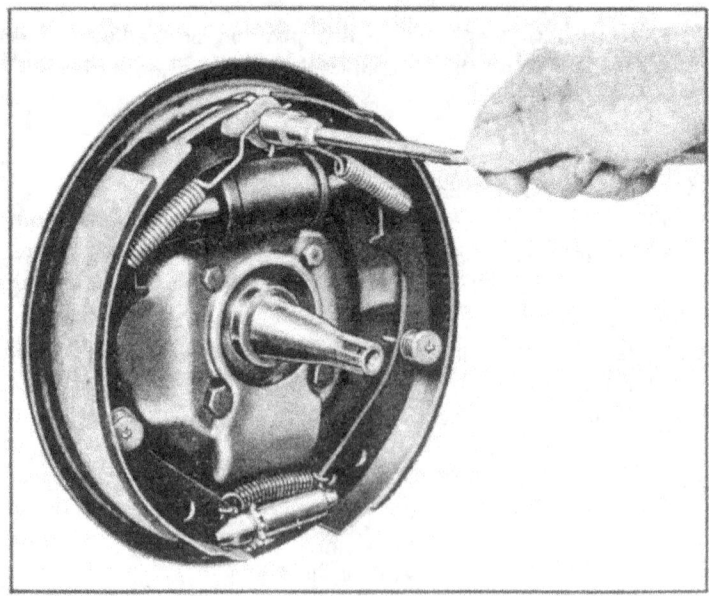

Fig. 15—Unhooking Pull Back Spring

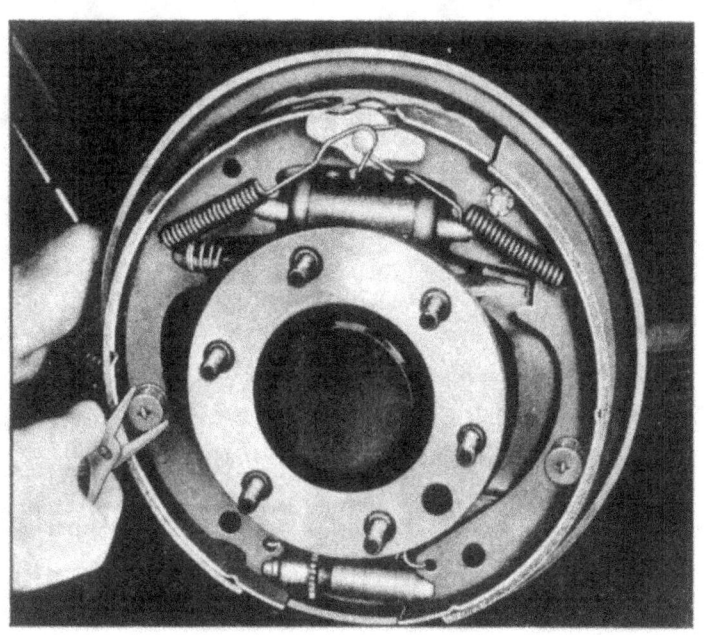

Fig. 16—Removing Hold Down Springs and Pins

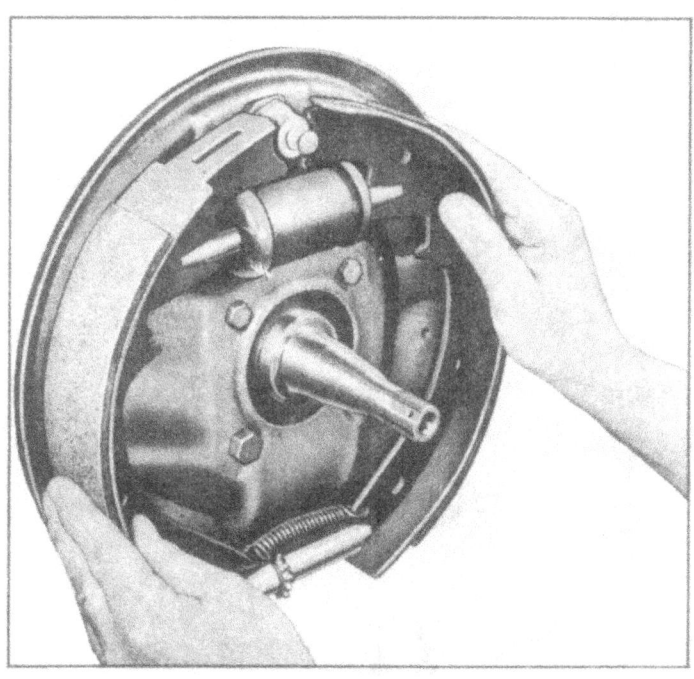

Fig. 17—Spreading Brake Shoes for Removal

7. Separate the brake shoes by removing adjusting screw and spring.
8. Remove parking brake lever from secondary brake shoe (rear only).
9. Clean all dirt out of brake drum using care to avoid getting dirt into front wheel bearings. Inspect drums for roughness, scoring or out-of-round. Replace or recondition drums as necessary.
10. Inspect wheel bearings and oil seal and replace any necessary parts.
11. Carefully pull lower edges of wheel cylinder boots away from cylinders and note whether interior is wet with brake fluid. Excessive fluid at this point indicates leakage past piston cups requiring overhaul of wheel cylinder.

NOTE: A slight amount of fluid is nearly always present and acts as lubricant for the piston.

12. If working at rear wheels, inspect backing plate for oil leakage past axle shaft oil seals. Install new seals if necessary.
13. Check all brake flange plate attaching bolts to make sure they are tight. Clean all rust and dirt from shoe contact faces on flange plate, using fine emery cloth (fig. 18).

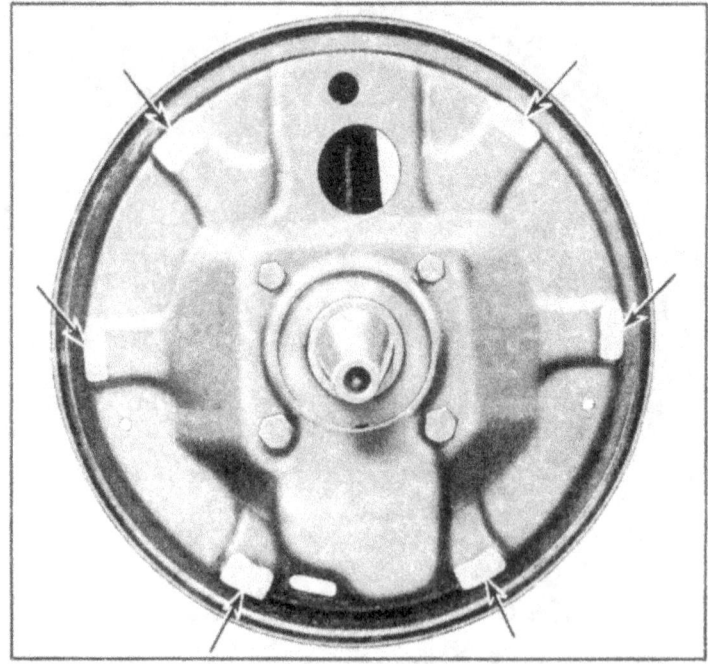

Fig. 18—Backing Plate Contact Faces

Installation

CAUTION: Make certain that when replacing with new shoe and lining assemblies, that the latest type linings are used. Otherwise, serious fade or permanent failure may occur.

1. Inspect new linings and make sure there are no nicks or burrs or bonding material on shoe edge where contact is made with brake flange plate or on any of the contact surfaces.

   NOTE: Keep hands clean while handling brake shoes. Do not permit oil or grease to come in contact with linings.

2. If working on rear brakes, lubricate parking brake cable.
3. On rear brakes only, lubricate fulcrum end of parking brake lever and the bolt with Bendix or Delco brake lube or Lubriplate, then attach lever to secondary shoe with bolt, spring washer, lockwasher, and nut. Make sure that lever moves freely.
4. Lubricate threads and socket end of adjusting screw with Bendix or Delco brake lube or Lubriplate.
5. Connect brake shoes together with adjusting screw spring then place adjusting screw, socket and nut in position.

   CAUTION: The socket and adjusting screw must be adjacent to the primary shoe (front) on the brakes on the left side and adjacent to the secondary shoe (rear) on the brakes on the right side.

6. Attach brake shoes to brake flange plates with the hold down pins and springs using a pair of needle-nosed pliers; at the same time engage shoes with wheel cylinder connecting links. The primary shoe (short lining) goes forward.
7. On rear brakes, connect cable to parking brake lever and install strut between lever and primary shoe as installation is made.
8. If old brake pull back springs are nicked, distorted, or if strength is doubtful, install new springs. Install guide plate over anchor, hook springs in shoes and using Tool J-8049, install spring connected to primary shoe over anchor (fig. 19), and then spring connected to secondary shoe over anchor.

   NOTE: The brake shoe release springs are color coded for identification. The secondary spring is colored black, and the primary spring is colored grey.

9. Pry shoes away from backing plate and lubricate shoe con-

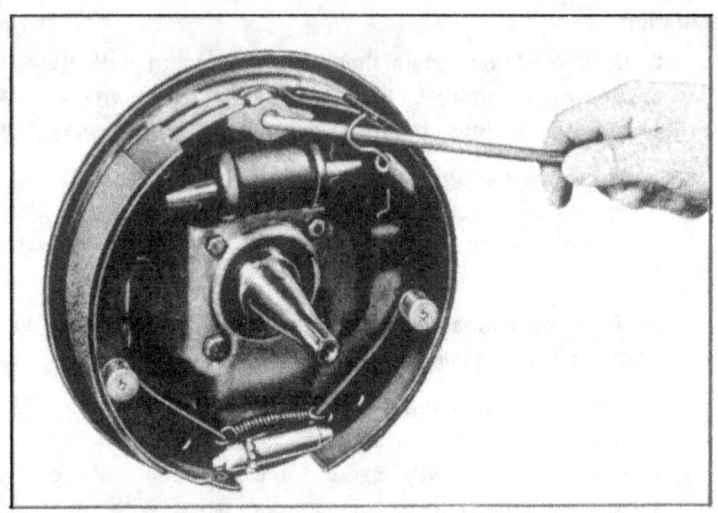

Fig. 19 — Installing pull-back spring

tact surfaces with a thin coating of Bendix or Delco brake lube or Lubriplate. On rear wheels, sparingly apply this same lubricant where brake cable contacts brake flange plate.

CAUTION: Be careful to keep lubricant off facings.

10. Install brake drums. If working on front brakes, lubricate and adjust wheel bearings and install front and rear wheel and tire assemblies. Remove adjusting hole covers from backing plates.
11. Adjust all brakes and brake cables as outlined under "Maintenance and Adjustments."

NOTE: The fixed anchor pins have eliminated need for anchor pin adjustment.

PUSH ROD TO MAIN CYLINDER CLEARANCE

This clearance very seldom needs adjustment. The brake pedal has a definite stop which is permanent and not adjustable. This stop consists of a rubber bumper at the release end of pedal travel. Before adjusting push rod to main cylinder clearance, make sure brake pedal returns to the fully released position freely, with no binding, and that the pedal retracting spring has not lost its tension.

1. Brake pedal clevis should be adjusted to give barely perceptible end play between main cylinder piston and the brake push rod.
2. Loosen check nut on the clevis.
3. Turn push rod in proper direction to secure the proper adjustment, barely perceptible movement of pedal before con-

tact of push rod and main cylinder piston (⅛" to ⅜" pedal movement should be felt.)
4. Tighten check nut on clevis.

HYDRAULIC BRAKE TUBING

Hydraulic brake tubing used on all models is a double layer annealed steel, copper coated and tin plated tubing which resists corrosion and also stands up under the high pressures which are developed when applying the brakes. All models use 3/16" tubing, except on the brake main cylinder pipe and front crossover pipe which are ¼". In making up hydraulic brake pipes, it is important that the proper size flaring to be used to flare the ends of the tubing for the compression couplings. Unless the tubing is properly flared, the couplings will leak and the brakes will become ineffective.

CAUTION: When necessary to replace brake tubing, always use special metal tubing which is especially designed to withstand high presure and resist corrosion. For this reason, ordinary copper tubing is not satisfactory and should not be used.

This safety steel tubing must be double-lap flared at the ends in order to produce a strong leak-proof joint.

BRAKE DRUMS

Front and rear brake drums are both removable, that is, the front drum is removable without disturbing the wheel hub, and the rear drum may be removed without disturbing the axle shaft.

Removal
1. Jack up front end of vehicle and remove wheel.
2. Remove brake drum assembly.
3. Jack up rear end of vehicle and remove wheel.
4. Remove brake drum from flange of axle shaft.

Inspecting and Reconditioning

Whenever brake drums are removed they should be thoroughly cleaned and inspected for cracks, scores, deep grooves, and out-of-round. Any of these conditions must be corrected since they can impair the efficency of brake operation and also can cause premature failure of other parts.

Smooth up any slight scores by polishing with fine emery cloth. Heavy or extensive scoring will cause excessive brake lining wear and it will probably be necessary to rebore in order to true up the braking surface.

An out-of-round drum makes accurate brake shoe adjustment impossible and is likely to cause excessive wear of other parts of brake mechanism due to its eccentric action.

A drum that is more than .008" out-of-round on the diameter is unfit for service and should be rebored. Out-of-round, as well as taper and wear can be accurately measured with an inside micrometer fitted with proper extension rods.

If drum is to be rebored for use with standard size brake facings which are worn very little, only enough metal should be removed to obtain a true smooth braking surface.

If drum has to be rebored more than .020" over the standard diameter, it should be rebored to .060" diameter oversize and the brake facing should be replaced with .030" oversize facings.

A brake drum must not be rebored more than .060" over the maximum standard diameter, since removal of more metal will effect dissipation of heat and may cause distortion of drum. Chevrolet brake facing is not furnished larger than .030" oversize and this will not work efficiently in drums bored more than .060" oversize.

Brake drums may be refinished either by turning or grinding. Best brake performance is obtained by turning drums with a very fine feed. To insure maximum lining life, the refinished braking surface must be smooth and free from chatter or tool marks, and run-out must not exceed .005" total indicator reading.

Cleaning

New brake drums in parts stock are given a light coating of rust proofing oil to prevent the formation of rust on the critical braking surfaces during the time that the drums are in storage.

This rust proofing oil must be carefully removed before the drum is placed in service to prevent any of this oil from getting on the brake shoe facings, which might cause an extreme brake grab condition.

It is recommended that a suitable volatile, non-toxic, greaseless type solvent be used to clean the oil from the braking surface of the new brake drums before they are placed in service to insure the cleanest possible surface.

Gasoline or Kerosene should not be used as there is danger that a portion of the diluted oily substance may be left on the braking surface that may later cause difficulty.

Installation
1. On front, install drum to wheel hub.
2. On rear, assemble drum over axle shaft studs.
3. Replace wheel assembly, adjust brakes and lower vehicle to floor.

Brake System

TROUBLES AND REMEDIES

SYMPTOMS & PROBABLE CAUSE	PROBABLE REMEDY

Pedal Spongy
  a. Air in brake lines.

  a. Bleed brakes.

All Brakes Drag
  a. Improper pedal to push rod clearance blocking compensator port.
  b. Compensating port in main cylinder restricted.
  c. Mineral oil in system.

  a. Adjust clearance.
  b. Overhaul main cylinder.
  c. Flush entire brake system and replace all rubber parts.

One Brake Drags
  a. Loose or damaged wheel bearings.
  b. Weak, broken or unhooked brake retractor spring.
  c. Brake shoes adjusted too close to brake drum.
  d. Parking brake adjustment too tight.

  a. Adjust or replace wheel bearings.
  b. Replace retractor spring.
  c. Correctly adjust brakes.
  d. Readjust parking brake.

Excessive Pedal Travel
  a. Normal lining wear or improper shoe adjustment.
  b. Fluid low in main cylinder.

  a. Adjust brakes.
  b. Fill main cylinder and bleed brakes.

Brake Pedal Applies Brakes but Pedal Gradually Goes to Floor Board
  a. External leaks.
  b. Main cylinder leaks past primary cup.

  a. Check main cylinder, lines and wheel cylinder for leaks and make necessary repairs.
  b. Overhaul main cylinder.

Brakes Uneven
  a. Grease on linings.
  b. Tires improperly inflated.

  a. Clean brake mechanism; replace lining and correct cause of grease getting on lining.
  b. Inflate tires to correct pressure.

Excessive Pedal Pressure Required, Poor Brakes
  a. Grease, mud or water on linings.
  b. Full area of linings not contacting drums.
  c. Scored brake drums.

  a. Remove drums—clean and dry linings or replace.
  b. Free up shoe linkage, sand linings or replace shoes.
  c. Turn drums and install new linings.

Wheels And Tires

INTERCHANGING TIRES

Normal tire wear is uneven between the front and rear wheels because of the difference in the functions of the front and rear tires. To minimize tire wear and tire noise, it is recommended that tires be interchanged both as to front or rear and as to change of direction at intervals of from 4,000 to 5,000 miles.

In addition, utilizing the spare tire in rotation with the other four tires gives 20% more total car mileage before replacement tires must be purchased.

The recommended plan for interchanging tires is based on the following steps.

CORRECTION OF IRREGULAR TIRE WEAR

Heel and Toe Wear—This is a saw-toothed effect where one end of each tread block is worn more than the other.

The end that wears is the one that first grips the road when the brakes are applied.

Heel and toe wear is less noticeable on rear tires than on front tires, because the propelling action of the rear wheels creates a force which tends to wear the opposite end of the tread blocks. The two forces, propelling and braking, make for more even wear of the rear tires, whereas only the braking forces act on the front wheels, and the saw-tooth effect is more noticeable.

A certain amount of heel and toe wear is normal. Excessive wear is usually due to high speed driving and excessive use of brakes. The best remedy, in addition to cautioning the owner on his driving habits, is to interchange tires regularly.

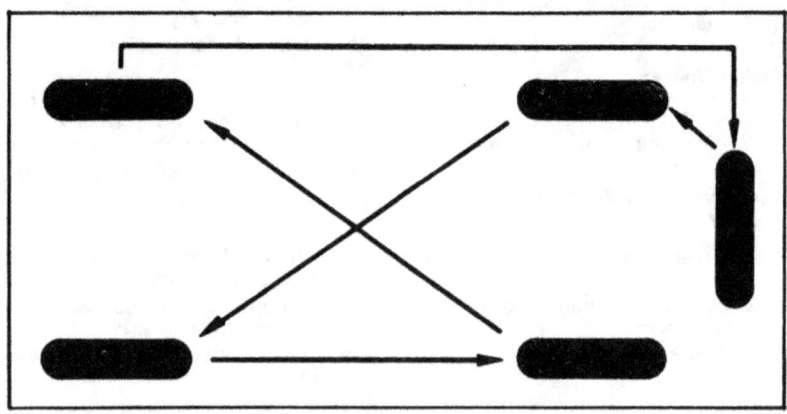

Tire Rotation Plan

Side Wear—This may be caused by incorrect wheel camber, underinflation, high cambered roads or by taking corners at too high a rate of speed.

The first two causes are the most common. Camber wear can be readily identified because it occurs only on one side of the treads, whereas underinflation causes wear on both sides. Camber wear requires correction of the camber first and then interchanging tires.

Move the left front wheel to left rear, left rear to right front, right front to spare, spare to right rear and right rear to left front.

In detail, the plan provides the changes as shown in Figure 34 each time the tires are interchanged.

There is, of course, no correction for high cambered roads. Cornering wear is discussed further on.

Misalignment Wear—This is wear due to excessive toe-in or toe-out. In either case, tires will revolve with a side motion and scrape the tread rubber off. If misalignment is severe, the rubber will be scraped off of both tires; if slight, only one will be affected.

The scraping action against the face of the tire causes a small feather edge of rubber to appear on one side of the tread and this feather edge is certain indication of misalignment. The remedy is readjusting toe-in within 1/16" to 3/32", or rechecking the entire front end alignment if necessary.

Uneven Wear—Uneven or spotty wear is due to such irregularities as unequal caster or camber, bent front suspension parts, out-of-balance wheels, brake drums out-of-round, brakes out-of-adjustment or other mechanical conditions. The remedy in each case consists of locating the mechanical defect and correcting it.

Cornering Wear—Since the introduction of independently sprung front wheels, improvements in spring suspension have enabled drivers to negotiate curves at higher rates of speed with the same feeling of security that they had with the older cars at lower speeds. Consequently, curves are being taken at higher speeds with the result that a type of tire wear called "Cornering Wear," frequently appears.

When a car makes an extremely fast turn, the weight is shifted from an even loading on all four wheels to an abnormal load on the tires on the outside of the curve and a very light load on the inside tires, due to centrifugal force. This unequal loading may have two unfavorable results.

First, the rear tire on the inside of the curve may be relieved of so much load that it is no longer geared to the road and it slips, grinding off the tread on the inside half of the tire at an excessive rate. This type of tire shows much the same appearance of tread wear as tire wear caused by negative camber.

Second, the transfer of weight may be also overload the outside tires so much that they are laterally distorted resulting in excessive wear on the outside half of the tire, producing a type of wear like that caused by excessive positive camber.

Cornering wear can be most easily distinguished from abnormal camber wear by the rounding of the outside shoulder or edge of the tire and by the roughening of the tread surface which denotes abrasion.

Cornering wear often produces a fin or raised portion along the inside edge of each row in the tread pattern. In some cases this fin is almost as pronounced as a toe-in fin, and in others, it tapers into a row of tread blocks to such an extent that the tire has a definite step wear appearance.

BALANCING WHEELS AND TIRES

A wheel and tire assembly may lose its original balance due to irregular tire wear, tire repair or some type of misalignment. Consequently, if front end instability develops, the tire and wheel assembly should be checked for static and in severe cases, dynamic balance. The assembly should also be checked for balance whenever any original tire is replaced or repaired, and especially in cases where nonstandard tire equipment, such as an extra ply casing, is used.

Static Balance (still balance) is the equal distribution of weight of the wheel and tire assembly about the axis of rotation so that the assembly has no tendency to rotate by itself. Static unbalance causes the pounding action of the front wheels that is called "tramp."

To correct static unbalance (front and rear):
1. Remove wheel and hub from spindle as a unit.
2. Clean all grease from wheel bearings and races.
3. Clamp a clean spindle in a bench vise, or if the spindle on the car must be used, clean it carefully.
4. Mount the wheel on the spindle and adjust the bearings loosely so that the wheel is just held in position and is practically frictionless.
5. Make sure that the tire is inflated to the correct pressure.
6. Start the wheel in motion and allow it to stop by itself. When it stops, the heavy side will be at the bottom.
7. Mark the heaviest point and also the uppermost or lightest point.
8. Install two balancing weights on the rim opposite each other and 180° away from the heavy point.
9. Move these weights equally in opposite direction toward the heavy side until the wheel is in balance.

10. Repack wheel bearings, reinstall and adjust bearings as explained in this section under "Front Wheel Bearings—Adjust."

Dynamic Balance (running balance) requires the wheel to be not only in static balance, but balanced and running smoothly while turning on an axis which runs through the centerline of the wheel and tire perpendicular to the axis of rotation.

The quickest and best methods of testing and correcting dynamic unbalance are by the use of dynamic wheel balancers include all necessary information on where and how the balancing weights should be placed. The following information, however, will help in the correction of dynamic balance.

NOTE: Before attempting to balance the wheels, check to be certain that no foreign matter has been trapped in the wheel ventilation slots or in the accessory wheel discs. This is especially important if the vehicle has been run in soft mud and then parked in freezing weather.

When a wheel that is statically unbalanced is dynamically in balance the dynamic balance can be retained while correcting the static balance by installing the corrective weights so that half of the weight required is placed on the inner edge of the rim and the other half on the outer edge of the rim.

Dynamic unbalance can be corrected without destroying static balance by installing weights so half of weight required for dynamic balance is placed on the rim opposite the heavy point, while the other half is placed 180° away and on the opposite side of the rim.

WHEEL RUN-OUT AND ECCENTRICITY

The wheels should not run out (wobble) more than 1/16" as measured on the side of the rim at the base of the tire. Excessive run-out is the result of a bent wheel, an improperly mounted wheel, worn knuckle bearings or steering connections. These parts should be checked for correct adjustment, proper alignment and wear whenever excessive run-out is encountered.

The wheels should also run concentric with the steering knuckle spindle within 1/16 inch as measured on the tire bead seat of the rim with the tire removed.

Wheel run-out, eccentricity and balance are closely associated with steering and front wheel alignment. Further information on these subjects will be found under "Standard Suspension."

TESTING FOR TIRE NOISE

Noise caused by the normal action of tire treads on various road surfaces is often confused with rear axle gears or other noises in the car.

The determination of whether tires are causing the noise complained of is relatively simple. The car should be driven at various speeds and note taken of part throttle, sudden acceleration and deceleration as axle and exhaust noises show definite variations under these conditions, while tire noise will remain constant. Tire noise is, however, most pronounced at speeds of approximately twenty or thirty miles per hour.

The tires may be further checked by driving the car over smooth pavement with the tires at normal pressure and again over the same stretch of pavement when the tires have been inflated to fifty pounds pressure. Reduce the tires to normal pressure (24 pounds) one at a time to determine faulty tire or tires. This high inflation pressure should immediately be reduced to normal after test. If the noise for which the test is being made is caused by tires it will noticeably decrease when the tire pressure is increased, whereas axle noise should show no change in volume.

If, on inspection, the tires on the front wheels are found to be creating most of the noise, the alignment of the front wheels should be checked, as excessive tire noise usually results from low tire pressure, incorrect alignment or from uneven tire wear.

DISMOUNTING AND MOUNTING TIRES

Dismounting tubeless tires presents no problems if the correct procedures are used and the following precautions observed.
1. Remove the valve cap and valve core. Let out all the air.
2. Press the **inner side** of the tire into the rim well. Use bead loosening tool or if regular tire irons are used, take particular care not to injure or tear the sealing ribs on the bead.
   CAUTION: Never use tire irons with sharp edges or corners.
3. Using tire irons on the opposite side, remove bead, taking small "bits" around the rim.
4. Turn the tire over, and use two tire irons, one between the rim flange and the bead to pry the rim upward, the other iron to pry outward between the beat seat and bead.

Mounting Tubeless Tires

The general procedure is the same as for tube and tire installation except that extreme care must be exercised to prevent injury to the sealing bead and circumferential bead when forcing tire over rim.

Newly designed tire mounting machines or tire irons should be used.
1. Apply a light film of Ruglyde or other suitable rubber lubricant to sealing bead of tire.
   NOTE: The use of excessive lubrication may lead to rim slippage and subsequent breaking of oil seal.

2. Carefully mount the **outer bead** in usual manner by using tire irons, taking small "bites" around rim, being careful not to injure the tire bead.

CAUTION: DO NOT use a hammer, as damage to the bead will result.

3. Install the **inner bead** in the same manner.

NOTE: If a seal cannot be effected in the foregoing manner with the rush of air it can be accomplished by applying to the circumference of the tire a tire mounting band or heavy sash cord and tightening with the use of a tire iron. On tire mounting machines, bouncing the tire assembly is not required. The tire should be lifted on the rim to force the top tire bead against the top rim flange. The weight of the tire will seat the bottom bead.

CLEANING WHITEWALL TIRES

A great deal of ordinary road dirt which collects on white sidewall tires may be sponged off with clear water or a mild soap solution.

Chevrolet Whitewall Tire Cleaner however, is a quicker and more effective cleaner for removing dirt and stains from whitewall tires and in many cases it will remove stains and discoloration that the simpler method of soap and water will not remove.

Under no circumstances should gasoline, kerosene or any cleaning fluid containing a solvent derived from oil be used to clean whitewall tires. Oil in any form is detrimental to rubber and a cleaner with an oil base will discolor or injure whitewall tires.

The antics of competition are of course not conducive to maximum tire life!

TROUBLES AND REMEDIES

WHEELS AND TIRES

Symptoms and Probable Cause

Hard Steering
a. Low air pressure in tires.
b. Lack of lubrication.
c. Improper wheel alignment.
d. Sagging front or rear spring.
e. Bent wheel or spindle.
f. Broken wheel bearings.
g. Tight spherical joints.
h. Underinflated tires.
i. Improper steering gear adjustment.
j. Tie rod ends out of alignment.

Front Wheel Shimmy
a. Underinflated tires.
b. Broken or loose wheel bearings.
c. Worn spherical joints.
d. Improper caster.
e. Unbalanced wheels.
f. Steering gear loose.
g. Tie rod ball loose.
h. Loose wheel lugs.
i. Bent wheel.
j. Improper alignment.
k. Wheel out-of-balance.

Excessive or Uneven Tire Wear
a. Wheels out of balance.
b. High speed cornering.
c. Improper air pressures.
d. Not rotating tires as recommended.
e. Improper acting brakes.
f. Improper alignment.
g. Rapid stopping.

Vehicle Too Flexible
a. Faulty shock absorber.

Hard Riding
a. Shock absorber broken or seized.
b. Excessive tire pressure.

Probable Remedy

a. Inflate tires to recommended pressure.
b. Lubricate according to instructions.
c. Front end alignment correction.
d. Replace springs as required.
e. Straighten or replace wheel or replace spindle.
f. Replace necessary bearings.
g. If not corrected by lubrication, replace joints.
h. Inflate tires to recommended pressure.
i. Adjust steering gear.
j. Align tie rod ends with ball studs.

a. Inflate tires to recommended pressure.
b. Replace or adjust wheel bearings.
c. Replace joints.
d. Adjust caster.
e. Balance wheel and tire assemblies.
f. Adjust steering gear.
g. Replace tie rod end.
h. Tighten lugs.
i. Replace or tighten wheel.
j. Front end alignment as per specifications.
k. Balance wheel.

a. Balance wheels.
b. Instruct driver.
c. Inflate tires to recommended pressure.
d. Rotate tires according to instructions.
e. Correct brakes as required.
f. Align front end as per specifications.
g. Apply brakes slowly on approaching stop.

a. Disconnect shock absorber and test action (there should be considerable and steady resistance in each direction when held in upright position), replace if necessary.

a. Disconnect shock absorber and test action, replace if necessary.
b. Check tire pressure, maintain 24 pounds (cold).

The Corvette Body

In contrast to the many components of the Corvette which have changed during the eight years, certain features have remained constant, notably the fiberglass resin body.

Use of fiberglass saves considerable weight in the Corvette body as compared with production in steel. Excellent resistance to corrosion is provided. Resistance to casual damage is also outstanding. And, of great importance, fiberglass permits the lowest possible retail price in limited, high quality production.

Corvette body panels are molded between matched metal dies for optimum accuracy and quality. Most body parts are one-tenth of an inch thick to give a structural rigidity comparable to steel panels of conventional thickness. Fiberglass panels are shipped by Chevrolet suppliers to St. Louis where Corvettes have been assembled since 1954.

The Corvette assembly line today is a far cry from the customer delivery garage at Flint, Mich., where the first 300 Corvettes were literally made by hand. Using jigs and fixtures for precision, craftsmen assemble the closely-formed body parts to build up the body shell. Assembly begins with placement of an underbody on a dolly which then travels through subsequent operations.

When the Corvette body is fully assembled, extensive wet and dry sanding is combined with sealing, priming and finish painting to produce a high-lustre and durable finish. Wiring and upholstery are then added, completing a body ready to install on the chassis.

As the bodies are assembled, chassis buildup takes place on the main assembly line. Suspension, drive-line, power-train, exhaust, steering and related components are added as the chassis moves down the line. At the point where preliminary chassis assembly is completed, the body arrives and is lowered into place. A short time later the Corvette rolls off the line ready for intensive final inspection prior to shipment.

In servicing the body, there are, naturally, a number of differences from the conventional all metal body.

Minor Service Operations

Body parts requiring lubrication are lubricated at the factory, and subsequent body lubrication should be determined by operating conditions rather than at specific intervals. Generally, twice a year is sufficient for most types of service. The following points require lubrication:

Lubrication Point	Lubricant
Hood Support	
Rails and Latches	Lubriplate or equivalent
Trunk Lock Catch	Lubriplate or equivalent
Side Door Lock Gear Teeth	Lubriplate or equivalent
Gas Tank Filler Door Hinge	Lubriplate or equivalent
Cowl Vent Linkage	Lubriplate or equivalent
Deck Lid and Folding Top Lid Hinges, Links, Bolts and Springs	Lubriplate or equivalent
Seat Adjuster and Seat Tracks	Lubriplate or equivalent
Side Door Hold-Open Clips	Lubriplate or equivalent

When access is available, side door lock mechanism and connecting links may be lubricated with Lubriplate or equivalent.

The various weather-strips on the body and top, both hard top and folding top, may be lubricated with Ru-Glide, a silicone lubricant or a similar material. This lubrication will improve seal performance, extend seal life, and make door closing an easier and smoother operation.

WINDSHIELD WIPER

The electric windshield wiper and associated linkage is essentially the same as used on passenger car and reference should be made to Section I of the Passenger Car Shop Manual for service operations.

BODY ADJUSTMENTS
Hood

The hood may be adjusted vertically at four points. The rear edge vertical adjustment is obtained by an adjustable bumper at each hood lock "A", Fig. 1. The front edge is adjusted vertically at each hinge by loosening the bolts holding the hinge to the radiator support "A", Fig. 2, and raising or lowering the hinge as required. If this range of adjustment is insufficient, shims may be added or removed as necessary between the hinge assembly and the hood.

The hood may be adjusted laterally at four points. The proper procedure is to loosen the two hood lock assemblies at the rear of the hood, "B", Fig. 1, loosen the bolts attaching the hinge to the hood, "B", Fig. 2, relocate hood as necessary, and retighten the hinge to hood bolts. The hood lock assemblies should then be adjusted to freely enter the hood catch assemblies. It is important that the hood lock bolts not be bent for alignment. Check for bent lock bolts before adjusting the lock assemblies. Lock bolts are now serrated to improve hood retention.

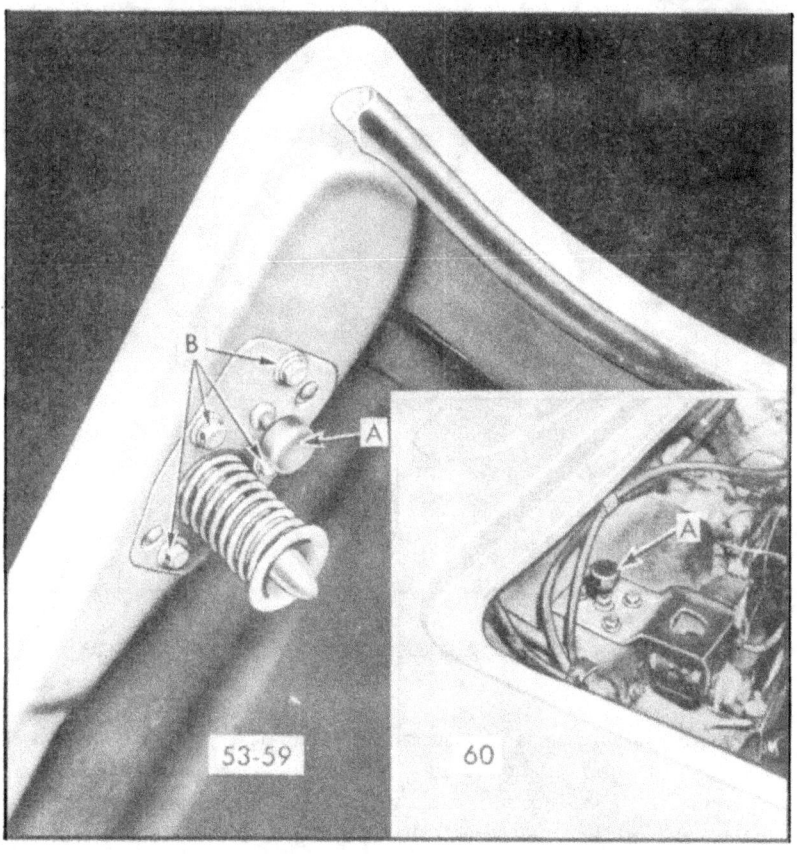

Fig. 1   Hood Adjustments - Rear Edge

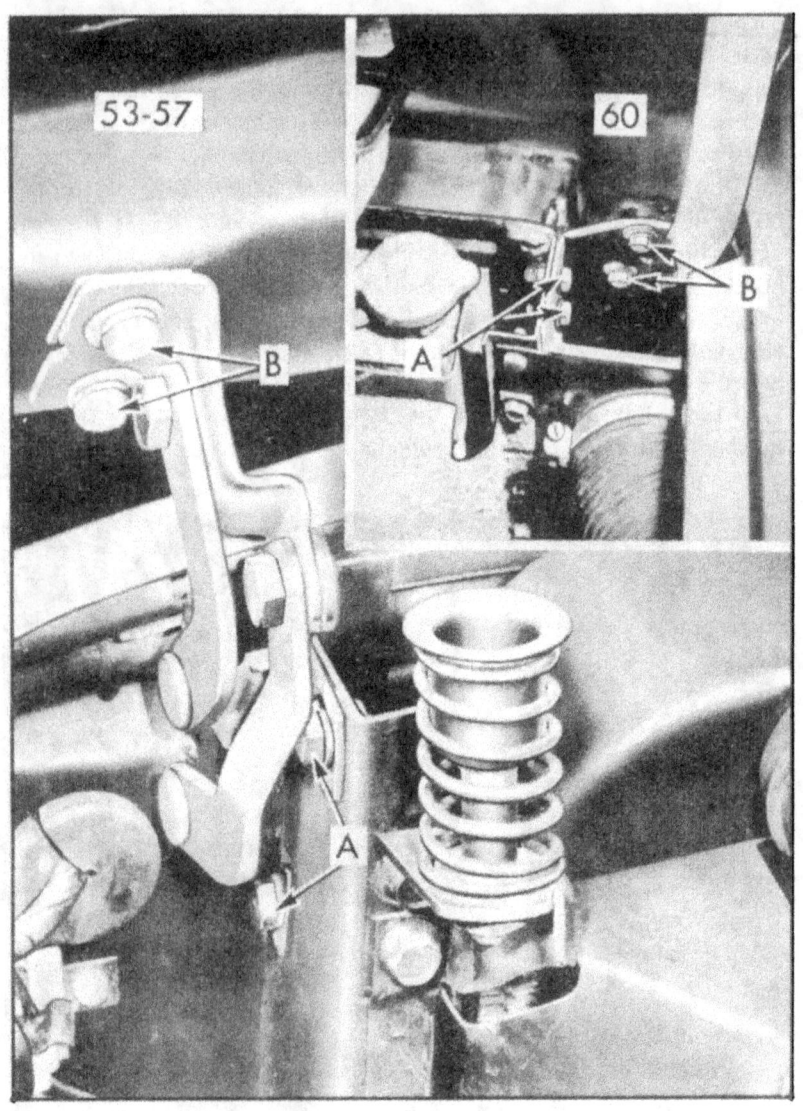

Fig. 2   Hood Adjustments - Front Edge

Doors

Door adjustment is provided at the hinges through the use of cage nuts and anchor plates. When checking a door for misalignment, remove the door lock striker and allow the door to hang free on its hinges, then check the spacing at the sides and top of the door. After determining the type of correction needed, correct in the following manner.

Up or Down and In or Out

1. Scribe location of hinge box on pillar.
2. Loosen bolts attaching hinge box to pillar, "A", Fig. 3.
3. Shift door to desired position and retighten bolts.

Up or Down and Fore or Aft
1. Remove trim pad.
2. Scribe location of hinge strap on door.
3. Loosen bolts attaching strap to inner panel, "B", Fig. 3. Shift door to desired position and retighten bolts.
4. Install trim pad and lubricate door hold opens and hinge pins with Lubriplate or its equivalent.

NOTE: After performing any door adjustment, the window and door post should be checked for alignment and adjusted as necessary. In addition, never slam the door after adjustment without first checking the door lock and striker plate engagement. An adjustment may be necessary.

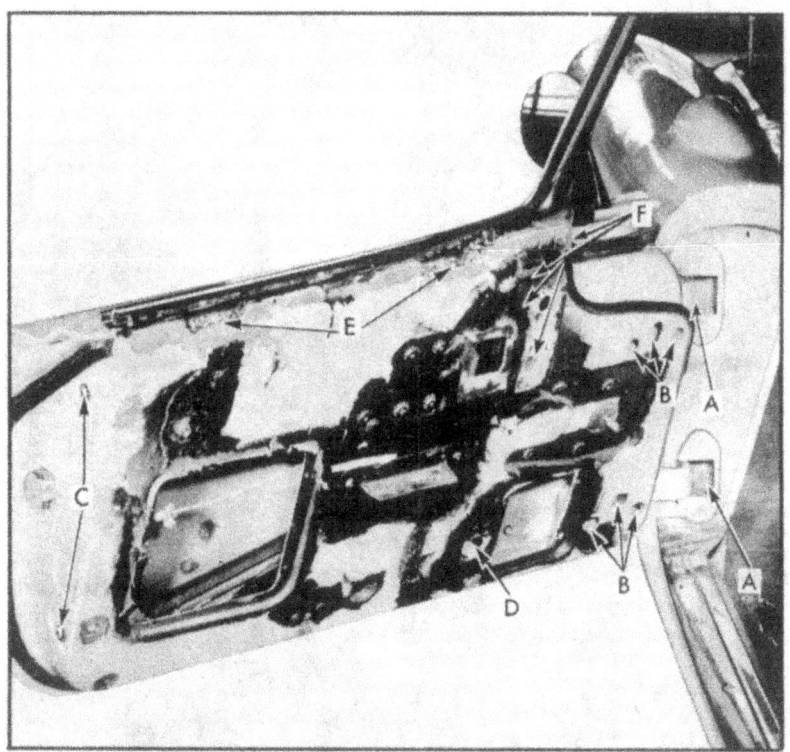

Fig. 3 Door and Window Adjustments

Door Lock

The door lock assembly is located at the factory and is not adjustable. The striker plate is adjustable. The door lock is basically the same as used on the Passenger Car, and reference should be made to Section I of the Passenger Car Shop Manual for Service Operations.

Door Lock Striker

Door lock strikers incorporate an inter-lock feature consisting of a notch in the striker into which the lock bolt housing extension engages. With the inter-lock feature it is very important that the lock extension engages properly in the striker notch and that, where necessary, the correct striker emergency spacers are used to obtain proper engagement.

Removal and Installation

1. With pencil, scribe position of striker on body pillar.

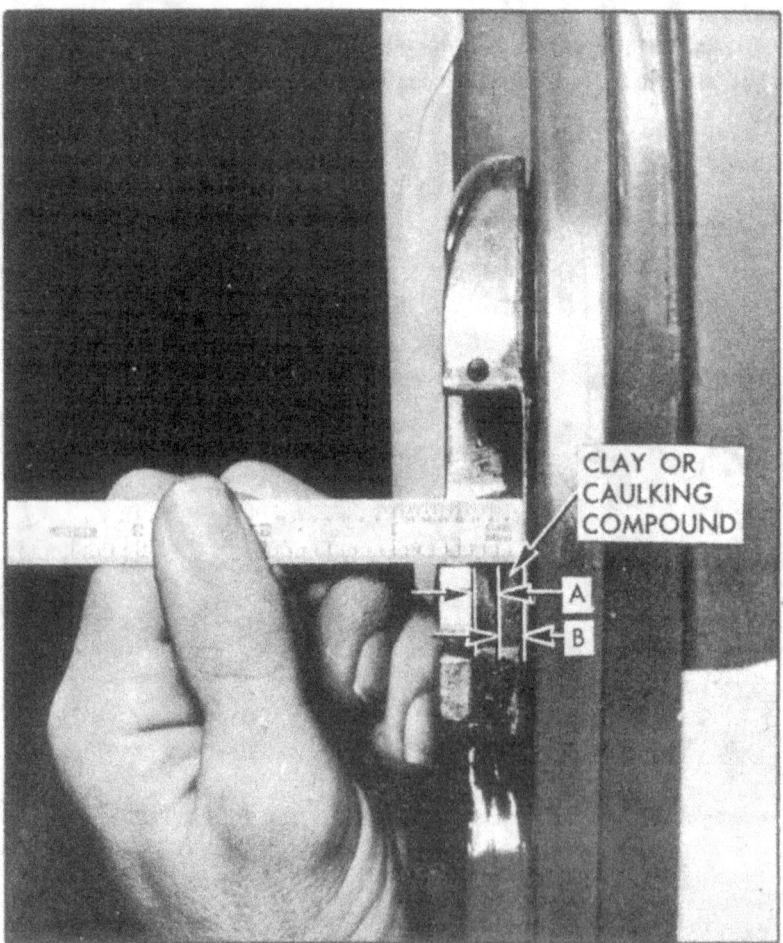

Fig. 4 Checking Adjustment of Door Lock Striker

2. Remove three door lock striker attaching screws and remove striker and adjusting plates from pillar.
3. To install, place striker and adjusting plates within scribe marks on pillar and tighten screws.

IMPORTANT: Whenever a door has been removed and installed, or realigned, the door SHOULD NOT be closed completely until a visual check is made to determine if the lock extension will engage in the striker notch. Where required, door lock striker emergency spacers should be installed so that door can be closed and an accurate check made to determine emergency spacer requirements.

Adjustments

1. To adjust striker "up", "down", "in", or "out" loosen striker plate screws and shift striker and adjusting plates as required, then tighten screws.
2. To determine if door lock striker emergency spacers are required, apply modeling clay or body caulking compound in the door lock striker notch where the lock extension engages, and then close the door to form a measurable impression in the clay or caulking compound, as shown in Fig. 4.

When dimension "A" from inside face of striker teeth to center of lock extension is less than 3/16", install emergency spacers and proper length striker attaching screws.

NOTE: Dimension "B" from center of lock extension to inside face of striker notch should never be less than 1/8".

Door Window and Post Adjustment

To move the top of the window in or out, the bottom ends of both run channels are adjustable. The rear channel is adjusted by loosening the lower of the two screws on the rear face of door, "C" Fig. 3, and moving channel as necessary. The front channel is adjusted by removing the trim pad and moving the channel in or out by a stud and nut adjustment, "D" Fig. 3. The top end of the rear channel is not adjustable in or out.

To adjust the height of the raised window, two vertically adjustable cushions, "E", Fig. 3, are located on the top of the door inner panel. These cushions may also be moved in or out to control window side movement by loosening the screw holding the cushion plates in place and moving the plates in or out as necessary.

The door post is adjustable to obtain good sealing at the windshield side frame. An in and out adjustment is provided by a stud and nut on the door inner panel, "D", Fig. 3. This is the same adjustment as for the lower end of the front run channel. No fore and aft adjustment is provided on 1956-1957 models. The door post is held to the door by the bolts indicated "F", Fig. 3.

Folding Top Lid and Rear Compartment Lid

Vertical adjustment of the folding top lid and the rear compartment lid is accomplished by the addition or removal of shims between each lid and its hinge assembly. A lateral adjustment of the lids is made by loosening the lid to hinge bolts "A", Fig. 5, and "A", Fig. 6 and repositioning the lid as necessary.

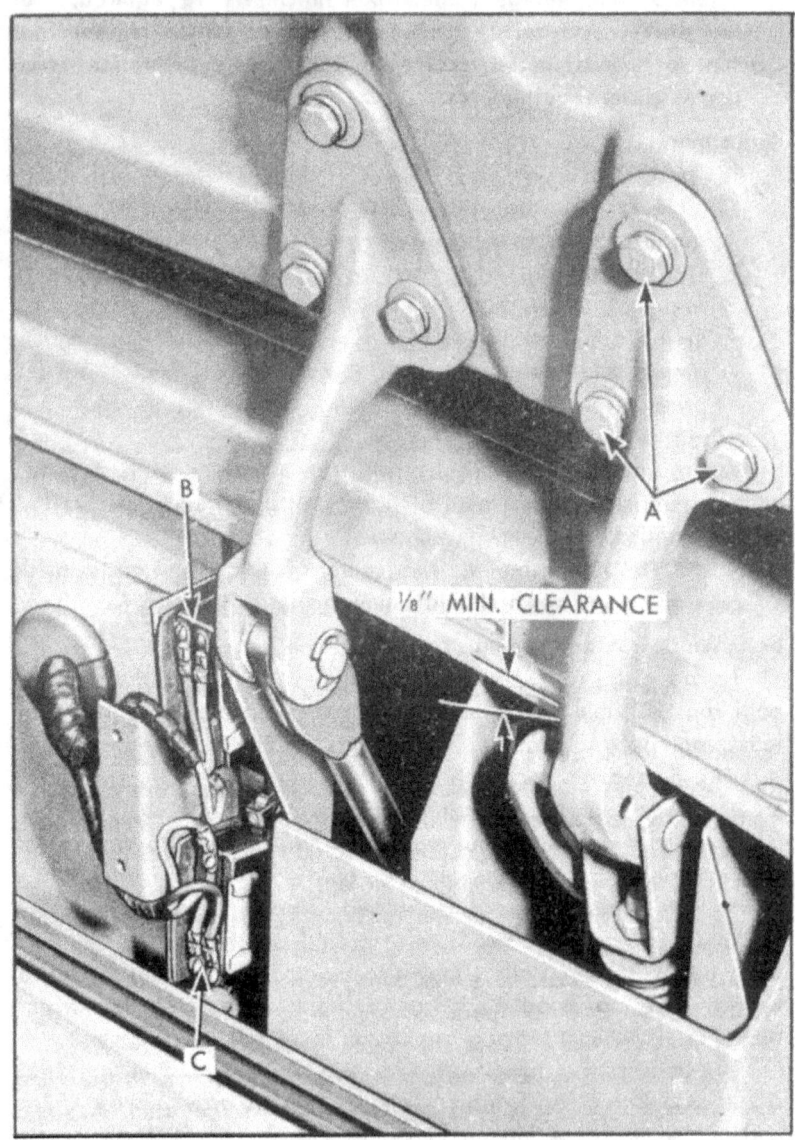

Fig. 5 Folding Top Lid Adjustments

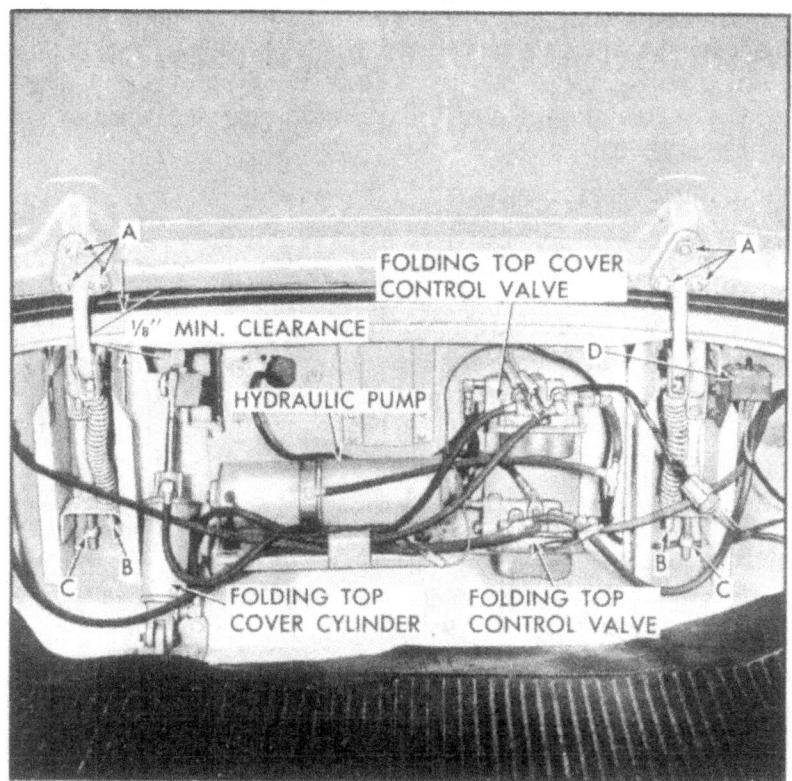

Fig. 6 Rear Compartment Adjustments

The folding top lid striker may be bent as necessary to obtain good engagement with the folding top lid lock assembly.

The hinges for both lids require adjustment to keep the hinges from striking the Body Rear Panel. Each hinge on each lid has a spring, thru-Bolt and nut, "B" Fig. 6, for Rear Compartment Lid, and "C" Fig. 6, for Folding Top Lid. The nut should be adjusted to contact the bottom bracket at each location when there is 1/8" clearance between the hinge and the gutter of the body rear panel. On models equipped with the power top, a further adjustment is required on the folding top lid.

After the folding top lid has been raised by power and is stopped by the limit switch, the bottom nut on each of the two spring thru-bolts "C", Fig. 6 should be backed-off 1/8".

Rear Compartment lid lock bolt and striker engagement check may be made by inserting modeling clay, as shown in Fig. 7. Close the lid with moderate force, open the lid and check the engagement by measuring the distance between the "U" in the clay and the base of lock. This dimension should be 1/8" to 5/32". If necessary, the striker lid lock engagement may be adjusted at the lid lock striker by loosening attaching bolts and shifting the striker plate on its beveled anchor plate. In extreme cases to obtain proper engagement a spacer or shim may be placed between the striker plate and beveled anchor plate.

WINDSHIELD REPLACEMENT
Removal
1. Underneath the instrument panel, remove twelve (12) nuts holding windshield assembly to cowl.
2. Remove windshield assembly from vehicle.
3. Remove one screw from the top of each side frame assembly.
4. Remove the rubber spacer at the bottom of each side frame assembly and remove the two screws located under each spacer.
5. Remove each side frame assembly from the glass and channel. Pull to the rear and out at the same time. It may be necessary to use a rubber hammer.
6. Remove the header molding and upper frame assembly as a unit. Fig. 8 shows an exploded view.

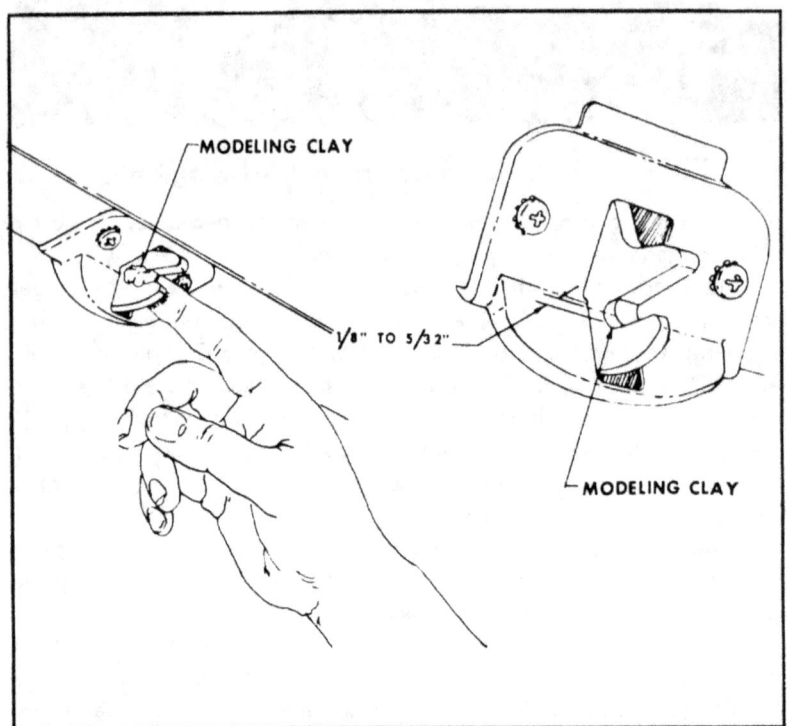

Fig. 7 Rear Compartment Bolt and Striker Check

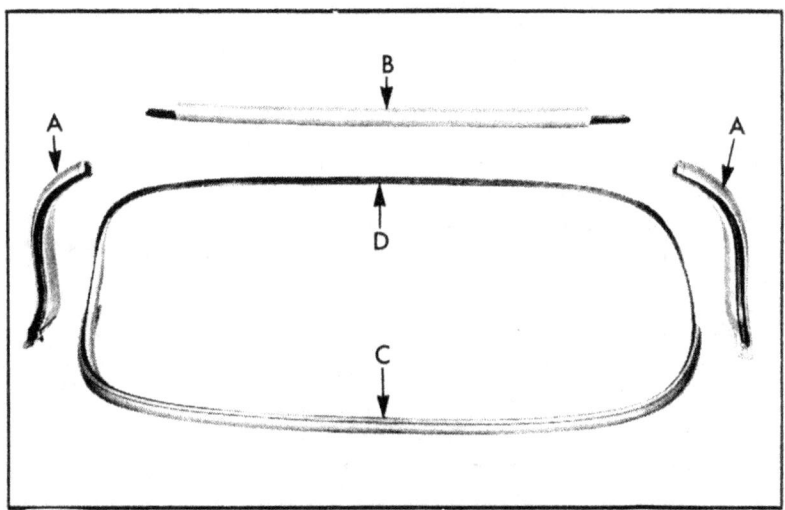

Fig. 8 Windshield Assembly - Disassembled

7. Remove rubber channel from top and sides of windshield.
8. Remove the windshield from lower frame, leaving the bottom of the rubber channel in the lower frame.

Installation

To install the windshield, reverse the removal procedure. Use a heavy ribbon of a medium bodied sealer between the rubber channel and the side frames and upper frame. A vegetable soap may be utilized to aid in installing the side and top frames over the rubber channel. Seal the outside lip of the rubber channel to the glass with a weatherstrip adhesive. Use body caulking compound between windshield assembly and cowl.

SIDE DOOR GLASS

Side door glass removal is similar for manually or electrically operated windows.
1. Remove trim pad, molding and trim rail from door. Remove door top reveal end molding and remove inner seal assembly (upper garnish molding retainer).
   NOTE: On electric window models, disconnect battery.
2. Remove two large access hole covers.
3. Remove rear glass run channel.
4. Loosen adjustable bumper and upper limit stops on door inner panel.
5. Remove two screws at each end of window cam track, holding glass channel to track.
6. Disengage window channel from window cam track and remove window from door. Use care not to damage lip seal

on window assembly. Rear end of lower edge of window assembly must leave door first, and window assembly must be moved rearward to clear roller guide at front of window assembly.
7. Remove two screws at each lower corner of window assembly. The glass may now be replaced.
8. To install, reverse the above procedure. Reseal the door inner panel at all locations where sealing was disturbed.

WINDOW REGULATORS

Both the manual and electric window regulators are similar to those used in the 1957 Passenger Car. Reference should be made to Section I, 1957 Passenger Car Shop Manual for Service Operations.

NOTE: On Electric Regulator models, if the regulator mechanism is to be removed, the motor must be separated from the regulator mechanism inside the door to permit removal.

SEATS

Each of the two bucket-type seats used in the Corvette are mounted on two seat tracks. The outer track of each seat contains the adjuster mechanism. Access to the tracks is obtained by removing the cushions and seat backs from the seat frame. The cushion is removed by lifting the front edge and pulling forward. The seat back is removed by bending up two tabs located under each back at the bottom. The seat back may then be lifted out. Each inner track is held to the floor pan by three bolts. Each outer track is held to the floor pan by three bolts and to a cross-support by a stud and nut. Each track is held to the seat frame by two bolts. Lubriplate or its equivalent may be used for lubrication of the seat tracks.

BODY MOUNTING

The body is fastened to the frame at ten locations. At each rear corner, the body is mounted to the frame with a cushion-spacer mounting similar to the Passenger Car Convertible. Four locations on each side of the body, at the corners of the "X" portion of the frame, are shim-type mountings similar to those used on Convertible models. Rubber shims are used at various locations between the underbody and the frame to prevent rubbing or oil canning of the underbody. All of the mounts should be torqued to 15-20 ft. lbs. These mounts should be checked periodically to prevent annoying squeaks and rattles and aid in maintaining the rigidity of the assembly.

Corvette Folding Top And Hard Top

The Corvette has a manually operated folding top as standard equipment. A hard top is available as an option, as in a power operated folding top. The manual top and the power top use the same linkage and operate in similar manners.

Procedures for raising and lowering the manually operated top are the same as described in the following power operated top instructions except that the top compartment cover and the top itself are operated manually instead of automatically.

Raising the Top
1. Unsnap the top compartment end straps at the outer edge of each seat back.
2. Push the button located on the seat separator panel. This unlatches the folding top compartment cover and at the same time completes the folding top electrical circuit.
   DO NOT ATTEMPT TO OPERATE THE TOP WITHOUT FIRST UNLATCHING THE TOP COMPARTMENT COVER.
3. Push the folding top control and hold it in until the folding top compartment cover opens, the top lifts out, and the cover closes.
4. Push the top compartment cover down until it latches.
5. Unhook the snap fasteners ("A", Fig. 9) allowing the rear bow to drop.

Fig. 9 Folding Top Rear Bow Straps

Fig. 10 Folding Top Rear Latches

6. Latch the rear bow to the body, Fig. 10.
7. Latch the header to the windshield, Fig. 11.
8. Snap both top compartment end straps.

Lowering the Top
1. Unlatch the header and rear bow. Double check to see that all latches are completely free and not caught in any way. Unsnap both top compartment end straps.
2. Hook the rear bow with the straps provided.
3. Push the button to unlatch the top compartment cover.
4. Pull the folding top control and hold until the top compartment cover opens, the top folds into the compartment, and the cover closes.
5. Push the cover to close on latch.
6. Snap the top compartment end straps.

   NOTE: Both the raising and lowering operations require about 20 seconds. The control must be held in place during these operations. A safety switch in the rear compartment breaks the folding top circuit and prevents the top mechanism from operating while the rear compartment lid is open. This will prevent damage to the finish of either the top compartment lid or the rear compartment lid. A second safety switch, in the top compartment, prevents operation of the top compartment cover or folding top operating mechanism unless the cover is unlatched. The hydraulic motor will run but a bypass prevents pressure build-up in the system. HOWEVER, NEVER OPERATE THE TOP CONTROL WITHOUT FIRST UNLATCHING THE TOP COMPARTMENT COVER.

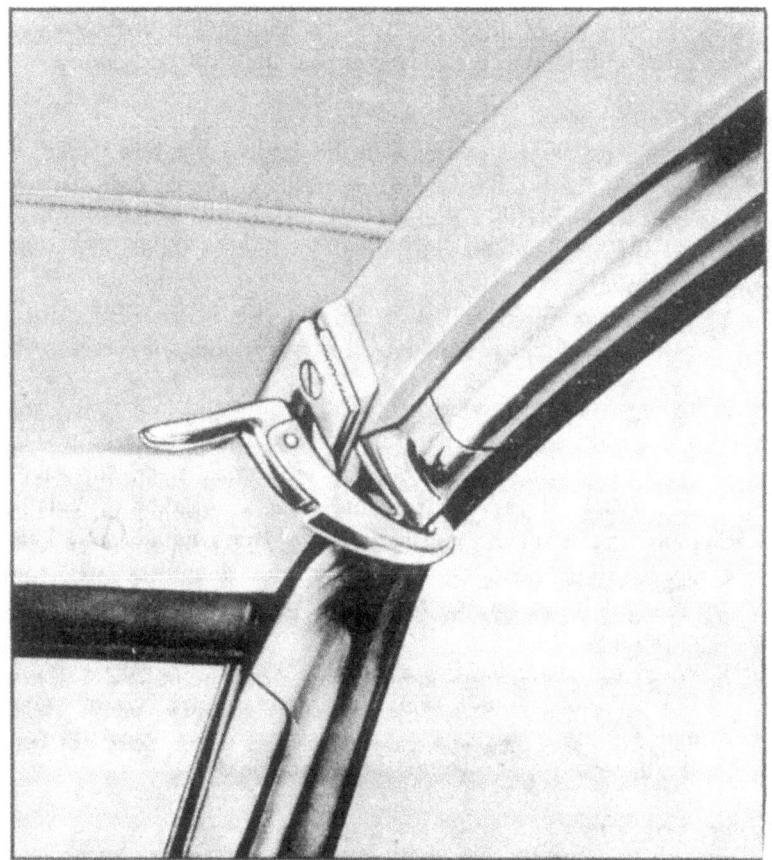

Fig. 11   Folding Top Front Latch

HARD TOP

The optional plastic hard top may be quickly and easily installed. Lower the folding top carefully, so as not to scratch the paint. Place the plastic top in position on the body, making sure that the guide pins at the front of the rear quarter windows are in place. Then guide pins into header. Tighten down rear bolts and fasten latches at header. When not in use, store the plastic top in a clean, dry place.

CAUTION: Do not use excessive torque on center rear bolt. Bolt bracket is riveted to backlight.

CARE OF THE FOLDING TOP

To avoid water stains, mildew, or possible shrinkage of the top material, do not keep the top folded for extended periods of time if it is damp or water soaked. Permit top to dry out in a raised position before stowing. Also avoid pasting advertising stickers, gummed labels or masking tape on the plastic back window. In addition to being difficult to remove, the adhesive on these stickers may also be injurious to the plastic composition of the window.

Care of Rear Window

The large plastic rear window in the folding top will remain in good condition for the life of the top if given proper care. Due to the texture of the plastic window, it is susceptible to scratches and abrasions; therefore, when cleaning the window, follow the steps outlined below.
1. To remove superficial dust, do not use a dry cloth. Use a soft cotton cloth moistened with water and wipe cross-wise of the window.
2. To wash the rear window, use cold or tepid (not hot) water and a mild neutral soap suds. After washing, rinse with clear water and wipe with a slightly moistened clean soft cloth.

    CAUTION: Never use solvents such as alcohol or volatile cleaning agents on the plastic window. These liquids may have a deteriorating effect on the plastic and if spilled, may spot the painted finish on the rear body panels directly below the rear window.
3. When removing frost, snow or ice from the plastic window, DO NOT USE A SCRAPER. In an emergency, warm water may be used. Use care that the warm water does not contact the actual glass windows or windshield.

HARD TOP CARE

The outside painted finish of the hard top should be cleaned the same way as the rest of the car. The inside headlining should be cleaned with a damp cloth.

When not using hard top, store it indoors where it can be kept clean and dry. If the top is to be stored for any period of time, keep it covered to avoid dirt settling on top and headlining.

FLUID LEVEL IN HYDRAULIC PUMP RESERVOIR

Proper fluid level must be maintained in the hydraulic system to insure proper operation of the top mechanism.
1. Operate the top to its raised position.
2. Disconnect the positive battery cable.
3. Remove the fibre panel shielding the top mechanism in the rear compartment.

4. Place absorbent rags below the pump reservoir at the filler plug (right end).
5. Remove the filler plug. Fluid level should be at bottom of filler plug hole.
6. If fluid level is low, add hydrauic fluid (G.M. Hydraulic Brake Fluid Super #11) to bring up to bottom of filler plug hole.
7. Install filler plug, shielding panel and battery cable.

FOLDING TOP LINKAGE

The regular production folding top and the optional power top use the same top and linkage and the same adjustments are used for both models.

To correct variations in the adjustment of the top, carefully examine the entire top to determine the necessary corrections. A combination of adjustments may be necessary, including door or window adjustments.

Adjustments
A. Front roof rail too far forward or too far to the rear for proper engagement of the guide studs in the windshield header.

Fig. 12 Folding Top Header Adjustments

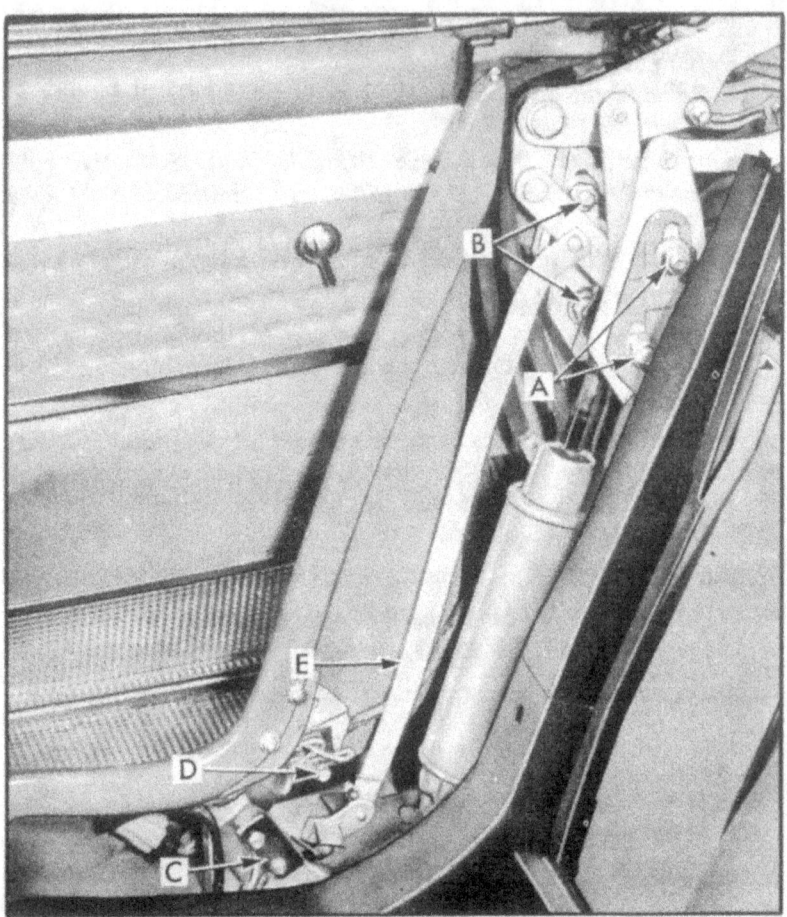

Fig. 13 Folding Top Linkage Adjustments

Correction:
1. Raise top slightly above windshield header and loosen screw at each front corner, "A", Fig. 12.
2. Adjust front roof rail fore or aft as required. Repeat on opposite side if necessary.
   NOTE: This adjustment is limited, should additional adjustment be required, it can be made at folding top male hinge, see location in D. below.
B. Difficult to lock top in raised position or loose fit between top front roof rail and windshield.

Correction:
1. Raise top slightly above windshield header and loosen screws holding latch to top header, "B", Fig. 12.

2. Adjust latch up or down as necessary for correct over-center action.
   3. Tighten screws.
C. Top will not stack properly in rear compartment or top does not meet windshield header.

Correction:
   1. Loosen two nuts at location "A" in Fig. 13 on each side.
   2. Adjust top link as necessary and retighten nuts.
D. Side roof rail too high or too low at top of door glass.

Correction:
   1. Loosen the two nuts at location "B" in Fig. 13.
   2. Raise or lower side roof rail as necessary and tighten nuts.
E. Excessive effort required to latch rear of folding top to folding top cover, or insufficient tension to seal top.

Correction:
   1. Loosen two screws holding catch assembly (wire loop) to top rear bow.
   2. Raise or lower catch as necessary to obtain proper effort and retighten.

   NOTE: Make this adjustment only after other top adjustments have been made. If this adjustment is not sufficient, holes in top lid for the lock assembly may have to be elongated to secure proper action.

POWER OPERATED FOLDING TOP

The electrical system of the power operated folding top consists of; one circuit breaker, one top control switch — manually operated, one deck lid safety switch, one folding top cover safety switch, two folding top limit switches, one 12 volt electric motor and hydraulic pump, one folding top solenoid, one folding top cover solenoid and two 14 amp fuses. The limit switches used on 1957 models are of the micro-type. Earlier models used toggle-type switches. Operation of each type is similar.

The electrical circuit is shown in Fig. 14.

Hydraulic-Electric Sequence of Operations
   1. The top is up and is to be lowered.

Pushing the folding top control switch closes the circuit from the battery (tan) to the motor (red). The motor is grounded to the frame and will operate regardless of the various limit and safety switches. Pushing the folding top control switch also closes the circuit thru the folding top cover safety switch (dark blue) to the folding top limit switch #2 (light blue) ("C" Fig. 13). With the top up, the folding top limit switch is closed to the folding top cover

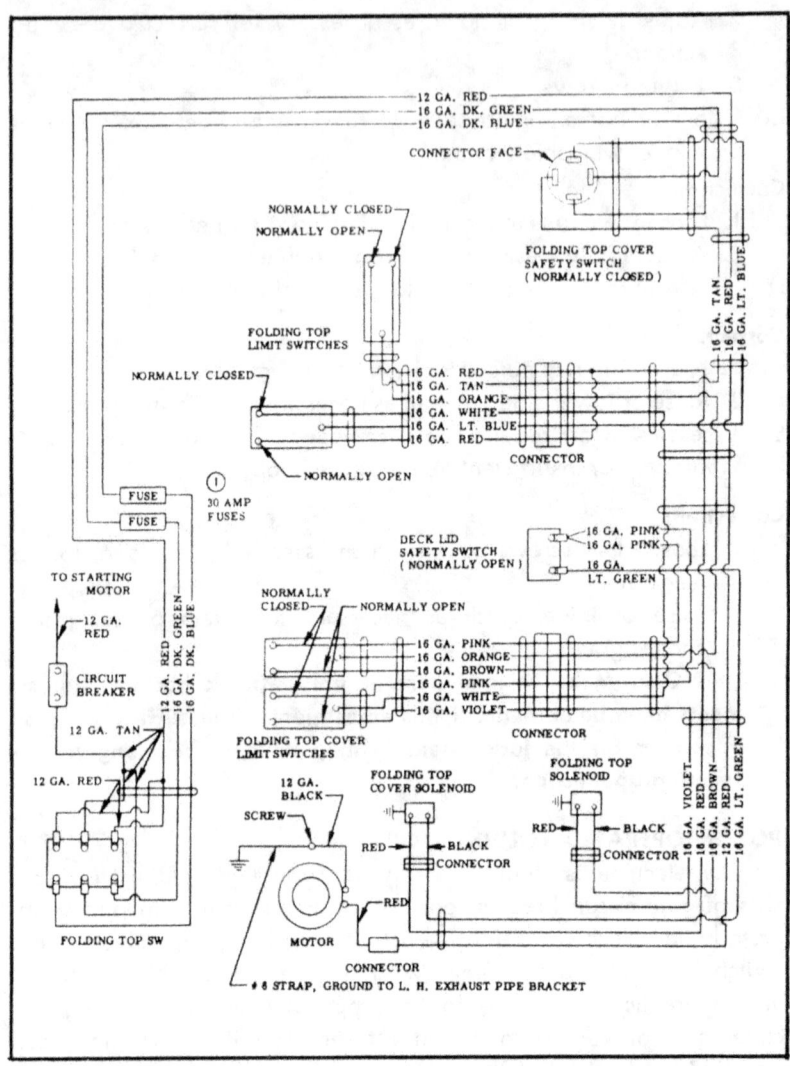

Fig. 14 Power Operated Folding Top Wiring Diagram

limit switch #3 (white) ("B" Fig. 5). With the folding top cover closed, the folding top cover limit switch #3 is closed to the Deck Lid safety switch (green). With the deck lid closed, the deck lid safety switch is closed to the folding top cover solenoid (light green). The folding top cover solenoid directs oil under pressure to the bottom end of the folding top cover hydraulic cylinder, raising the folding top cover. When the folding top cover is fully open, it contacts the folding top cover switch #3, opening the circuit to the folding top cover solenoid and closing the circuit to the folding top solenoid (violet). The folding top solenoid directs oil to the top of each of the two folding top hydraulic cylinders, lowering the top. The top lowers until a top control link ("E" Fig. 13) contacts folding top limit switch #2, opening the circuit to the folding top solenoid (white) and closing the circuit to the folding top cover solenoid (red). The folding top cover solenoid directs oil under pressure to the top end of the folding top cover hydraulic cylinder, closing the folding top cover. There is no limit switch for the closed position of the folding top cover.

2. Top is down and is to be raised.

Pulling the folding top control switch closes the circuit from the battery (tan) to the motor (red). The motor is grounded to the frame and will operate regardless of the position of the various limit and safety switches. Pulling the folding top control switch also closes the circuit thru the folding top cover safety switch (dark green) to the folding top cover limit switch #1 (tan) ("D" Fig. 13). With the top down, the folding top limit switch is closed to the folding top cover limit switch #4 (orange) ("C" Fig. 5). With the folding top cover closed, the folding top cover limit switch #4 is closed to the deck lid safety switch (pink). With the deck lid closed, the deck lid safety switch is closed to the folding top cover solenoid (light green). Energizing the green lead of the folding top cover solenoid directs oil under pressure to the bottom of the folding top cover hydraulic cylinder, raising the folding top cover. When the folding top cover is fully open, it contacts the folding top cover limit switch #4, opening the circuit to the folding top cover solenoid and closing the circuit to the folding top solenoid (brown). The folding top solenoid directs oil under pressure to the bottom of each of the two folding top hydraulic cylinders, raising the top. When the top reaches the full "up" position, a top control link ("E" Fig. 13) contacts folding top limit switch #1, opening the circuit to the folding top solenoid and closing the circuit to the folding top cover solenoid (red). Energizing the red lead of the folding top cover solenoid directs oil under pressure to the top of the folding top cover hydraulic cylinder, closing the folding top cover. This completes the hydraulic-electric sequence of operations.

POWER OPERATED FOLDING TOP LIMIT SWITCH ADJUSTMENTS

Folding Top Cover Limit Switches

The two folding top cover limit switches ("B" and "C", Fig. 5) are located under the folding top cover at the rear of the top compartment. Access to the switches is made by removing the sheet metal shield, held in place by three sheet metal screws.

Each of the two switches is held in place by a strap and double stud. Adjustment is made by loosening the two stud nuts and positioning the switch as necessary. Both switches should be actuated by the lever at the top cover hydraulic cylinder rod bracket at the same time. They should be adjusted to actuate just before the top cover reaches its upper stop.

Folding Top Limit Switches

The two folding top limit switches are located at the lower right side of the passenger compartment, ("C" and "D", Fig. 13). A sheet metal shield is used to protect the switches, held in place with three sheet-metal screws. Each switch, mounted by a strap and double stud arrangement, is adjustable by loosening the stud nuts and positioning the switch as necessary. The upper switch should be adjusted to actuate just as the top header strikes the windshield header during the top raising cycle. Similarly, the lower switch should be adjusted to actuate when the top reaches its full down or stack position in the top well during the top lowering cycle.

Deck Lid Safety Switch

The deck lid safety switch Fig. 6, is a protective device, used to prevent operation of the top if the deck lid is raised. The protection is necessary because of possible interfrence between the deck lid and folding top cover. The switch is adjustable vertically and should be set so the deck lid will close the circuit thru the switch when the deck lid is fully closed.

Folding Top Cover Safety Switch

The folding top cover safety switch Fig. 15, is included in the circuit to prevent operation at the folding top cover solenoid and hydraulic cylinder with the top cover in the latched position. The switch is adjustable vertically and should be set to prevent top operation with the top cover latched, and to allow top cover operation with the top cover latch tripped.

Motor and Pump Assembly

The motor and pump assembly used on the power operated folding top is basically the same as used on the 1957 Passenger Car Convertible. Section I of the 1957 Passenger Car Shop Manual should be referred to as a guide for any necessary service operations. The motor used on the Corvette is not reversible.

Trouble Diagnosis

Failure of the hydraulic-electric system where the cause is not readily evident, should be checked in the following sequence: Mechanical, Electrical and Hydraulic systems.

Mechanical Check

If top action is slow, check for mechanical bind.

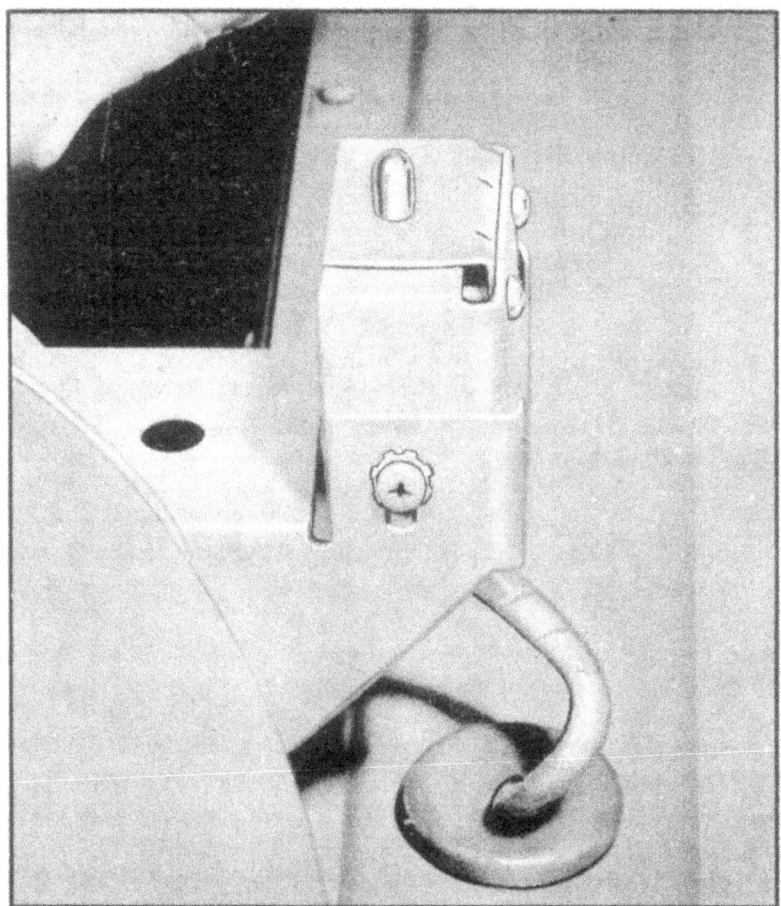

Fig. 15 Folding Top Cover Safety Switch

1. Disconnect piston rods at top linkage attachment and raise and lower the top by hand through the cycle, noting any binding action of the top linkage.
2. While locking top at header, if binding action is noted, check alignment of door windows, ventilators and rear quarter windows in relation to the side roof rail weatherstrips. Make necessary adjustment to correct.

Electrical Check

1. Check battery condition, a partially discharged battery will result in a sluggish operating pump.

Folding Top Switch

1. Connect one lead of test light to feed wire terminal of control switch and ground the opposite lead. If tester does not

light, there is an open or shorted circuit between battery and switch, or a defective circuit breaker.
2. Disconnect lead to motor (red) at switch terminal and place one lead of tester to terminal and other lead of tester to ground. Push control knob forward, if tester fails to light switch is defective. Check down cycle side of switch by pulling control knob out. Failure of tester to light in either case indicates a faulty switch. Replace switch.
3. Disconnect leads to folding top cover safety switch (green and blue). Use test lamp on each terminal of switch and operate switch. With switch in lowering position, the terminal for the green wire should light the test lamp. Failure of this check indicates a faulty switch. Replace switch.

Switch to Motor Lead Wires
1. Disconnect switch to motor lead at motor in rear compartment. Connect tester to red motor wire and ground, operate control knob in and out to check. If tester fails to light in either case the circuit from switch to motor is either open or shorted.

Motor Unit
Check the operation of the motor by connecting the lead of motor via a jumper wire directly to the positive post of the battery; if the motor operates check the motor ground lead in a similar manner. If motor operates, but will not operate when hooked into the wiring harness, check back over the wiring harness for shorts. A sluggish operating motor when hooked into wiring harness could be indicative of low voltage at the motor resulting from poor connection, poor motor ground or a short.

Limit Switches and Safety Switches
1. Any of the limit or safety switches may be checked using the same procedure.
2. Disconnect the leads from the switch and connect a ground lead to one terminal.
3. Connect a test lamp to the positive battery post and to each of the ungrounded terminals of the switch.
4. Figure 14 shows which contacts are normally open and which are normally closed. Operate the switch manually and replace any defective units.

   NOTE: A quick check on the limit switches is to operate the switch arm manually. If the switch does not click, it is probably defective. If it clicks, it is probably in good condition.

Additional Checks
If the above checks do not disclose the electrical trouble, addi-

tional checks may be made in a similar manner by referring to the Power Operated Folding Top Wiring Diagram, Fig. 14.

Hydraulic Checks

Hydraulic system failure can be caused by lack of fluid in the system, leaks, obstruction or kinks in lines, faulty lift cylinders, faulty solenoid valves or pump. Troubles in the hydraulic system can be readily located with a pressure gauge. Pressure should read between 240 psi and 280 psi when pressure relief valve opens.

Pump
1. Install pressure gauge (300 psi min.) in line leading from pump to solenoid valves, and block or plug the line at the tee connector leading to the solenoid valves.
2. Operate the top control switch. Pressure should rise to 240 psi to 280 psi.
3. If pressure is low, check wiring and battery by using a fully charged battery and jumper leads, and recheck.

Lift Cylinder and Solenoid Valves
1. Operate the folding top, while watching action of the lift cylinders. If operation is sluggish or a binding is evident, check for a kinked hydraulic line. Remove the lines and inspect for obstruction within the lines.
2. Vent the system by removing the filler plug, then install pressure gauge between line and fitting at bottom of cylinder. Check one at a time, the top cover cylinder and the two lift cylinders. With the top in the up position, push the control knob in and hold for several seconds. Note reading on pressure gauge, (240 psi to 280 psi). This check is based on the assumption that pump pressure and lines have been checked and found satisfactory.
3. If the reading is substandard, install the gauge on the end of the same line being checked, without hooking the line up to the cylinder. Repeat the test. If the pressure rises appreciably, the cylinder is defective and should be replaced. If the reading is still low, and the pump and lines are all right, the solenoid valve for that cylinder is probably defective.
4. Repeat this test at each cylinder port. When the down cycle is being checked, have the top locked at header and pull the control knob out.

WATER LEAK CORRECTION

Checking for water leaks and then applying the right correction are two operations that often require considerable skill or ingenuity on the part of the service man. Water which shows up at a certain place in the body may actually be entering at a point other than where the water is found. In locating and correcting a water leak, it is only by a thorough knowledge of body construction, the use of proper sealing compounds, and knack of locating points at which a potential leak may occur, that enables the serviceman to make a successful correction.

Basic Water Leak Correction Procedure
   1. Make certain that all of the various body, window and top adjustments have been made to obtain proper clearances at all sealing locations.
   2. Inspect all of the weatherstrips for deterioration, tearing or failure of adhesive bond to the body. Replace or repair if necessary.
   3. Carefully water test for leaks noting any locations affected.
   4. Examine in detail any leakage location to determine the cause. Each problem encountered may require a slightly different correction.
   5. Replace the seal affected with the latest parts as indicated in the Chevrolet Master Parts Catalog. Minor but important changes are made from time to time in these seals, and identification as to latest production is difficult.
   6. Some leakage problems may require building up the body beneath the weatherstrip with Plastic Solder Repair Kit materials to obtain a good seal.

It has been found that through the use of the complete procedure as described above, particularly the first five steps, effective sealing of the Corvette Body may be obtained.

Individual Corrections

Test the windshield or side window for leakage by spraying water under medium pressure against the face of the glass. Direct a heavy stream along weatherstrip while an assistant inside the body marks points of leakage, paying particular attention to whether leakage occurs between the glass and weatherstrip or between weatherstrip and other body sections.

If the leakage is between the glass and the rubber apply 3-M Weatherstrip Adhesive, or its equivalent using a cement gun between lip of rubber weatherstrip and glass. Allow adhesive to set and then retest with a water spray.

If water leaks occur around door opening, check to make sure door seats on rubber weatherstrip. If door does not alignment should be checked and corrected.

If water leaks occur at the top or sides of the windows, the windows may need adjusting. If the vehicle is equipped with a hard top, the windows should be adjusted to the hard top. The folding top should than be adjusted to the windows.

NOTE: The moldings that receive the rear locating pins of the hard top were revised to use elongated holes in late 1957 production, Fig. 16. This will aid hard top alignment and sealing. Where interference is indicated on earlier models, the holes may be elongated or the moldings replaced with the revised parts.

Wet floor mats are not a definite indication of a leakage problem. Water collecting in the cowl gutter at the lower rear corner of the windshield Fig. 17, may run into the vehicle when the door is opened. A longer gutter, part number 3746117-8 is available to combat this problem. This change entered production on late 1957 models. The long gutter (dotted lines in Fig. 17) is applied to the under side of the cowl lip. The short gutter used previously was applied to the top of the cowl lip, and should be removed if the long gutter is installed.

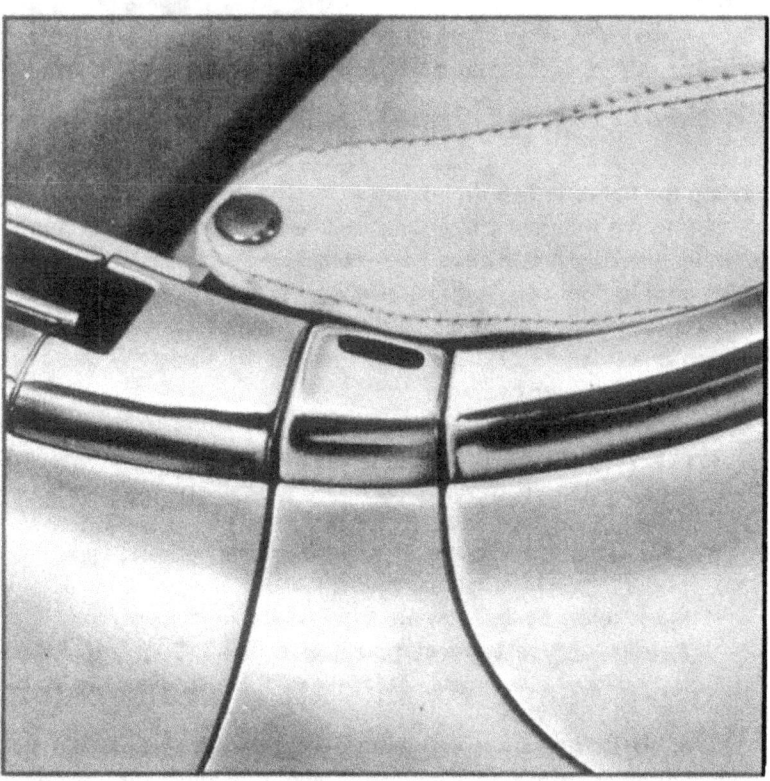

Fig. 16   Hard Top Rear Guide Pin Molding

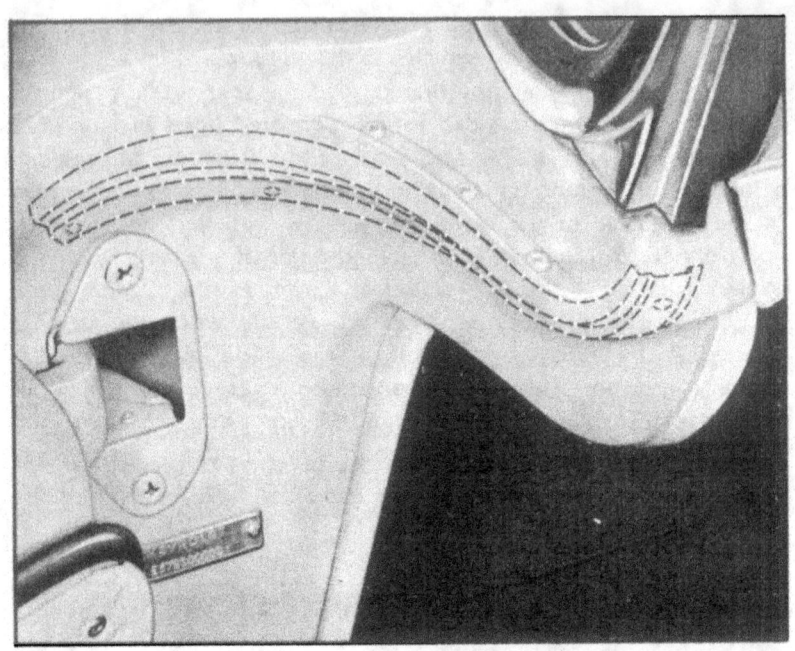

Fig. 17 Cowl Drain Gutter

Sealing the Corvette Top

Due to the inherent characteristics of a convertible top, a degree of water wicking has always been considered normal. In the event a convertible top with excessive water wicking stains or normal dirt and wear is encountered, the stains may be removed and the wicking characteristics substantially reduced by using the materials and procedures given below.

1. Paint: "Color Coat", Chevrolet Reconditioning Material. Color coat is available in 12 colors plus black and white. This material, listed in group 8.800 in the Chevrolet Master Parts Catalog, will seal and dye the top material, is fast-drying and easy to handle. The paint is applied with a spray gun.
2. Sealer: "Convertible Top Sealer" or equivalent. Available in black color. Sealer may be brushed on or dispensed through a pressure type applicator such as a Plews Oiler, a K-P Controlled-Flow Oiler, etc. This material is supplied in a kit, Part No. 3630951.

CAUTION: Exercise extreme care during application, as sealer is highly injurious to trim, paint and the vinyl rear window.

3. Silicone Waterproofing Solution: such as "Silicone Anti-Wick Material". Apply with a ½ inch paint brush. This material is also included in the kit, Part No. 3630951.

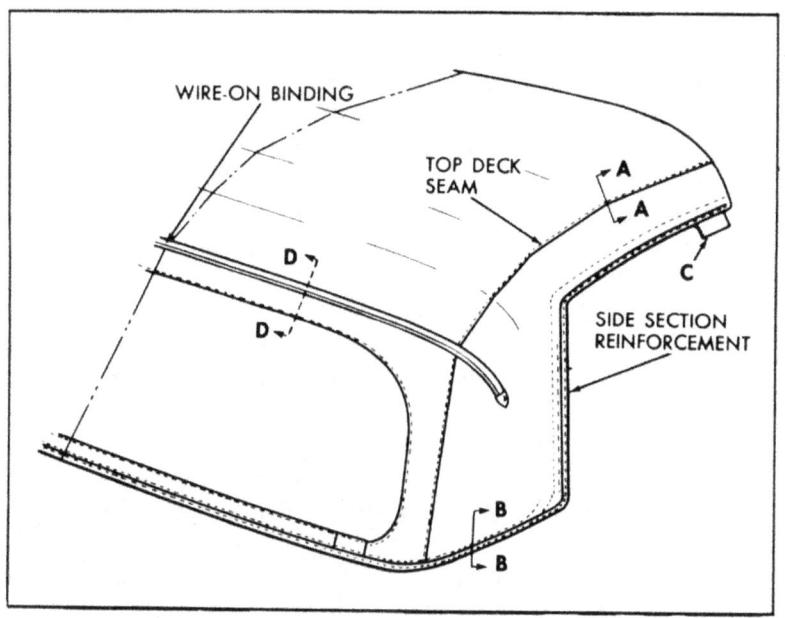

Fig. 18   Corvette Top Sealing

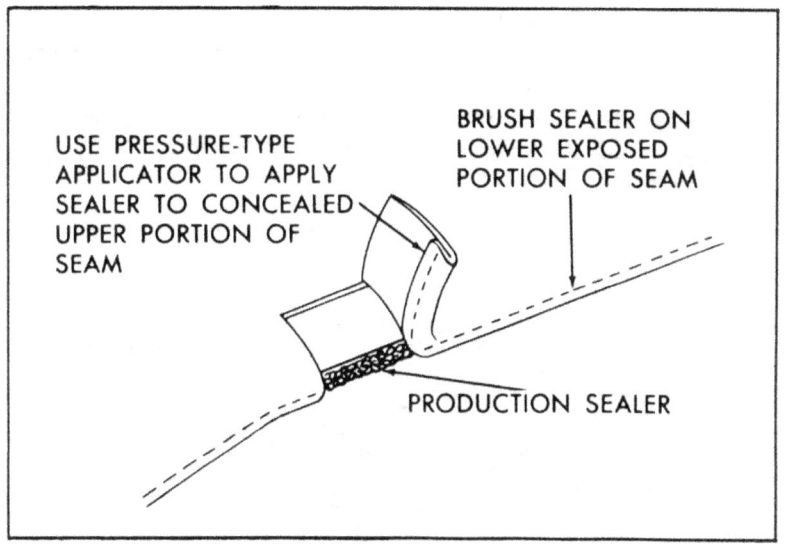

Fig. 19   Top Deck Seam Construction

CAUTION: Silicone solution is highly flammable. Apply in a well ventilated area, away from excessive heat or flame.

Procedure for Sealing Top

1. Place protective coverings on seat cushion, seat back and on painted surfaces.
2. Remove rear roof bow wire-on binding (Fig. 18). Wipe roof bow area to remove dust and moisture. Inspect trimmed edge of top deck material. Trim, if necessary, so that resealed edge of the top deck material and the tack heads will be completely concealed when wire-on binding is reinstalled. Cement any loose or gapped sections of the top deck material to the rear roof bow using 3 M Super Weatherstrip Adhesive or its equivalent. Allow adhesive to dry. Using a pressure-type applicator, apply sealer to the trimmed edge edge of the top material, around each tack head, into each tack hole and into the two screw holes used for attaching the metal retainer at each end of the wire-on binding. Allow approximately 15 minutes for sealer to dry, then install wire-on binding.
3. Position top assembly so that top material may be propped in a position to avoid contact with stay pads. Check top center section to side section seams for proper application of production sealer. Reseal, if necessary, with 3 M Super Weatherstrip Adhesive. When adhesive is dry, apply sealer to top deck seams. Use a pressure type applicator to reach the concealed upper portion of seam and a brush to cover lower, exposed portion of seam. See section "A-A", Fig. 19.
4. With top in same position as in step 3, apply two beads of sealer to side section reinforcement seam. See section "B-B", Fig. 20.

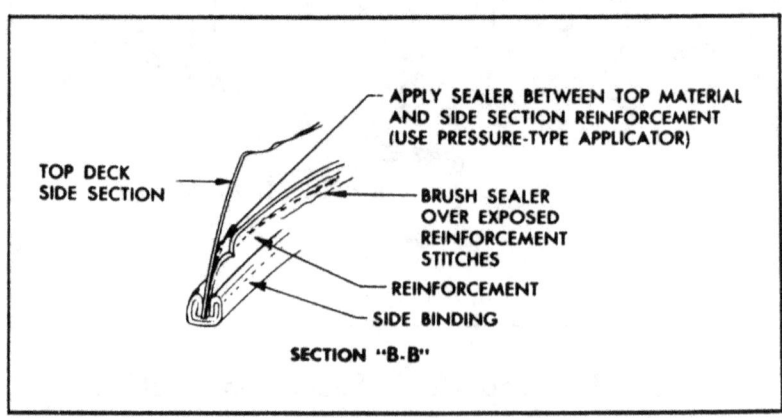

Fig. 20 Side Section Reinforcement

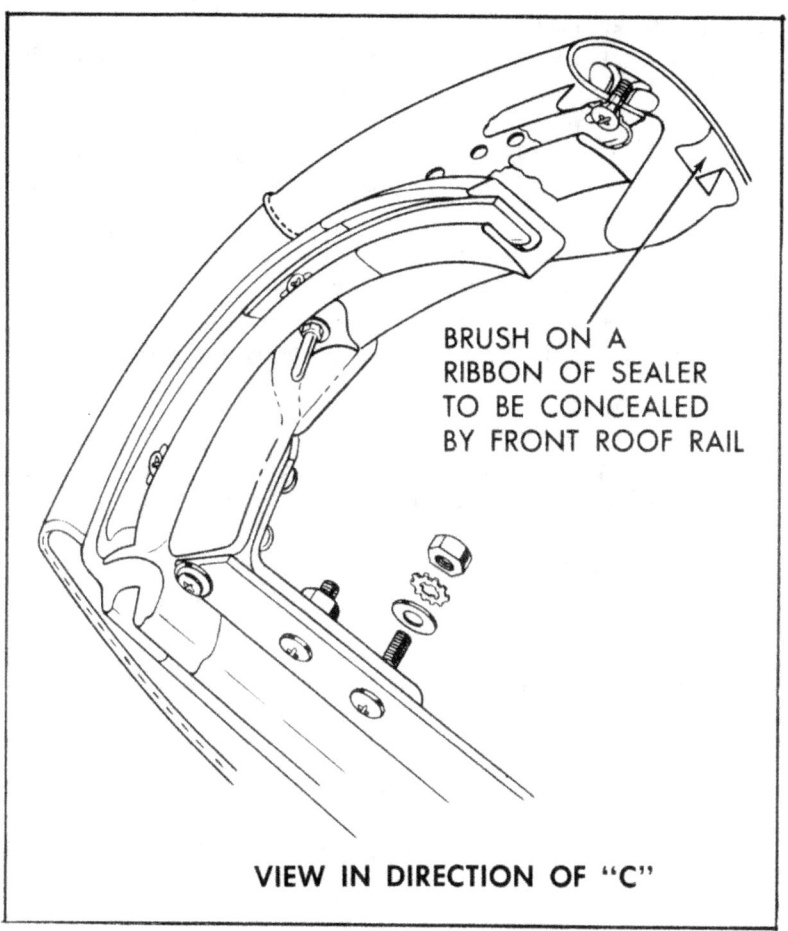

Fig. 21 Header Bar Sealing

5. Brush a ribbon of sealer between front roof rail and top material. See location "C", Fig. 21.
6. Brush a silicone waterproofing solution to upper surface of folding top stay pads.

   CAUTION: Silicone solution is highly flammable. Apply in a well ventilated area, away from excessive heat or flame.
7. While silicone is drying, using a pressure-type applicator, very carefully apply a bead of sealer at forward edge of rear roof bow between bow and top material. Use sealer sparingly to avoid sealer from oozing out and presenting an unsightly appearance. See section "D-D" Fig. 22.

NOTE: Allow approximately 30 minutes for sealer and silicone to dry before allowing stay pads to contact top material.

Removing Wicking Stains

1. When all sealers are thoroughly dry, wet stained area with clear warm water using a sponge as the applicator. Avoid rubbing stained area during application of water.
2. Slowly run a metal-ended attachment from a tank-type vacuum cleaner over stained area to remove excess water and stains.
3. Allow wetted area to thoroughly air-dry.
4. If stains persist, repeat above three steps.
5. If severe stains cannot be satisfactorily removed from the material, follow procedure for coloring top material.

Coloring Top Material

Before dying the top, place car in a well ventilated area. Open both doors and lower door windows for maximum ventilation within car. Top material must be thoroughly dry before applying Chevrolet "Color Coat".

1. Place protective covers over interior trim, plastic window and painted surfaces. Mask as necessary to guard against over-spray.

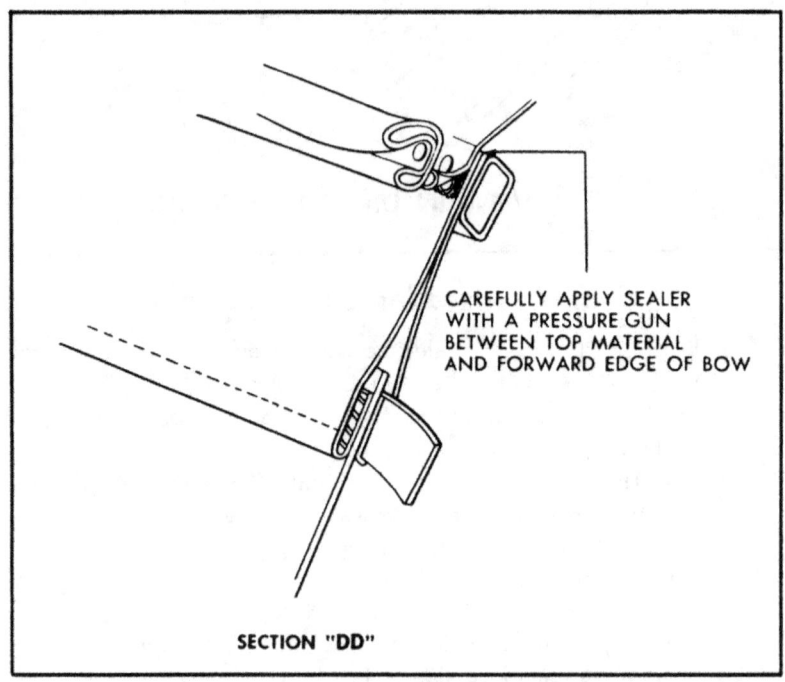

Fig. 22 Rear Bow Area Construction

2. Wipe surfaces clean, using a rag saturated with a solvent to remove wax and other foreign matter.
3. Spray on a mist coat of Color Coat (using twenty pounds air pressure at gun).
4. Allow to become tack-free.
5. Spray on a full second coat of Color Coat. Allow to dry.

NOTE: Over-spray may be wiped clean while wet with a solvent saturated rag.

A forecast of things to come? CERV-1: Chevrolet Experimental Research Vehicle, at Riverside Raceway. Stirling Moss turned a few quick demonstration laps with the potent machine.

Corvette Body Repair And Paint Refinishing

The Corvette plastic body presents, at first glance, numerous problems involving panel repairs and refinishing. Actually, the panel repair procedures are simple and the paint refinishing procedure is the same as recommended for metal bodies.

Basically, the Corvette body is formed from laminated sheets of fibre glass mats held together with a Polyester resin, (liquid plastic). When the liquid resin cures or hardens, it binds the filaments of glass in the mats to create a solid panel. The strength of the panel is provided by the fibre glass and the liquid plastic only acts as the bond, supplying very little additional strength to the panel.

In general, all repairs to the Corvette body consist of filling the damaged area with either glass and resin or plastic solder. The plastic is then allowed to harden and then the finish operations are performed. Use of the various materials is determined by the type of repair to be made.

The Resin Repair Kit, part number 987341, contains Epoxy resin, hardener, Thixatrope, fibreglass cloth, protecting creams and mixing untensils. The resin repair kit is to be used for major repairs on the fibreglass reinforced plastic body. Such repairs as large holes, torn panels and separated joints require the adhesive qualities of the resin and the reinforcing qualities of the glass fibres.

The Plastic Solder Repair Kit, part number 987511 Fig. 23, contains one quart of resin and one quart of hardener. The Plastic solder Repair Kit is to be used for minor repairs on the Corvette Body. These materials will produce an easy, quick and lasting repair in the case of small cracks, surface imperfections and small holes.

GENERAL INSTRUCTIONS
Precautions

    1. Creams are supplied to protect you from a condition known as occupational, or contact dermatitis. This type of dermatitis is very common and not contagious. While improved resin formulas in the approved kit have practically eliminated the irritation, use of creams is recommended. Kerodex 71 and 55 protective creams are supplied with the kit for men who may have a tendency toward skin irritation from the resins or dust.

        The application of these creams is recommended whenever the Resin Repair Kit materials are being used. Generally,

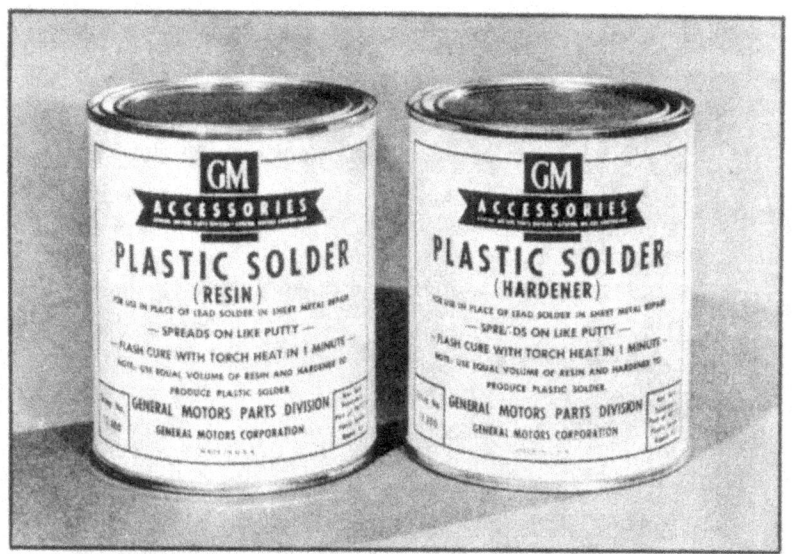

Fig. 23   Plastic Solder Kit

the creams are not required when the plastic solder kit is being used.

Follow the Instructions:
   a. Wash hands clean. Dry thoroughly.
   b. Squeeze about ½ inch (or ½ teaspoonful) of number 71 into palm of hand.
   c. Spread evenly and lightly until cream disappears. Work cream into cuticle, between fingers, and around wrists.
   d. Repeat application as in b and c above.
   e. Hold hands briefly under cold running water to set cream.
   f. Apply number 55 over the 71 in the same manner, but do not wash hands. (Cream 55 will wash off. After sanding operations, hands may be rinsed under water to remove cream and dust. Do not rub hands together while rinsing.)
2. Remove resin mixture from hands as soon as possible and imperatively before mixture starts to gel. This can be observed by the action of the material being used. Resin may be removed with lacquer thinner followed by washing in soap and water.
3. Respirators are recommended when grinding. Also some minor skin irritation from glass and powdered cured resin may be evident. Washing in cold water will help to minimize.
4. Use a belt sander with a vacuum attachment for dust control if possible.

5. Resin mixtures may produce toxic fumes and should be used in well ventilated areas.
6. Be careful not to get any resin material on clothing.
7. Use the right materials for the job. It is important to use the approved kits because Chevrolet's rigid quality standards assure you the right material to do the job. Other materials available may not meet the required engineering and safety standards.
8. Keep the materials, utensils and work area clean and dry. These repairs involve chemical reactions, and dirt or moisture may upset the chemical balances and produce unsatisfactory results.
9. Before starting repair operations, look for hidden damage by applying pressure around the damaged area, looking for hairline cracks and other breakage. Check for minor damage at other points in the vehicle such as around exhaust pipes, grille, headlamps and points of wear or rub. Early repair of this minor damage may prevent major repair later.

Basic Procedure for use of Resin Repair Kit

The following procedure is basic for repairing any plastic (fibreglass) component or panel.

1. Look for hidden damage. Apply pressure by hand around the damaged area.

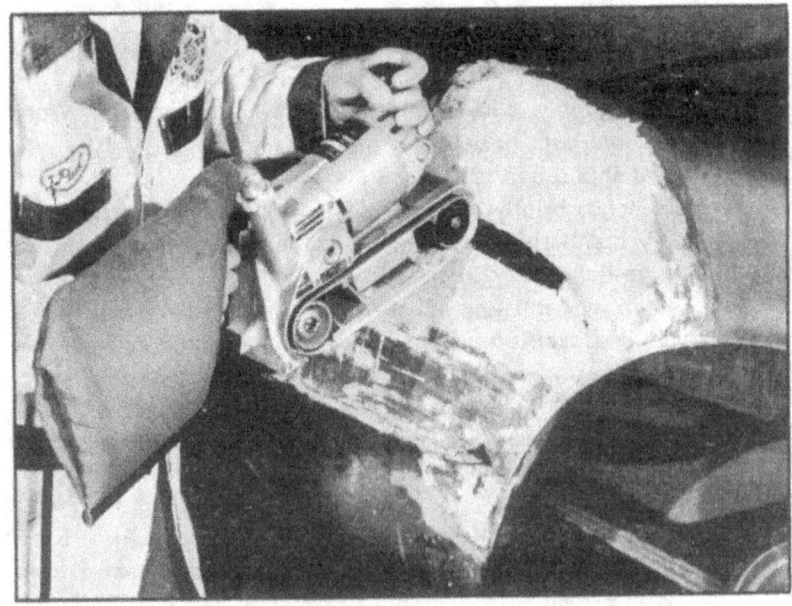

Fig. 24 Grinding "V" at Damage

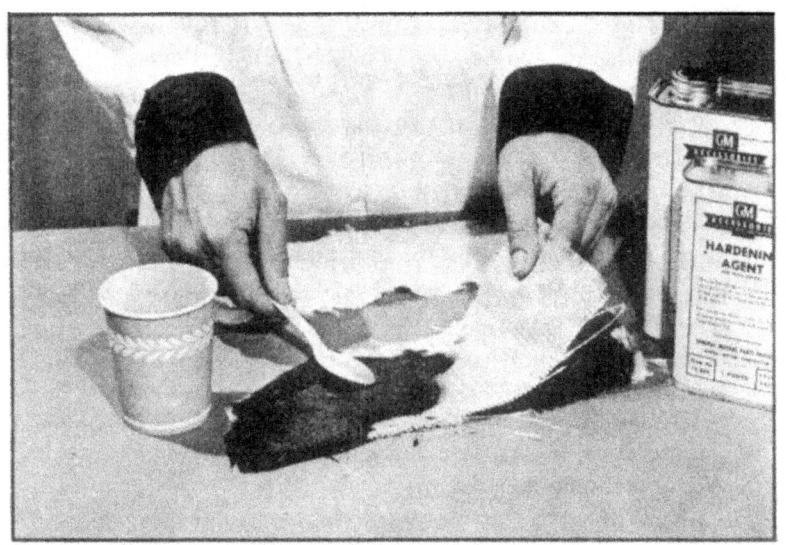

Fig. 25 Mixing Resin and Hardener

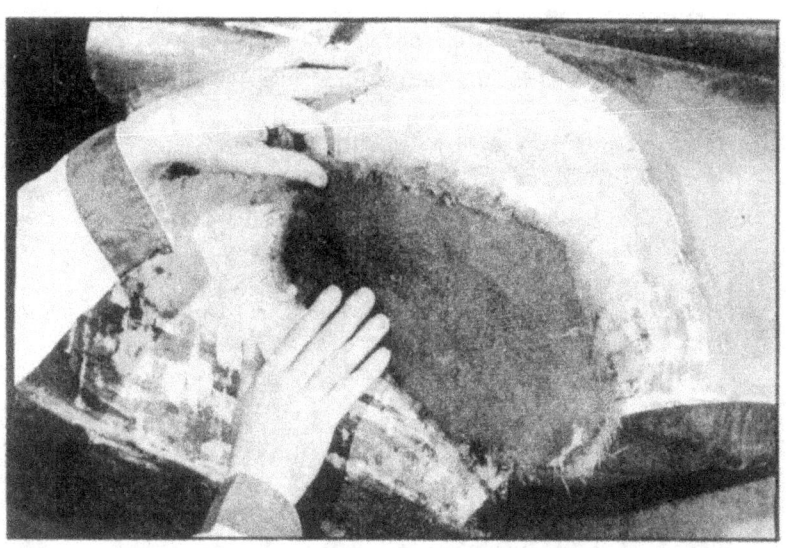

Fig. 26 Applying Laminate

2. Use paint remover and remove finish from around damage area. Inspect area again for signs of other damage.
3. Grind or file the damaged area to form a "V" at the broken or cracked portion. Side of "V" should have a shallow pitch for maximum bonding surface. A belt sander with a vacuum attachment will minimize the dust problem, Fig. 24.

4. If rear of damage is accessible, use a button-type repair. Clean back of area to permit the use of laminate (resin-saturated glass-cloth) on both sides of damaged area.
5. Cut fibreglass cloth to size. Make certain a minimum of five layers is cut for the average repair.
6. Mix resin and hardener, 1 part hardener to 4 parts resin, Fig. 25. Add Thixatrope to the mix to give the mix body and reduce the "runniness" of the material. Caution: Cleanliness is most important. Be certain all containers are dry and clean and the resin and hardener cans are kept closed when not in use. Do not use waxed cups for mixing and do not allow resin to enter hardener can or vice versa.
7. Saturate layers or fibreglass. Place laminate over damage area. Smooth out wrinkles and make sure general contour of area is maintained, Fig. 26.
8. Apply heat to repair area. Heat lamps are recommended, used at least 12" away from repair, Fig. 27. Allow 15 to 20 minutes curing time. Trim repair to shape at gel stage.
9. After the repair is cured, grind, file or sand to contour. Files other than body files may be more suitable. A belt sander with a vacuum cleaner attachment will minimize the dust problem. Feather edge and finish sand.

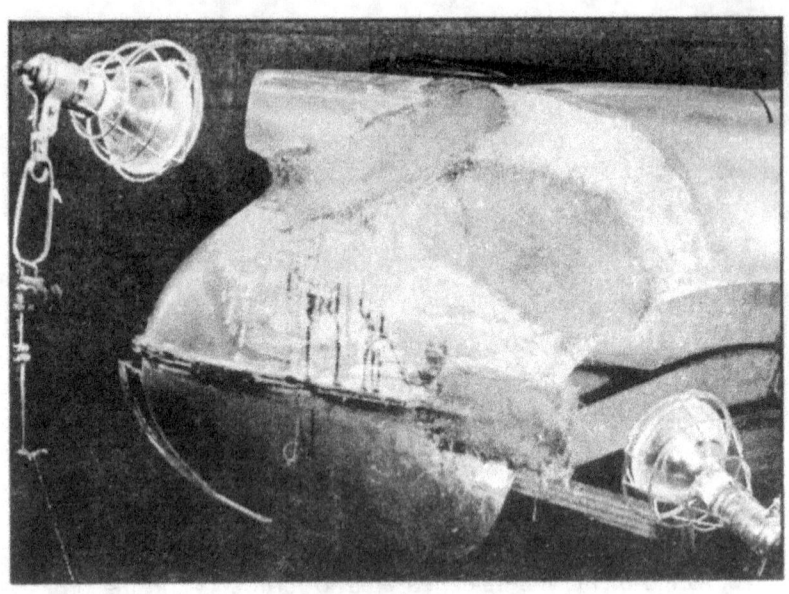

Fig. 27 Using Heat Lamps

NOTE: After Resin Repair, small pits or irregularities may appear in finished surface. Imperfections should be repaired using the Plastic Solder Repair Kit as shown below.

Fig. 28   Mixing the Plastic Solder Materials

Basic Procedure for use of Plastic Solder Repair Kit

The following procedure is basic for using Plastic Solder on repairing all types of surface imperfections.

1. Use paint remover or power sander, and remove finish from damaged area. Carefully inspect for other areas requiring repair.
2. Mix the materials. Each kit consists of one quart of Plastic Resin and one quart of Hardener. The plastic is a light gray aluminum shade. The hardener is black. Mix equal proportions of each material on a clean piece of cardboard, Fig. 28. Stir the material until all light streaks disappear and the mixture is an even color. Caution: If the same utensil is used to ladle out both materials, wipe the utensil clean of one material before dipping into the other material to prevent crusting in the can. Always keep the cans tightly covered when not mixing material. The hardener may attract moisture and upset the chemical balance of the reaction.
3. Preheat the repair area with heatlamps to remove any moisture and to speed up the repair.
4. Apply the material, using a putty knife or rubber squegee, Fig. 29. Work the material into the repair and build the material up to the desired contour. For deep filling and on

vertical surfaces, several layers may be used, each about ½" thick.
5. Focus heat lamps on the repair at a 12" distance. Curing time will be approximately 10 minutes. After the lamps are set, wash hands in soap and water to remove any mixture before it cures.
6. Finish the repair by grinding, sanding and painting in the usual manner, Fig. 30.

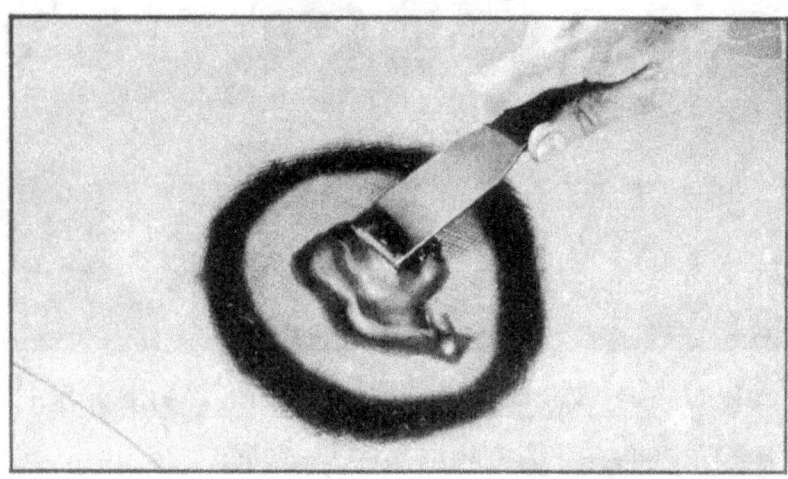

Fig. 29　Applying Plastic Solder

Fig. 30　Finishing the Plastic Solder Repair

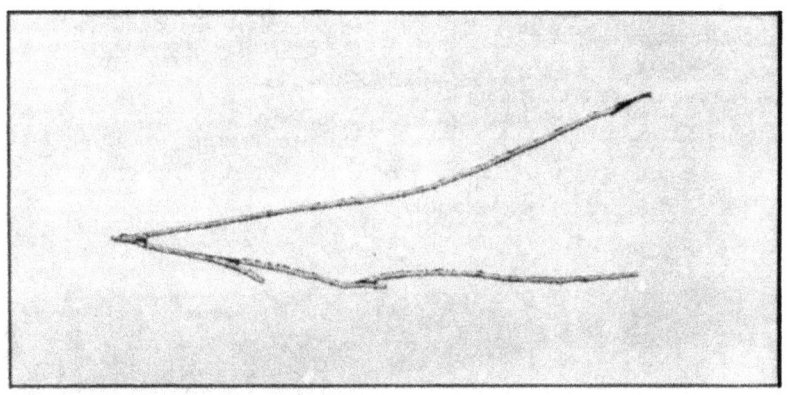

Fig. 31 Typical Scratched Panel

SPECIFIC REPAIRS
Scratched Panels, Spot Refinishing

In many instances, a scratched panel will involve only a paint refinishing job. Fig. 31 shows the top of a fender panel which has been scratched through to the plastic.
1. Remove all paint down to the plastic from the area surrounding the scratch with Lacquer Removing Solvent, Dupont number 39012, or some similar solvent.
2. Featheredge the repair area with No. 220 wet or dry sandpaper and finish block sand with No. 320 wet or dry paper, Fig. 32.

CAUTION: Do not sand too deeply into fibre glass mat. Should it be necessary to cut fairly deep into the glass mat use the repair procedure suggested for dents and pits in plastic panels.
3. Clean up repair area Prep-Sol or its equivalent, then finish the clean-up with a tack rag.
4. Protect surrounding panels by masking before performing paint refinishing operations. Use only non-staining type masking tapes on Corvette plastic body.
5. Refinish panel as described in paint refinishing portion of this manual.

Dents or Pits in Panels, Cracks in Glaze Coat

Fig. 33 shows a panel which has received a heavy glancing blow, resulting in an identation or large pit in the panel. The following procedure is advised for a repair on this type of damage. Cracks in the glaze or finish coat of plastic and paint may also use this procedure.

NOTE: This repair may be used wherever the damage is not extensive and the plastic is not pierced, but the damage area does require a plastic build-up.

1. Remove paint down to the plastic from area surrounding the damage with Lacquer Removing Solvent, Dupont number 39012, or its equivalent.
2. Scuff area surrounding damaged area to provide a good bonding surface.

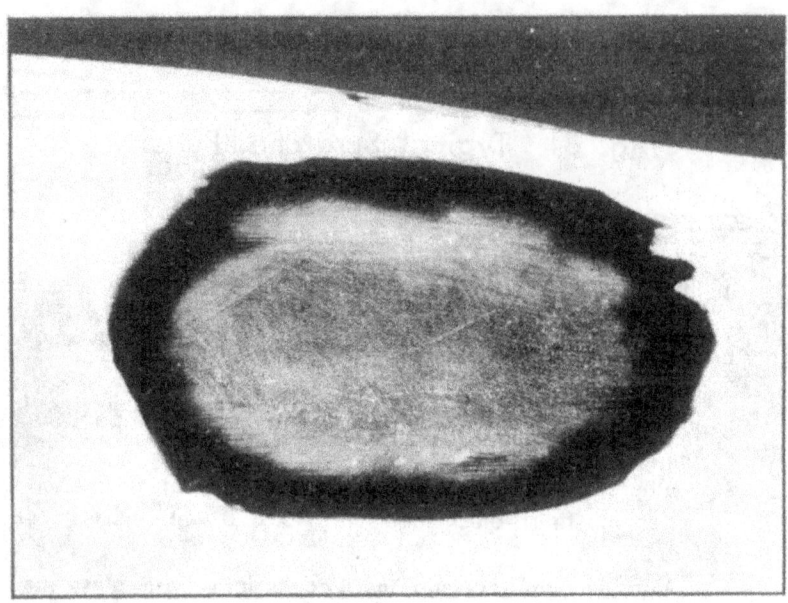

Fig. 32   Repair Area Finish Sanded

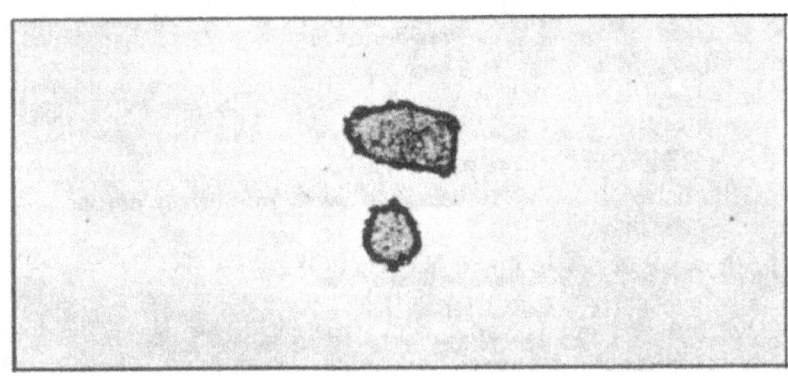

Fig. 33   Typical Pitted Panel

Fig. 34   Typical Cracked Panel

3. Clean up work area with Prep-Sol then use tack rag for finish clean-up.
4. Use the Plastic Solder Repair (previously described) to fill the imperfections.
5. Feather sand damaged area with No. 220 sandpaper and finish sand with No. 320.
6. Prepare repair area for paint refinishing operation (see paint refinishing operation in this manual).

Cracked Panels

Where a fender panel, Fig. 34 or the like, has a fractured or broken off, the following repair operations are recommended.

NOTE: For best results, ambient temperature should be at least 70° - 75° F.

1. In the case of a cracked panel, such as shown in Fig. 34, cut along the break line with a hacksaw blade and remove broken portion of the panel.
2. Remove the paint down to the plastic from both portions of the panel with Dupont Lacquer Remover No. 39012 or its equivalent.
3. Remove dirt and deadener thoroughly, back approximately 2 to 3 inches from the fracture, on the under side of both portions of the panel. Also, remove paint and scuff area clean to provide a good bonding surface.
4. Remove all cracked and fractured material along the break. Bevel the attaching edges of the panels at approximately a 30° angle with a file or grinder and scuff plastic surfaces along edges of break.

NOTE: Mask surrounding panels using a non-staining masking tape.

5. Use "C" clamps to align panel portions allowing approximately 1/8" between the panels or as necessary to provide proper alignment of panels, Fig. 35.
6. With scissors, cut two pieces of woven glass fibre cloth for backup, of sufficient size to overlap the fracture by ap-

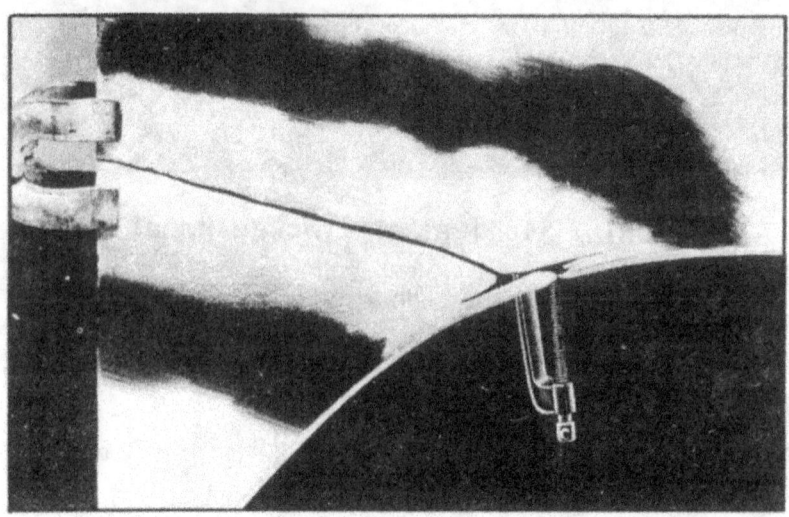

Fig. 35   Cracked Panel Preparation

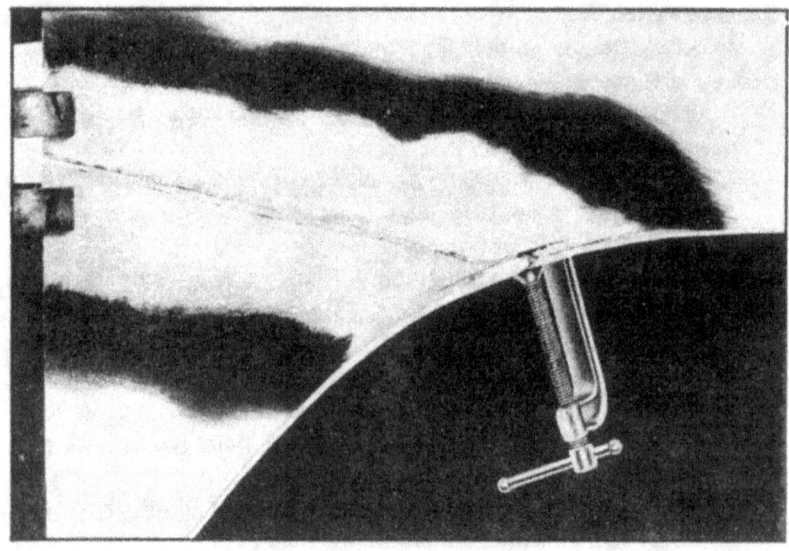

Fig. 36   Use of Back-Up Laminations

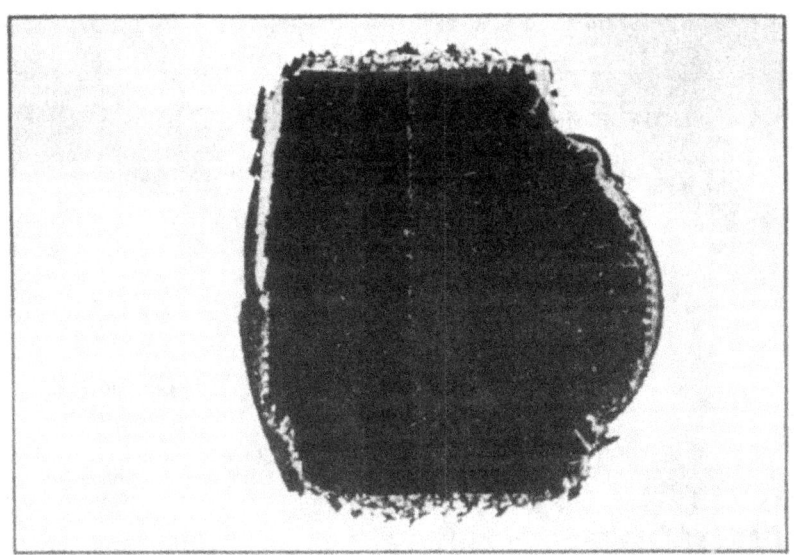

Fig. 37   Hole in Fender Panel

proximately two inches, Fig. 36.
7. Clean up repair area with Prep-Sol, then use tack rag for finish cleanup.
8. Use the Resin Repair Procedure previously described.

NOTE: In some cases it may be desirous to proved additional reinforcements along a fracture. This may be accomplished by placing glass cloth strips in the panel break before applying the plastic mixture.

Holes in Panels

Fig. 37 shows a hole in the side of a fender panel. This type of damage will be rare in the field, due to the unusual strength of the plastic panel. The following procedure may also be applied to a fractured area.
1. Prepare the damaged area by grinding or filing all cracked and splintered material away from around the hole.
2. Bevel the edge of the hole at approximately a 30° angle.
3. Remove the paint with Dupont Lacquer Solvent #39012 or its equivalent, Fig. 38.
4. Thoroughly remove dirt, paint, and deadener from underside of panel for a distance of approximately 4" from the break.
5. Scuff plastic surface on both sides of panel with #80-D sandpaper.
6. Clean up work area with Prep-Sol and wipe dry and mask

surrounding panels using a non-staining masking tape.
7. Cut two pieces of glass cloth, which will overlap the hole. These pieces of cloth will be used for the backup lamination.

NOTE: If the plastic section is rather thick, tailor a suitable number of pieces of glass cloth to the approximate shape of the hole.

8. The size of the area will determine the amount of resin needed for backup and insert laminations (if used). Use two backup laminations on the underside of the panel Fig. 39, and follow previously described Resin Repair procedures. Plastic solder may be used for further filling.
9. Block sand the plastic fill with 80-D sandpaper and finish sanding with #220 and #320 wet or dry sandpaper.
10. Prepare repair for paint refinishing (see Paint Refinishing Operations).

Fractured Panels

Occasionally, some damage will occur to panels where the underside is inaccessible or for reasons of panel contour it is impractical to use back plies of fibre glass cloth. The following repair operations are typical of this type of damage.
1. Prepare the damaged area by grinding or filling all cracked and splintered material away from the fracture.

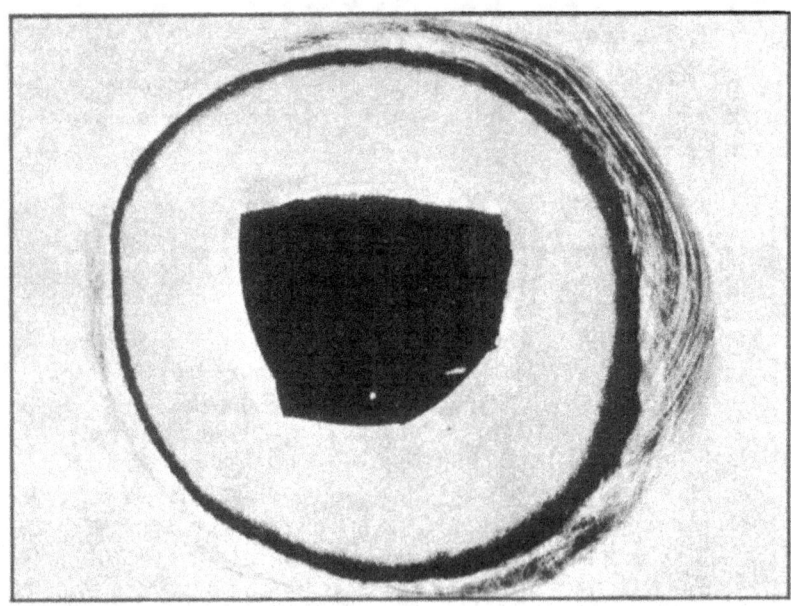

Fig. 38   Preparation of Hole-Type Damage

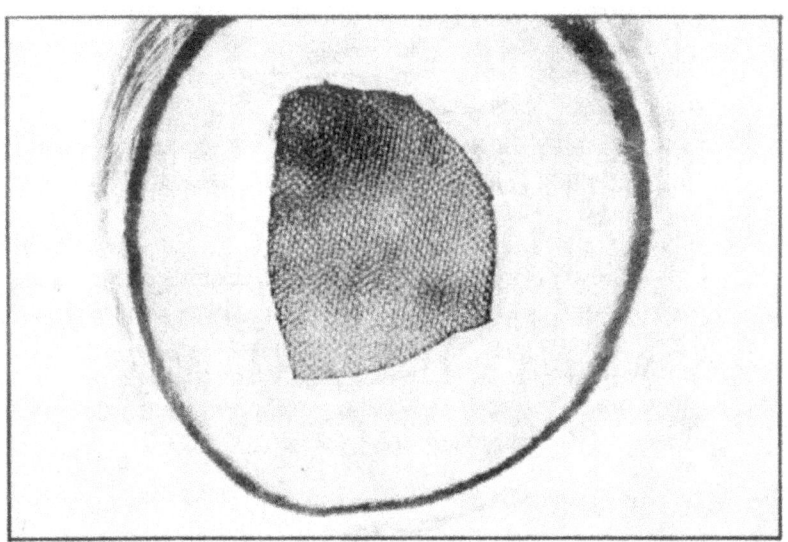

Fig. 39 Back-Up Laminations in Place

2. Bevel the edge of the fracture at approximately a 30° angle.
3. Remove paint from area surrounding fracture with Dupont Lacquer Solvent, No. 39013 or its equivalent.
4. Scuff surface to provide a good bonding surface. Then, clean up area with Prep-Sol and wipe dry.
5. Protect adjacent panels by masking, use non-staining masking tape.
6. Cut a strip of fibre glass cloth of sufficient size, so the fracture will be lapped from 1 to 2 inches on all sides.
7. Prepare plastic mixture in an unwaxed paper cup. (See Resin Repair Kit procedure.)
8. Impregnate glass fibre cloth by brushing or dipping in plastic mixture. Squeeze excess mixture from cloth.

NOTE: Avoid over-rich plastic areas in the glass cloth, as the strength of the patch is directly proportional to the glass content of the patch.

9. Position plastic impregnated fibre glass over the fracture on the exterior of the panel, lap the break by 1 to 2 inches, and depress into fracture.
10. Carefully work excess plastic out of woven glass by "squeegeeing" from the center of the break outward.

NOTE: Hold woven glass in place until plastic resin "gels" with Saranwrap or some similar material.

11. Trim excess or loose strands of fibre glass from patch.
12. If low spots exist, prepare another plastic mixture of resin

and hardener and mix thoroughly. To this mixture add short fibres cut from glass cloth to give the mixture a putty-like consistency.
13. Liberally apply the plastic mixture with a spatula to fracture and surrounding area. Deposit enough material build-up to allow the filing and sanding operations.
14. Allow the patch to harden.
15. File or grind patch to match the general contour of the panel. Exercise care when performing these operations to avoid gouging the patch or surrounding panel.
16. Use plastic solder as necessary to fill any imperfections.
17. Allow fill to harden, then sand finish preparatory to paint operation, (see Paint Refinishing Section).

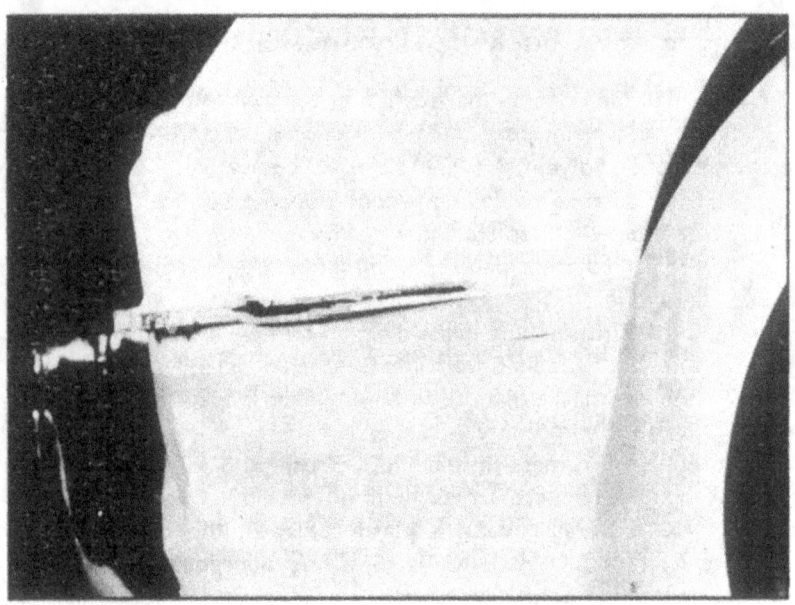

Fig. 40   Cracked Panel Junction

Cracked at Panel Junction

Fig. 40 shows a crack at the junction of two panels. This type

of repair requires a minimum of time and effort.
1. Cut all splintered material from break and sand area to provide a good bonding strip.
2. Prepare a mixture of Plastic Solder.
3. Fill crack with Plastic Solder and allow patch to harden.
4. Sand area to surrounding panel contour.
5. Prepare surface for paint. (See Paint Refinishing in this manual.)

PANEL REPLACEMENT

To install a replacement panel, the following method may be used. Various repair panels are available for service. These complete panels may be used or sections may be cut to accommodate the type of repair necessary. The panels should be fitted in and all attaching parts installed to insure proper alignment and fit of all pieces before plastic applications. See the Chevrolet Master Parts Catalog for available panels.
1. Cut out damaged panel with a hacksaw blade and thoroughly remove all dirt, deadener and paint from the underside of the old panel or panels for a distance of approximately 2 to 3 inches back from the attaching line.
2. Remove the paint from the finish side, for a distance of 2 to 3 inches on the panel adjacent to the replacement panel location with du Pont Lacquer Solvent #39012, or its equivalent.
3. Scuff the surface on both the replacement panel and adjacent panel for a distance of 2 to 3 inches back from the attaching line and wipe clean.
4. Bevel all attaching edges at approximately 30° across the entire thickness of the plastic so a single "V" butt joint will be formed on the finish surface when the pieces are joined. If the replacement panel does not fit closely to the break, reshape to suit.
5. Cut two backup pieces of woven glass fibre cloth to run the entire length of the joint or shorter lengths of fibre cloth may be lapped over entire length of joint, also cut wide enough to lap the junction line on either side by two or three inches.
6. Prepare a sufficient amount of liquid plastic in an un-waxed paper cup by mixing resin with hardener (See Resin Repair procedure).
7. Align replacement panel, then clamp panel in place to form a closed "V" butt joint at the panel junction. When panel cannot be clamped, use 3/16" bolts with large washer on inner and outer of panel to hold panels in alignment or use straps and sheet metal screws, Fig. 41.

Fig. 41   Use of Straps in Panel Replacement

Fig. 42   Filling Panel Replacement

8. Impregnate backup plies of woven glass cloth with prepared plastic mixture by dipping or brushing. Remove excess plastic from cloth by squeezing.
9. Place impregnated backup plies on underside of panels. If necessary, hold backup plies in place with paper until plastic "gels".
10. Prepare another plastic mixture of resin and hardener and mix thoroughly. To this mixture add cut glass fibre (½" lengths) until mixture has a putty-like consistency, or utilize glass cloth.
11. Fill "V" groove with reinforced plastic material or saturated

glass cloth. Build up surrounding area with sufficient material to allow for finish operations, Fig. 42.
12. Allow patch to harden.
13. File or sand (#80-D sandpaper) to general panel contour.
14. Remove plastic skin from all air pockets and fill pockets with Plastic Solder as previously described.
15. Allow plastic fill to harden, then sand, preparatory to paint operations. (See Paint Refinishing in this manual.)

PAINT REFINISHING

The same lacquer preparations and painting procedures used on metal bodies are recommended for the Corvette plastic body. When refinishing a panel, it seems advisable to refinish to the nearest break line, although suitable spot repairs may sometimes be made. This is the same recommendation made for refinishing Metallic-Chrome Lacquered panels.

The following paint procedure is recommended for panel or complete paint refinishing of the plastic Corvette body.

NOTE: When it is desired, small pits in the plastic may be filled before primer-surfacer is applied to the plastic. After sanding and wiping it clean, the imperfections may be filled with Plastic Solder. See the "Basic Procedure for use of the Plastic Solder Repair Kit" Section for the application procedure. This material is faster than body glazing compound when used on the Corvette Plastic Body, although both materials are satisfactory.

1. Wipe the entire work area with clean cloth soaked with Prep-Sol, this will remove all traces of wax, polish and grease, then wipe surface dry with a clean cloth.
2. Remove old paint finish with either du Pont Lacquer Solvent #39012, its equivalent, or by sanding with coarse sandpaper.
3. Feather sand edges of paint with #220 wet or dry sandpaper and finish feathersanding with #440 wet or dry paper.

NOTE: For the best results, feathersand from the outside of the paint break toward the center, this will eliminate the possibility of low spots in the paint.

4. Clean up job with Prep-Sol, then finish the cleanup with a tack rag.

CAUTION: Avoid touching the job from this point on with bare hands, as the skin oil deposited on the surface of the panel might affect the adhesion of the paint to the body.

5. Spray the bare plastic and feathered areas with Duco-Primer-Surfacer or its equivalent, reduced 1 part Duco Primer Surfacer to 2 parts Duco Thinner. Apply two or more medium coats allowing each to "Flash" (become dull) before applying the succeeding coat.

6. Allow the final coat to dry at least one hour before starting sanding operations.
7. For best sanding results, water sand with #320 wet or dry sandpaper. If dry sanding is preferred, use #360 paper.
8. Should pin point imperfections still show, knife out with PX putty and allow to dry for one to two hours. Sand the putty-glaze. Plastic solder may be used to produce a faster repair.

NOTE: Most glazing putty failures are the result of two common errors on the operators part. First, not enough drying time is allowed for the glazing putty, and secondly, the glazing putty is applied too heavily.

9. Dust job off, then spray entire area to be refinished with one coat of Make-Ready Sealer or its equivalent, reduce 1 part Make-Ready to 1½ parts thinner. Allow at least thirty minutes for drying. This will give maximum sealing.
10. If necessary, scuff lightly with #440 sandpaper to remove nibs, dust off panel and tack wipe.
11. Spray the Duco which has been reduced 1 part Duco to 1½ parts Duco Thinner, in three or four wet double coats. Allow each color coat to flash before applying the succeeding coat.
12. Allow at least four hours for drying, or, if possible, overnight; then hand rub with Duco Rubbing Compound No. 2 or machine polish with Machine Compound #14 or equivalent.
13. Polish by hand or machine with Duco Liquid Polish or dry buff with "Amcor" Disc No. 5, or lambs wool bonnet.
14. It is advisable to allow at least thirty days for the Duco Lacquer to harden before performing a waxing operation. This permits all trapped solvents to disperse before wax is applied.

Trim body work on a competition Corvette. (Note added taillights.)

CORVETTE PAINT CHART
(EXTERIOR)

MODEL YEAR	COMBINATION NO.	COLOR	ACRYLIC LACQUER			REGULAR LACQUER	
			Du Pont Lucite Stock No.	R-M Stock No.	Ditzler Code No.	Du Pont "Duco" Stock No.	R-M Stock No.
60	523-A	Honduras Maroon Met.	4034-LH	A-1221R	DDL 50568	4066-H	1221R
60	509-A	Sateen Silver Met.	4023-L	A-1203	DDL 31905	93988	1203
60	510-A	Ermine White	4024-L	A-1199	DDL 8259	94001	1199
60	504-A	Tasco Turquoise Met.	4025-L	A-1211	DDL 12228	93996	1211
60	502-A	Horizon Blue Met.	4030-L	A-1210	DDL 12234	93998	1210
60	517-A	Cascade Green Met.	4029-L	A-1214	DDL 42693	93997	1214
59-60	506-A	Roman Red	2931-LH	A-1138R	DDL 70961	2967-H	1138R
59	504-A	Crown Sapphire	2930-L	A-1137	DDL 12001	92945	1137
59	502-A	Frost Blue	2925-L	A-1150	DDL 12018	92808	1150
59	508-A	Classic Cream	2924-L	A-1148	DDL 81092	92810	1148
59-60	503-A	Tuxedo Black	88-L	A-946	DDL 9300	44	400
58	506-A	Signet Red	2704-LH	—	DDL 70826	—	58V52
58	508-A	Panama Yellow	2705-LH	A-1108D	DDL 80986	—	58V74
58	504-A	Regal Turquoise	2702-L	—	DDL 11836	—	58V26
58	502, 514	Silver Blue	2696-L	A-992D	DDL 11755	—	992D
58-59	510-A	Snowcrest White	2697-L	A-986	DDL 8160	—	986
58	500-A	Charcoal	2703-L	—	DDL 31742	—	58V11
58-59	509-A, 512-B	Inca Silver	2436-L	A-696	DDL 31425	94260	56V13
56-57	714	Venetian Red	—	—	DAL 70694	2415-H	56V52
56-57	713,720	Arctic Blue Met.	—	—	DAL 11537	2413	56V29
56-57	712	Cascade Green	—	—	DAL 41973	2416	—
56-57	709	Aztec Copper Met.	—	—	DAL 21295	2414	56V84
56-57	704	Onyx Black	—	—	DAL 9200	44	400
55	596	Gypsy Red	—	—	DAL 70575	1973-H	443R
55	632	Harvest Gold	—	—	DAL 80739	2004-H	491G
54	573	Corvette Copper	—	—	DAL 21207	2187-H	55V84
54	570	Pennant Blue	—	—	DAL 11238	1927	—
53-57	718	Polo White	—	—	DAL 8011	1783-H	54V91
53-54	569	Sportsman Red	—	—	DAL 70418	1905-H	—

(INTERIOR)

MODEL YEAR	COLOR	Du PONT "DUCO"	R-M STOCK NO.	DITZLER CODE NO.
59-60	Light Blue Met.	92808	U-2471	DAL 12018
60	Med. Turq. Met.	93996	A-1211	DAL 12228
59-60	Red	2967-H	59C51	DL 70961
59-60	Black	44	400	DAL 9200
59	Turquoise Met.	92945	59C24	DL 12067
58	Silver Blue	2696-L	992-D	DAL 11755
58	Charcoal	2703L	58V11	DAL 31742
58	Signet Red	2704-LH	8V52	DAL 70826
56-57	Venetian Red	2415-H	56V52	DAL 70694
55	Autumn Bronze	2002	56V84	DAL 21151
55	Harvest Gold	2004-H	55V71	DAL 80739
54-57	Shoreline Beige	1726	356	DAL 21054
54	Corvette Copper	1925-H	—	DAL 21207
54	Pennant Blue	1927	—	DAL 11238
53-55	Polo White	1783-H	54V91	DAL 8011
53-55	Sportsman Red	1905-H	—	DAL 70418

To reduce gloss add Du Pont 4528 "DUCO" Lacquer Flattening Compound or equivalent.

Corvette Regular Production Options

Corvette owners are sometimes curious about the designation R.P.O. before certain component descriptions. These letters are the abbreviation of **Regular Production Option** and are always followed by a three digit number of identification. Regular Production Option indicates that the part or unit is specified and manufactured for the car and has been homologated in accordance with International competition regulations. These options are, in other words, accepted as indigenous to the Corvette by racing groups all over the world.

They grew out of the effort to make the Corvette a true sports-competition machine as well as a sporty car. Realizing that every Corvette owner has his own definitions of the use to which his car will be put, Chevrolet has tried to anticipate the requirements of a wide variety of conditions to be imposed by individual owners. As we mentioned in the opening segment of this handbook, the "improving of the breed" tactics resulted in the development of numerous components not ordinarily associated with passenger cars. And, while the Chevrolet standard passenger car brakes, for example, are more than adequate for the lighter Corvette under even extreme highway usage, a superior stopping ability is required for the hot competition encountered in road racing. These improved brakes are offered as a Regular Production Option. The Corvette can be ordered so equipped or the brakes can be installed on any model for which they are specified without penalty if the owner desires to compete under the rules of the Sports Car Club of America or other sanctioning organizations.

The descriptions of the various R.P.O's are included to help the the owner of a Corvette who may have not purchased it new to determine how his car is equipped. Service of certain R.P.O's varies from the technique employed on standard components and this information is included.

Use of the right RPO's is almost mandatory if you hope to reach the front of the grid.

Heavy Duty Brakes and Suspension

Several heavy-duty suspension and heavyduty brake options have been available on Corvettes since 1957. The following description covers these Regular Production Options by their respective R.P.O. numbers.

Fig. 50—Ceramic-Metallic Brake Linings (Typical of units before 1960)

R.P.O. 684, used on 1957, 58 and 59 models included heavy-duty front and rear suspension, described below, and special brake equipment built around Ceramic-Metallic, segmented linings (fig. 50). The lining widths are 2½" front and 2" rear. Special finned drums (fig. 51) were used in conjunction with vented brake backing plates. In addition, on 1957, 58 and early 59 models, a duct system (fig. 52) utilizing the body rocker panels was used to direct air at the rear brakes. Special brake shoe hold-down springs and pull-back springs were incorporated for heat resistance. This brake material produces a pedal feel that is extremely "hard" when the brakes are cold, and exhibits some tendency to be erratic even when hot. This option should be used primarily for competitive events or extremely high speed driving.

Fig. 51—Finned Brake Drums

In 1959 and 60, a separate brake option R.P.O. 686, was available which used a Sintered-Metallic, segmented lining material. This option applied to brakes only, and standard drums with a specially ground, smooth finish on the lining contact surfaces were used. Special low-rate brake shoe hold-down springs and pull-back springs were used to provide long life under high-temperature conditions. The lining widths are 2" front and 1¾" rear. This brake material exhibits a tendency toward a "hard" brake pedal feel when the brakes are cold.

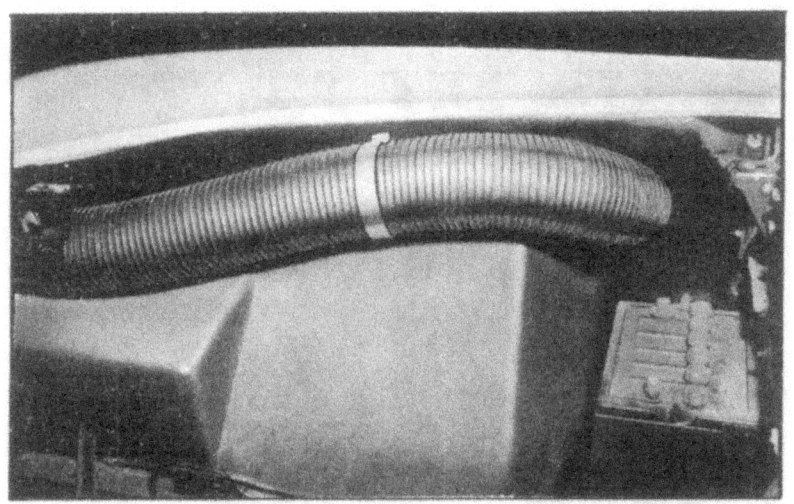

Fig. 52—Brake Cooling Duct (ex. 1960)

In 1960, R.P.O. 687 was made available for maximum brake effectiveness. This option applies only to the brakes plus a steering adapter to produce a faster steering ratio. The lining material is sintered-metallic, and the lining widths are 2½" front and 1¾" rear. Very special, temperature resistant brake shoe hold-down springs and pull-back springs were used for service under high temperature conditions. The brake backing plates were vented for cooling purposes. Special finned drums were used with a 24 vane fan inside the drums to assist in air circulation. The shoe contact area of each drum is specially ground to a very smooth finish. I the owner of a Corvette with R.P.O. 684 should desire to convert the brake linings to the R.P.O. 687 material, it would be necessary to use new shoes and linings, new rear wheel cylinders, new hold-down and pullback springs and to remove a welded-on spacer that was used between the rear brake backing plates and the rear brake anchor pins. In addition, it would be necessary to provide a smooth ground surface in the brake drums.

The Corvette for 1960 feature a redesigned suspension that eliminate the need for a special suspension option.

FRONT SUSPENSION

The front suspension changes (special option except 1960) include high-rate coil springs, larger shock absorbers (1⅜") with stiffer valving, a heavier, 13/16 inch stabilizer bar and a fast steering adaptor, Fig 53. The fast steering adaptor changes the overall steering ratio from 21.1: to 16.3:1. These revisions affect service procedures only in the matter of part numbers of pieces to be replaced. The basic service procedures are similar to those on the 1954

Passenger Car and reference should be made to the 1949-54 Passenger Car Shop Manual for procedures.

Fig. 53—Fast Steering Adapter (typical)

REAR AXLE AND SUSPENSION

The rear suspension changes include heavier rear springs (5 leaf) and larger shock absorbers (1⅜") with stiffer valving, Fig. 54.

The rear axle housing incorporates special baffles and vent tube to control lubrication during fast cornering. The Heavy Duty Suspension option is used only in conjunction with one of the three Positraction Rear Axles options.

In 1960, a stabilizer bar was added (as standard production) immediately rearward of the rear axle. This eliminated the need for heavy-duty springs and shock absorbers. A redesigned front stabilizer added greater strength to the front suspension.

No special service problems should be encountered in servicing the Corvette rear suspension, and basic 1957 Passenger Car Procedures should be used.

BRAKE SERVICE
Minor Brake Adjustment

The minor brake adjustment is made in the same manner as with conventional brakes with the exception that the adjusting screw must be backed-off 27-32 notches on R.P.O. 684, Ceramic-Metallic brakes, and 12 notches on R.P.O.'s 686 and 687, Sintered Metallic brakes. This back-off specification is from a light drag condition. Refer to one of the Chevrolet Passenger Car Shop Manuals for further details to provide proper running clearance.

Fig. 54—Rear Suspension and Brakes (typical)

CAUTION: These adjustments will produce a low pedal for normal driving, but must be maintained to give the proper clearance for heavy-duty operation.

Drum Refinishing

Brake drums used with R.P.O. 684, Ceramic-Metallic brakes, can be refinished in a conventional manner. The brake drums used with R.P.O. 686 or 687, Sintered-Metallic brakes, must have a specially ground finish. These drums should be finish-turned with a light cut and fine feed, and then ground twice, using a fine feed. Use a grinding wheel of #46 or #80 grit. The final drum finish should be of the same quality as an engine cylinder bore.

Major Brake Adjustment

The major brake adjustment, performed on the adjustable anchor pin, is called for when an unequal or severe braking condition is present. The procedure is as follows.

1. Loosen anchor pin just enough so that pin can be shifted in anchor plate.

CAUTION: Do not loosen pin excessively, as the pin may then tilt instead of shift.

2. Turn brake adjusting screw to expand brake shoes until a heavy drag is felt on the drum.

3. Tap anchor pin and flange plate to allow shoes to center in drum. If the drag or the drum decreases, expand the shoes a few notches and repeat the tapping operation. When the drag remains constant, tighten the anchor pin nut to 60-80 ft. lbs.

4. Adjust brake shoes to a light drag and back off the specified number of notches.

NOTE: The Corvette with the standard brake system uses an anchor pin with a vertical adjustment only (front and rear). The units with the R.P.O. (optional) brake system utilize an eccentric pin on the front wheels and a vertical moving pin on the rear wheels.

Wide Base Wheels

Wide base wheels are available as an option. These wheels are of conventional design but are built to take larger tires. The 15 x 5½K wheels will accept 7.10/7.60 x 15 tires. Conventional 6.50/6.70 x 15 tires may be mounted on these optional wheels or on the standard production 15 x 5K wheels.

Close-Ratio Transmission

The three speed close-ratio transmission used in 1956-60 Corvettes is basically the same as the conventional three speed transmission. Design changes in the clutch gear, counter gear and second gear account for the numerically lower ratios. Ratios in first gear are 2.2-to-1, second gear 1.31-to-1, third gear 1-to-1 and reverse gear 2.2-to-1.

A higher capacity clutch gear bearing and mainshaft rear bearing provide greater durability, and a stronger snap ring better retains the synchronizer ring for rapid shifting. A neoprene "O" ring replaces the cork seal used on the shifter shaft for lower shifting friction. General service procedure remains the same as for the regular three speed transmission with the exception of clutch drive gear removal. Because of the larger diameter gear, the extension housing and mainshaft are removed first. The counter gear must then be dropped to the case bottom after which the clutch gear and bearing are removed toward the rear of the transmission case. On installation, the countergear is placed in the case bottom and then the clutch gear is installed from inside of case. The counter-gear is then raised and shaft installed, after which the mainshaft and extension housing are installed. Repair operations of unit components are serviced as outlined for the regular three speed transmission, in the 1957-60 Chevrolet Passenger Car Shop Manuals.

Standard And Optional Engine Construction

The standard engine in the Corvette is a single 4 barrel carburetor equipped engine.

This engine is basically the same as the 4 barrel carburetor, 283 cu. in. passenger car engine for each model year (263 cu. in. in 1956). Minor differences in ignition coils, fan blades, generators, etc. are incorporated to adapt it for Corvette use.

Another feature which sets the standard Corvette engine apart from the 283 cu. in. passenger car engine is the thickness of the chrome plate used on the piston rings. The top compression ring and the oil control ring on the passenger car are chrome-flashed to produce a coating approximately .0005" thick. On the Corvette, the chrome plate on these rings is approximately .004" thick. These rings are used on all Corvette engines.

The engine oil pan on all Corvette engines is of a five quart capacity, 1 quart more than conventional passenger car V-8 engines.

The pistons used on all Corvette engines with the exception of the special cam, Fuel Injection engine, are of the notched type, with cut away areas or "eye-brows" machined into piston tops to insure valve clearance. The passenger car 283 cu. in. V-8 engine is equipped with flat pistons.

Corvette engines with special camshafts have heavy-duty crankshaft main bearings and connecting rod bearings.

The 1956 225 h.p. and 1957-1960 245 h.p. engine is basically the same as the standard Corvette engine, with the addition of the dual four-barrel carburetor equipment.

The 250 h.p. engine (275 h.p. in 1960) is also similar to the standard engine, with the addition of the Fuel Injection equipment.

The 270 h.p. engine has the basic equipment of the 245 h.p. dual four-barrel carburetion engine and has, in addition, a different camshaft utilizing solid valve lifters. Used in conjunction with the solid lifters and different camshaft are lightweight valves with modified contours.

The 1957, 283 h.p. engine (290 h.p. in 1958-59, 315 h.p. in 1960) has the basic equipment of 250 h.p. (275 h.p. in 1960) Fuel Injection engine plus the camshaft, solid lifters and valves of the 270 h.p. engine, and utilizes domed pistons to boost the rated compression ratio to 10.5 to 1 (10.0 in 1958, 11.0 in 1960). The crankshaft of this engine is specially strengthened and balanced for use with the heavier, domed pistons. This crankshaft is not serviced, and if replacement is necessary, a standard crankshaft must be used. A balance weight kit, Part Number 3716306 must be used to balance the replacement crankshaft for proper engine balance. Instructions on installing the weights are provided in the kit.

With the exception of the adjustment of the valve clearances on the special cam engines, and the piston clearance on the special cam, fuel injection model, the service procedure and tools as shown in the 1957-60 Passenger Car Shop Manual may be used on the Corvette engines.

The valve clearance on the engines with solid lifters should be adjusted, with the engine normalized, to .012" (.008" for 1960) for intake valves and .018" for exhaust valves. On engines with aluminum cylinder heads, the valves should be adjusted to .006" intake and .014" for the exhaust valves.

On the special cam, fuel injection engine, the domed pistons are fitted .001" looser than specified for all other 283 cu. in. Chevrolet V-8 engines. The piston clearance should be .0016" to .002".

ENGINES!

210 H.P.

RECOMMENDED IDLE........................
DISTRIBUTOR PART NUMBER................
BREAKER POINTS..........................
ADVANCE SYSTEM..........................
BREAKER ARM SPRING TENSION..............
POINT GAP...............................
CAM ANGLE (dwell).......................

1956 Standard Engine,
4-Barrel Carburetion,
Regular Camshaft (1)
475 r.p.m. (2)
1110866, 1110869, 1110878
Single
Centrifugal & Vacuum
19-23 oz.
New —.019"; Old —.016"
28"—32"

SPARK ADVANCE...........................
  Initial setting @ recommended idle
  Centrifugal advance (5)   Start
                         Intermediate
                              Maximum
  Vacuum advance   Start
                              Maximum

4° BTDC
0° @ 600 r.p.m.
14° @ 1500 r.p.m.
28° @ 3700 r.p.m.
0° @ 8" Hg.
13.75" @ 15" Hg.

220 H.P.

1957 Standard Engine,
4-Barrel Carburetion,
Regular Camshaft
475 r.p.m. (2)
1110891
Dual
Full centrifugal
19-23 oz.
Set by dwell (4)
29" each breaker;
33" ≈ 1° total

4° BTDC
0° @ 600 r.p.m.
14° @ 1500 r.p.m.
28° @ 3700 r.p.m.
None

225 H.P.

1956 Optional Engine,
2 X 4-Barrel Carburetion,
Special Camshaft (1)
600 r.p.m. (3)
1110872, 1110879
Dual
Full centrifugal
19-23 oz.
Set by dwell (4)
29" each breaker;
33" ≈ 1° total

4° BTDC
0° @ 600 r.p.m.
15° @ 1500 r.p.m.
28° @ 3700 r.p.m.
None

230 H.P.

RECOMMENDED IDLE........................
DISTRIBUTOR PART NUMBER................

BREAKER POINTS..........................
ADVANCE SYSTEM..........................
BREAKER ARM SPRING TENSION..............
POINT GAP...............................
CAM ANGLE (dwell).......................

1958-1960 Standard Engine,
4-Barrel Carburetion,
Regular Camshaft
475 r.p.m. (2)
1110946 ('59)
1110890 ('58)
Single
Centrifugal & Vacuum
19-23 oz.
New —.019"; Old —.016"
28"—32"

SPARK ADVANCE...........................
  Initial setting @ recommended idle
  Centrifugal advance (5)   Start
                         Intermediate
                              Maximum
  Vacuum advance   Start
                              Maximum

4° BTDC
0° @ 600 r.p.m.
14° @ 1500 r.p.m.
28° @ 3700 r.p.m.
0° @ 8" Hg.
15° @ 15.5" Hg.

245 H.P.

1957-1960 Optional Engin
2 x 4-Barrel Carburetion,
Regular Camshaft
600 r.p.m. (3)
1110891

Dual
Full centrifugal
19-23 oz.
Set by dwell (4)
29" each breaker,
33" ≈ 1° total

4° BTDC
0° @ 600 r.p.m.
14° @ 1500 r.p.m.
28° @ 3700 r.p.m.
None

250 H.P.

1957-1959 Optional Engine,
Ramjet Fuel Injection,
Regular Camshaft
500 r.p.m. (3)
1110915 ('58-'59)
1110906 ('57 with
Powerglide) (6)
Single
Centrifugal & Vacuum
19-23 oz.
New —.019"; Old —.016"
28"—32"

4° BTDC
0° @ 600 r.p.m.
14° @ 1500 r.p.m.
28° @ 3700 r.p.m.
0° @ 4.75" Hg.
24° @ 13.5" Hg.

270 H.P.

RECOMMENDED IDLE........................
DISTRIBUTOR PART NUMBER................
BREAKER POINTS..........................
ADVANCE SYSTEM..........................
BREAKER ARM SPRING TENSION..............
POINT GAP...............................
CAM ANGLE (dwell).......................

1957-1960 Optional Engine,
2 x 4-Barrel Carburetion,
Special Camshaft (1)
800-850 r.p.m.
1110891
Dual
Full centrifugal
19-23 oz.
Set by dwell (4)
29" each breaker;
33" ≈ 1° total

SPARK ADVANCE...........................
  Initial setting @ recommended idle
  Centrifugal advance (5)   Start
                         Intermediate
                              Maximum
  Vacuum advance   Start
                              Maximum

7° BTDC
0° @ 600 r.p.m.
14° @ 1500 r.p.m.
28° @ 3700 r.p.m.
None

275 H.P.

1960 Optional Engine,
Ramjet Fuel Injection,
Regular Camshaft
600 r.p.m.
1110915
Single
Centrifugal & Vacuum
19-23 oz.
New —.019"; Old —.016"
28"—32"

4° BTDC
0° @ 600 r.p.m.
14° @ 1500 r.p.m.
28° @ 3700 r.p.m.
0° @ 4.75" Hg.
24° @ 13.5" Hg.

283 H.P.

1957 Optional Engine,
Ramjet Fuel Injection,
Special Camshaft (1)
700 r.p.m.
1110889, 1110905, 1110908
Dual
Full centrifugal
19-23 oz.
Set by dwell (4)
29" each breaker;
33" ≈ 1° total

4° BTDC
0° @ 600 r.p.m.
15° @ 1550 r.p.m.
28° @ 5000 r.p.m.
None

290 H.P.

RECOMMENDED IDLE........................
DISTRIBUTOR PART NUMBER................
BREAKER POINTS..........................
ADVANCE SYSTEM..........................
BREAKER ARM SPRING TENSION..............
POINT GAP...............................
CAM ANGLE (dwell).......................

1958-1959 Optional Engine,
Ramjet Fuel Injection,
Special Camshaft (1)
700 r.p.m.
1110914
Dual
Full Centrifugal
19-23 oz.
Set by dwell (4)
29" each breaker;
33" ≈ 1° total

SPARK ADVANCE...........................
  Initial setting @ recommended idle
  Centrifugal advance (5)   Start
                         Intermediate
                              Maximum
  Vacuum advance

18° BTDC
0° @ 1000 r.p.m.
5° @ 1500 r.p.m.
22° @ 6000 r.p.m.
None

315 H.P.

1960 Optional Engine,
Ramjet Fuel Injection,
Special Camshaft (1)
700 r.p.m.
1110914
Dual
Full centrifugal
19-23 oz.
Set by dwell (4)
29" each breaker;
33" ≈ 1° total

18° BTDC
0° @ 1000 r.p.m.
5° @ 1500 r.p.m.
22° @ 6000 r.p.m.
None

FOOTNOTES

(1) Mechanical valve lifters
(2) 450 r.p.m. with Powerglide (in "Drive")
(3) Synchro-Mesh and Powerglide (in "Drive")
(4) Should give .014"-.018" point opening
(5) Does not include initial setting. Curve is a straight line between specified points.
(6) 1110889, 1110905, full centrifugal distributors, used with Synchro-Mesh in '57 models. Specifications same as for 283 h.p. engine except recommended idle is 500 r.p.m.

Corvette 4-Speed Transmission

The four speed synchromesh transmission, special option equipment for use with the Corvette, incorporates helical gears specially designed to provide high torque capacity without additional weight, and gear teeth proportioned to operate at high speeds with neither excessive heat generation nor excessive frictional losses. Shafts, bearings, high capacity synchronizers and other precision parts are held to close limits, providing proper clearances necessary for durability and during extended heavy usage.

The rear end of the clutch gear is supported by a heavy duty ball bearing at the front end of the transmission case and is piloted

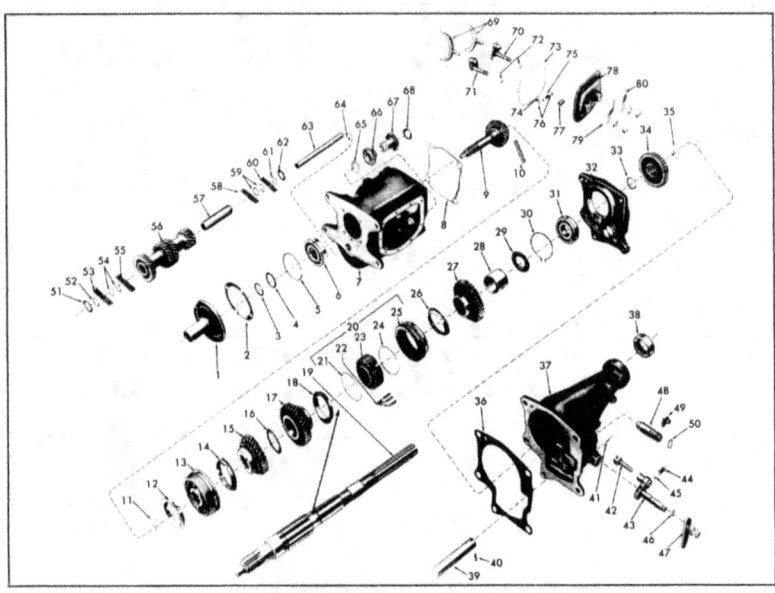

Fig. 57—4-Speed Transmission-Exploded View

1. Front Bearing Retainer
2. Gasket
3. Selective Fit Snap Ring
4. Spacer Washer
5. Front Bearing Snap Ring
6. Front Bearing
7. Transmission Case
8. Case to Rear Bearing Retainer Gasket
9. Clutch Gear
10. Roller Bearings (14)
11. Snap Ring (.086" to .088")
12. Fourth Speed Gear Synchronizer Blocker Ring
13. Third and Fourth Speed Gear Synchronizer Assembly
14. Third Speed Gear Synchronizer Blocker Ring
15. Third Speed Gear
16. Second and Third Speed Gear Spacer (Needle Roller Bearing)
17. Second Speed Gear
18. Second Speed Gear Synchronizer Blocker Ring
19. Mainshaft
20. First and Second Speed Gear Synchronizer Assembly
21. Energizing Spring
22. Synchronizer Keys
23. Synchronizer Hub
24. Energizing Spring
25. Synchronizer Sliding Sleeve
26. First Speed Gear Synchronizer Blocker Ring
27. First Speed Gear
28. First Speed Gear Sleeve
29. First Speed Gear Thrust Washer
30. Rear Bearing Snap Ring
31. Rear Bearing
32. Rear Bearing Retainer
33. Selective Fit Snap Ring
34. Reverse Gear
35. Speedometer Drive Gear
36. Rear Bearing Retainer to Case Extension Gasket
37. Case Extension
38. Rear Oil Seal
39. Rear Idle Shaft
40. Rear Idler Shaft Lock Pin
41. Reverse Shifter Shaft Lock Pin
42. Reverse Shifter Fork
43. Reverse Shifter Shaft and Detent Plate
44. Reverse Shifter Shaft Ball Detent Spring
45. Reverse Shifter Shaft Detent Ball
46. Reverse Shifter Shaft "O" Ring Seal
47. Reverse Shifter Lever
48. Speedometer Driven Gear and Fitting
49. Lock Plate and Bolt
50. "O" Ring Seal
51. Tanged Washer
52. Spacer (.050")
53. Roller Bearings (20)
54. Spacers (2-.050")
55. Roller Bearings (20)
56. Countergear
57. Countergear Roller Spacer
58. Roller Bearings (20)
59. Spacers (2-.050")
60. Roller Bearings (20)
61. Spacer (.050")
62. Tanged Washer
63. Countershaft
64. Countershaft Woodruff Key
65. Reverse Idler Front Thrust Washer (Flat)
66. Reverse Idler Gear (front)
67. Reverse Idler Gear (rear)
68. Tanged Thrust Washer
69. Forward Speed Shift Forks
70. First and Second Speed Shifter Shaft and Detent Plate
71. Third and Fourth Speed Shifter Shaft and Detent Plate
72. "O" Ring Seals
73. Gasket
74. Interlock Pin
75. Poppet Spring
76. Detent Balls
77. Interlock Sleeve
78. Transmission Side Cover
79. Third and Fourth Speed Shifter Lever
80. First and Second Speed Shifter Lever

at its front end in an oil impregnated bushing mounted in the engine crankshaft. The front end of the mainshaft is piloted in a row of roller bearings set into the hollow end of the clutch gear and the rear end is carried by a heavy duty ball bearing identical to the one which supports the clutch gear.

The counter gear is carried on a double row of roller bearings at both ends while thrust is taken on thrust washers located between the ends of the gear and the front and rear of the case.

The two-piece reverse idler gear is carried on bronze bushings while thrust is taken on thrust washers located between the front of the gear and the back of the reverse idler thrust boss and between the rear of the gear and the reverse idler shaft boss in the case extension.

Gearshifting is manual through shift control rods to the transmission cover shifter levers for first through fourth gears, and to the reverse lever located in the case extension. The shifter lever to the rear of the transmission cover controls first and second gears while the lever to the front controls third and fourth gears.

All four forward gears are provided with synchronizers which can be engaged while the car is in motion. Closely spaced gear ratios of 2.2 (first), 1.68 (second), 1.30 (third) and 1.00 (fourth) provide excellent ratio matching with minimum loss of engine R.P.M. at the shift points.

The transmission may be used as an aid in deceleration by downshifting in sequence without double clutching or gear clashing, due to all forward speeds being synchronized.

Reverse gear (2.25 ratio) is not synchronized.

Minor Service Operations

SHIFT LINKAGE ADJUSTMENT

The 4-speed transmission shift linkage, Fig. 55 utilizes three shift rods and levers. A simple gage block, shown in Fig. 56, will aid in making the proper adjustments. The adjustments can be made without the gage block by having an assistant hold the manual shift lever in the neutral positions.

1. Remove transmission selector plate and shift lever escutcheon plate from floor pan.
2. Place transmission in neutral and install gage block in position shown in Fig. 55.
3. Remove the cotter pin and clevis pin at each shift lever.
4. On each shift rod, adjust the threaded clevis to permit free entry of the clevis pin into the hole in the transmission shift lever.
5. Reconnect the clevises to the shift levers.
6. Remove the gage block and check the shifts. If any roughness

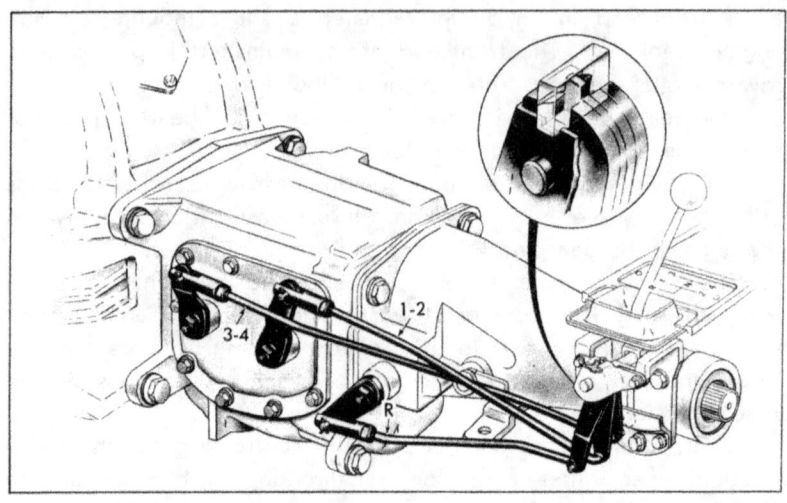

Fig. 55—4-Speed Transmission Shift Linkage

still exists, one of the clevises may require adjustment of approximately one-half turn. Determine the rod and clevis requiring adjustment by sighting along the slot where the gage block was used in step 2.

SPEEDOMETER DRIVEN GEAR
Disassembly

Disconnect speedometer cable, remove lock plate to housing bolt and lock washer and remove lock plate. Insert screwdriver in

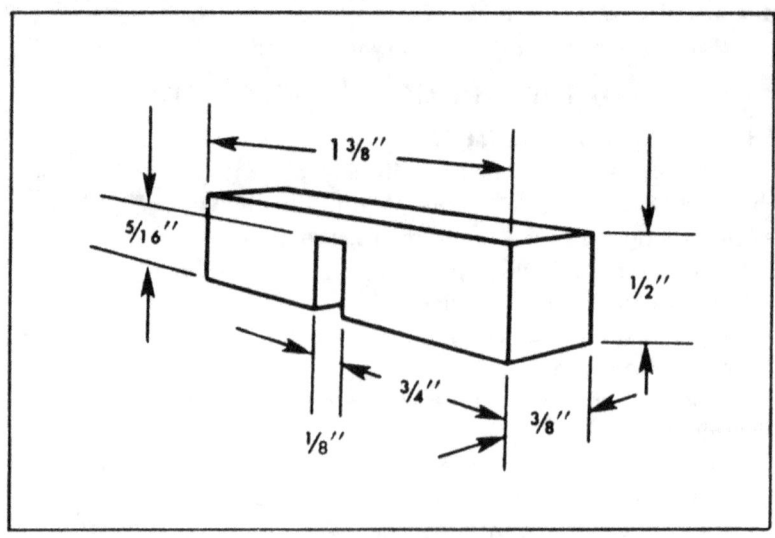

Fig. 56—Linkage Gage Block

lock plate slot in fitting and pry fitting, gear and shaft from housing. Pry "O" ring from groove in fitting.
Assembly

Install new "O" ring in groove in fitting and insert shaft. Hold the assembly so slot in fitting is toward lock plate boss on housing and install in housing. Push fitting into housing until lock plate can be inserted into groove and attached to housing.

TRANSMISSION SIDE COVER
Removal

1. Drain transmission and disconnect control rods from levers.
2. Remove cover assembly from transmission.
3. Remove the outer shifter lever nuts and lockwashers and pull levers from shafts.
4. Carefully push the shifter into cover, allowing the detent balls to fall free, then remove both shifter shafts.
5. Remove interlock sleeve, interlock pin and poppet spring.
6. Replace necessary parts.

Assembly and Installation

1. Install interlock sleeve and one shifter shaft. Place steel detent

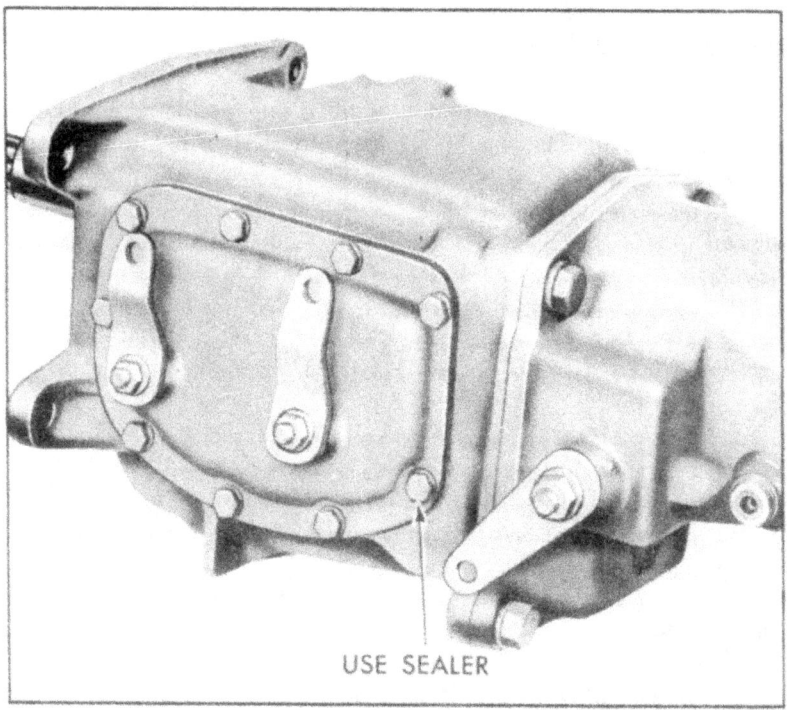

Fig. 58—Sealing Side Cover Assembly

ball into sleeve followed by poppet spring and interlock pin.

2. Start second shifter shaft into position and place second detent ball on poppet spring. Compress ball and spring with screwdriver and push the shifter shaft fully in.

With synchronizers in neutral and shifter forks and levers in place, lower side cover into place. Install attaching bolts (using sealer on the lower right bolt, Fig. 58), and tighten evenly.

4. Remove the filler plug and add 1½ pints of SAE 90 "Multipurpose" Gear Lubricant. This quantity should bring the lubricant level to a point approximately ½" below the filler plug hole.

MAINSHAFT OIL SEAL
Removal

1. Remove nuts and U-bolts retaining rear universal joint trunnion bearings to the drive flange. Lower the rear of the propeller shaft and slide front joint off the mainshaft.

2. Use Tool J-5859 to remove the mainshaft oil seal.

Installation

1. Press new oil seal carefully into place in extension.

NOTE: Do not force the seal against the seat in the extension.

Major Service Operations

REMOVAL FROM VEHICLE

1. Drain lubricant from transmission.

2. Disconnect the speedometer cable from speedometer driven gear-fitting and disconnect shift control rods from the shifter levers at the transmission.

3. Disconnect propeller shaft at the rear universal joint, lower the rear of the shaft and slide to the rear, pulling the front universal joint off the transmission output shaft.

4. Remove the two top transmission to clutch housing cap screws and insert two transmission guide pins in these holes.

5. Remove the two lower transmission to clutch housing cap screws.

6. Slide the transmission straight back on guide pins until the clutch gear is free of splines in the clutch disc.

NOTE: The use of the two guide pins during this operation will support the transmission and prevent damage to the clutch disc through springing.

7. Remove the transmission from under the body.

DISASSEMBLY

1. Remove nine bolts from the transmission side cover and remove cover, gasket and shifter forks.

2. Remove four bolts from front bearing retainer and remove retainer and gasket.

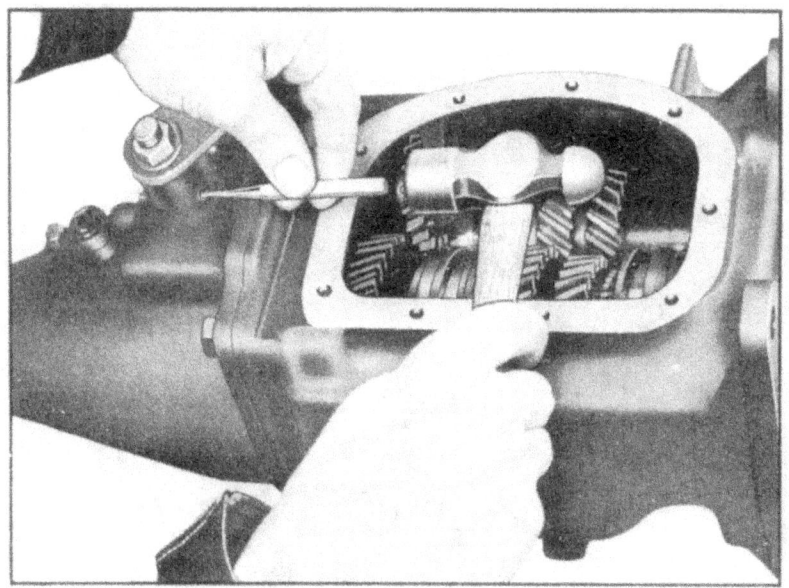

Fig. 59—Removing Reverse Shifter Shaft Retaining Pin

3. Drive retaining pin from reverse shifter lever boss, Fig. 59, and pull shifter shaft out about ⅛". This disengages the reverse shifter fork from reverse gear.

4. Remove five bolts attaching the case extension to the rear bearing retaining plate. Tap extension with soft hammer in a rearward direction to start. When the reverse idler shaft is out as far as it will go, move extension to left so reverse fork clears reverse gear and remove extension and gasket.

5. Rear half of the reverse idler gear and tanged thrust washer may now be removed.

6. Remove speedometer gear and reverse gear. The speedometer gear may be removed with a puller, J-5184, Fig. 60.

7. Remove the self locking bolt attaching the rear bearing retainer to transmission case. Carefully remove the entire mainshaft assembly.

8. Unload needle bearings from clutch gear and remove fourth speed synchronizer blocker ring.

9. Lift front half of reverse idler gear and its thrust washer from case.

10. Remove the clutch gear retaining snap ring, Fig. 61 and

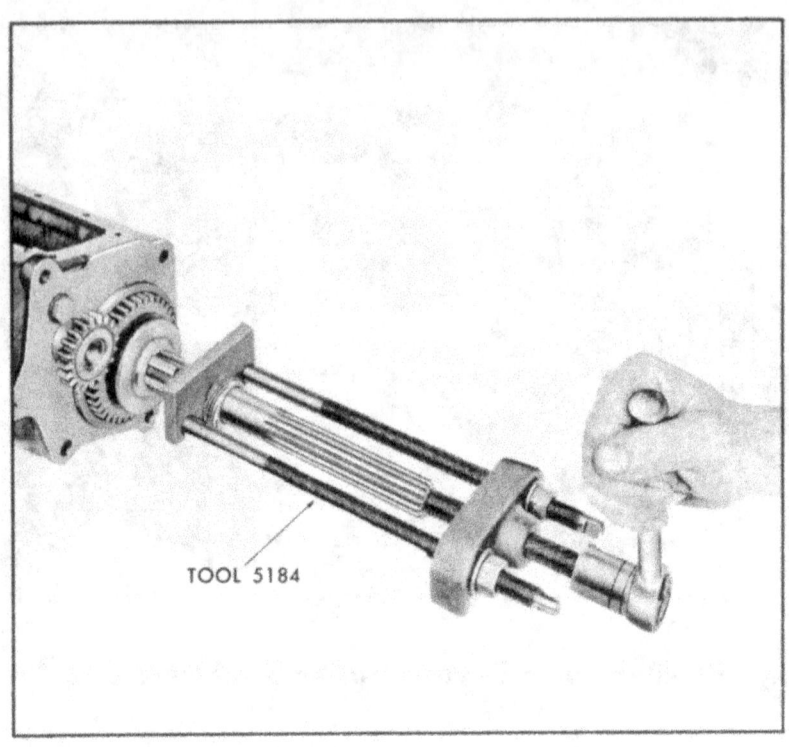

Fig. 60—Removing Speedometer Gear

spacer.

11. Press clutch gear down from front bearing, Fig. 62.
12. From inside case, tap out front bearing and snap ring.
13. From the front of the case, press out the countershaft, Fig. 63. Then remove the countergear and both tanged washers.
14. Remove the 80 rollers, six .050" spacers and roller spacer from countergear.
15. Remove mainshaft front snap ring Fig. 64, third and fourth speed clutch synchronizer assembly, third speed gear and synchronizer blocker ring, second and third speed gear spacer (needle roller bearing), and second speed gear and synchronizer blocker ring.
16. Spread rear bearing retainer snap ring and press off the retainer, Fig. 65.
17. Remove the mainshaft rear snap ring. Support first and second speed synchronizer assembly and press on rear of mainshaft to remove rear bearing, first speed gear thrust washer, first speed gear and synchronizer blocker ring, first and second speed synchronizer assembly and first speed gear sleeve, Fig. 66.

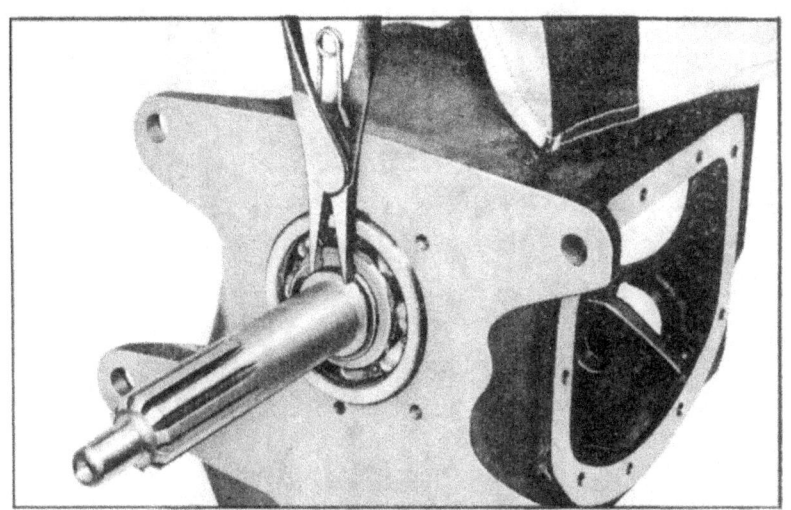

Fig. 61—Removing Clutch Gear Retaining Snap Ring

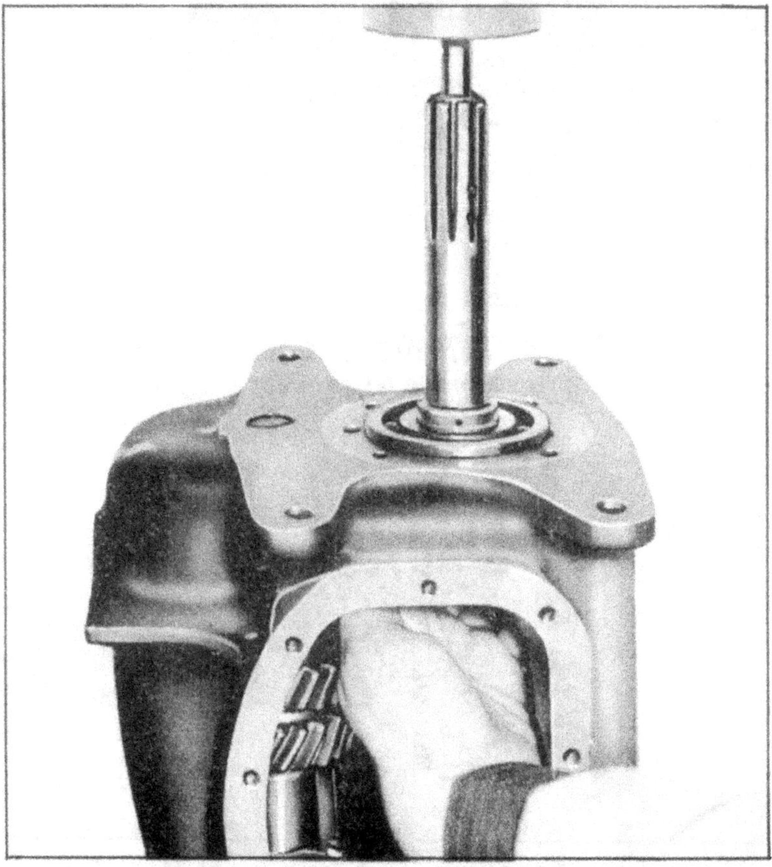

Fig. 62—Removing Clutch Gear

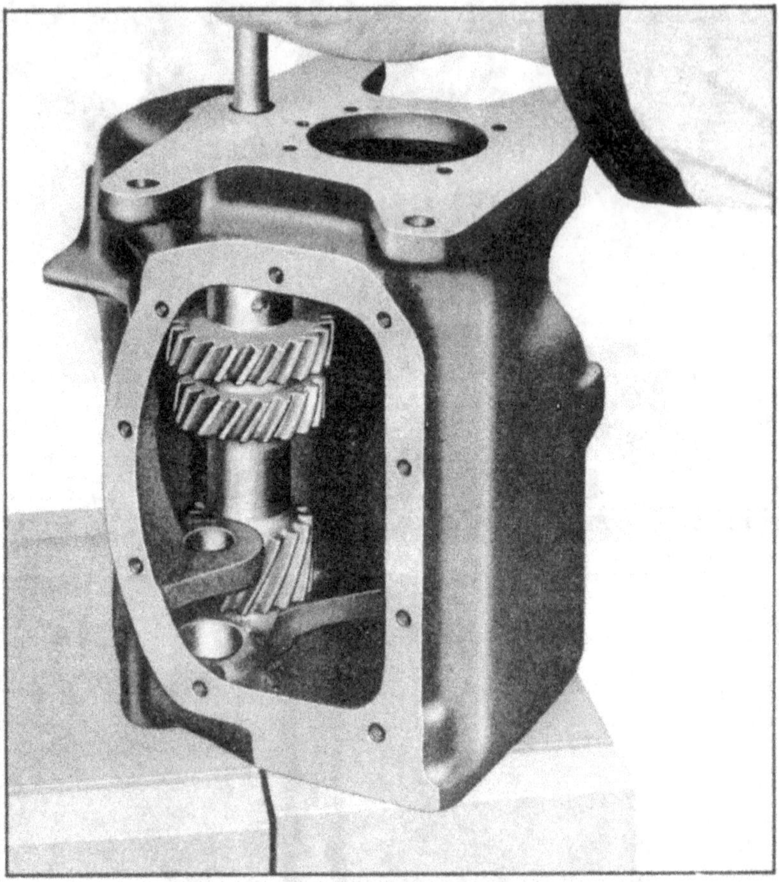

Fig. 63—Removal of Countershaft

Fig. 64—Removing Mainshaft Front Snap Ring

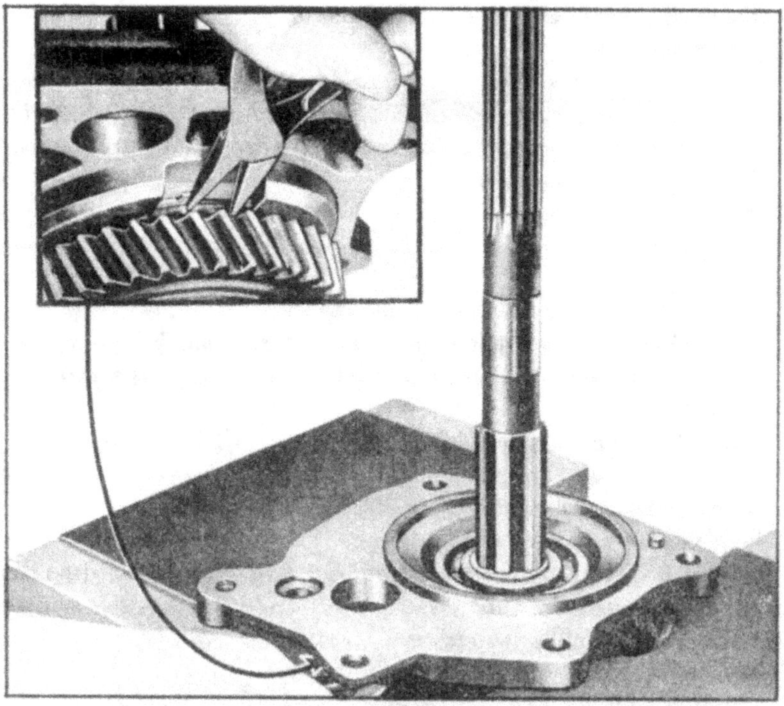

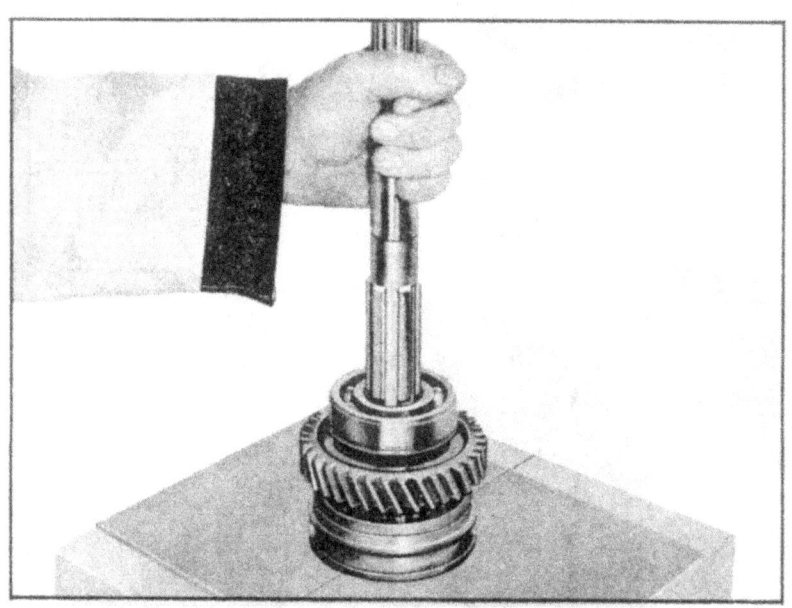

Fig. 65—Removal of Rear Bearing Retainer

Fig. 66—Pressing Out Mainshaft

CLEANING, INSPECTION AND REPAIRS
Transmission Case

Wash the transmission case inside and out with a cleaning solvent and inspect for cracks. Inspect the front face which fits against clutch housing for burrs and if any are present, dress them off with a fine cut mill file.

Front and Rear Bearings

1. Wash the front and rear bearings thoroughly in a cleaning solvent.

2. Blow out bearings with compressed air.

CAUTION: Do not allow the bearings to spin, but turn them slowly by hand. Spinning bearings will damage the race and balls.

3. Make sure the bearings are clean, then lubricate them with light engine oil and check them for roughness. Roughness may be determined by slowly turning the outer race by hand.

Needle Bearings, Spacers and Bushings

All clutch and counter gear needle bearings should be inspected closely and replaced if they show wear. Inspect countershaft at the same time and replace if necessary. Replace all worn bushings.

Gears

Inspect all gears and, if necessary, replace all that are worn or

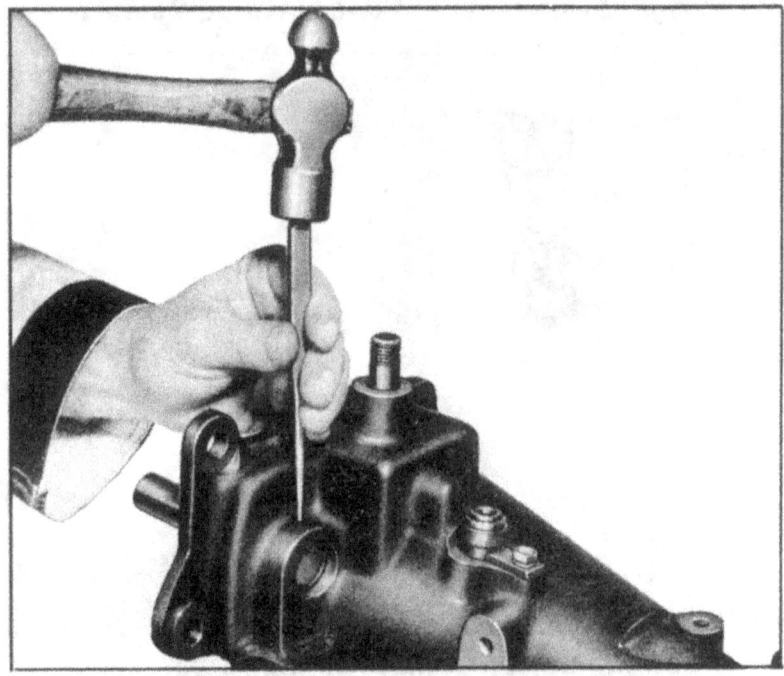

Fig. 67—Driving Out Rear Idler Shaft Lock Pin

damaged.
Rear Idler Shaft
REMOVAL
1. With case extension removed from the transmission, drive the rear idler shaft lock pin into the boss until it falls into the clearance hole in the shaft, Fig. 67.

2. Pry out the extension plug at the end of the shaft and press the shaft from the extension.

INSTALLATION
1. Line up the locking pin hole in the shaft with the hole in the boss. Install idler shaft and lock in place with pin.

2. Install new expansion plug behind idler shaft and use sealer on plug.

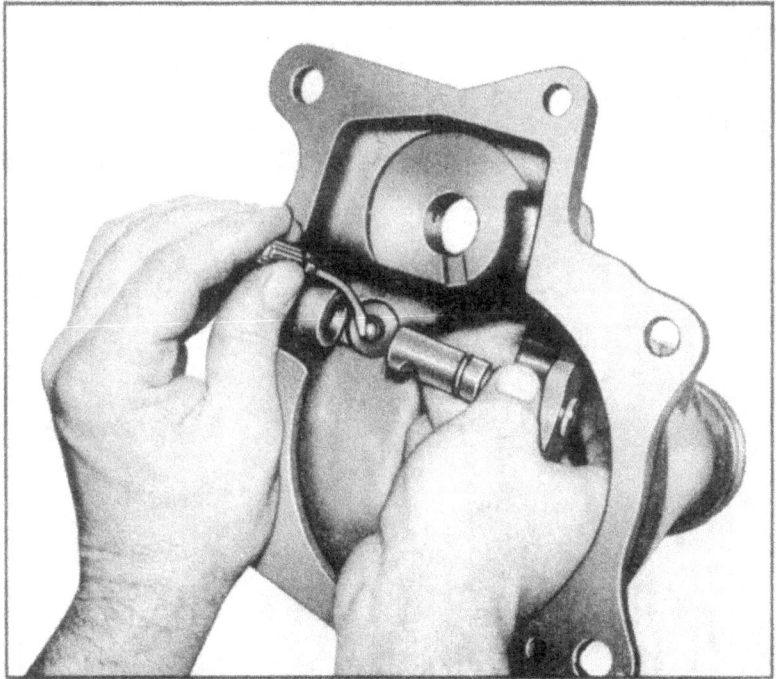

Fig. 68—Replacing Reverse Shifter Shaft

Reverse Shifter Shaft
REMOVAL
1. With case extension removed from transmission the reverse shifter shaft retaining pin will already be removed. (See Step 3 under Disassembly.)

2. Remove shifter fork.

3. Carefully drive shifter shaft into case extension, allowing ball detent to drop into case. Remove shaft and ball detent spring.

INSTALLATION

1. Place ball detent spring into detent spring hole and start reverse shift shaft into hole in boss.

2. Place detent ball on spring and, holding ball down with a suitable tool, Fig. 68, push the shifter shaft into place and turn until the ball drops into place in detent on the shaft detent plate.

3. Install shifter fork.

NOTE: Do not drive the shifter shaft locking pin into place until extension has been installed on the transmission case.

Synchronizer Keys and Energizing Springs

The synchronizer hubs and sliding sleeves are a selected assembly and should be kept together as originally assembled, but the three keys and two energizing springs may be replaced if worn or broken.

REMOVAL

Push the hub from the sliding sleeve. The keys will fall free and the energizing springs may be easily removed.

ASSEMBLY

Place the two energizing springs in position (one on each side

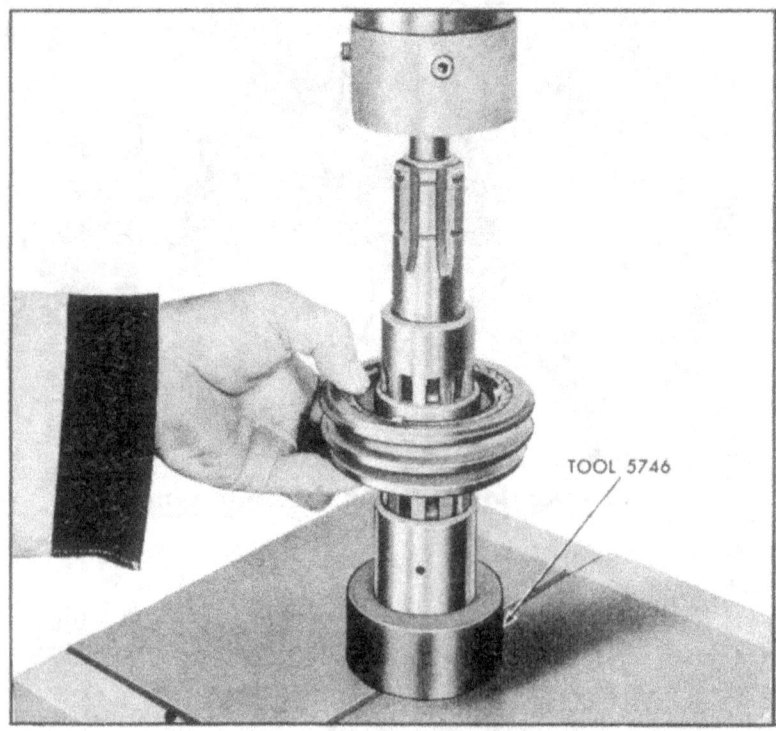

Fig. 69—Installing First Speed Gear Sleeve

of the hub), so that a tanged end of each spring falls into the same keyway in the hub. Place the keys in position and, holding them in place, slide the hub into the sleeve.

ASSEMBLY
Mainshaft Assembly

1. From rear of mainshaft, assemble first and second gear synchronizer assembly to mainshaft (siding clutch sleeve taper toward the rear hub to the front), and, using Tool J-5746, press on the first gear sleeve, Fig. 69.

2. Install the first speed gear synchronizer blocker ring so that the notches in the ring correspond to the keys in the synchronizer hub, Fig. 70.

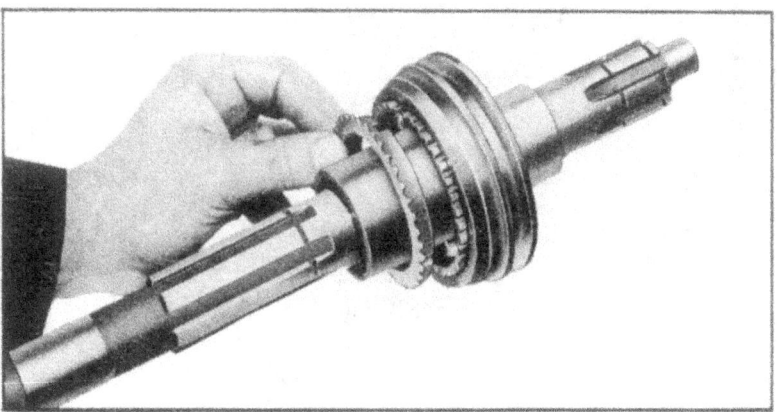

Fig. 70—Installing Blocker Ring

3. Install first speed gear (with hub toward the front) and the first speed gear thrust washer. Make certain that the grooves in the washer are facing the first speed gear.

4. Using Tool J-5746, press on the rear bearing with the snap ring groove toward the front of the transmission, Fig. 71. Firmly seat the bearing against the shoulder on the mainshaft.

5. Choose the correct selective fit snap ring and install it in the groove behind the rear bearing. This snap ring is available in three thicknesses, .087", .093" and .099". Use the ring that will produce from no clearance to .005" clearance between the rear face of the bearing and the front face of the snap ring.

NOTE: Always use new snap rings when reassembling transmission and do not expand the snap ring further than is necessary for assembly.

6. From the front of the mainshaft, install the second speed gear synchronizer blocker ring so that notches in the ring correspond to the keys in the synchronizer hub.

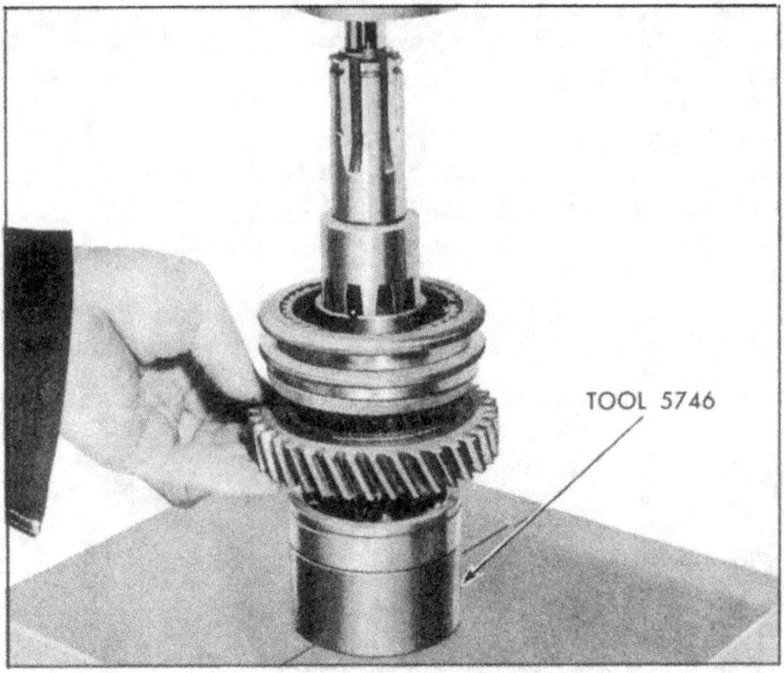

Fig. 71—Installing Rear Bearing

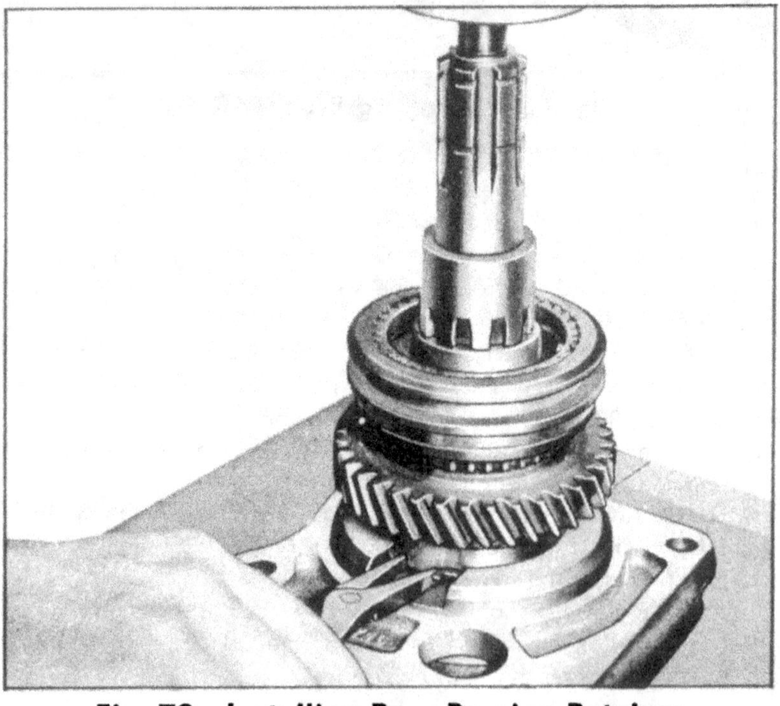

Fig. 72—Installing Rear Bearing Retainer

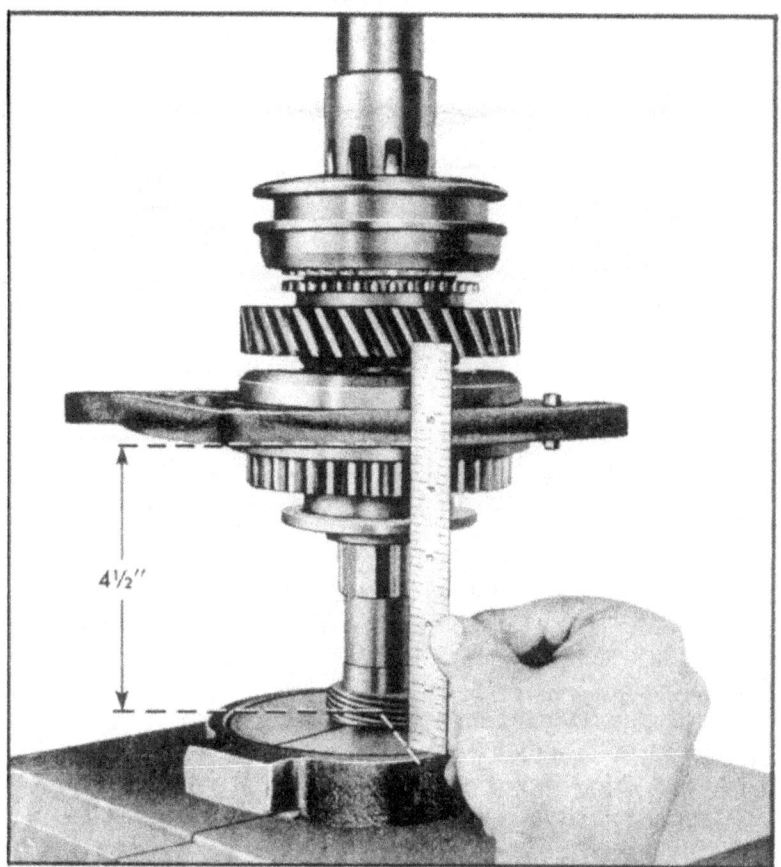

Fig. 73—Installing and Positioning Speedometer Drive Gear

7. Install the second speed gear (with the hub of the gear toward the back of the transmission) and install the second and third speed gear spacer (needle roller bearing).

8. Install the third speed gear (hub to front of transmission) and the third speed gear synchronizer blocker ring (notches to front of transmission).

9. Install the third and fourth speed gear synchronizer assembly (hub and sliding clutch sleeve taper toward the front) making sure that the keys in the synchronizer blocker ring correspond to the notches in the third speed gear synchronizer blocker ring.

10. Install snap ring (.086" to .088" thickness) in the groove in front of the third and fourth speed synchronizer assembly.

11. Install the rear bearing retainer plate, Fig. 72. Spread the snap ring on the plate to allow the snap ring to drop around the rear bearing and press on the end of the mainshaft until the snap

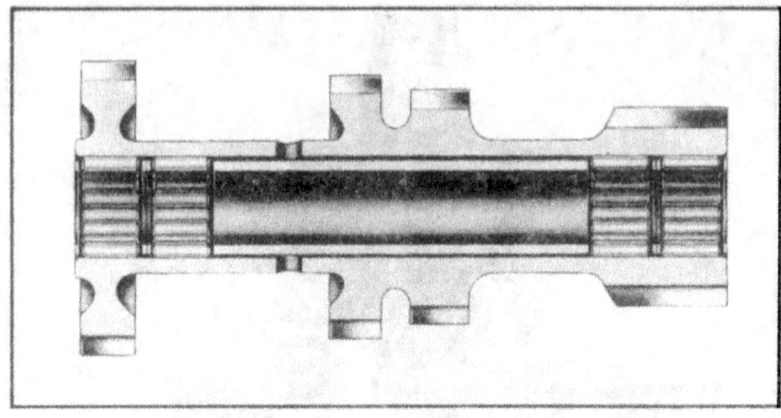

Fig. 74—Cross Section of Countergear Assembly

ring engages the groove in the rear bearing.

12. Install the reverse gear (shift collar to rear).

13. Press speedometer drive gear onto the mainshaft using a suitable press plate. Position the speedometer gear to get a measurement of 4½" from the center of the gear to the flat surface of the rear bearing retainer plate, Fig. 73.

Assembly of mainshaft is now complete.

Countergear Assembly

1. Install roller spacer in countergear.

2. Using heavy grease to retain them, install 20 rollers in the first gear end of the countergear, two .050" spacers, 20 more rollers, and one .050" spacer on top of the second race of rollers. Install in the other end of the countergear, 20 rollers, two .050" spacers, 20 more rollers, and another .050" spacer.

This completes assembly of the countergear, Fig. 74.

Transmission Assembly

1. Rest the transmission case on its side with the side cover opening toward the assembler. Put countergear tanged thrust washers in place, retaining them with heavy grease, making sure that tangs are resting in notches in case.

2. Set countergear in place in bottom of transmission case, making sure that tanged thrust washers are not knocked out of place.

3. Press front bearing onto clutch gear (snap ring groove to front) using Tool J-5746, Fig. 75. Firmly seat bearing against shoulder on clutch gear.

4. Install spacer washer and selective fit snap ring in groove on clutch gear ahead of front bearing. This snap ring is available in three thicknesses, .087", .093" and .099". Use the ring that will

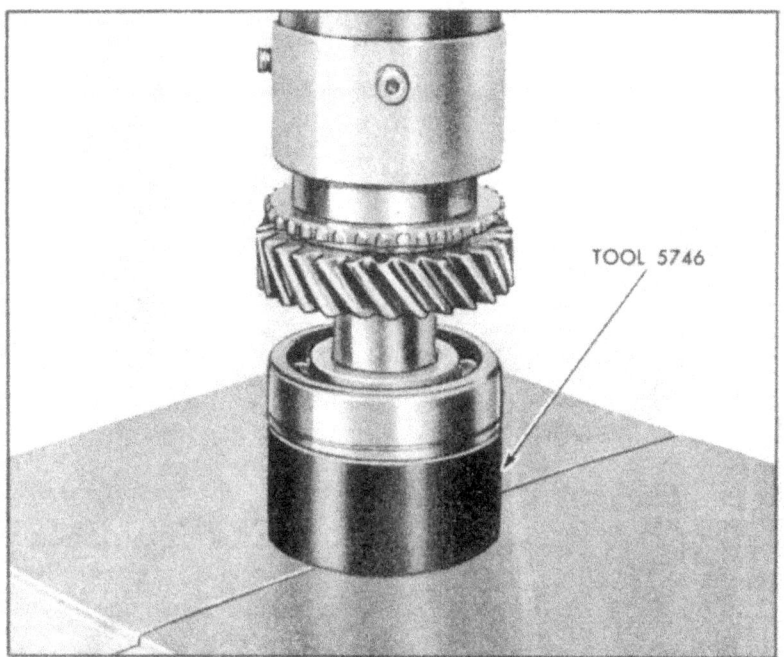

Fig. 75—Installing Front Bearing

produce from no clearance to .005" clearance between the rear face of the snap ring and the front face of the spacer washer.

5. Install the clutch gear and bearing assembly through the side cover opening and into position in transmission front bore. Tap lightly into place, if necessary, with plastic hammer. Place snap ring in groove in front bearing.

6. With the transmission case resting on its front face move countergear into mesh with clutch gear. Be sure thrust washers remain in place. Install woodruff key into end of countershaft and press shaft, Fig. 76, until end of shaft is flush with rear face of transmission case.

7. Attach a dial indicator as shown in Fig. 77, and check the end play of the countergear. End play must not be in excess of .025".

8. Install the fourteen (14) pilot roller bearings into clutch gear, using heavy grease to hold the bearings in place.

9. Using heavy grease, place gasket into position on front face of rear bearing retainer.

10. Install the fourth speed synchronizer blocker ring on clutch gear with the notches toward the rear of the transmission.

11. Position the reverse idler gear thrust washer (untanged) on the machined face of the ear cast in the case for the reverse idler

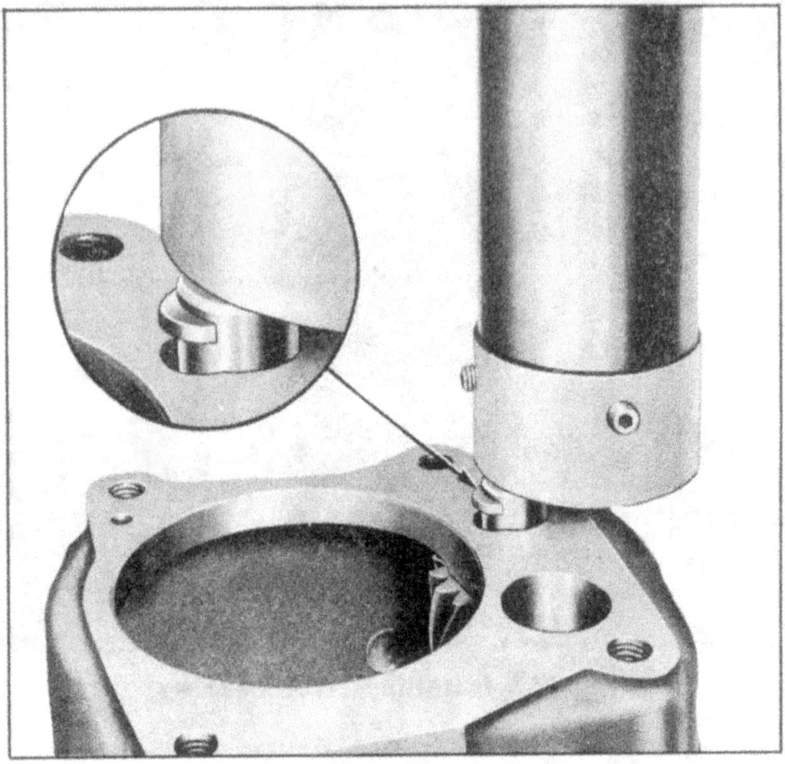

Fig. 76—Installing Countershaft

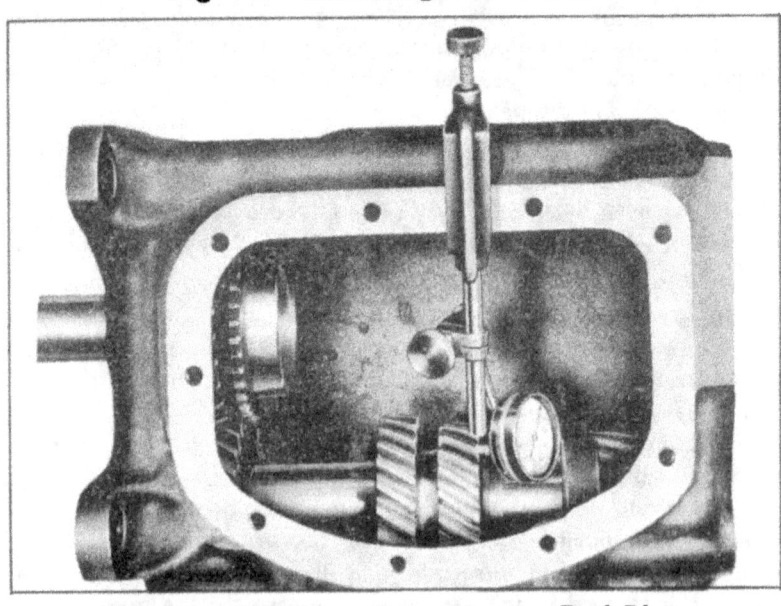

Fig. 77—Checking Countergear End-Play

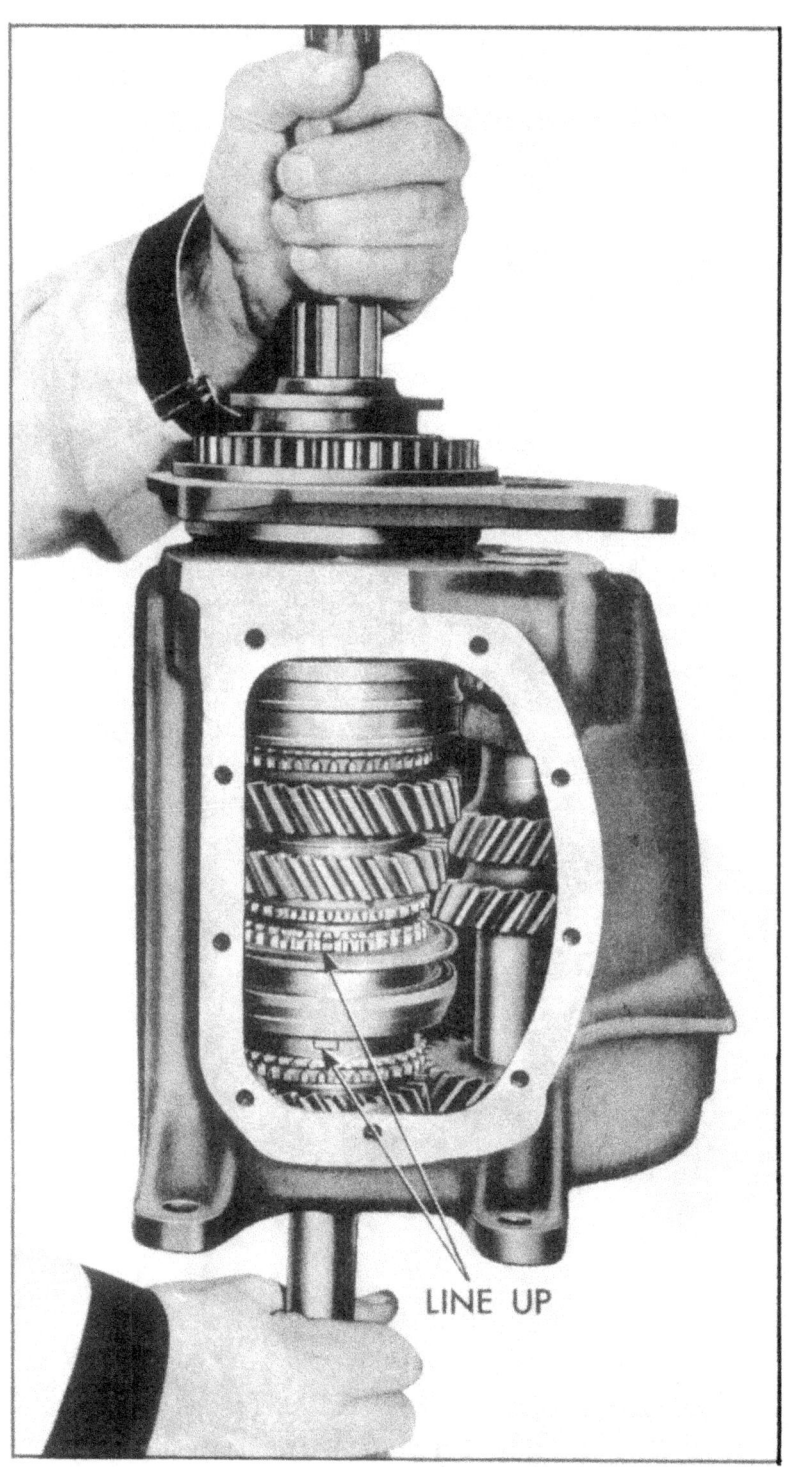

shaft. Position the front half of the reverse idler gear on top of the thrust washer, with the notched hub facing up toward rear of the case.

12. Lower the mainshaft assembly into the case making certain that the notches on the fourth speed synchronizer assembly, Fig. 78.

13. Install the self locking bolt attaching rear bearing retainer to transmission case, Fig. 79. Torque to 20 to 30 foot-pounds.

14. From the rear of the case, insert the rear half of the reverse idler gear, engaging the notches with the portion of the gear within the case.

15. Using heavy grease, place gasket into position on rear face of rear bearing retainer.

16. Using heavy grease, install the remaining thrust washer into place on rear idler shaft making sure that the tang on the thrust washer is in the notch in the idler thrust face of the extension.

17. Place the two synchronizer sleeves in neutral position. Pull reverse shifter shaft to left side of extension and rotate shaft to bring reverse shift fork as far forward in extension as possible. Start to lower the extension onto the transmission case, Fig. 80, while slowly pushing in on the shiter shaft to engage the shift fork with the reverse gear flange. When the fork engages, rotate the shifter shaft to move the reverse gear rearward permitting the extension to slide down onto the transmission case.

18. Install 3 extension and retainer to case attaching bolts

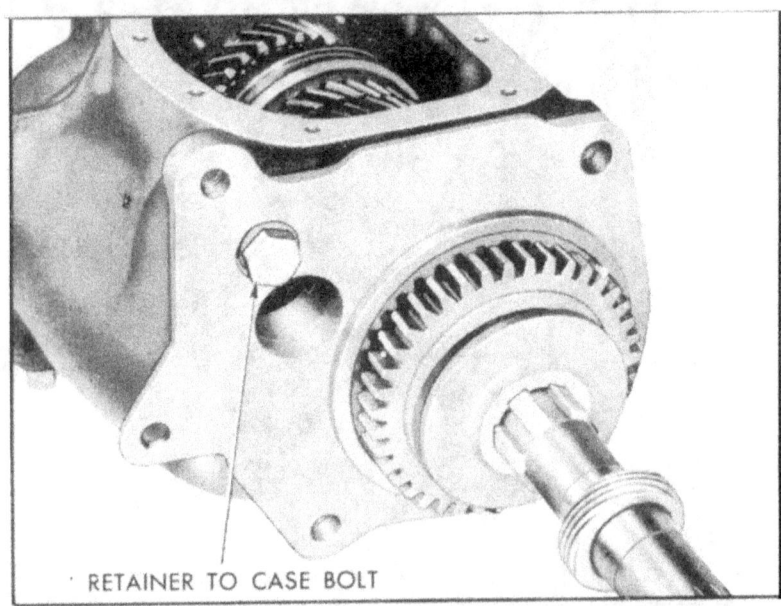

· RETAINER TO CASE BOLT

Fig. 79—Bearing Retainer to Transmission Bolt

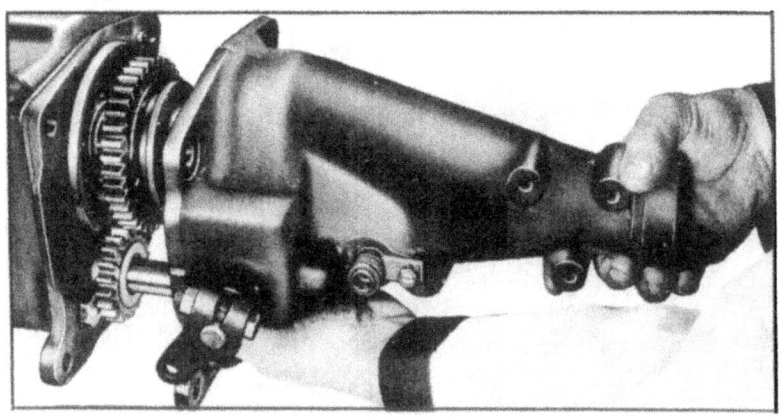

Fig. 80—Installing Case Extension to Transmission Case

(Torque to 35 to 45 foot-pounds), and 2 extension retainer attaching bolts (Torque to 20 to 30 foot-pounds). Use suitable sealer on the lower right attaching bolt as viewed from rear, Fig. 81.

19. Push or pull reverse shifter shaft to line up groove in the shaft with the holes in the boss and drive in the locking pin. Install shifter lever.

20. Install the front bearing retainer, gasket and four attaching bolts using a suitable sealer on bolts. Torque to 15 to 20 foot-pounds.

21. Install a shifter fork in each synchronizer.

22. Place both synchronizers in neutral; install side cover gasket and carefully lower side cover into place. Install attaching bolts and tighten evenly to avoid side cover distortion. Use suitable sealer when installing the lower right bolt.

NOTE: The transmission should "overshift" slightly in all ranges.

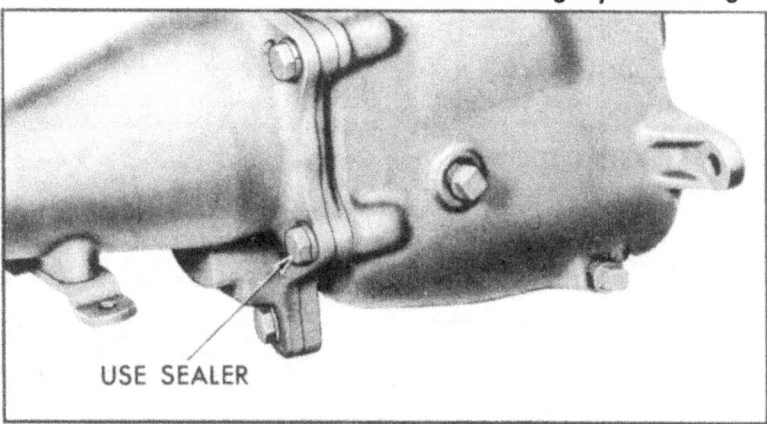

Fig. 81—Sealing Case Extension Attaching Bolt

Installation In Vehicle

1. Install guide pin in upper right transmission-to-clutch housing bolt hole for alignment and place transmission on guide pin. Rotate transmission as necessary, start clutch gear shaft into clutch disc and slide transmission forward.

2. Install the two lower transmission mounting bolts and lockwashers and tighten securely. Remove guide pin and install upper mounting bolts and lockwashers and tighten securely.

3. Install propeller shaft. Align yokes and install U-bolts and nuts which retain rear trunnion bearings to pinion flange and tighten securely.

4. Connect shifter lever rods at the transmission.

5. Check and adjust linkage.

6. Connect speedometer cable to driven gear and tighten securely.

7. Remove filler plug and add 1½ pts. of SAE 90 "Multi-purpose Gear Lubricant". Lubricant level should be approximately ½" below the filler plug hole.

TROUBLES AND REMEDIES

Symptom and Probable Cause — **Probable Remedy**

Shifts hard
1. Clutch not releasing engine or slow to release.
2. Shift linkage binding or selector not properly adjusted.

    1. Adjust or repair clutch.
    2. Free up and adjust as required.

Shifts hard on downshift
1. Downshifting at too high an engine speed.

    1. Shifting into low gear above 45 MPH and second above 65 MPH causes extra work for synchronizers and will require extra time or more force on lever to complete. There is also danger of over-speeding the engine if low or second is used at high car speeds.

Disengages from gear
1. Clutch housing misaligned with engine.
2. Does not fully engage.
3. Clutching teeth worn or defective and or clutch hub spline worn.

    1. Shim transmission or replace clutch housing.
    2. Check linkage for interference. Adjust or replace damaged shift linkage.
    3. Replace gear, clutch sleeve and clutch hub.

Noisy
1. Gears worn, scored or broken.
2. Bearing dirty, worn.
3. Interference of clutch sleeve with countergear of idler gear.

    1. Replace gears.
    2. Flush transmission with kerosene. If noise is still present, replace bearings and examine gears as above.
    3. Replace worn shift forks, countergear, and idler gear thrust washers to restore gears and clutch sleeve to proper location. Examine thrust faces on these gears for wear. Replace if worn excessively.

Positraction Rear Axle

Chevrolet's Positraction Rear Axle available optionally on Corvettes provides built-in safety through controlled driving power. It keeps delivering safe, managed torque where it will do the most good, always adjusting automatically to conditions of the road.

The conventional rear axle divides the torque equally between both driving wheels and will always drive the wheel which is easiest to turn. This is a definite disadvantage under conditions of driving where the traction of one wheel is limited.

The main purpose of the Positraction rear axle is to overcome this limitation and provide many times the torque of the slipping wheel to the driving wheel resulting in improved operation under all driving conditions.

In the Positraction rear axle Fig. 82, engine power is trans-

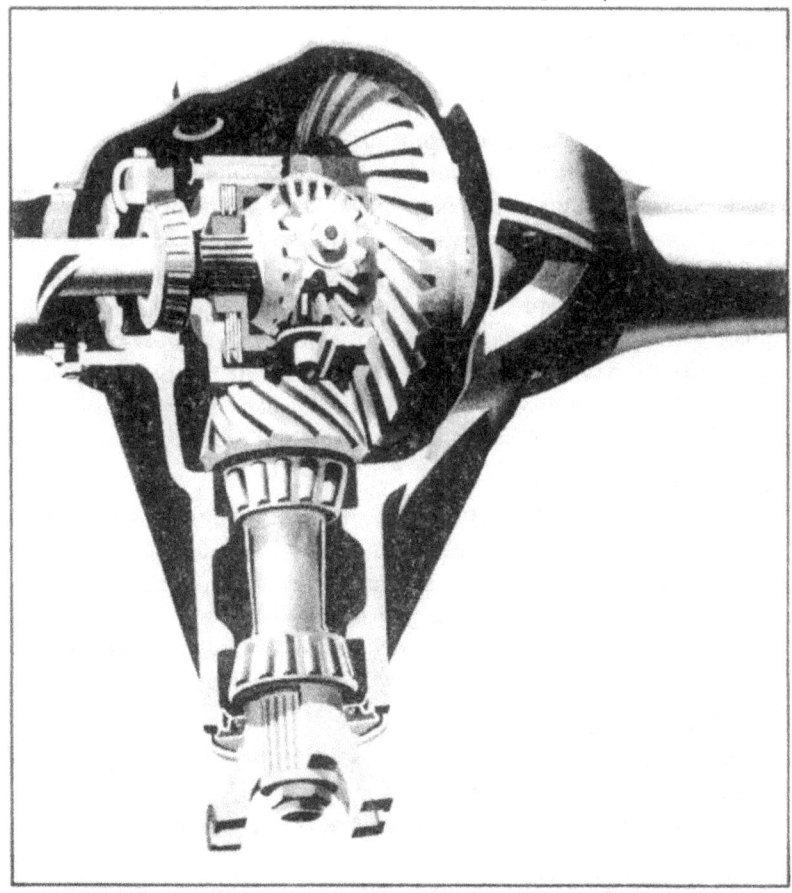

Fig. 82—Positraction Rear Axle, Cross-Section

mitted from the ring gear to the differential case. The driving force couses cross pins to move up the ramps of cam surfaces applying a load to the clutches. This, in effect, locks the axle shafts in normal, straight ahead driving, thus preventing momentary spinning of the wheels when leaving the road or when encountering poor traction. The division of torque between axle shafts varies in accordance with the traction of each rear wheel. When cornering, however, the faster turning outer wheel relieves the load from the clutch surfaces so that wear is reduced to a minimum and the action is effectively that of a conventional rear axle. The unit is available in three ratios; 3.70:1, 4.11.1 and 4.56:1.

The Positraction rear axle is available as a factory option and the differential assembly is also available as a parts package for field installations. Adjustments are the same as for the conventional unit.

There are two types of Positraction units used on Corvettes:

1957, 1958, 1959 and Early Production 1960

The early production 1960 vehicles are equipped with a unit similar to the 1957-59 type except for a change in the friction plates. The change consists of the substitution of a Belleville or "dished" plate for each outboard friction plate. Service kits for 1957-1959 four plate units contain the Belleville plate which can be installed in all four plate stack Corvette Positraction units. The installation of the Belleville plate changes the clearance requirements of the pinion mate shaft to the "V" notch in the case. Those units with the Belleville conversion require 0 clearance at this point. Original four plate stack units without the Belleville plate retain the necessity for the clearances outlined in the following procedures.

Later Production 1960

The later production, 1960 Corvettes are equipped with a Positraction unit incorporating two friction discs and two friction plates plus a Belleville plate. As in the converted early models, the mate shaft-to-"Vee" clearance is no longer required.

The case screws on this unit are ⅜ x 24 left hand thread, instead of ⅜ x 16 right hand thread used on the early units.

COMPLAINT DIAGNOSIS

Improper operation of the Positraction differential is generally indicated in one of three ways:

1. Improper drive with one wheel having less traction.
2. Differential chatter.
3. Excessive backlash or lost motion in the vehicle driveline.

(1) Improper Drive With One Wheel Having Less Traction.

Under some operating conditions where one rear wheel is on excessively slippery surface and the opposite wheel is on a good traction surface, it may be necessary to lightly apply the parking brake (usually three or four notches) to produce enough resistance to the spinning wheel to cause axle lock-up.

Lock-up is independent of acceleration; therefore, light throttle application on starting is recommended to provide maximum traction by preventing "break away" of the non-slipping wheel.

The Positraction unit can be effectively tested for correct operation by placing one rear wheel on good dry pavement and the other on ice, mud, grease, etc.

It can easily be determined whether or not the non-slipping wheel is providing pulling power. The procedure can then be repeated with the opposite wheel on the dry and slippery surface.

CAUTION: The warning posted in the luggage compartment regarding operation of the unit while on a jack should not be interpreted as a means of testing. Its only intention is to point out that a possibility does exist that the axle could lock-up under certain conditions and force the vehicle off the jack.

(2) Differential Chatter.

Differential chatter is due to the wrong lubricant being used in the axle. The special lubricant available thru Chevrolet Dealers must always be used for this unit. In some cases, the slightest bit of contamination of the lubricant by any foreign lubricant is enough to cause considerable chatter.

(3) Excessive Backlash

Driveline backlash is inherently more noticeable with Positraction axles because of the greater looseness required between the clutch plates and side gears to insure sufficient clearance for full release of the clutches during coast. The backlash results in a slight "clunk" as the driveline goes from drive to coast or from coast to drive.

To determine if Positraction backlash is abnormal, proceed as follows:

1. Remove one rear wheel, then tighten brake adjustment on the opposite rear wheel until it is fully locked.
2. Wedge the propeller shaft to hold it stationary.
3. On the side with the wheel removed, turn the brake drum forward until it stops. Mark both the brake drum and flange plate while holding drum in this position.
4. Turn brake drum its full limit rearward and place a second mark on the brake drum opposite the mark on the flange plate.

5. Measure distance between marks on the brake drum. Distance between marks should not be more than ½-inch; otherwise rear axle backlash is considered excessive.

Backlash found by the preceding check is confined to the rear axle as driveline and transmission backlash was eliminated by blocking the propeller shaft. If backlash is excessive, remove the Positraction differential, check for worn or scored parts, and replace as necessary, paying particular attention to the mate shaft "V" notch clearance.

REMOVAL

1. Remove axle shafts from car as outlined in Section 4 of the 1957 Chevrolet Passenger Car Shop Manual, or Section 5 of the 1958 manual.

NOTE: Corvettes equipped with Positraction have a 1957 Passenger Car type rear axle shaft bearing. All other Corvettes have a construction similar to the 1954 Chevrolet Passenger Car Rear Axle Shaft Bearing.

2. Remove the carrier from under the car.
3. Remove the differential bearing caps. Mark each cap for reassembly. Mark the bearing adjustment nut for reasonably. Keep bearing cups with the bearings if they are reusable; replace if worn or damaged.

Fig. 83—Checking Mate Shaft Clearance

DISASSEMBLY

Before disassembly, check the clearance between the pinion mate shaft "V" and the cam surface in the case This must be done using shim stock or feeler gauges under both sides of the "V" on both ends of the pinion mate shaft at the same time. Note that this involves placing feeler gages at four positions (Fig. 83). As closely as possible, the same thickness feeler gage must be used at all four positions. The clearance of the maximum feeler thickness at each of the four positions on original 1957 to 1959 units without Belleville plate should not exceed .015" (Fig. 84). Both pinion mate shafts must be checked in this manner.

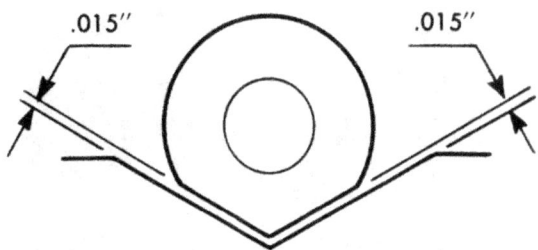

MAXIMUM PERMISSABLE SHIM THICKNESS AT <u>BOTH ENDS</u> OF THE PIN AT THE SAME TIME

Fig. 84—Pinion Mate Shaft Clearance

NOTE: On 1957 to 1959 units with Belleville conversion, and on all 1960 units, there should be no clearance (metal to metal).

If a clearance of more than .015" on 1957, 1958 and 1959 units without Belleville (dished) plate, or zero on converted and 1960 units is found, the unit should be disassembled as follows:

NOTE: If clearance is found to be excessive on the 1957 to 1959 original units. installation of the Belleville plate conversion is suggested.

1. Check that the differential case halves are marked with a number or letter to aid aligning the case when assembling. If not, scribe an alignment mark as shown in Fig. 85.

2. With unit on bench, remove eight bolts securing the end case to the ring gear case.

NOTE: Bolts used to assemble 1960 units with the number 22-159X or 22158X stamped on end case are left hand thread. All others are right hand.

3. Remove end case.

4. Remove clutch plates from side gear retainer and note the re-

lation of these clutch plates.

5. Remove side gear retainer and side gear.
6. Remove pinion mate shafts and gears.
7. Remove remaining side gear, side gear retainer and clutch plates.

Fig. 85—Differential Case Alignment Marks

CLEANING AND INSPECTION

All parts, before reassembly, must be clean and free from all foreign substance. All parts must be inspected. See that there are no worn, cracked or distorted clutch plates. All parts must be free of nicks, burrs, or any imperfections that will reduce the efficiency of operation of this unit. Lubricate all parts before assembly, using the special lubricant.

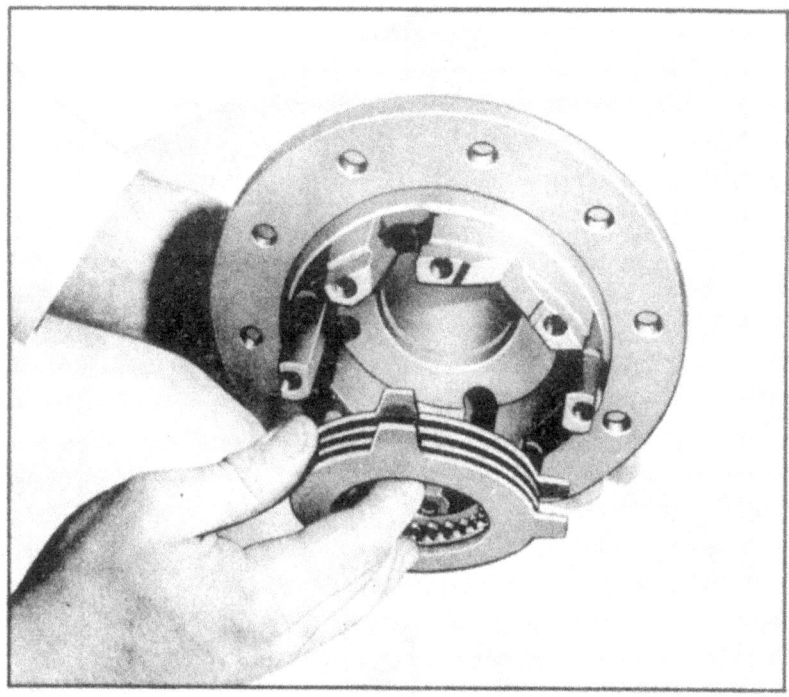

Fig. 86—Installing Clutch Plates

ASSEMBLY

1. Hold ring gear half of case on its side, Fig. 86. Install side gear retainer and clutch plates as follows.

FOUR STACK UNITS WITH BELLEVILLE PLATE (Fig. 87)

A. Belleville type (dished) plate positioned so concave side rests against case.

B. Two internally splined plates.

C. Eared clutch plate (flat plate) against side gear ring.

NOTE: Clutch stack may be varied for certain driving conditions. See "Clutch Stack Arrangement."

FIVE STACK UNITS (Fig. 88)

A. .061/.059 friction plate against case.
B. Friction disc.
C. .096/.094 Belleville friction plate.
D. Friction disc.
E. .096/.094 friction plate.

Make sure the side gear retainer will rotate with a slight drag when in the case. Repeat for opposite side.

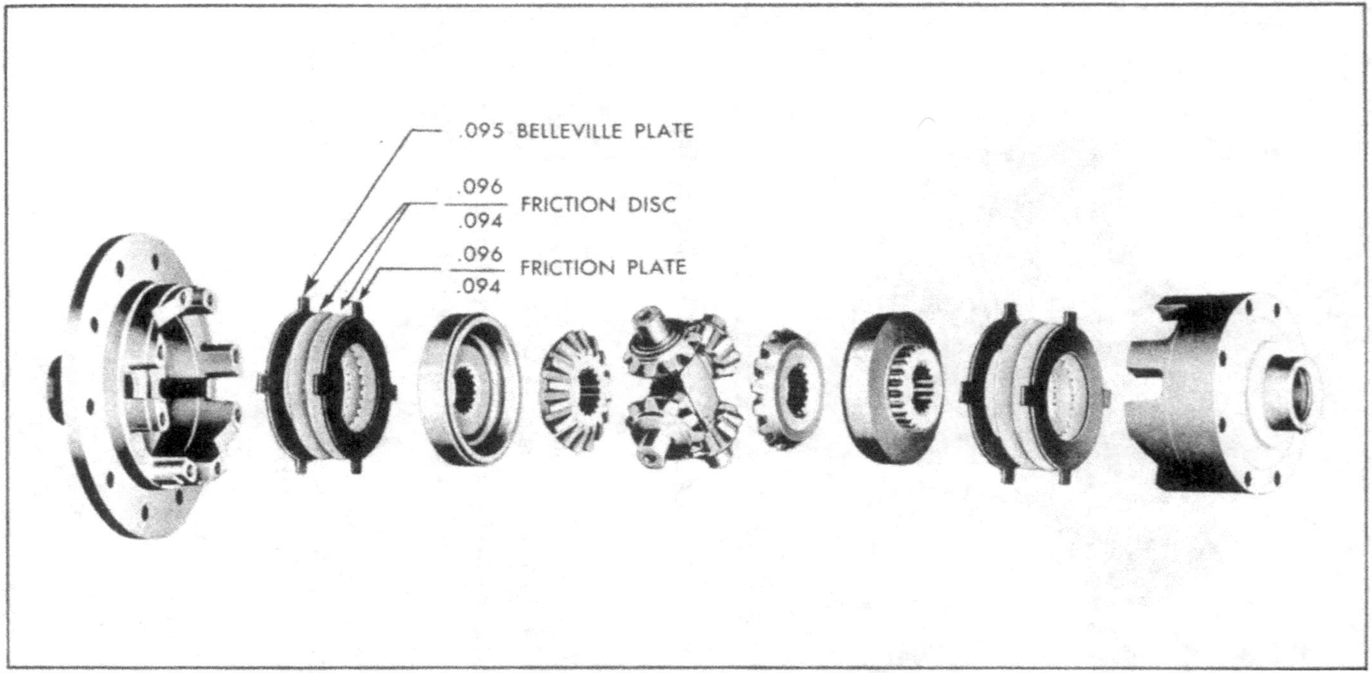

.095 BELLEVILLE PLATE
.096 FRICTION DISC
.094
.096 FRICTION PLATE
.094

Fig. 87—Four Stack Plate Arrangement

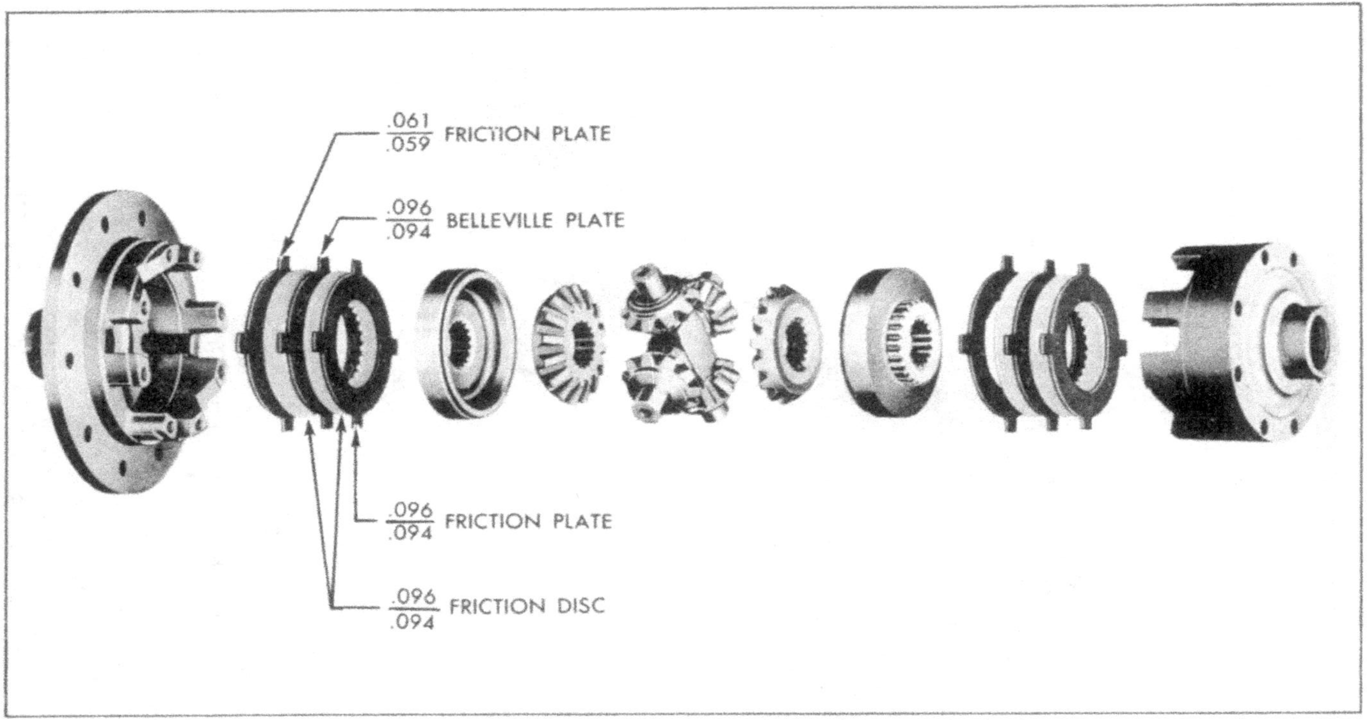

.061 / .059 FRICTION PLATE

.096 / .094 BELLEVILLE PLATE

.096 / .094 FRICTION PLATE

.096 / .094 FRICTION DISC

Fig. 88—Five Stack Plate Arrangement

2. Install side gear on ring gear case half.

3. With the ring gear case half of the differential case in a vertical position, install one mate shaft and gears as shown in Fig. 89. Make certain that notch in shaft is up, and shaft is 90° from "V" notches in case.

4. Install remaining shaft and gears over the first with the center notch down, as shown in Fig. 90.

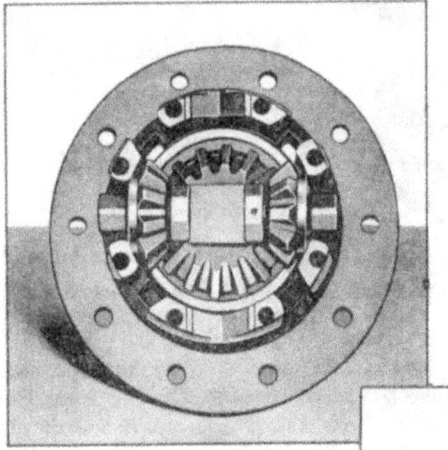

Fig. 89—Installing Mate Shaft

Fig. 90—Pinion and Side Gear Installation

5. Install side gear in other half of case.

6. Hold the remaining end case through the bearing trunnion and install it on the ring gear flange half as shown in Fig. 91.
Make certain that identification marks are in alignment.

7. Tighten eight attaching bolts evenly to 35-45 pounds torque to avoid distortion to case assembly. On some units, it will be necessary to turn bolts until bolt head flats are tangent to O.D. of case (Fig. 83) in order to install ring gear.

8. Check the clearance between each pinion mate shaft and the "V" of the case as follows:

Converted units and 1960 production units require a "no clearance" metal to metal contact between mate shafts and case "V" notches.

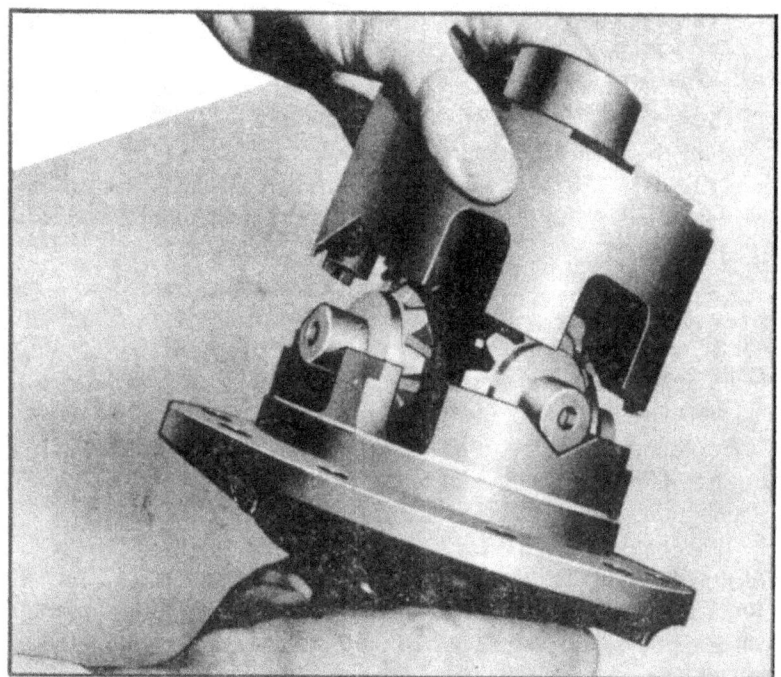

Fig. 91—Installing Differential Case Cover

If clearance exists in these units, disassemble and check friction plates and discs for correct thickness and position. Also examine cases and internally splined drums for excessive wear.

9. Check for clutch plate freedom on each side by using a discarded and cut-off axle shaft. The shaft should turn firmly but should not lock.

Installation

1. Install the Positraction differential with the ring gear and bearings assembled as outlined in Section 4 of the 1957 Chevrolet Passenger Car Shop Manual or Section 5 of the 1958 Manual for standard differential.

2. Use the same instructions and specifications for ring gear bolts, bearing cap bolts, backlash, and bearing preload as used for the standard differential.

NOTE: Make sure the spline end of the axle shaft does not interfere with the pinion mate shafts. This is best determined by measurment. Use a steel tape, and with the aid of a flashlight, measure from the bottom of the axle shaft bearing bore to the pinion mate shafts. Then measure the axle shafts from the corresponding point of the bearing to the end of the spline. The minimum clearance required is 1/8 of an inch. Grind off the spline end of the axle shaft if it is too long Check the other axle shaft in the same manner.

WARNING: Do not spin wheels with one elevated as it is possible to have sufficient driving load due to friction, etc to actuate the Positraction unit and cause the car to move.

CAUTION: Use only Special Hypoid gear lube available through parts under GM Part Number 3758791 for filling Positraction Rear Axles.

OPTIONAL CLUTCH STACK ARRANGEMENT

FOUR STACK UNITS ONLY

Two clutch stack arrangements can be made as shown in Fig. 92 to tailor axle operation to owner's preference on four stack units.

For general service, the arrangement used in production, with the two internally splined plates placed between the externally tanged plate and the Belleville plate (Belleville plate against case), provides ample traction. In cases where the owner desires maximum traction for off-highway operation or heavy duty operation, the clutch plates should be stacked alternately starting with an internally splined friction disc against the differential case, followed by the Belleville plate. However, owners should be cautioned that in order to obtain the benefits of the maximum traction arrangement, tire squeal on turns and a tendency toward oversteer is to be expected.

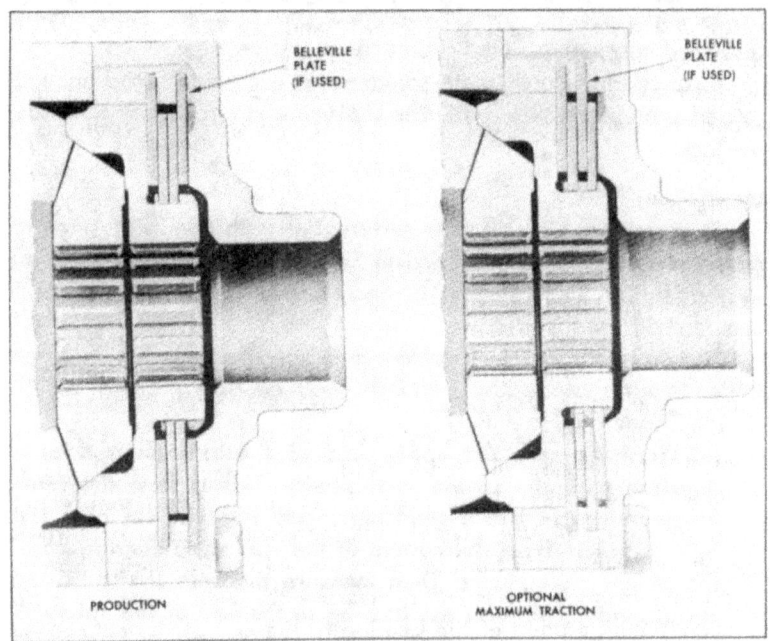

Fig. 92—Clutch Stack Arrangement

Fuel Injection

INTRODUCTION

The following pages provide theory of operation and maintenance procedures for all Chevrolet fuel injection units which have been used since their introduction in 1957.

The theory of operation and specific overhaul procedures cover the 7014800 units. This injection unit is the simplest unit of the various models that have been used. An undertanding of the functions of the individual components is a "must" for practically all diagnosis. Once the 7014800 unit is understood, the refinements of manufacture included in later units are easily understood and are described briefly.

For repair procedures, only the 7014800 is fully covered, but the differences between the 7014900 unit (which is the basis of all later units except 7017300 and 7300 R units) and this original unit are fully described and illustrated. Actually, the physical differences

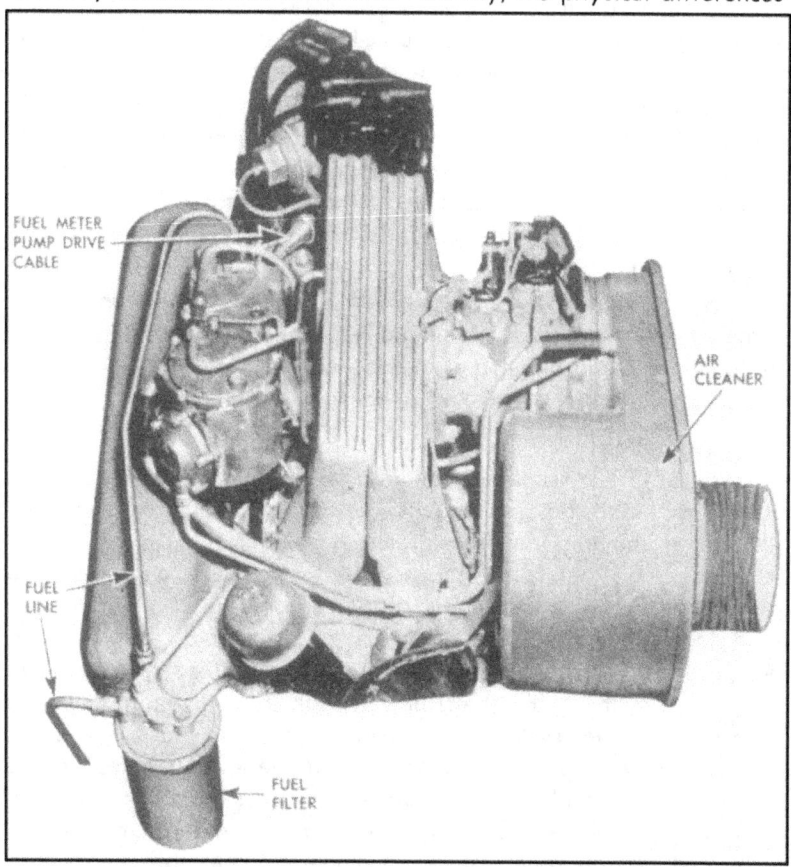

Fig. 93—Fuel Injection Installed on Engine

are so slight that even a complete novice should not encounter any confusion working from the 7014800 procedures.

Fuel flow recalibration, which must be performed after any fuel meter overhaul, is completely described and data for all units ever produced by Chevrolet is listed at the end of this section.

As all units produced to date by Chevrolet are basically modifications of either the 7014800 or 7014900 units, a brief description of each later unit will be found following the complete procedures for the 7014800 unit. This capsule information will tell you for example, that a 7017200 or 7250 unit operates and is repaired exactly like a 7014900 unit as its primary difference is only that a siphon-breaker has been incorporated into the fuel meter casting. Knowing this and understanding the slight differences between the 4800 and 4900 units, the unit can then be diagnosed and repaired by following the procedures provided.

ADVANTAGES OF FUEL INJECTION

Fuel injection has been a Chevrolet production option on Corvette and passenger car 283-cubic-inch V-8 engines since 1957 (fig. 93.). Used in conjunction with hydraulic valve lifters and 9½--to-1 compression ratio cylinder heads, the engine produces 250 hp. @ 5000 rpm (275 hp for 1960) whereas when combined with a special camshaft, mechanical valve lifters, and high compression ratio cylinder heads, the rating is increased to 290 horsepower @ 6200 rpm, (283 hp for 1957, 290 hp for 1958 and 1959, and 315 for 1960).

The potentialities of fuel injection are based on elimination of some of the more apparent limitations of carburetor equipped engines, these being equal fuel distribution, air supply, mixture heating, and horsepower. Let's examine these one at a time.

Fuel Distribution

One of the most important advantages of fuel injection is its ability to divide the fuel equally between all cylinders. From the illustration showing an exaggerated 8-cylinder manifold (fig. 94), it can be seen that when the manifold carries fuel/air mixture to a variety of sizes and lengths of passages, it is very difficult to feed each cylinder in equal amounts. As a matter of fact, it would not be uncommon to have 15% difference in fuel/air ratio between the leanest cylinder and the richest cylinder of a given engine with a carbureted fuel system. The main difficulty is that air is quite willing to flow around corners and through various shaped passages but the fuel, being heavier, is bothered by obstructions, curves, etc. In fuel injection fuel can be fed under pressure through a set of calibrated nozzles, one for each cylinder so that the fuel charge for each cylinder is virtually equal.

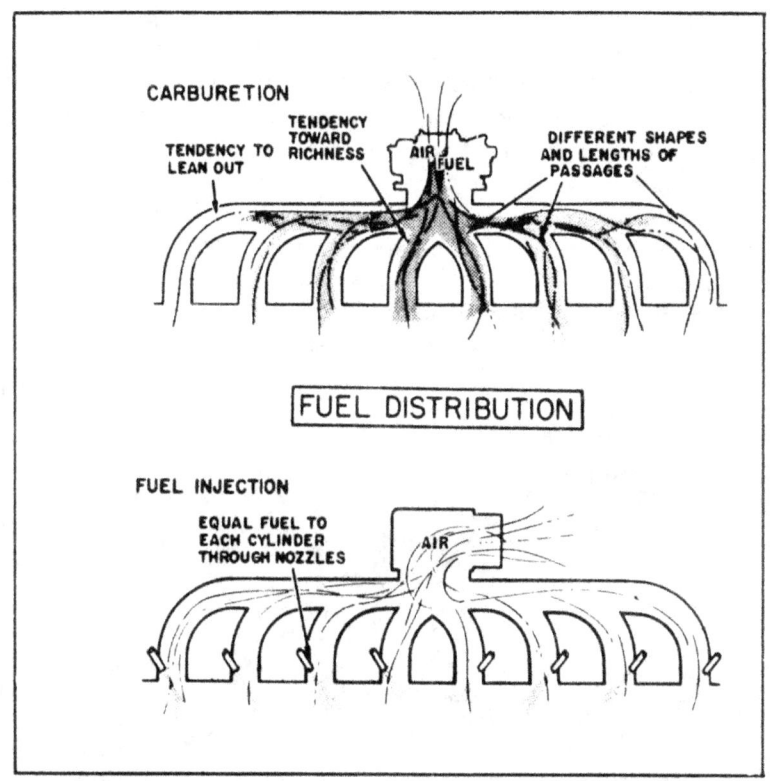

Fig. 94—Fuel Distribution Comparison Diagram

You can see that in the carbureted system it would be necessary to supply mixtures rich enough so that no cylinders were too lean, which means that there would be waste in the cylinders which were already rich enough. The engine equipped with fuel injection can often be run as much as 10% leaner than it would have to be with a carburetor and manifold.

Air Flow

In a carbureted fuel system, the intake manifold must strike a happy medium between low and high speed requirements (fig. 95). At idle, for instance, air flow is very slight and in order to keep the gasoline mixed with the air it is necessary to have small passages to keep up the air velocity. On the other hand, when power is required, we would like to have as big a manifold passage as possible to allow maximum breathing of the engine. Naturally, to supply both of these requirements, the manifold must be compromised between small and large passages which results in passages of medium size which limit both the low and high speed performance, but provide enough of each to get by.

In the case of fuel injection, the manifold (fig. 95) does not have to carry a fuel/air mixture and, therefore, can be designed to give the best breathing possible. In fact, the manifold can be made to actually supercharge the engine at certain speeds. This is done by having a ram pipe for each cylinder so that the air on its way to the cylinder will be traveling in a long column, while the valve is open and air is entering the cylinder, the air flow gets quite a lot of momentum in the ram pipe. As the piston reaches bottom dead center and starts back up, air will continue to flow into the cylinder because of air velocity in the ram pipe. At the particular engine speed where the valve just closes as the air stops flowing,

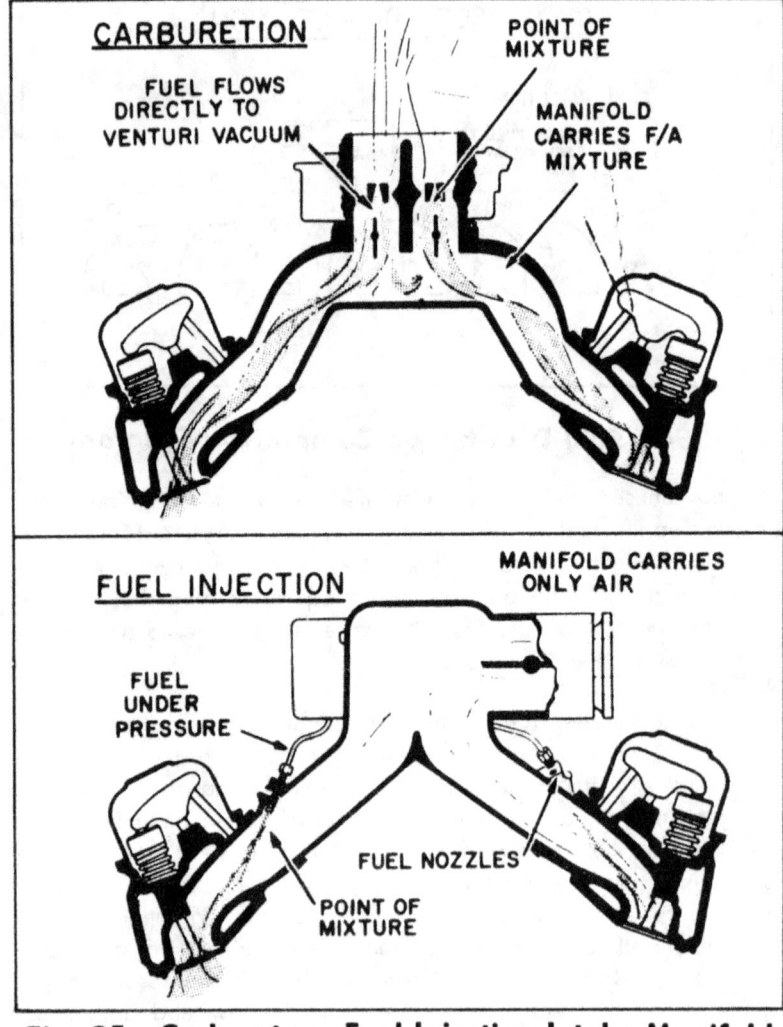

Fig. 95—Carburetor—Fuel Injection Intake Manifold

an extra charge of air has been trapped in the cylinder. This effect is called dynamic super charging. By design of the ram tubes, a particular engine speed can be picked for this effect to occur and quite a boost results at that particular point.

Mixture Heating

Mixture heating is a fuel distribution problem in many respects. First, it is necessary to heat the carburetor from the intake manifold to assist initial fuel vaporization and to overcome fuel condensation from the mixture striking cold surfaces of the intake manifold during delivery to the combustion chambers. However, this same heat creates carburetor problems because the heat continues when the engine is warmed, creating vapor problems plus requiring periodic service to keep the heat passages clear.

In fuel injection, the need for mixture heating is virtually eliminated because of the separation of air and fuel until induction into the combustion chamber. Since the combustion chamber area heats quickly after initial starting of the engine, the period in which richer fuel mixtures are required is shortened considerably due to the excellent varporization conditions at the point of air-fuel mixing.

Horsepower

Many engineers feel that we are approaching practical limits of carburetion in size of venturi, number of cores, etc., and of course the farther we go in this direction the more difficult it becomes to maintain efficiency in the part throttle operation.

Since a fuel injection system could supply almost unlimited quantities of fuel and air, more efficient engine performance can be realized with today's engines. This allows considerable room for further advances in engine design.

Other Advantages of Fuel Injection

Since fuel delivery does not depend on level of fuel injection system is very little affected by maneuvers like tight turns and steep hill climbing.

Since the fuel is sprayed into the warm part of the engine, much less extra fuel is required before the system is operating at normal performance.

Response to the trottle is instantaneous since the fuel is under pressure at all times and neels only to be released for acceleration. With the current interest in sports cars and stock car racing, this in itself has created one of the major demands for fuel injection.

Another possibility in fuel injection is that fuel, since it is supplied separately from the air, can be shut off completely during deceleration if desired. This could reduce the amount of unburned hydrocarbons exhausted to the air and could also offer some improvement in fuel economy. Chevrolet units do not provide any coasting shut-off device at this time.

Finally, fuel injection offers definite engine height reduction possibilities for continuing lower trends of automobile styling.

Types of Fuel Injection

Three basic types of fuel injection are in use today. These are direct timed injection, timed port injection, and continuous flow port injection.

Direct timed injection is that used with Diesel engines. In this system, the nozzle sprays fuel directly into the combustion chamber at the instant that the piston reaches top dead center and the mixture is fired.

Timed port injection systems mount the nozzle outside the combustion chamber and the fuel is sprayed into the combustion chamber at the moment the intake valve is opened.

Continuous flow port injection systems, which we use, mount the injection nozzle outside the combustion chamber as in timed port injection systems. However, with this system, fuel flows from the nozzle continuously at such a rate that the desired charge has accumulated by the time the intake valve opens at the start of the cylinder. The built up fuel charge is carried into the combustion chamber with the air flow created by intake valve opening and by direct spray from the nozzle during the valve opening period.

Tests conducted by G. M. engineers during development of our fuel injection system failed to show any economy advantage of timed injection as compared to continuous flow injection. This allowed elimination of the expensive and complicated timing devices without sacrifice of efficiency. Direct combustion chamber injection is not practical from an optional production standpoint due to the engine adaptations which would be required to mount the injection nozzle in the combustion chamber plus the timing devices that would be needed.

FUNDAMENTALS OF OPERATION

Fuel Injection Components

Three basic assemblies comprise the G. M. fuel injection system (fig. 96). These are (1) the fuel meter, (2) air meter, and /3) the intake manifold. Let's look at the roles of each of these units.

Fuel Meter

As the name indicates, the job of the fuel meter is to supply the desired fuel delivery to the engine for all operating conditions (fig. 97). The fuel meter contains a fuel reservoir, high pressure pump, and fuel control system plus diaphragms which control the fuel rate according to speed and load. Also in the fuel meter are

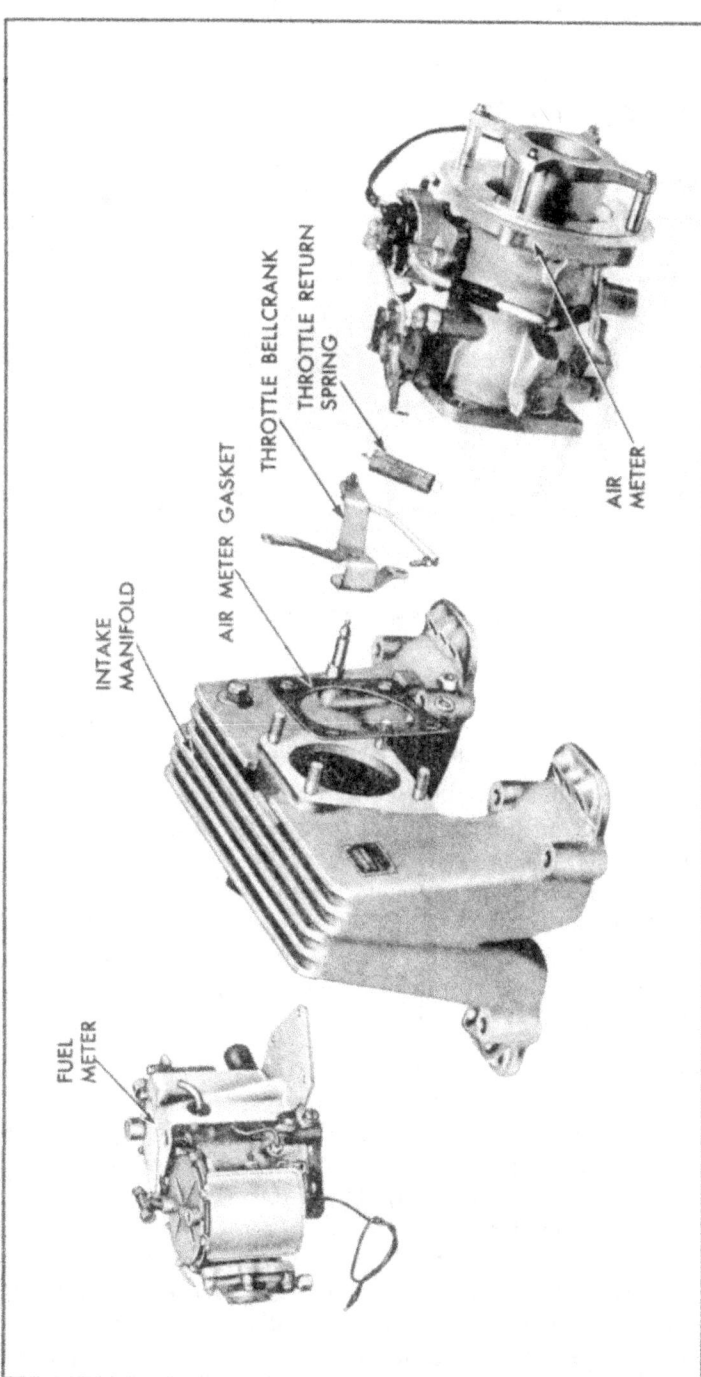

Fig. 96—Fuel Injection Components

auxiliary controls for starting. Fuel from the fuel meter goes through a distributor to eight nozzles, one for each cylinder.

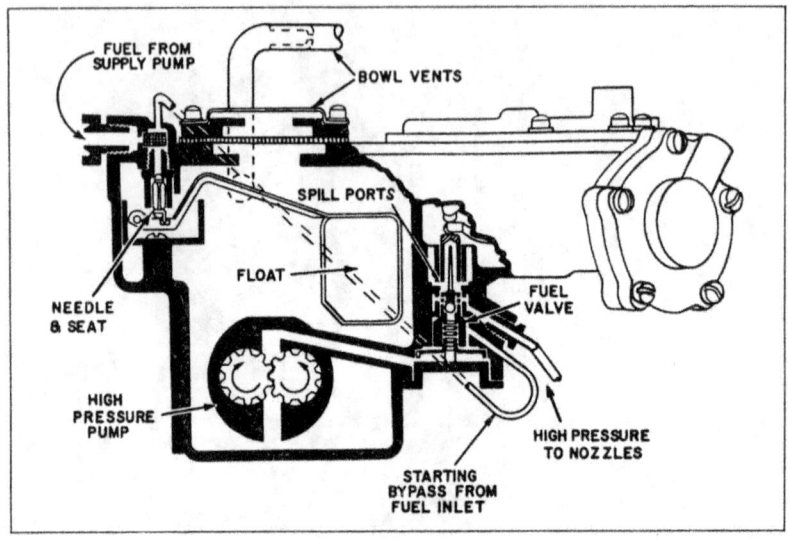

Fig. 97—Fuel Supply and Regulation

Fuel Supply

The fuel meter (fig. 97) contains a float controlled fuel bowl, very asimilar to those used in carburetion. Fuel is supplied to the fuel meter by a conventional diaphragm type fuel pump and passes through a ten micron filter before it reaches the fuel meter. Incoming fuel from the needle valve splashes directly into a nylon cup where it spills over more evenly into the fuel bowl to avoid getting bubbles in the fuel which might be picked up by the gear pump. Float level, although important, is not as critical as in carburetion because the reservoir is merely a supply for the gear pump and does not affect final fuel delivery to the engine.

Gear Pump

Submerged in the fuel reservoir is a gear pump (fig. 97) driven by a flexible cable from the engine distributor at one-half engine rpm. The gear pump picks up fuel from the reservoir and delivers it at high pressure through a passage to the fuel valve where fuel delivery rate to the nozzles is determined by a fuel control valve. Excess fuel is spilled back to the main fuel reservoir. Although the gear pump is manufactured to very close tolerances, its delivery rate is about twice engine requirements at any speed to prevent any losses in effectiveness due to pump wear. Pump delivery pressures can be as high as 400 psi.

Fuel Valve—Normal Operation

As mentioned, the rate of fuel delivery to the nozzles is governed by a fuel valve (fig. 98), which in turn is controlled through linkage by venturi vacuum signals from the air meter. The incoming fuel from the gear pump passes through a filter screen and travels upward through the center of the fuel valve where it lifts a check ball and flows through small holes into the metering chamber. At this point, the fuel flow splits: Some fuel flows through holes directly to the line supplying the nozzles and the remaining fuel flows upward into the area beneath the spill plunger. Of this fuel, some will be spilled back into the fuel bowl through the spill ports with the amount of spill depending on the position of the spill plunger. As a result, the total fuel delivery to the fuel nozzles becomes the difference of two factors:

- The rate of fuel delivery by the gear pump which runs at at one-half engine speed.
- Less the amonut of fuel spilled back to the fuel reservoir by the position of the spill plunger.

By this means, it is easily understood that for a given pump output the fuel delivery to the nozzles can be decreased by increasing the amount of spill or increased by decreasing the amount of spill. Obviously, when the spill plunger is up as shown in figure 99, the spill rate will be high and fuel flow to the nozzles will be lowered. Conversely, depressing the spill plunger covers the spill ports and fuel delivery to the nozzles is increased (fig. 100).

This description covers operation of the fuel valve in all operational phases while the engine is running. During starting however, fuel delivery must be altered to meet and overcome conditions present at only that time.

Fuel Valve Operation—Starting

During normal operation, all fuel must enter the metering chamber by lifting the fuel valve check ball off its seat. However, at engine cranking speeds the fuel pressure delivered by the gear pump is insufficient to lift the check ball, therefore other means must be used to supply fuel for starting (fig. 101).

During engine cranking, the spill plunger and fuel valve are fully depressed by a lever activated by a solenoid energized by the starting circuit. This action does two things: First, the fuel valve depression opens a passage for fuel delivery to the nozzles from the fuel tank fuel pump and second, the spill ports are fully closed off at the same time so that the rich fuel mixtures required for starting will be delivered. A small external fuel line delivers fuel from the fuel tank fuel pump to a port in the fuel meter normally closed off by the fuel valve which is held up by a small spring.

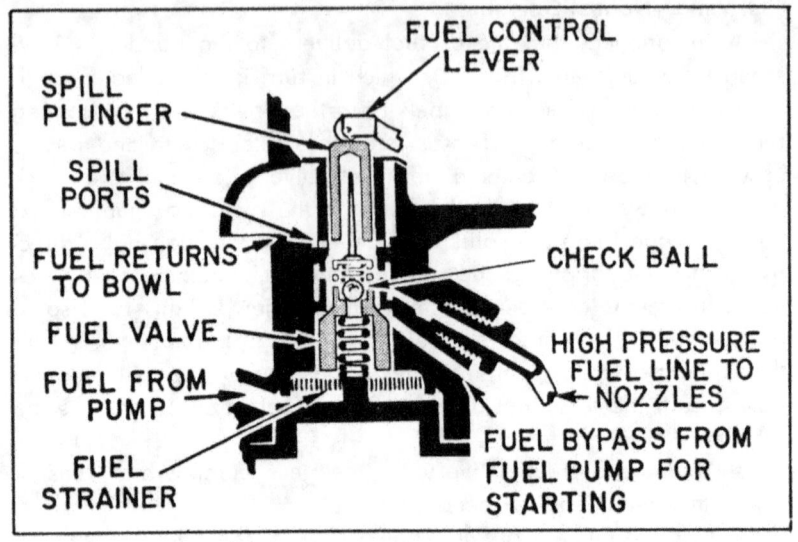

Fig. 98—Fuel Valve Components Identification

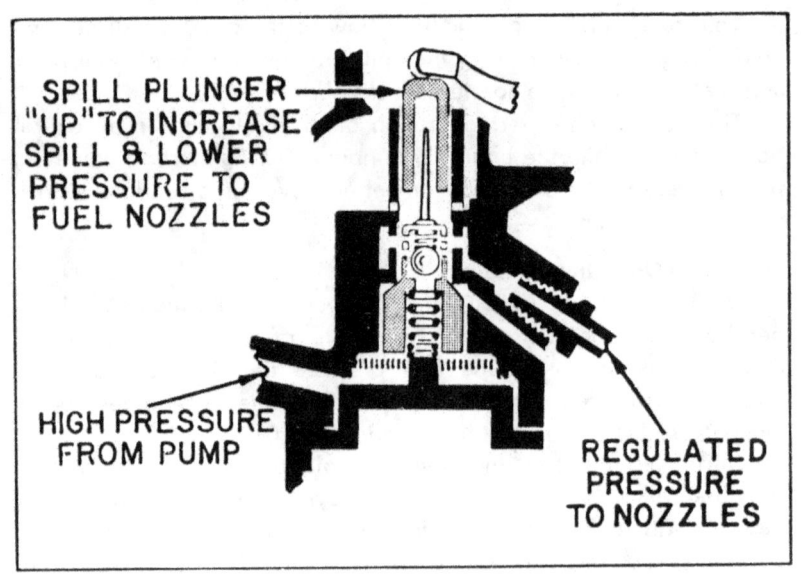

Fig. 99—Fuel Valve—Low Fuel Flow

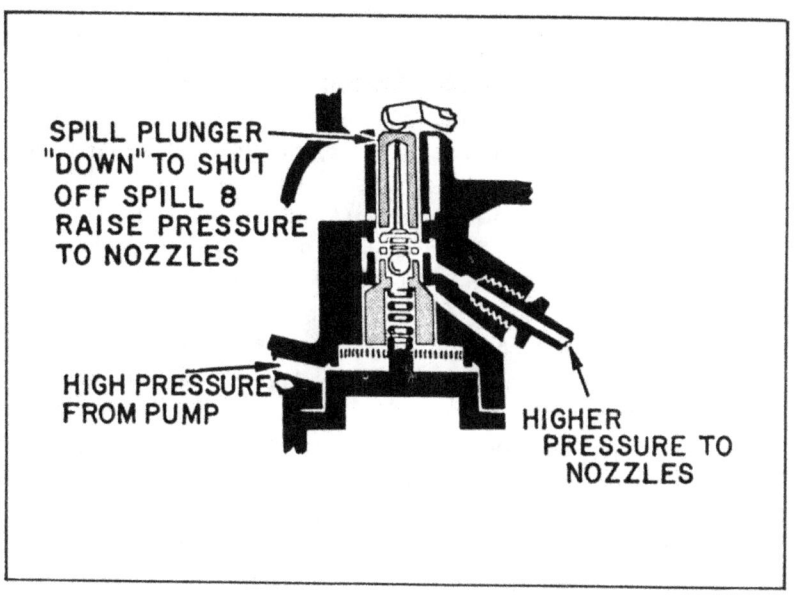

Fig. 100—Fuel Valve—High Fuel Flow

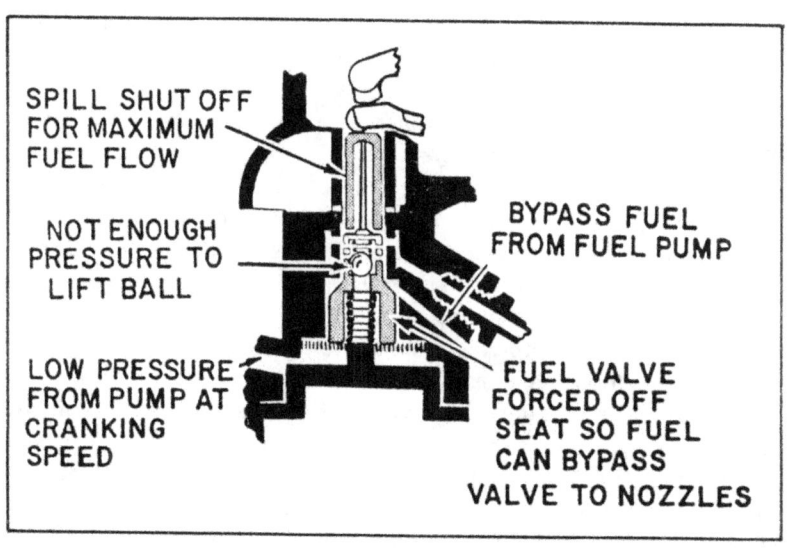

Fig. 101—Fuel Valve—Starting By-pass

When the fuel valve is depressed by the solenoid activated linkage during cranking, this port is uncovered which allows engine fuel pump pressure to be delivered directly to the nozzles. As soon as the engine starts and the ignition switch is returned to its "RUN" position, the solenoid linkage releases and the fuel valve moves back up to once again close-off the by-pass fuel passage.

To provide unloading in the event of a flooded engine, a small micro switch is provided which cuts the electrical circuit to the solenoid when the throttle blade in the air meter is held ¾ open or more. By this means, almost all fuel supply to the engine is cut off while the maximum amount of air is admitted for fast restarting.

Summarizing the operation of the fuel valve, one could consider that the driver is actually controlling its position with his foot. That is, at light throttle the spill plunger is up, the spill rate is high, and fuel delivery to the nozzles is relatively low. As the accelerator is depressed, the spill plunger moves downward to increase fuel delivery to the nozzle by reducing the spill rate. While this analogy is not quite true as there is no direct connection between the spill plunger and the accelerator pedal, the driver does control the spill plunger indirectly as the position of throttle valve in the air meter controlled by the driver causes a venturi vacuum signal relative to the throttle position and this vacuum, in turn, controls the position of the spill plunger.

Fuel Control Linkage

The position of the spill plunger is always the direct result of two opposed forces and thus becomes a state of balance. From below, pressure from the fuel meter gear pump pushes upward on the spill plunger and this pressure increases and decreases with engine speed Opposing this force is downward pressure exerted by a lever acuated by a venturi vacuum controlled diaphragm.

As shown (fig. 102), one end of the fuel control lever rests directly on the spill plunger and controls spill plunger position. The other end of the lever is connected by a link to the control diaphragm and the lever pivots around another part which is called the ratio lever. When the diaphragm pulls the link upward due to increased venturi vacuum, the lever end pushes downward on the spill plunger to increase fuel pressure. As venturi vacuum decreases due to lower air flow into the engine, the diaphragm allows the link to fall and fuel pressure forces the spill plunger upward to open the spill ports and lower fuel pressure. This linkage system is so designed that it will balance at the particular point where the fuel pressure is correct for the amount of vacuum "pull" on the diaphragm. The linkage system is carefully counter-balanced so that the only forces acting are fuel pressure and diaphragm vacuum.

The small counterweight balances the weight of the fuel control lever itself and the large counterweight compensates for the weight

For normal driving, the ratio lever is positioned at the approximate center of the fuel control. This means that the force applied by the fuel control lever to the spill plunger will be just the force applied to the main control diaphragm which will result in a high rate of spill. During power operation, the ratio lever is moved closer to the spill plunger. With the same vacuum applied to the diaphragm, the spill plunger will be depressed further due to the increased leverage and the spill rate will be reduced. It is easly seen that by changing the fulcrum we can directly control fuel delivery for a given venturi vacuum signal thus allowing us direct control of the air-fuel ratio. Power mixtures are obtained by moving the ratio lever closer to the spill plunger and economy mixtures are obtained by centering the ratio lever.

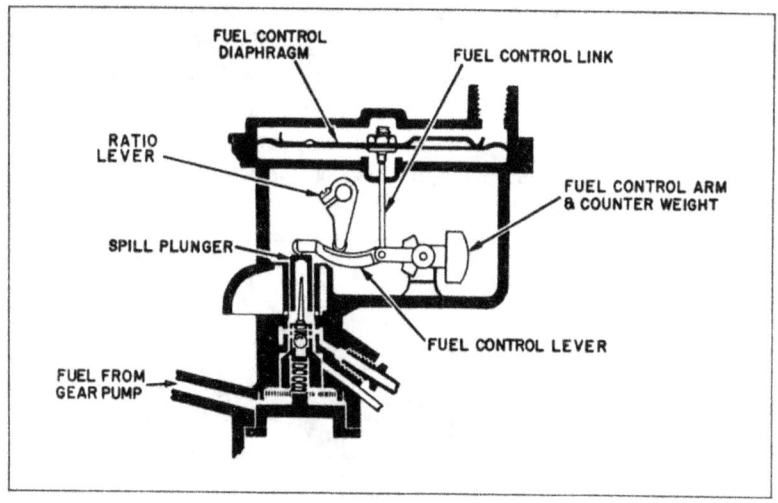

Fig. 102—Fuel Control Linkage

The position of the ratio lever is controlled through linkage by a diaphragm actuated by manifold vacuum and a spring. The tension holds the diaphragm in the power position but whenever manifold vacuum is above 9" Hg, the spring tension is overcome and the ratio lever is held in its economy position. By this means, the fuel meter is able to deliver the best mixture for the drivers demand; when manifold vacuum drops below 9" Hg due to extreme throttle opening, the fuel meter automatically delivers the power mixture required for best power and acceleration. However, as soon as the engine catches up to the throttle demand, manifold vacuum increases which moves the ratio lever to the lean stop and the fuel meter once again delivers economy mixtures. Manifold vacuum is prevented from reaching the diaphragm during engine warm-up, thus helping provide the richer fuel mixture required at that time by keeping the enrichment lever on the rich stop.

Fuel Nozzles

The design of the fuel nozzles is one of the prime factors in the success of the G.M. continuous flow injection system. In the past attempts at continuous flow injection, control of fuel delivery became a problem due to percolation in the nozzles and erratic flow at lower engine rpm due to vacuum pulsations.

As shown in the nozzle cross section (fig. 103), the nozzle in the G. M. system discharges to atmospheric pressure by means of air ducted to the nozzles from the air meter. By this means, the ducts act as a suction breaker to effectively nullify vacuum pulsations plus providing an anti-percolation feature by venting the nozzles to atmosphere during heat soak periods.

Fuel entering the nozzle passes through a domed strainer screen and then is squirted through a metering orifice drilled in a small disc, across the air duct through a larger nozzle opening and on into the area immediately above the intake valve. As covered previously, fuel is delivered continuously at such a rate that the desired fuel change has accumulated for induction by the time the intake valve is ready to open.

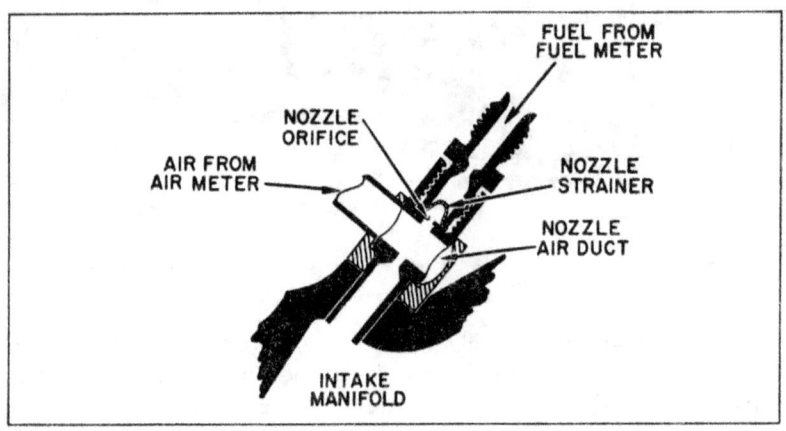

Fig. 103—Fuel Nozzle

Air Meter

The primary purpose of the air meter, in conjunction with the intake manifold, is to measure, control, and deliver all air used for combustion (fig. 104). As in the carburetor, air flow is measured by a venturi and air flow is controlled by a throttle valve operated through linkage by the accelerator pedal. Air is delivered to the cylinders via individual ram tubes housed in the intake manifold fed from a common plenum by the air meter.

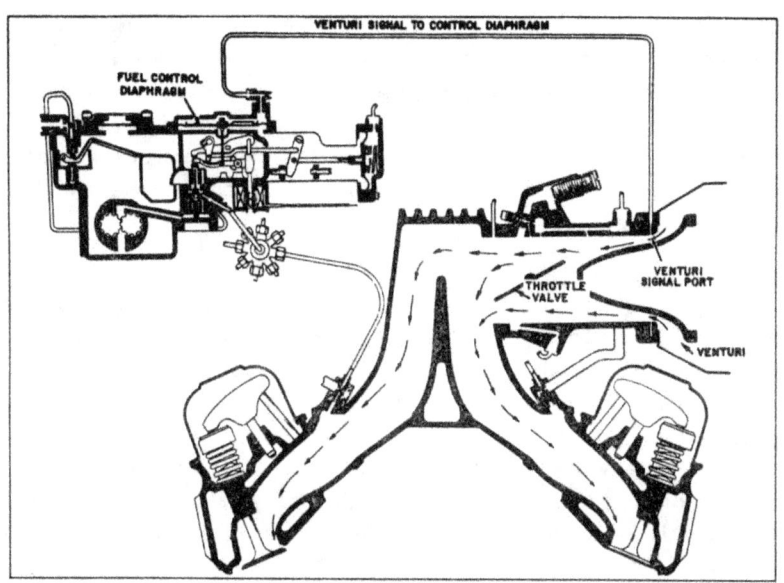

Fig. 104—Air Supply and Control

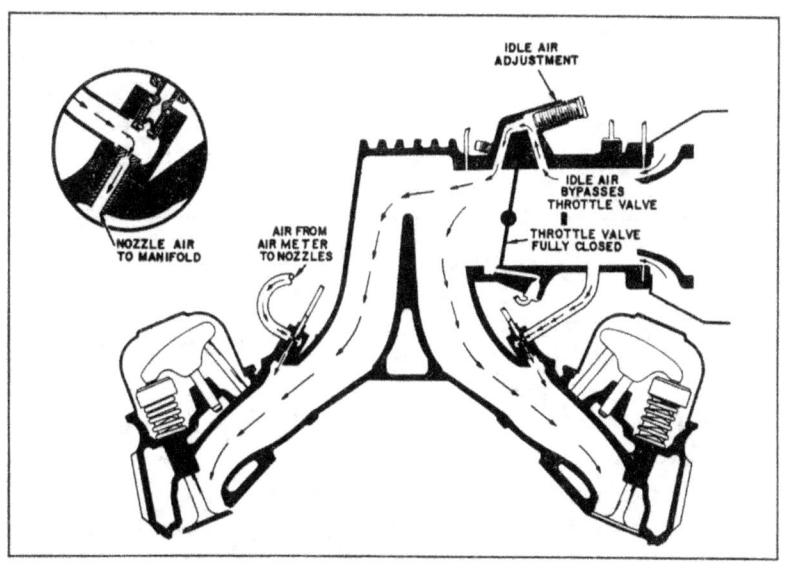

Fig. 105—Idle Air Flow

To reduce air meter length, an annular venturi is formed by a cone-shaped diffuser mounted at the mouth of the air meter. Incoming air causes a low pressure or vacuum at the venturi just as in the venturi of a carburetor and the amount of vacuum will be an indication of the amount of air entering the air meter. In a carburetor, this venturi vacuum is used to draw fuel from the fuel bowl into the air stream. In the injection system, this vacuum is used instead as a signal to the main control diaphragm in the fuel meter which, as we just covered, controls the position of the spill plunger to regulate fuel flow. In effect then, the amount of air flow is sensed at the venturi signal port and this signal is passed along through the venturi signal line to the main control diaphragm so that fuel can be fed in the right proportion for the air flow into the engine.

Idle Air

During idle operation, the throttle valve is closed against the bore within .0015-.002" of the air meter and air is introduced to the manifold through a by-pass system (fig. 105). Air is taken into the by-pass system above the throttle valve and is fed through passages to a point below the throttle valve. Idle speed adjustment is obtained by turning the idle air screw to regulate the amount of air allowed to flow through the by-pass system. In addition to this air through the air meter, one-third of the air for idle is taken in directly through each of the eight fuel nozzles via the nozzle block air ducts mentioned earlier.

Idle Fuel Control

The venturi signal is naturally very slight at idle speeds because the throttle is almost tightly closed (fig. 106). Since a higher signal is required to provide the richer fuel mixtures required for idle, the venturi signal must be strengthened. This is done by the addition of a regulated amount of manifold vacuum. Vacuum is

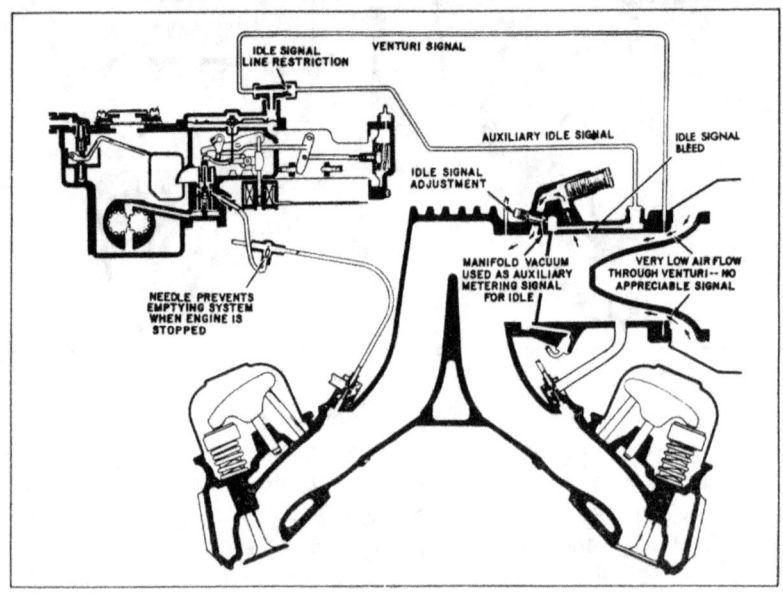

Fig. 106—Idle Fuel Metering Signal

applied to this system at the idle needle hole and is controlled by turning the needle in or out to obtain the best operation. This auxiliary signal vacuum is transmitted through a tube to a "T" at the main control diaphragm where it passes a restriction and combines with the main venturi signal to operate the control diaphragm. Thus the fuel flow is increased by strengthening the effective venturi signal at the main control diaphragm.

As the throttle valve is opened, vacuum is introduced to the system through an off-idle signal port and, at this point, the vacuum is controlled by the restriction in the tube. As the throttle valve continues to open, vacuum at the auxiliary signal ports decreases until there is no noticeable auxiliary signal and the main venturi signal operates the diaphragm. This decrease of idle and off idle port signals is comparable to the transfer between idle and main metering system operation in carburetors.

Because the strength of the manifold vacuum signal which can be picked up at the off-idle port is far stronger than those which can usually reach the main control diaphragm, a signal bleed is drilled into idle signal channel in the air meter. This allows air to bleed into the line and thus weaken the off-idle vacuum signal to a safe level. This bleed is effective during all operational phases, therefore any partial blockage will result in stronger vacuum signals and reduce fuel economy.

Fig. 107—Acceleration Fuel Metering Signal

Acceleration

For acceleration, an extra charge of fuel is added to make up for any lag in the fuel control system in answering the higher venturi signal (fig. 107). Here again the idle signal system is used. It can be seen that the signal on the fuel control diaphragm at any time will be a combination of the main venturi signal and the signal from the idle and off-idle ports. As the throttle valve is opened for acceleration, the air flow and the main venturi signal increase immediately. Because of the wider opening of the throttle valve, vacuum on the signal system decreases and if some measure were not provided, the idle and off-idle ports would back-bleed air and reduce vacuum signal at the main control diaphragm. However, the restriction at the signal end of the "Tee" fitting delays the loss of idle vacuum signal above the main control diaphragm momentarily. Since the venturi vacuum signal increased immediately, the total vacuum above the control diaphragm becomes momentarily high to provide the richer fuel mixture required for smooth acceleration to higher speeds. By the time the engine reaches speed, the excessive vacuum has bled back through the restriction and only the normal control signal remains.

Power

As mentioned earlier, the ratio lever in the fuel control linkage system controls the fuel air mixture, thus for power operation, the ratio lever must be moved to its rich position to supply the required richer mixtures for power operation (fig. 108). The ratio lever is connected by a shaft to an outside enrichment lever which, in turn, is connected by a rod to a diaphragm exposed to manifold vacuum. The power enrichment diaphragm operates much as the power valve and power piston in a carburetor. When manifold vacuum is high and lean mixtures can be used, the diaphragm is held in the lean position. When power is called for and engine vacuum drops below 9" Hg, a calibrated spring moves the diaphragm to the rich position and holds it there until manifold vacuum rises above 9" Hg, at which time power ratios are no longer required. Stops on the fuel meter casting which determine the rich and lean ratios are adjusted at the factory to provide proper fuel flow to a matched set of nozzles. These stops should not be moved in the field unless the need for recalibration is indicated through the use of test equipment described later in these pages.

Application of manifold vacuum to the power enrichment diaphragm is limited to periods when the engine is warmed-up as the vacuum apply to the diaphragm is controlled by a valve in the cold enrichment housing. During warm-up, the power enrichment valve remains closed which keeps the enrichment lever on the rich (power) stop due to power enrichment diaphragm spring tension. As the engine warms-up, a bimetal thermostat spring in the cold enrichment housing opens the power enrichment valve and allows manifold vacuum to reach the power enrichment diaphragm. Once the coil is heated, the valve remains open so long as the engine is kept running and the position of the power enrichment diaphragm is controlled entirely by manifold vacuum; at signals of 9" Hg or above, the diaphragm holds the enrichment lever on the economy (lean) stop whereas at lower vacuum the lever is moved to the rich (power) stop by tension of the power enrichment diaphragm spring.

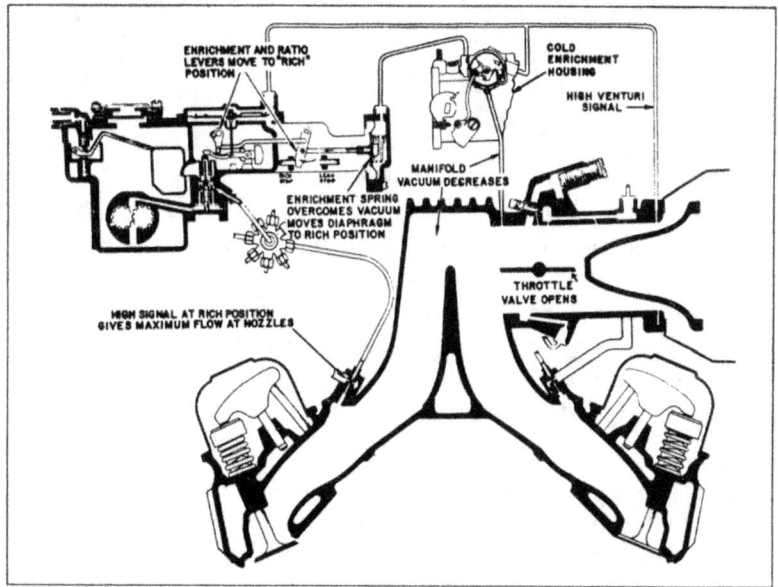

Fig. 108—Power Enrichment

Starting

While the operation during starting was basically covered during discussion of fuel valve operation, it is reviewed at this time so that the attitudes of all components can be seen (fig. 109).

At cranking speed, there is very little fuel pressure from the gear pump due to the fact it runs at one-half engine rpm. A special provision must be made to feed sufficient fuel to the nozzle at cranking rpm so that the engine can start. To obtain the maximum amount of fuel at these low pressures, the fuel valve is mechanically forced off its seat so that fuel can by-pass the valve and flow directly to the nozzles. This action is accomplished by a solenoid which is energized by the starting circuit and which operates through linkage to force the spill plunger downward until it forces the fuel valve off its seat.

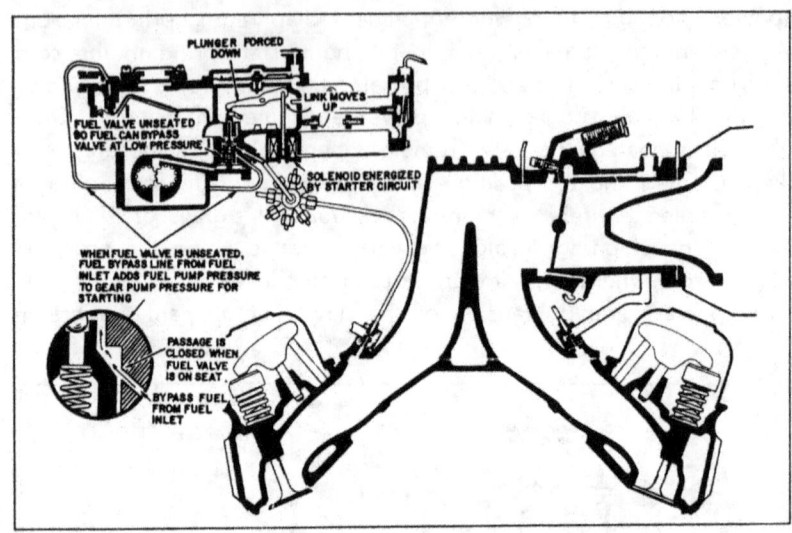

Fig. 109—Starting

When the fuel valve is unseated, it uncovers a special by-pass fuel line from the fuel meter intake which delivers engine fuel pump pressure to the metering chamber to combine with gear pump pressure in supplying sufficient fuel for starting. As soon as the engine has started and the ignition switch is returned to "RUN" position, solenoid current is cut off and the fuel valve returns to normal position, shutting off all by-pass fuel flow.

Unloading

To allow cranking without use of the fuel by-pass, a solenoid cut-off switch (fig. 110) is attached to the air meter next to the throttle lever. Whenever the throttle valve is opened ¾ or wider, a cam on the throttle lever operates the micro switch to break the circuit to the fuel by-pass solenoid. Thus, by opening the throttle wide, a flooded engine can be "unloaded" and restarted as starting by-pass fuel flow is cut-off and air intake is maximum.

Cold Enrichment

Fuel enrichment and higher initial idle speeds to provide smooth engine operation and prevent stalling during warm-up is accomplished through use of a cold enrichment housing and a fast idle linkage much like that used on carburetors. In effect, the cold enrichment assembly is the counterpart of a carburetor choke, however it enriches fuel mixture delivery without restricting air flow.

The cold enrichment housing, mounted on top of the air meter, contains four parts (fig. 111). These are (1) signal boost valve, (2) power enrichment valve, (3) thermostatic coil, and (4) an electric heat element. The thermostatic coil is mounted on a shaft, the lower end of which has an arm that operates the boost valve and the enrichment valve. Mounted on the upper end of the shaft are a trip lever and counterweight which operate the fast idle cam to control idle speed during engine warm-up.

The thermostatic spring, as mentioned, is heated electrically as compared to the exhaust manifold heat applications used on choke thermostatic springs for carburetors. Electrical heating is possible due to shorter warm-up required by fuel injection equipped engines because of the direct fuel delivery to the combustion chamber area. The electrical source for the heat element is the 12 volt side of the ignition resistor on the dash. By this connection, current flows to the heat element at all times when the engine is running or the ignition switch is in the "ON" position.

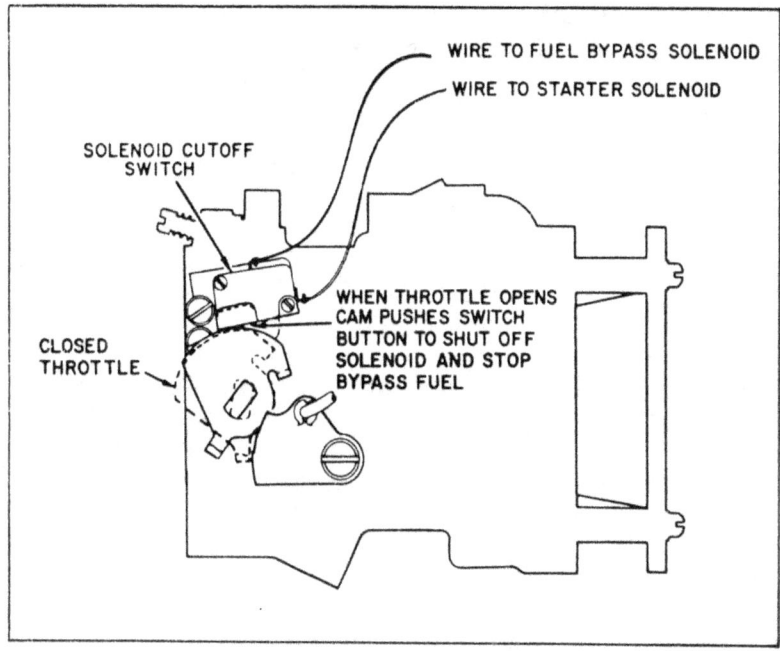

Fig. 110—Starting Fuel Cut-Off (Unloading)

Operation

The cold enrichment housing has a twofold purpose. First, it "boosts" the vacuum signal to the main control diaphragm during warm-up by supplementing the usual signals with manifold vacuum through a bleed valve. During the "boost" stage, it prevents manifold vacuum from reaching the power enrichment diaphragm, thus keeping the enrichment lever on the rich stop. Second, once signal

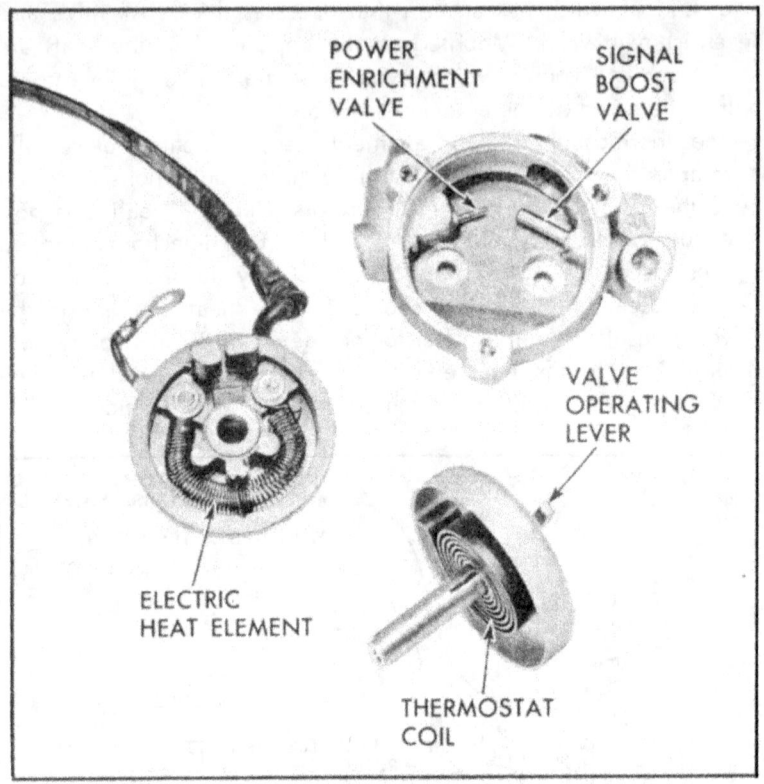

Fig. 111—Cold Enrichment Housing Components

boost is no longer needed, the boost signal is shut off and manifold vacuum is allowed to react on the power enrichment diaphragm to move the enrichment lever from the power stop to the economy stop. Manifold vacuum is constantly fed to the cold enrichment housing through a hole in its base connected to a passage in the air meter open to manifold vacuum. This sequence is easily understood by following the basic stages of operation.

1st Stage

The first stage of operation shown in figure 112 illustrates the attitudes of all parts when the engine is first started. The bi-metal thermostat coil, being cold, is under tension and holds the boost valve in cold enrichment housing open by means of an attached lever. This allows manifold vacuum, after passing through a restriction in the lower hose of the boost tube, to combine with the venturi vacuum to strengthen the signal and cause richer fuel mixtures. With the enrichment vacuum valve closed, the enrichment lever is held against the power stop by spring tension. This first, or "boost," stage of operation continues so long as the fast idle screw remains on the high step of the cam although the boost vacuum declines slowly as the coil heats and the cam rotates toward the second step.

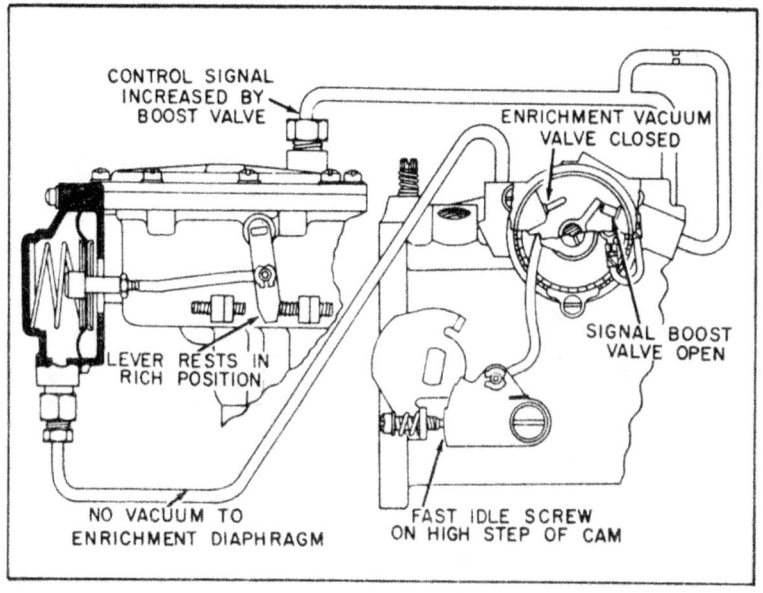

Fig. 112—Cold Enrichment 1st Stage

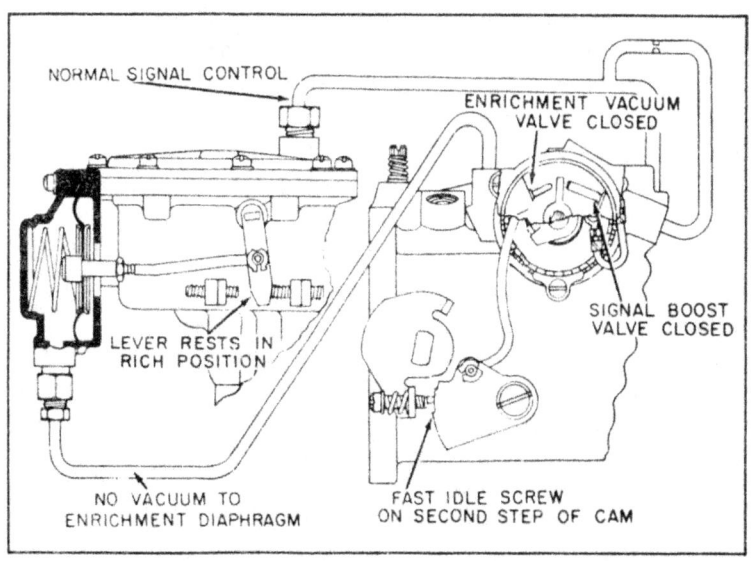

Fig. 113—Cold Enrichment 2nd Stage

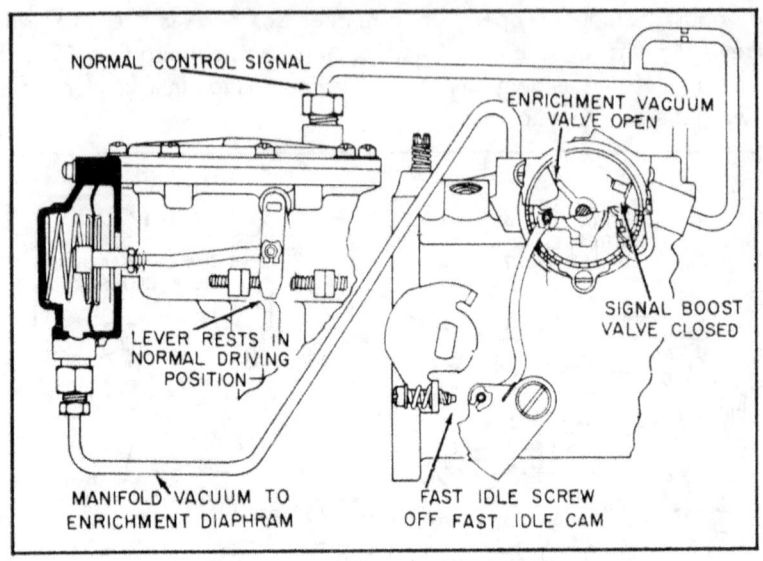

Fig. 114—Cold Enrichment 3rd Stage

2nd Stage

When the thermostat coil heats sufficiently to rotate the cam so that the fast idle screw rests on the second step, signal boost ceases. As shown in figure 113, the signal boost and enrichment valves are both fully closed during this second stage so the main control diaphragm will receive only the normal venturi and idle signal. Since the power enrichment valve remains closed, the enrichment lever on the fuel meter remains on the rich, or power stop. Actually, the only effect caused by the cold enrichment housing at this time is to keep the throttle blade at a slightly greater opening by means of the second and third cam steps to maintain a higher idle speed and prevent manifold vacuum from reaching the power enrichment diaphragm until the engine warm-up is complete.

3rd Stage

Further heating of the thermostat coil finally rotates the fast idle cam completely clear of the fast idle screw. This is the third stage or normal operation (fig. 114). With the coil completely relaxed, its operating lever depresses the enrichment vacuum valve to allow manifold vacuum to react on the enrichment diaphragm. any vacuum of 9" Hg (mercury) or above, the tension of enrichment diaphragm spring will be overcome and the enrichment lever will rest on the economy stop. Only normal control signals from the venturi will react on the main control diaphragm for driving or from the needle controlled orifce behind the throttle blade during idle as the boost valve is closed. Since engine vacuum generally stays above 9" Hg, the enrichment lever will nearly always be on the economy stop except for those momentary demands when the driver suddenly opens the throttle wide for acceleration from a standstill or for passing.

7014800 Fuel Injection Service Procedures

MAINTENANCE AND ADJUSTMENTS

Periodic maintenance requirements of the Chevrolet Fuel Injection are limited to replacement of fuel and air filter elements. Adjustments are limited to idle fuel and idle air (idle speed), cold enrichment rod length, cold enrichment coil index setting, and fast idle speed.

Fuel cleanliness is a major factor in maintaining the Chevrolet Fuel Injection unit at peak operating efficiency. The best assurance of fuel cleanliness and a reduced tendency toward gasoline gum and varnish formation is to use a reputable, premium fuel.

Servicing The Air Cleaner

The element should be replaced each 15,000 miles or more often in dusty areas. To replace air cleaner element, perform the following steps:
1. Remove aid cleaner flexible duct.
2. Remove fuel bowl vent pipe at air cleaner.
3. Remove wing nut attaching cleaner to stud in air meter.
1. Remove wing nut attaching air cleaner stud to bracket at front of engine, lift out air cleaner, then remove nut from opposite end of stud to allow removal of element.
5. Replace element and reinstall air cleaner by reversing the preceding steps.

Servicing The Fuel Filter

The fuel filter element should be replaced semiannually—in the spring and fall.

To remove the element, remove the filter cover and insert three pieces of shim stock about .040" thick between the element and the clips inside the filter as shown in figure 115. Now the element can be removed by simply pulling upward. Install new element in the same manner.

Idle Speed and Mixture Adjustment

Before attempting to adjust the idle speed and mixture, allow the engine to warm-up so that the throttle tab is completely off of the fast idle cam. If these adjustments are being performed after servicing the Fuel Injection unit, fully close both the idle air and idle fuel adjusting screws (fig. 116), and then back off each screw approximately two (2) turns as an initial setting for warm-up. A tachometer and vacuum gauge should be used to obtain the best possible adjustment.

1. Once engine is warmed-up, adjust idle air screw as required to give a moderate idle speed.
2. Adjust the idle fuel screw as required to give the highest steady vacuum reading and highest engine rmp. If instruments are not available, adjust idle fuel needle as necessary to obtain the best engine operation.
3. Reduce idle speed by turning the idle air screw inward. Idle speed should be finally adjusted to 500 rmp in "Drive" range on Powerglide and Turboglide models and to 600 rpm in neutral on standard transmission jobs.
4. Repeat the above adjustments as required to obtain the highest vacuum, and smoothest idle possible at the specified idle speeds.

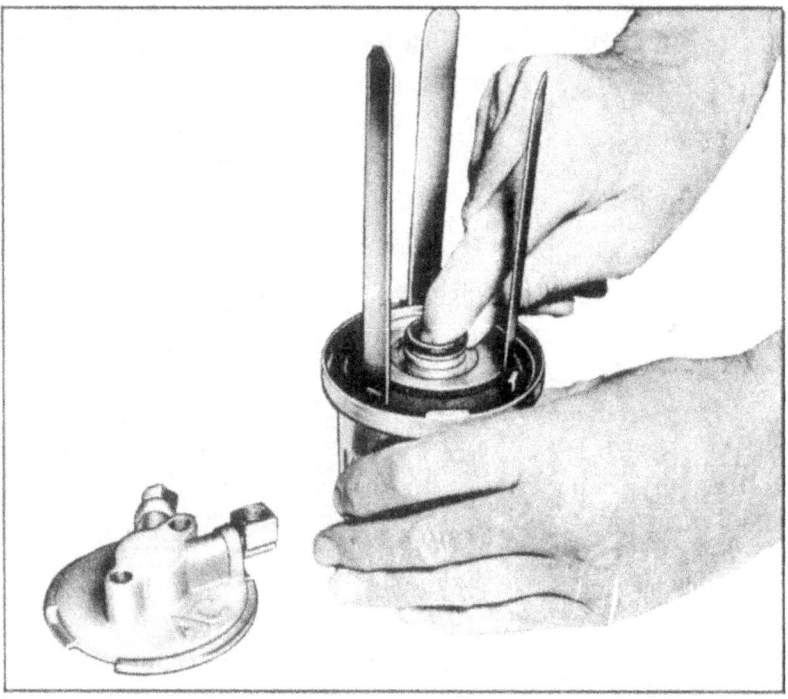

Fig. 115—Replacing Fuel Filter Element

Cold Enrichment Adjustments

These adjustments will normally only be required at the time of rebuild but the adjustments may be checked as follows:

Cold Enrichment Coil Setting

Scribe mark on the coil cover should be set 1½ notches rich from the scribe mark on the cold enrichment housing. (Notches are small radial marks on flange of coil cover.)

Fig. 116—Adjusting Idle Mixture and Speed

Cold Enrichment Adjustment
1. With the engine off and cool, disconnect the rubber sleeve from the cold enrichment housing signal boost tube and install a short length of rubber hose over the tube such as windshield wiper hose.
2. Crack the throttle valve as necessary to place the throttle tab just on the high step of the fast idle cam, then close the throttle.
3. Holding the trip lever against the counterweight tab as illustrated in Figure 117, blow into the hose while listening at the air meter. If choke rod length is correct, slight air flow should be heard. Repeat check but with throttle tab on second step of fast idle cam. No air flow should be heard. If necessary, bend rod as required with bending Tool J-6492 to shorten or lengthen rod in order to meet the above requirements.

Fast Idle Speed Setting
1. Normalize the engine to operating temperature.
2. With tachometer hooked up to measure rmp, start engine and place throttle tab on high step of fast idle cam.
3. Speed should be 1660-1700 rpm in neutral. If unit does not meet this specification, bend the throttle tab in or out as required.

TROUBLE SHOOTING

In general, the following procedures cover most of the malfunctions which may be encountered with the 7014800 Fuel Injection unit and basically apply to the two preceding models, 7014520, and the later 7017300 units.

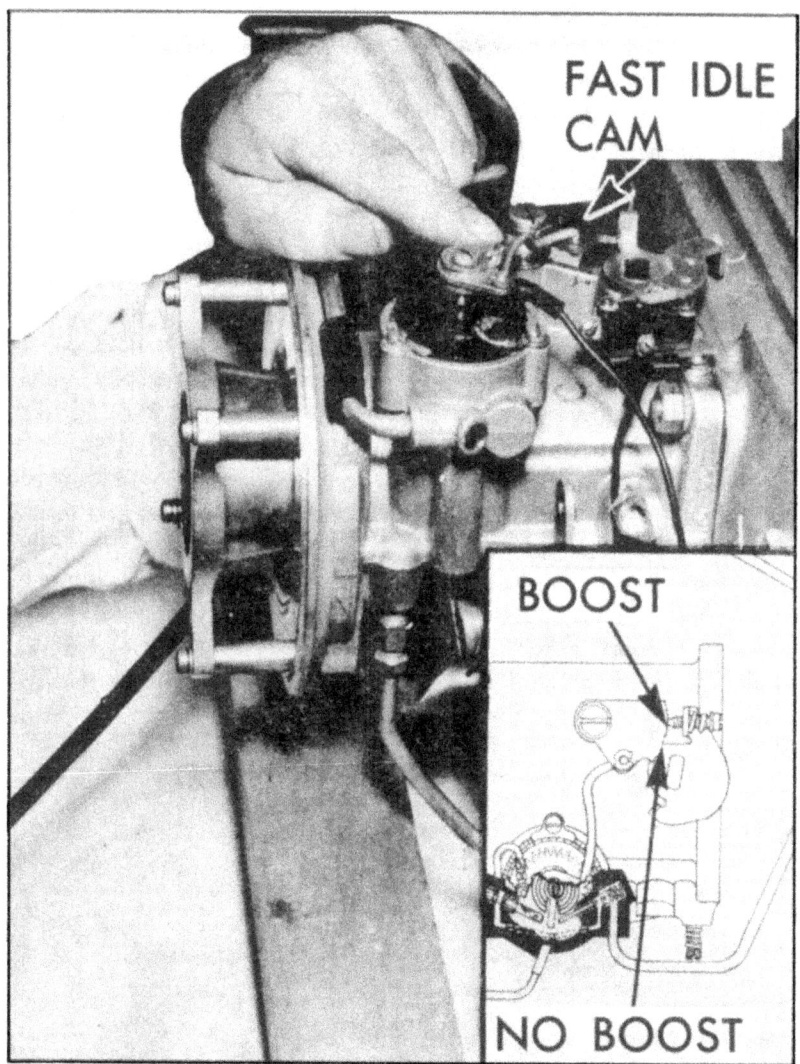

Fig. 117—Cold Enrichment Rod Length Adjustment

Probable causes of trouble are listed under each complaint heading by the order in which they should be checked.

Always make sure that the engine and ignition systems have been eliminated as the trouble possibilities by thorough checks before blaming the Fuel Injection system.

In many instances in the following trouble possibilities, it is necessary to check for air leaks at the signal line connections and nozzle blocks, or to check for leaks in the enrichment or main control diaphragms. The following procedures should be used to make these checks:

CONNECTION LEAK CHECK

The quickest check for possible air leakage into vacuum signal lines, nozzle blocks, and rubber sleeve-type connections is to spray the connections, one by one, with water from a pump-type oil can while the engine is idling. If leaks are present, a sucking sound will be heard as the water is pulled in by the vacuum.

Diaphragm Leak Check.

To check for leaks in the enrichment or main control diaphragm, disconnect the vacuum signal line at the end opposite the diaphragm connection end and attach a hose from a manometer with a vacuum source to the tube as shown in Figure 118. Then with the vacuum release valve on the manometer unit shut, apply and hold a vacuum on the diaphragm and watch the manometer dial. If the diaphragm leaks, the manometer dial needle will slowly slip to lower readings. When testing the main control diaphragm, disconnect the vacuum signal line from the opposite end of the tee and install a plug. If a main control diaphragm leak is found, replace the fuel meter; if the enrichment diaphragm leaks, replace the diaphragm.

Never apply a vacuum greater than 4" Hg (mercury) to the main control diaphragm as this may damage fuel meter! The enrichment diaphragm should be checked by applying 12-16" Hg. (mercury).

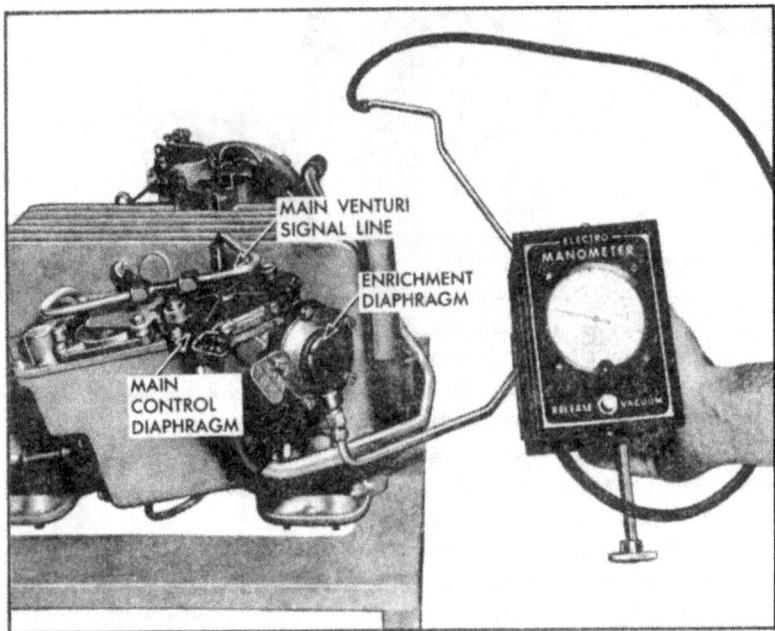

Fig. 118—Checking for Diaphragm Leaks

If an instrument such as shown in Figure 118 is not available, a substitute set-up may be made.
1. Connect a "Tee" fitting to the signal tube with windshield wiper hose.
    wiper hose.
2. Connect a sensitive vacuum gage or manometer to one outlet of the tee.
3. Connect a vacum pump to the other outlet of the tee. The vacuum pump that is a part of most Distributor Analyzers will work satisfactorily.
4. Turn on the vacuum pump and allow the vacuum to reach the levels specified above.

CAUTION: It is mandatory that the specified levels of vacuum are not exceeded even momentarily. Excessive vacuum on the main control diaphragm may irreparably damage the fuel meter.

5. When the desired vacuum is obtained, tightly close or seal the line leading to the vacuum pump. The best means of closed the vacuum line is to double the hose.
6. Observe the vacuum gauge connected to the tee. Any drop of vacuum indicates a ruptured or leaking diaphragm. Recheck the test equipment for leakage to be certain the diaphragm is a fault.

DIAGNOSIS

Won't Start

1. Check for correct cold starting procedure: The accelerator should be depressed once to index the fast idle cam, then the accelerator should remain released until the engine has started. If hot starting trouble is encountered, check that the starting cut-off switch (micro-switch) is being actuated by the throttle cam at approximately ¾ throttle. Bend the switch bracke as necessary. Also make certain that the driver understands that holding the throttle wide open during cranking will unload the system.
2. Observe the starting solenoid on the fuel meter to make certain it operates when the starter is engaged (closed throttle). If it does not, check out the starting cut-off switch and solenoid.
3. Check that fuel is flowing to the fuel distributor by loosening the distributor line at the fuel meter. Fuel should leak from the loosened fitting during cranking; otherwise the fuel valve is sticking and should be cleaned. Push the solenoid plunger to free fuel valve or remove valve and clean thoroughly.
4. To check that the fuel line to the fuel distributor is not

clogged, remove one set of nozzles from a nozzle block and check for fuel flow while cranking the engine. If fuel flow is not observed, check the fuel distributor check valve for sticking or a clogged fuel meter-to-distributor fuel line.
5. If fuel flows from the nozzles and the car still won't start, check for large air leaks, such as loose or crocked nozzle blocks. If the system is tight and fuel is present, there is either a very unusual flooding condition or the trouble is not in the fuel system.

Starts and Dies
1. This problem is often the result of residual vapors in the engine and exhaust system. In all cases after initially starting the engine, accelerate the engine several times to purge the system. This procedure is especially important in hot weather.
2. If engine will not take throttle as in Step 1 above, check for a broken or improperly connected fuel meter pump drive cable. Also, check that the enrichment lever rests on the power (rich) stop. In all cases when the engine is stopped, the enrichment lever should rest on the power stop. After the engine is started, the enrichment lever should remain on the power stop as long as the throttle tab is on the fast idle cam; otherwise check for leakege past the enrichment housing as described in "CLEANING AND INSPECTION." If leakage exists, attempt to remedy by cleaning; otherwise replace cold enrichment housing.
3. Be sure the solenoid releases after engine starts; otherwise check for binding or improper wiring.
4. Check for vacuum leaks, especially the vacuum lines to the main control diaphragm.
5. If trouble occurs on a cold start, check the cold enrichment coil cover for proper index (1½ notches rich) and check fast idle cam rod adjustment. Also check that the cold enrichment linkage is free to move and that the throttle tab rests on a stop of the fast idle cam for the first few minutes of engine operation. If the engine seems to be "starving," disconnect the enrichment line at the cold enrichment housing and start the engine. This will provide full enrichment. If disconnecting the enrichment line eliminates the trouble, the enrichment valve in the cold enrichment housing is not seating properly; clean or replace the cold enrichment housing as required.
6. The spill plunger may be sticking. It can be moved manually by pushing on the solenoid plunger. If the condition per-

sists, the spill plunger can be checked only by partial disassembly of the fuel meter.
7. Check for a leak in the main control diaphragm. Disconnect the main control diaphragm line and impose a vacuum of not over 4" Hg on the diaphragm and check for leakage by observing manometer. If leak is found, the fuel meter must be replaced as changing the main control diaphragm requires recalibration of the Fuel Injection unit which is not possible currently in field service.
8. Check the engine fuel pump for capacity and pressure as described in the Checrolet Passenger Car Shop Manual. The pressure specifications are 5¼ to 6½ psi.

Hesitation or Flat Spot
1. Check for vacuum leaks in the signal lines and fittings.
2. In the air meter, check the main control diaphragm venturi signal passage for cleanliness and see that the auxiliary signal passages are clean.
3. Check that the restriction in the main control diaphragm tee is clear.
4. Check the main control diaphragm for leaks with a manometer.
5. Check for sticking spill plunger.
6. Apply a vacuum of 12-16" Hg to the enrichment diaphragm to check for leakage.
7. Check that the enrichment control diaphragm rod length allows proper cut-in for power and economy as described in Step 2 of "Assembly of Fuel Meter." Enrichment lever should leave the economy stop at 9" Hg or below and reach the power stop at 3" Hg or above.
8. Check to be sure the enrichment diaphragm is receiving vacuum from cold enrichment housing. If not, look for trouble in the cold enrichment housing such as broken heat element posts, burned out heat element, or a stock ball in enrichment valve.

Surge
1. Check the engine fuel pump and the ignition system, especially the spark plugs, for proper operation and adjustment. If the engine is equipped with a vacuum advance distributor, the spark advance must be set with the vacuum disconnected to 4° BTDC @ 500 rmp idle speed.
2. Check that the fuel filter in the fuel supply line to the Fuel Injection unit is not obstructed and causing spasmodic fuel flow.
3. Check for vacuum signal line leaks.

4. If surge seems to result from over enrichment, check the enrichment control diaphragm for leaks; if surge is caused from too lean a mixture, check the main control diaphragm for leaks. If the main control diaphragm is leaking it is necessary to replace the fuel meter assembly.
5. Check the spill plunger for free operation as described under "Starts and Dies."

Rough Idle

1. Check for correct idle speed and mixture adjustments and correct distributor spark advance setting.
2. If adjustment of the idle fuel adjusting screw has little or no effect on engine operation, check for a sticking spill plunger.
3. Check that there is no perceptible vacuum signal from the boost tube at the cold enrichment housing when the rubber sleeve is disconnected and a finger is placed over the tube. This check must be made when the throttle tab is completely off the fast idle cam.
4. Check for leaks in the signal and fuel lines as described previously.
5. Check for a plugged nozzle by shorting out one spark plug at a time. If a plugged nozzle is present, there would be no change in engine operation when the spark plug to that cylinder was shorted out. Remove the nozzle and clean as described in "Cleaning and Inspection." This is likely to be extremely rare and a check of the spark plugs and leads should be made first.
6. Check that the enrichment lever leaves the economy stop at 9" Hg vacuum or below and arrives at the power stop at 3" Hg or above with a manometer as described under "Fuel Meter—Assembly."
7. Check for vacuum leaks, especially around the nozzle blocks and vent tubes. If a vacuum leak was not found by the water method but the nozzle area is still suspected, it will be necessary to remove the nozzles in sets and check that the small nozzle as described in "Installation of Signal, Fuel and Vent Lines."
8. Check for obstructions in the nozzle block vent tubes.

Poor Fuel Economy

1. Be sure the enrichment lever rests on the economy stop during normal operation after a 5-8 minute warm-up period.
2. After the throttle tab is completely off the fast idle cam, check that there is no perceptible signal at the signal boost tube by disconnecting the rubber sleeve and placing a finger

over the tube. If suction is felt, the signal boost valve in cold enrichment housing is leaking and should be cleaned so that complete signal boost valve seating is obtained; otherwise replace the cold enrichment housing.
3. Check that accurate manifold vacuum signals are reaching the enrichment diaphragm by first taking an engine vacuum check and then by performing the same check at the enrichment signal line connection at the cold enrichment housing. Signal indications at the cold enrichment housing should be within 1" Hg of manifold vacuum reading; otherwise check for partially closed enrichment valve in the cold enrichment housing or a leaking gasket between the cold enrichment housing and air meter.
4. Check for an enrichment diaphragm leak by applying approximately 12-16" Hg to enrichment diaphragm signal tube with a manometer and vacuum source. Manometer indications should hold steady; otherwise a diaphragm leak is indicated.
5. Visually check that the ratio stop screw positions have not been altered. These stops are pre-set at the factory and their positions should never be altered in the field unless fuel flow recalibration set J-7090 is available.

MAJOR SERVICE OPERATIONS
REMOVAL OF FUEL INJECTION UNIT FROM ENGINE

1. Disconnect and remove fuel injection pump drive cable by unscrewing nut attaching cable housing to distributor, pull housing and cable out of distributor, and then pull housing and cable free of fuel injection pump (fig. 119). Use care not to lose small fiber washer from drive cable assembly.
2. Disconnect fuel line at the fuel meter.
3. Remove air cleaner as described under "MAINTENANCE AND ADJUSTMENTS."
4. Disconnect the accelerator control rod and transmission TV rod (if automatic transmission) from the bellcrank on the Fuel Injection manifold.
5. Disconnect electrical connector (fig. 119) for the starting cut-off switch and cold enrichment coil.
6. Loosen the spark control pipe (fig. 119) at the distributor, then disconnect pipe at air meter end. Pipe should be loosened to allow its movement during removal of the Fuel Injection unit.
7. Remove the eight nuts and lockwashers attaching Fuel Injection intake manifold to adapter plate on engine and lift off Injector. Ports in adapter plate should be sealed off with masking tape immediately after removal of the Fuel Injec-

Fig. 119—Fuel Injection—Installed View

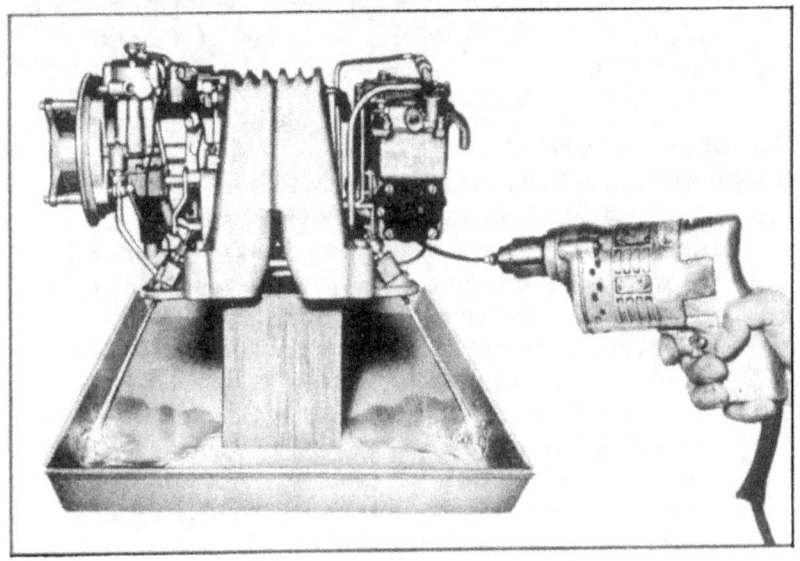

Fig. 120—Fuel Injection Fuel Flow Check

jection unit to prevent loose nuts etc., from falling into the combustion chambers.

Fuel Injection Flow Check

When the Fuel Injection unit is removed from the engine, it may be worth while to perform a fuel flow check. This is accomplished by filling the fuel meter with fuel and spinning the fuel meter pump (fig. 120). It is recommended that a geared hand-drill or air-powered drill be used to minimize any fire hazard. If a hand drill is used, it will be necessary to push up on the starting bypass solenoid plunger to permit full flow. Full fuel flow may also be obtained by disconnecting the main control diaphragm venturi signal line and applying a very light vacuum to the main control diaphragm. This may be done by applying oral vacuum to the main control diaphragm.

Properly operating, the streams of fuel from the nozzles should be practically perfectly aligned as viewed from the end of the unit and of equal volume.

This test should be performed after any rebuild of the unit and is sometimes helpful as a final diagnostic check of a complaint stemming from poor or erratic fuel flow.

The following are the most probable causes if all fuel streams are not in alignment:

  a. Kinked nozzle fuel lines.
  b. Partial blockage of one or more fuel distributor outlets.
  c. Partial blockage of the affected nozzles.
  d. Unlike coded nozzle installed in error during replacement.

Less probable possible causes are miscoded nozzles and odd size apertures in one or more fuel distributor outlets.

The above check will reveal only differences in fuel flow from the nozzles. It will not aid in uncovering problems arising from excessively lean mixtures, as all fuel flowing into the distributor, regardless of quantity, is distributed equally to all eight nozzles.

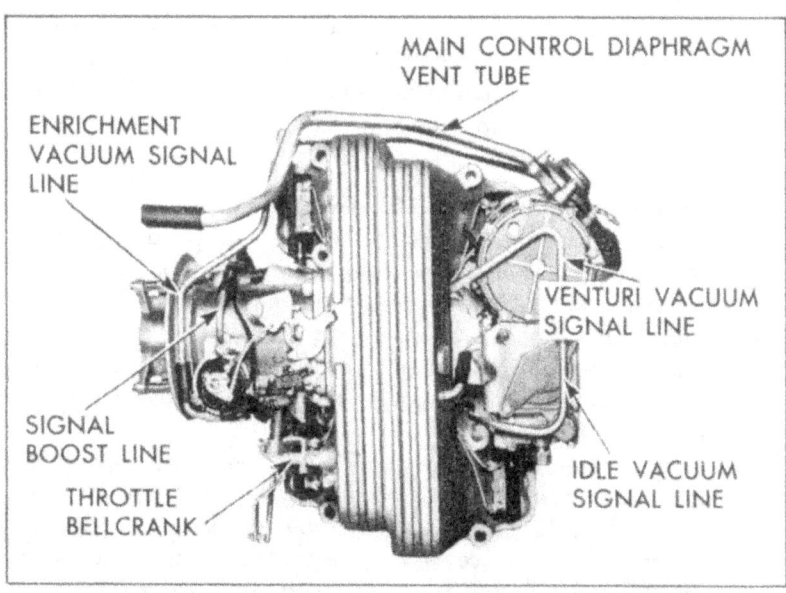

Fig. 121—Signal and Fuel Meter Vent Lines

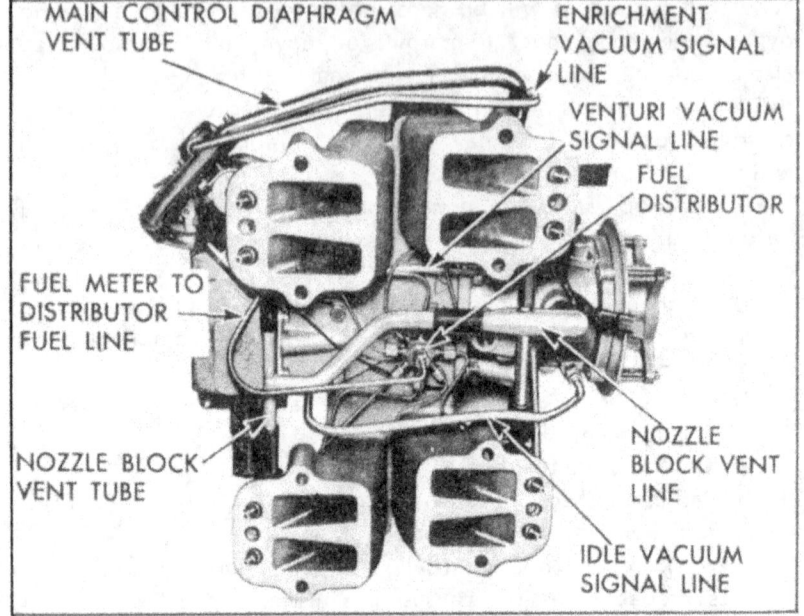

Fig. 122—Fuel and Nozzle Vent Lines

REMOVAL OF ASSEMBLIES

Throttle Control Linkage

1. Remove throttle return spring.
2. Remove nut and external toothed washer securing linkage to the throttle valve shaft lever beneath the air meter.
3. Remove hairpin retainer attaching accelerator linkage levers to post and manifold casting and remove linkage. Do not further disassemble.

Signal, Fuel and Vent Lines (figs. 121 and 122)

1. Remove enrichment vacuum signal line by disconnecting the rubber sleeve at the cold enrichment housing on the air meter and at the enrichment diaphragm on the fuel meter (fig. 121).
2. Disconnect main diaphragm vent tube at the rubber sleeve at the fuel meter and remove tube. Do not remove short tube fixed in the fuel meter.
3. Remove the fuel meter-to-distributor fuel line, leaving the the brass adapter fitting installed in the fuel meter casting (fig. 122). This fitting should not be removed from the fuel meter unless replacement is required. Exercise caution in removing this line at fuel meter end. Tube extends through adapter fitting into casting about 1¼".

4. To remove the venturi signal vacuum line, pull line out of its rubber sleeve at the air meter end and unscrew the fitting on top of the main control diaphragm cover.
5. Remove idle signal vacuum line by unscrewing fittings at both the air meter and main control diaphragm cover ends. Do not remove adapter from air meter casting unless replacement is required.
6. Remove the signal boost line (fig. 121).

CAUTION: Lower hose contains a calibrated restriction. If a replacement hose is required, press restriction out of old hose and install in new hose. On 7014800 units, this restriction should be .036" in diameter.

7. Remove nozzle block vent tubes from both the fuel meter and air meter sides.
8. Unscrew the cap screw securing the nozzle retainer, then lift the nozzles clear of the intake manifold and nozzle blocks. Remove nozzle blocks and gasket, then remove the other three sets of nozzles in the same manner.
9. Invert unit and carefully push fuel distributor toward air meter side to free from its retaining bracket. Remove distributor, fuel lines, and nozzles as an assembly, using care not to break or sharply kink lines. This completes the re-

Fig. 123—Disconnecting Starting Cut-Off Switch

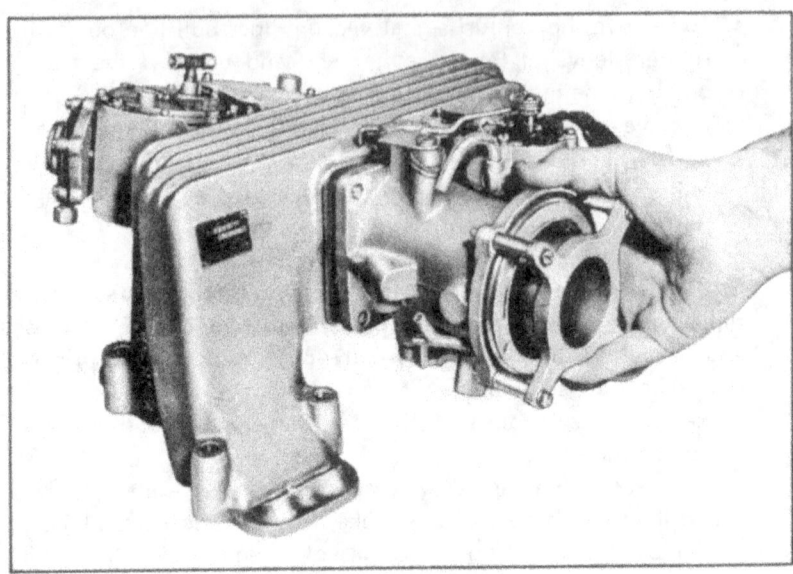

Fig. 124—Removing Air Meter

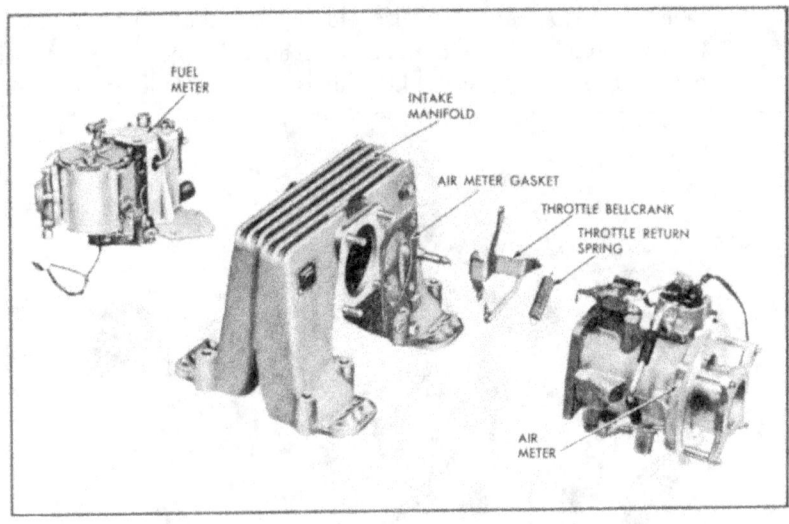

Fig. 125—Fuel Injection Basic Components

moval of the signal, fuel, and vent lines.

Air Meter
1. Disconnect lead from solenoid at starting cut-off switch (fig. 123).
2. Remove four nuts and lock washers securing air meter to the intake manifold and remove the air meter assembly and gasket (fig. 124).

Fuel Meter

To detach fuel meter, place intake manifold on end and remove three cap screws and lock-washers fastening the fuel meter bracket to the manifold (fig. 125). Complete removal by pulling fuel bowl vent tube free of rubber sleeve connecting it to the intake manifold.

DISASSEMEBLY

Air Meter

1. Remove the idle air and idle fuel adjusting screws and springs (fig. 126).
2. Unscrew four diffuser cone attaching screws and remove diffuser cone, spacers, venturi ring, rubber gasket, and attaching screws (fig. 127).

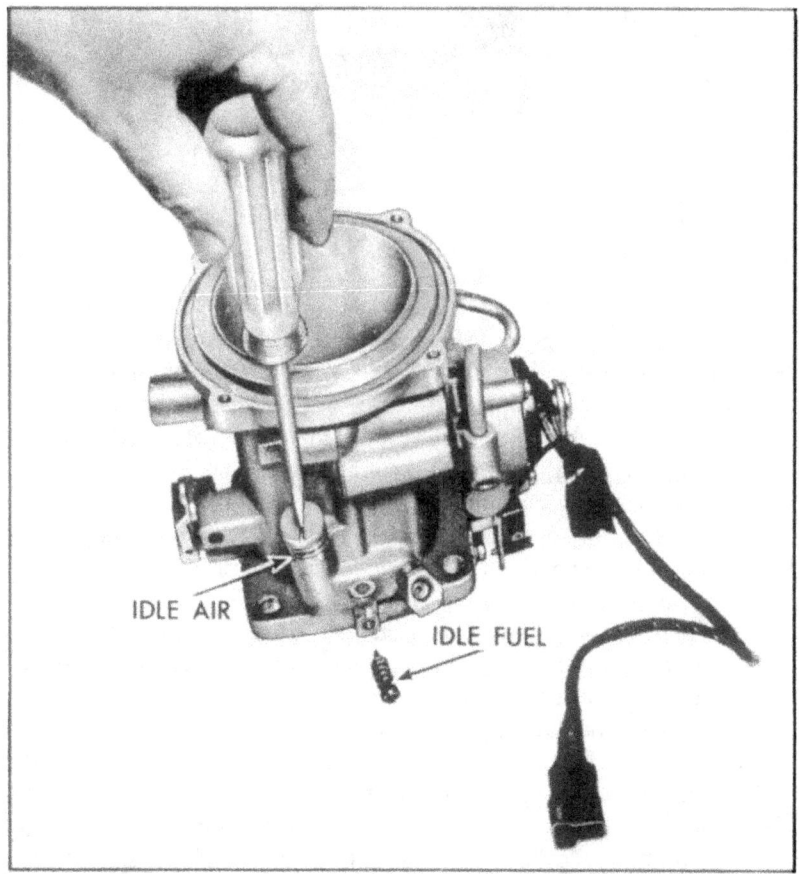

Fig. 126—Removing Idle Fuel and Idle Air Adjusting Screws

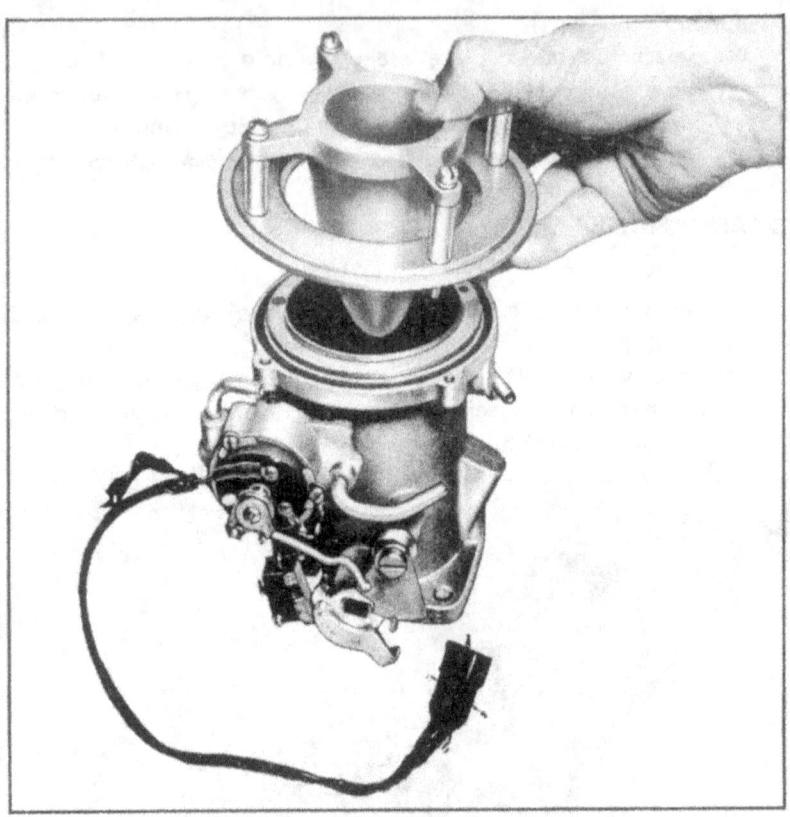

Fig. 127—Removing Diffuser Cone and Venturi Ring

3. Remove the fast idle linkage and cold enrichment coil as an assembly by first removing the screw attaching the fast idle cam (fig. 128). Then remove three screws and retainers securing thermostatic coil to the housing and lift out the cam, spring, linkage, and coil as an assembly. Further disassembly of these components is unnecessary unless replacement is required.
4. Remove both the starting cut-off switch and its bracket by removing the two screws and lockwashers securing the bracket to the boss on the air meter.
5. The above operations complete usual air meter disassembly. Under no circumstances should the throttle valve, throttle valve shaft lever, or lever stop screw be removed as these parts are not serviced separately and their position should not be altered. To prevent possible thread damage to the air meter casting, neither the 45-degree spark control pipe fitting nor the female fitting at the auxiliary idle signal location should be removed unless replacement is required.

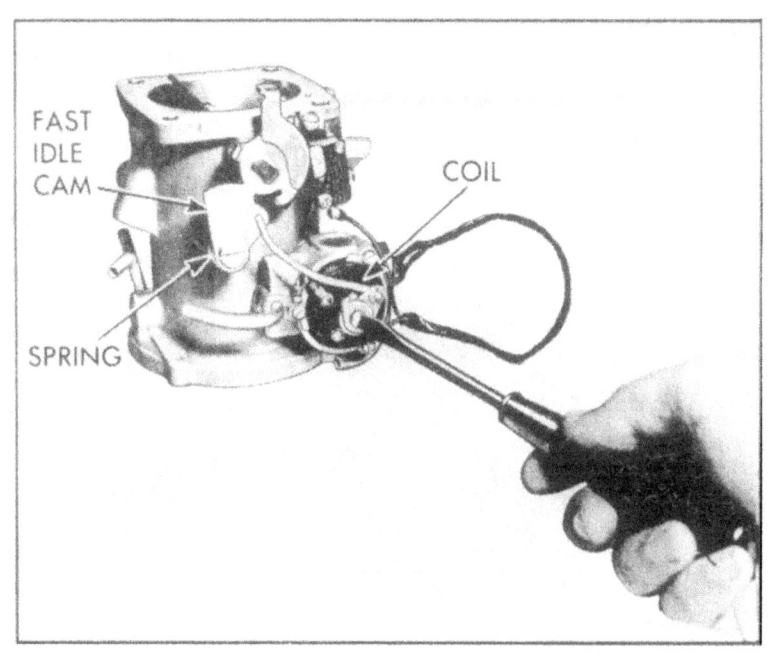

Fig. 128—Removing Cold Enrichment Coil

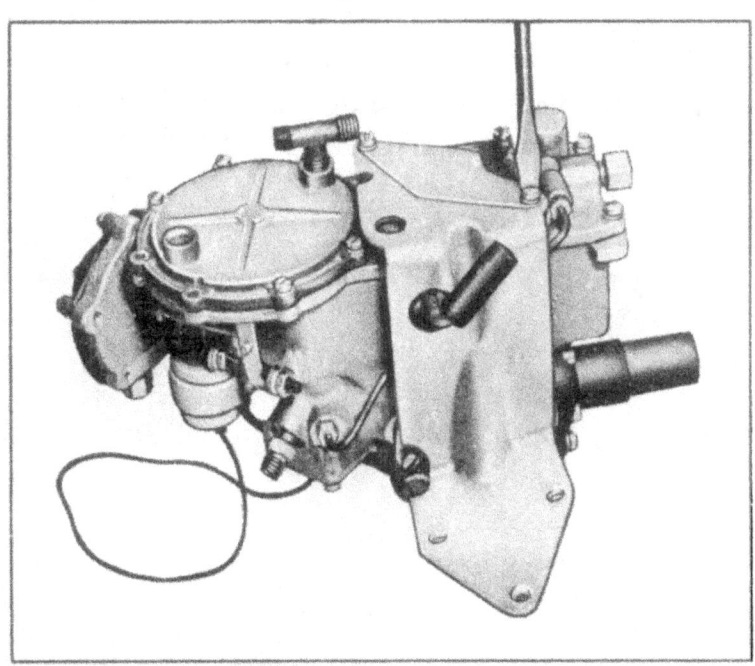

Fig. 129—Removing Fuel Meter Mounting Bracket

FUEL METER

1. Remove fuel meter mounting bracket by removing four attaching screws (fig. 129). Be careful not to lose the spacers used at the bowl cover attachment.
2. Remove starting by-pass fuel line (fig. 130).

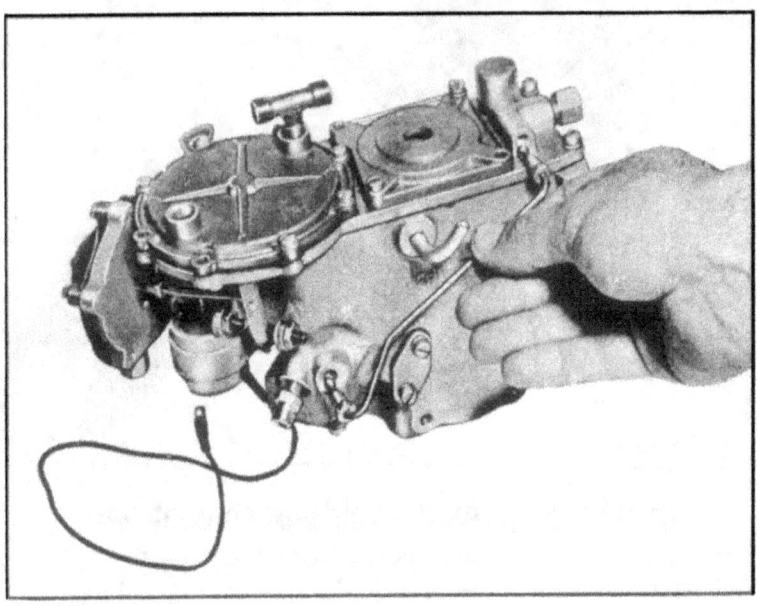

Fig. 130—Removing Starting By-pass Fuel Line

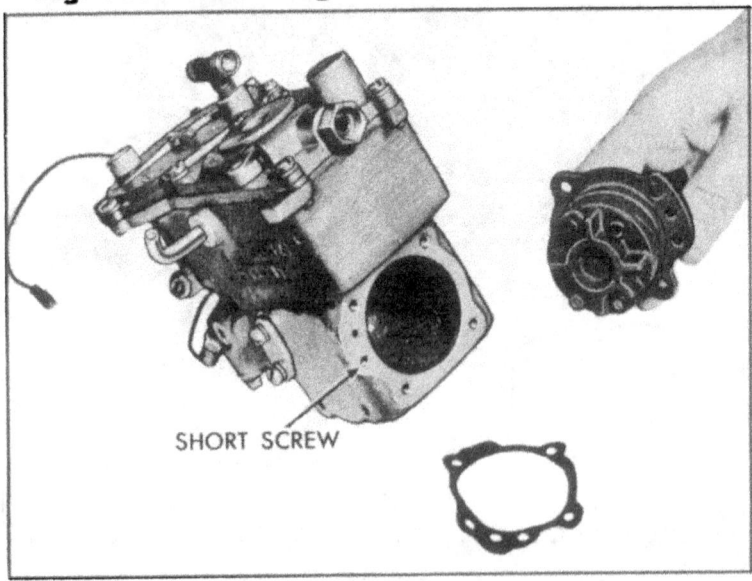

Fig. 131—Removing Fuel Meter Fuel Pump

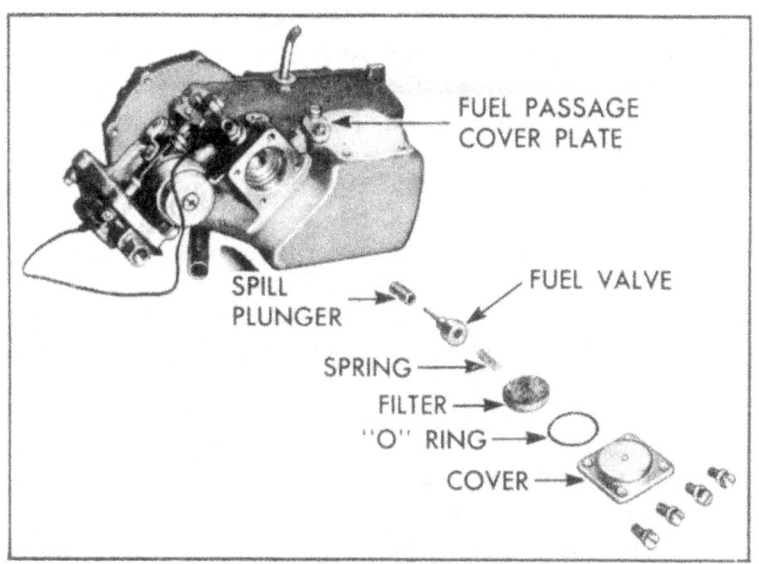

Fig. 132—Fuel Valve Components—Exploded View

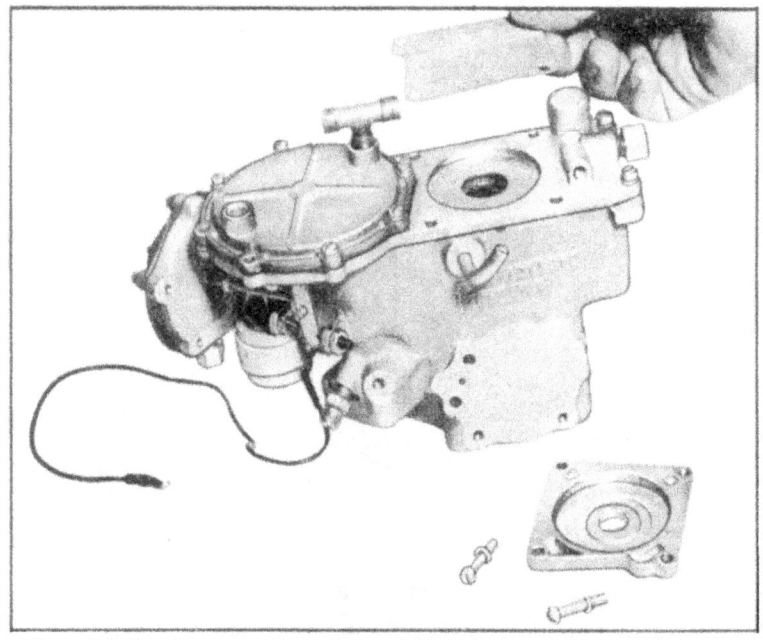

Fig. 133—Removing Bowl Vent Cover and Screen

3. Remove high pressure fuel pump and gasket (fig. 131) by removing five attaching screws. **Do not further disassemble fuel pump!**
4. Invert the fuel meter and remove the four screws and lock-

washers securing the fuel valve cover. Remove the cover and "O" ring, then remove the filter, fuel valve, spring, and the spill plunger (fig. 132). Be especially careful not to drop or lose the spill plunger as it is individually matched to the fuel meter casting and is not serviced separately.

5. Detach the fuel passage cover plate by removing the two attaching screws and lockwashers (fig. 132).
6. Remove the two remaining screws attaching the bowl vent cover and remove the cover and screen (fig. 133). It is good practice to inspect and clean the screen and replace immediately to minimize the possibility of dirt entry to the fuel meter.
7. If checks performed during "Trouble Shooting" indicate that the enrichment diaphragm is leaking and requires replacement, remove the two screws securing the shield to the main control diaphragm cover and remove the shield.
8. To remove the enrichment diaphragm, first remove the hairpin retainer securing the diaphragm rod to the enrichment lever. Then remove the five screws securing the enrichment diaphragm cover while holding the cover in place to prevent

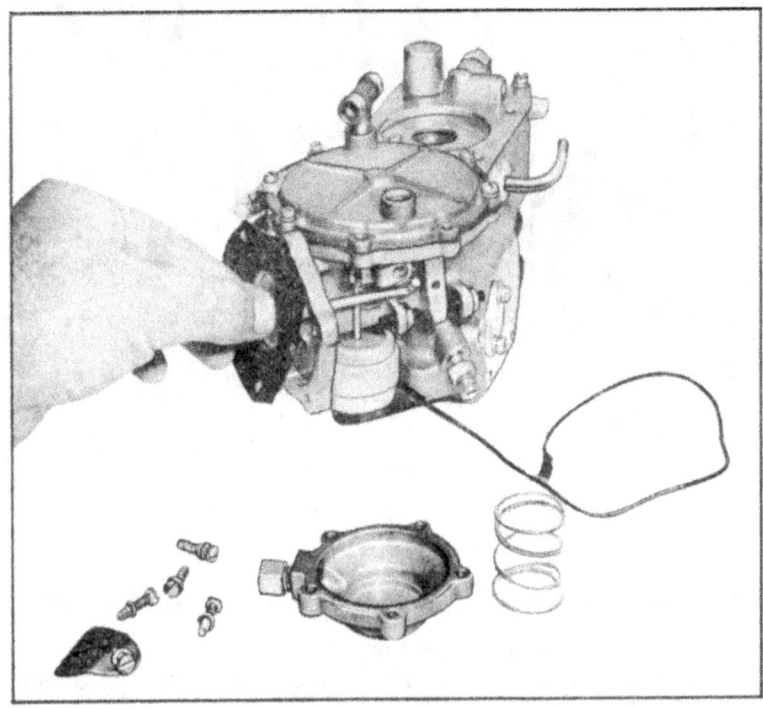

Fig. 134—Removing Power Enrichment Diaphragm

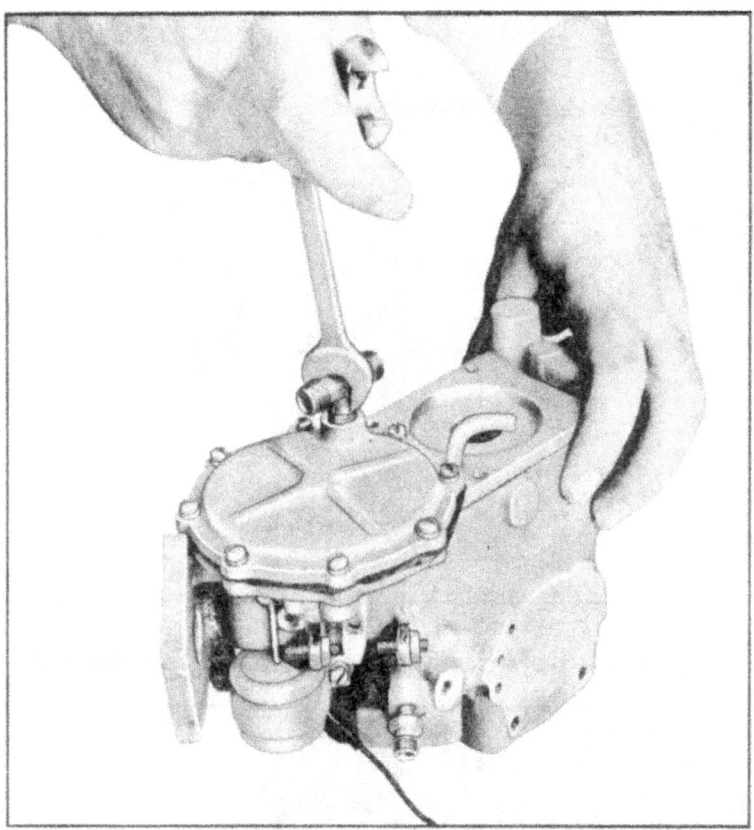

Fig. 135—Removing Main Control Diaphragm Tee

losing the spring when the cover is released (fig. 134). Once the cover is removed, turn the diaphragm slightly to free the rod from the enrichment lever.

9. If replacement is required, remove tee fitting from main control diaphragm cover by using two wrenches as illustrated in Figure 135. It should be noted that the restriction in the tee is toward the rear of the fuel meter assembly.
10. Remove eight screws and lock washers attaching main control diaphragm cover and remove cover and cover gasket. Discard gasket.
11. Using a small screwdriver and a 7/32" wrench, remove the nut securing the main control diaphragm to the link (fig. 136). It is imperative that the link be held fast while removing the nut to prevent damage to the fuel control linkage. Remove the main control diaphragm.
12. Remove the nylon shield from the link by lifting and tipping

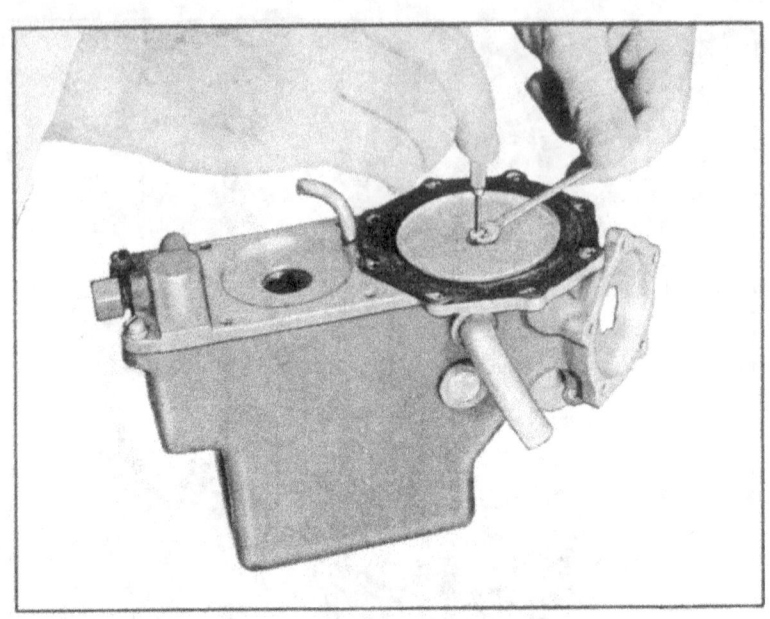

Fig. 136—Unfastening Main Control Diaphragm

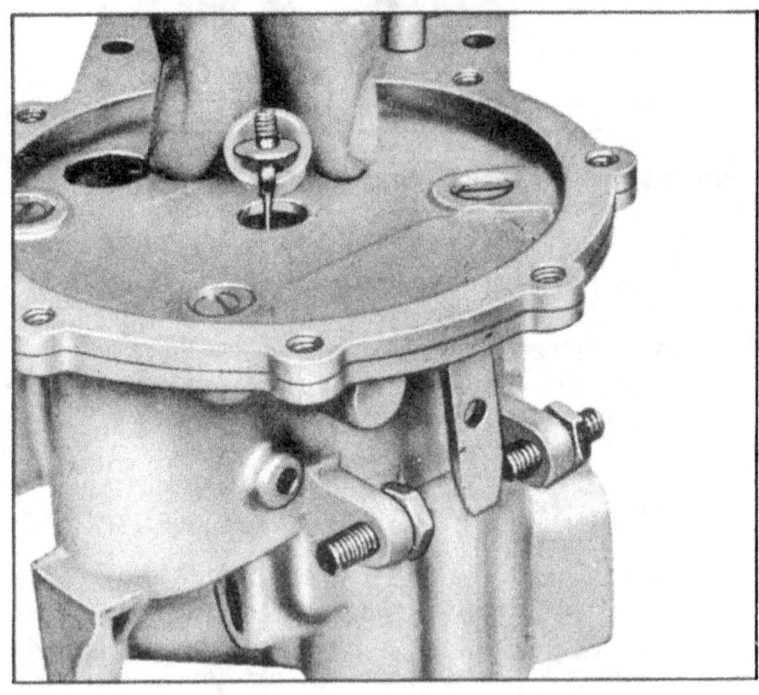

Fig. 137—Removing Nylon Shield

it to one side so that the slot in the shield will clear the link (fig. 137).

13. Remove the fuel meter cover by unscrewing the three self-locking screws at the main control diaphragm location and the two cover attaching screws at the fuel inlet end of the assembly. Lift cover up and then slightly rearward to prevent damage to the float (fig. 138). Remove and discard cover gasket.
14. Remove nylon splash cup (fig. 138) from fuel bowl by removing attaching screw.
15. Loosen set screw in ratio lever (fig. 139), then remove ratio lever by pulling enrichment lever shaft out of fuel meter housing.
16. Using a ¼" wrench, remove elastic nut securing solenoid inner lever (fig. 139). Remove inner lever and small brass washer from solenoid outer lever shaft.
17. Remove hairpin clip (fig. 140) securing solenoid shaft to solenoid outer lever, disconnect shaft and outer lever, then complete removal by removing two screws attaching solenoid to fuel meter.

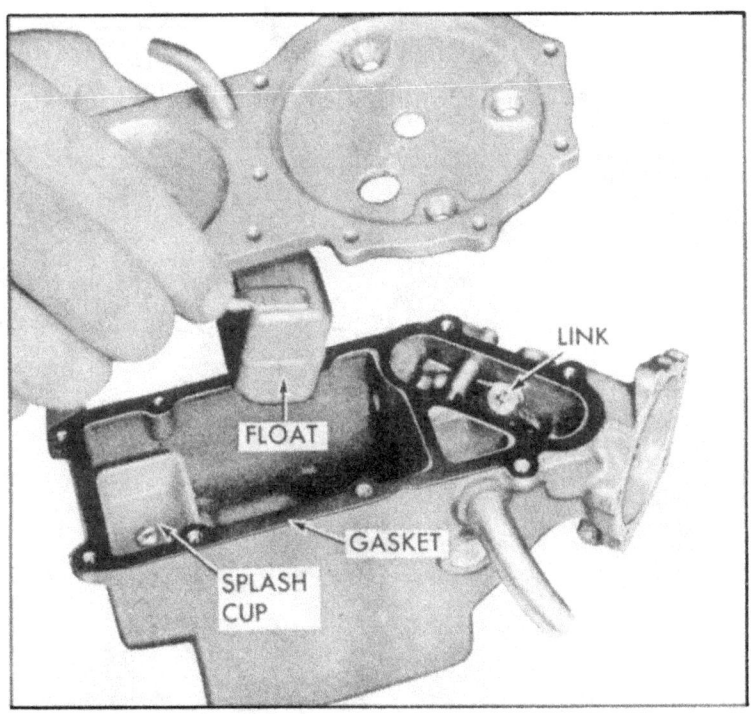

Fig. 138—Removing Fuel Meter Cover

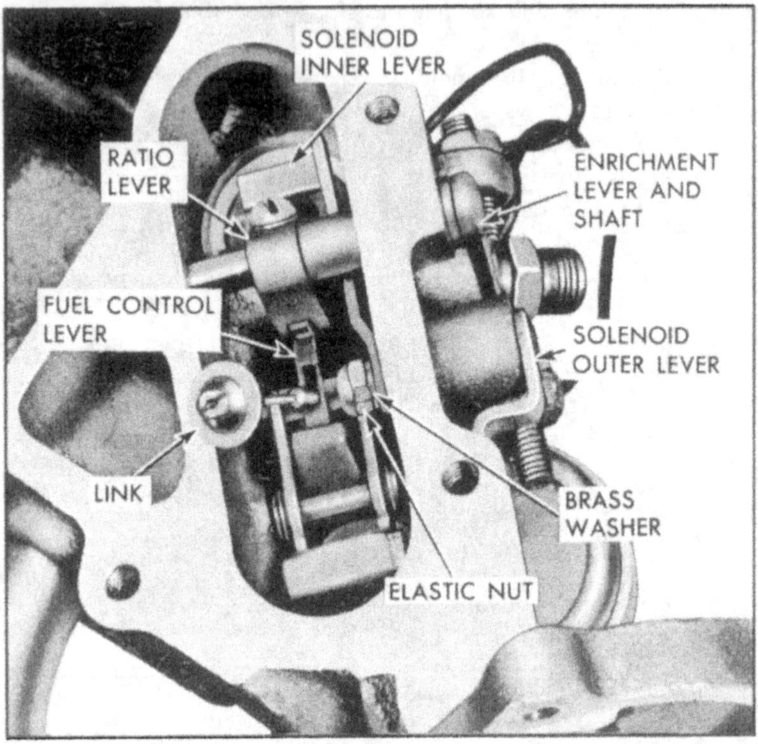

Fig. 139—Fuel Control Components Linkage

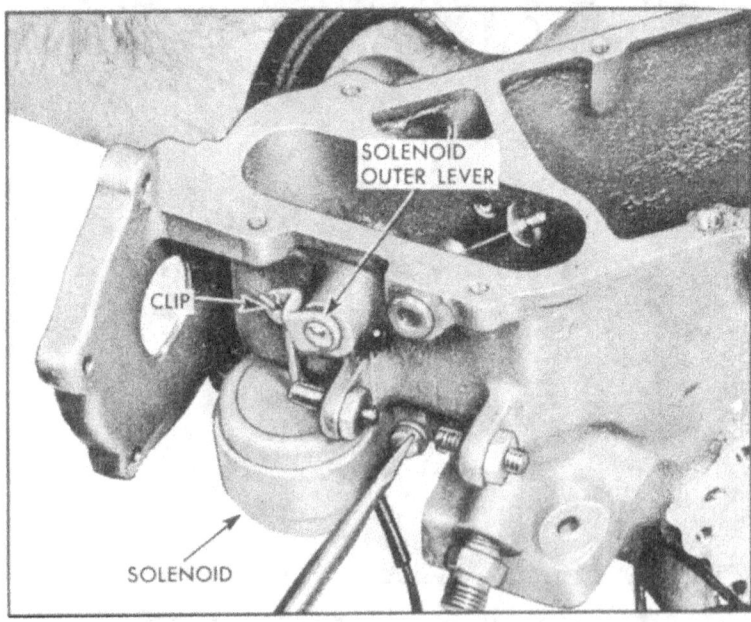

Fig. 140—Removing Solenoid and Outer Lever

18. Remove the float hinge pin and lift out the float and inlet needle. Using a wide screwdriver, remove the needle seat and gasket.
19. To remove fuel strainer screen remove nut at inlet port.

The above steps complete the usual fuel meter overhaul. However, if the fuel control linkage (fig. 139) is broken or otherwise damaged, the linkage can be replaced by forcing the linkage shaft through the side of the fuel meter housing with long nosed pliers from the inside.

Reinstall the new linkage in the same manner and check that it is free on the shaft and does not bind against the side walls. If binding exists, polish the brass bearings of the new linkage with crocus cloth until the required clearance is obtained.

Cleaning and Inspection

All metal parts should be thoroughly washed in clean solvent and blown dry. Under no circumstances should wires or drills be passed through any orifce as this would enlarge the openings and upset calibration. All gaskets should be discarded and replaced with new ones except the intake manifold-to-adapter plate gasket.

The rubber hose sleeves used to attach various vent and signal tubes may be reused after a careful check of condition. It is always best to replace any hose connection which shows the slightest sign of deterioration.

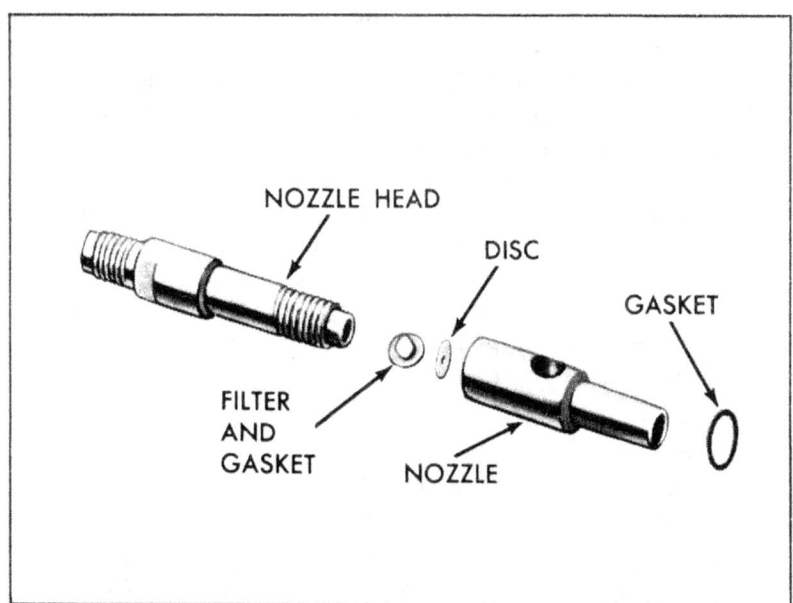

Fig. 141—Injection Nozzle—Exploded View

CAUTION: If it is necessary to replace the rubber hose connecting the signal boost line to the venturi signal line, be sure to remove the restriction plug from the old hose and install it in the new one.

Vent, signal, and fuel lines should be checked for cracks and plugging. Blowing into the tubes is the simplest check for obstructions.

Check nozzle blocks closely for cracks. A very slight over-tightening of the nozzle block can start fine cracks which will enlarge by vibration and cause an air leak, resulting finally in missing and rough idle.

The filter screen should be checked very closely for holes or plugging.

Free operation of the spill plunger is imperative as this regulates the amount of fuel delivered to the nozzles as signaled by the main control diaphragm. Because the fuel plunger is continually immersed in gasoline, sticking can result from gasoline gum and varnish formations. Thoroughly clean the fuel valve and the valve sleeve in the fuel meter with clean solvent and a small bristle brush. Dry with compressed air to protect against introduction of lint or dirt.

If a fuel flow or Trouble Shooting check reveals one or more faulty nozzles, remove faulty nozzle and adjacent nozzle and observe flow from nozzle lines. Also interchange nozzles and again observe fuel flow. If nozzle is definitely established as being faulty, disassemble as follows:

Hold the nozzle holder body with a 3/16" or slightly smaller drill or rod, and unscrew the upper half. Carefully remove the filter screen and the orifice disc. Inspect the disc for cleanliness. Do not attempt to clean the orifice with drills or wires. Clean the filter screen and reassemble as shown in Figure 141. The disc must be placed in the nozzle body with the bright surface down.

If it is necessary to replace a nozzle due to lost parts or from mutilation, check the nozzle code and replace with a like letter coded nozzle as shown in the following chart. Each nozzle carries a letter and number code at the upper end.

Production Nozzle Code	Use Replacement Nozzle	Part Number
Q-11 or Q-12	Q-12	7014856
R-12 or R-13	R-13	7014857
S-13 or S-14	S-14	7014858

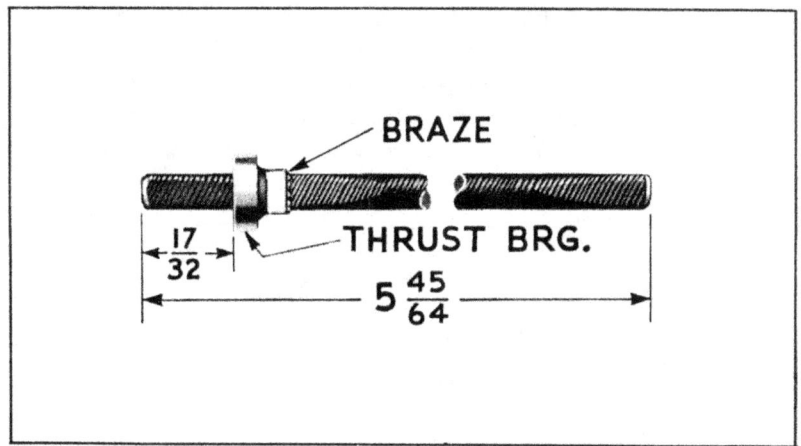

Fig. 142—Fuel Pump Drive Cable Dimensions

After carefully washing the air meter casting, check that the small drillings near the throttle blade are not clogged. These too should be cleaned by using a small bristle brush and cleaning solvent.

Checks should also be made to be sure that the two valves in the cold enrichment housing fully open and close. The simplest check is to blow into the base of the housing while depressing the signal boost valve. Air flow should be out of signal boost tube. Then repeat the check while depressing the enrichment vacuum valve. Air flow should be from the enrichment outlet. As a final check, blow into the housing without depressing either valve. No air should flow; otherwise reclean the housing until valves fully seat. Replace housing if necessary.

Check thrust member of fuel pump flexible drive cable. Thrust member should be firmly secured to the cable 17/32" from the end (fig. 142). If loose, replace drive cable with a new one or if a new part is not available, carefully braze the thrust bearing in place.

ASSEMBLY
Fuel Meter
1. Install fuel strainer screen in fuel meter cover inlet port and install fuel fitting nut.
2. Using a new gasket, install needle seat (fig. 143) in fuel meter cover with a wide blade screwdriver. Then hook float needle onto float and install float by inserting hinge pin through mounting bosses.
3. Check float level and drop adjustment as follows:
    a. **Float level.** With the fuel meter cover inverted measure the distance between the cover and the bottom of the float

(fig. 144). If float level is correct this dimension will be 2 9/32". Bend float arm as required to adjust.

b. **Float drop.** Holding the cover upright, measure the distance from the bottom of the cover to the lowest point on the float (fig. 145). Correctly adjusted, this distance would be 2 27/32". Bend float tang to adjust, if necessary.

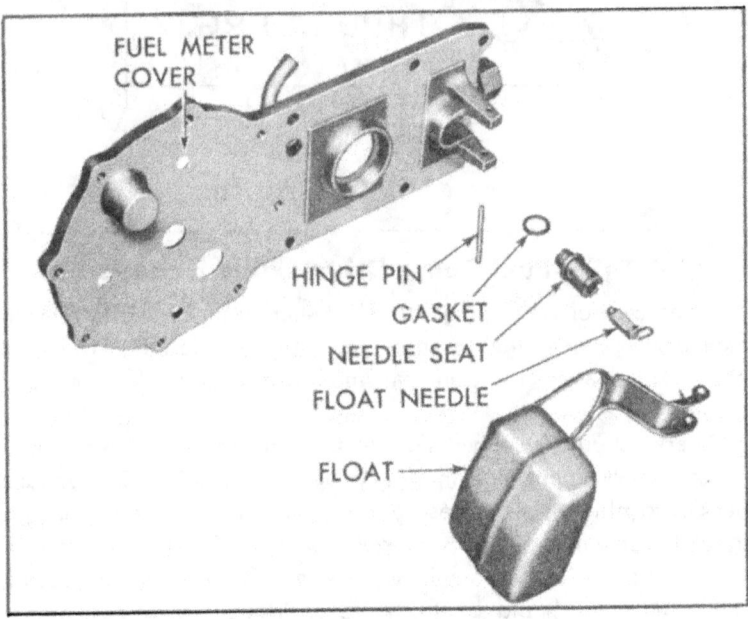

Fig. 143—Float Components—Exploded View

Fig. 144—Measuring Float Level

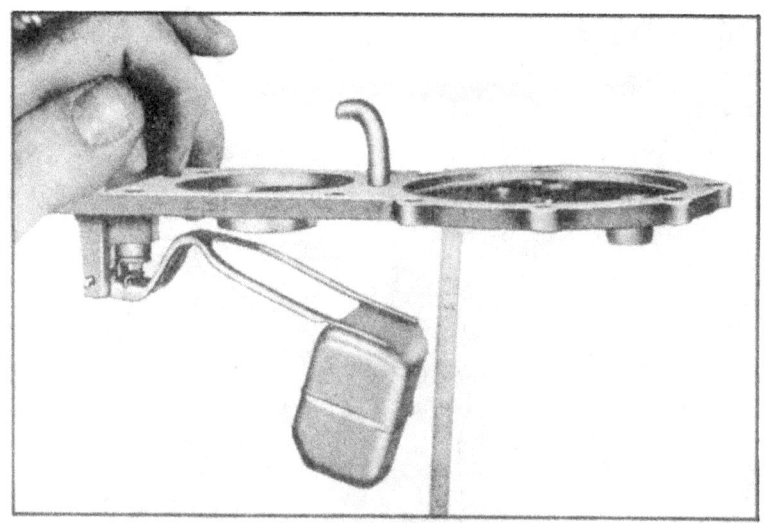

Fig. 145—Measuring Float Drop

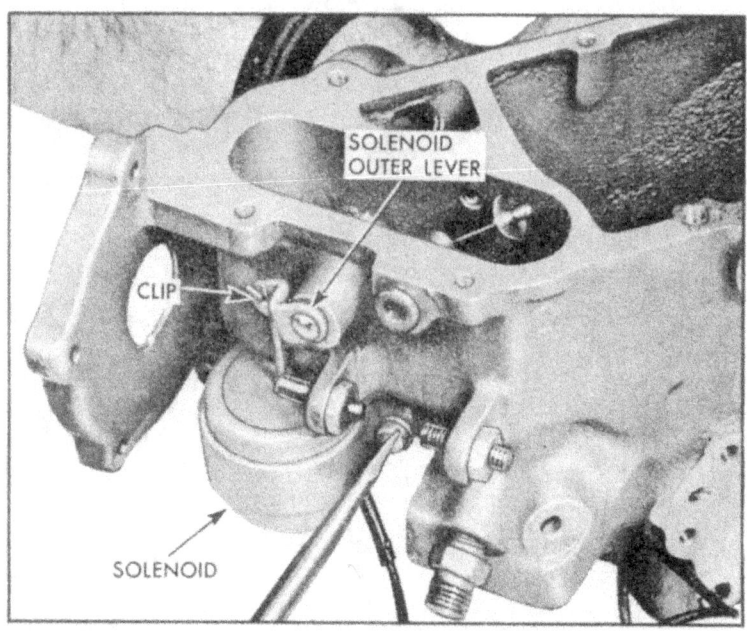

Fig. 146—Installing Solenoid and Outer Lever

4. Insert solenoid shaft through hole in solenoid outer lever (fig. 146) and connect with hairpin clip. Then insert shaft of solenoid outer lever into hole in fuel meter casting and secure the solenoid assembly to the fuel meter with two screws.

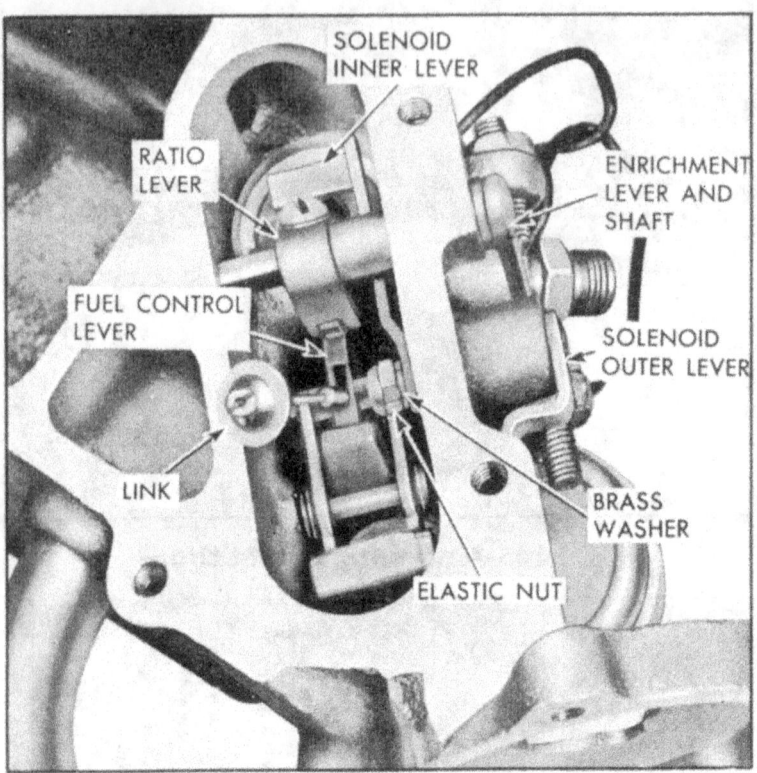

Fig. 147—Fuel Control Components

5. Position small brass washer (fig. 147) and solenoid inner lever on the outer lever shaft inside fuel meter and secure inner lever with ¼" elastic nut.
6. Position ratio lever (fig. 147) inside fuel meter, then insert enrichment lever shaft through side of fuel meter and through ratio lever. Be sure enrichment lever shaft is inserted its full distance and that ratio lever is centered over fuel control lever, then tighten set screw in ratio lever.
7. Position nylon splash cup (fig. 148) in fuel bowl and secure with attaching screw.
8. Position a new fuel meter cover gasket (fig. 148) on the fuel meter, then carefully lower the fuel meter cover assembly onto the fuel meter being careful not to bend the float and being sure that the fuel control link is through the hold at the center of the main control diaphragm location (fig. 149). Carefully align attaching screw holes in cover, gasket, and fuel meter. Then install three self-locking screws at the main control diaphragm location and two screws at the fuel inlet end of the assembly.

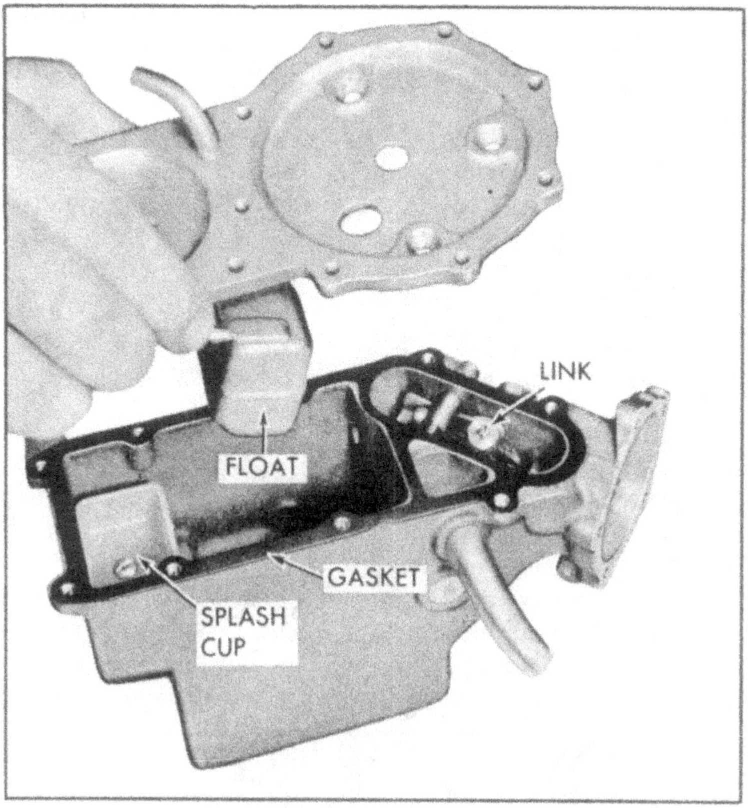

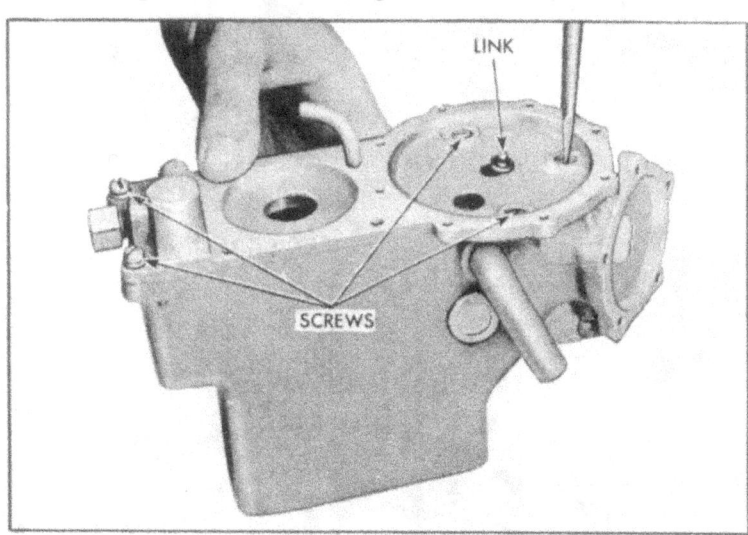

Fig. 148—Installing Fuel Meter Cover

Fig. 149—Fuel Meter Cover Attachment

9. Insert nylon shield (fig. 150) onto main control diaphragm link and push it flush into hole in fuel meter cover.
10. Position main control diaphragm onto link, turn diaphragm so that elongated holes are centered on attaching holes in fuel meter and secure with diaphragm nut while holding link with a screwdriver as shown (fig. 151).

NOTE: Be sure to install nut with countersink upward to allow clearance to hold link with screwdriver.

Once the diaphragm nut is fully tightened, recheck for centering of diaphragm holes and loosen nut and readjust if required. It is important that the diaphragm holes be perfectly centered so that it will not be necessary to stretch the diaphragm when the cover is installed.

11. Before installing main control diaphragm cover, check for full travel of the main control diaphragm and link. Lift assembly gently by diaphragm nut and drop. Diaphragm should bottom completely of its own weight. If it does not, loosen nut and rotate diaphragm until it will bottom on a free fall.
12. Position a new main control diaphragm cover gasket (fig. 152) on main control diaphragm cover, making sure that the holes in diaphragm and gasket align with attaching holes in fuel meter. Then position main control diaphragm cover and

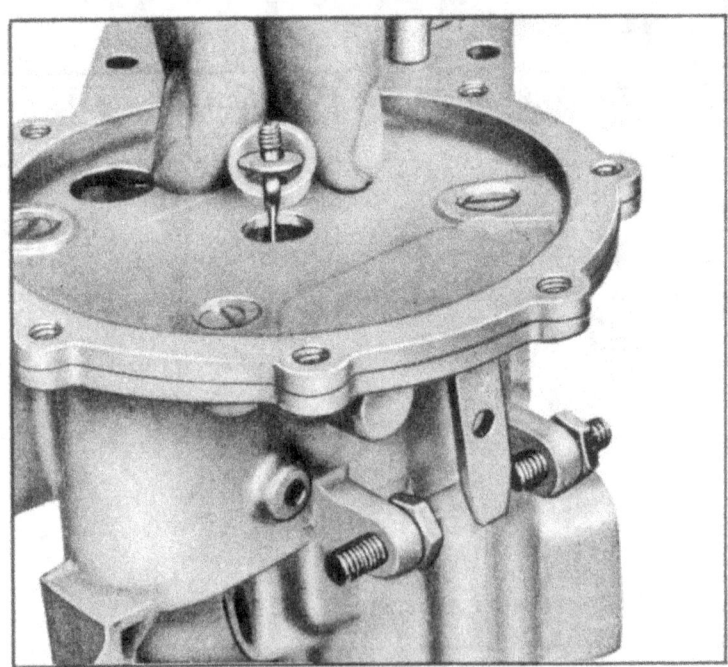

Fig. 150—Installing Nylon Shield

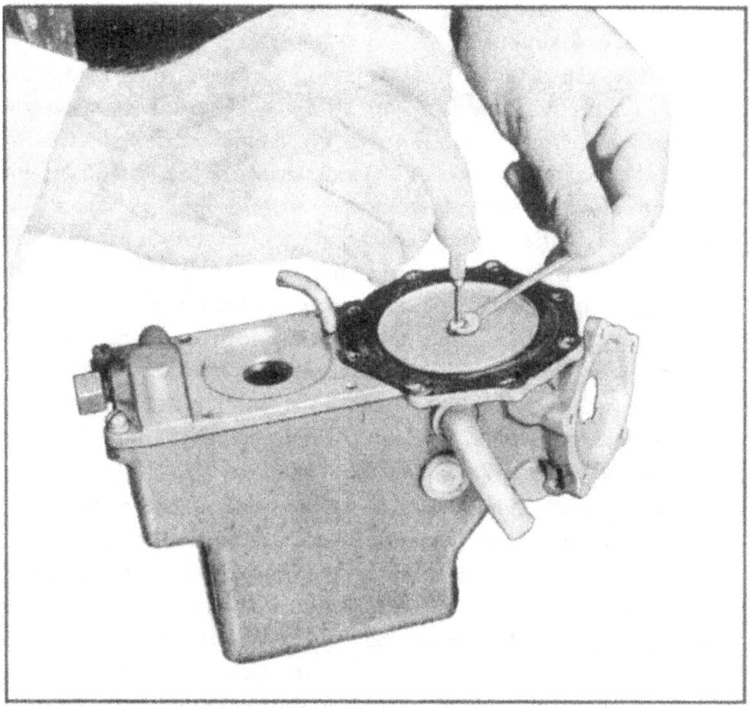

Fig. 151—Installing Main Control Diaphragm

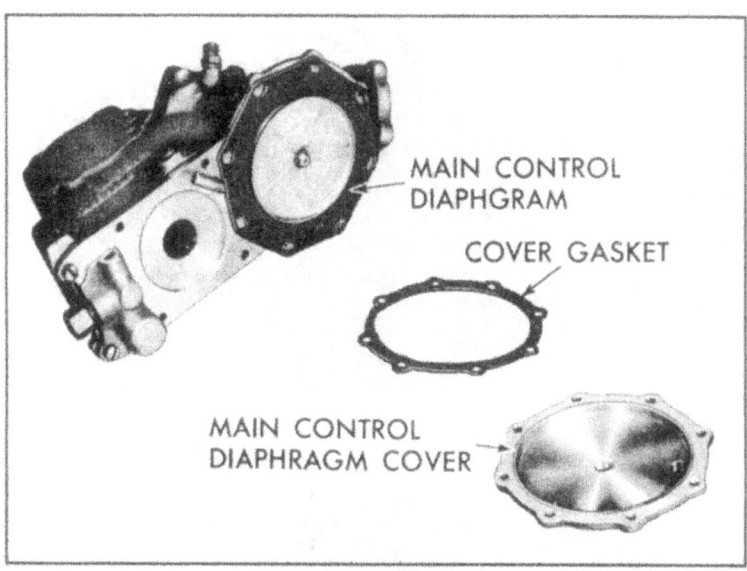

Fig. 152—Main Control Diaphragm Gasket and Cover

secure with eight screws and lockwashers tightened evenly in a criss-cross pattern.
13. If the restriction tee was removed from the main control diaphragm cover, reinstall it, using two wrenches as shown earlier in figure 135. Tee should be finally positioned so that the restriction end of the tee is toward the rear (fuel inlet end) of fuel meter assembly.
14. Connect enrichment diaphragm rod by slightly twisting the enrichment diaphragm rod to hook into enrichment lever, then secure rod with hairpin retainer (fig. 153). Complete installation by placing diaphragm return spring between enrichment cover and diaphragm and secure with five attaching screws. Use care to align diaphragm holes with holes in fuel meter to prevent a twisted diaphragm installation.
15. Check length adjustment of enrichment diaphragm rod by connecting a manometer with vacuum source to the enrichment vacuum line which should be temporarily installed for this adjustment. Apply and hold a vacuum of 12-15" Hg (mercury), then slowly release the vacuum, noting the readings at which the enrichment lever leaves the economy stop (forward) and arrives at the power stop (rear). If rod length is correct, enrichment lever should leave the economy stop

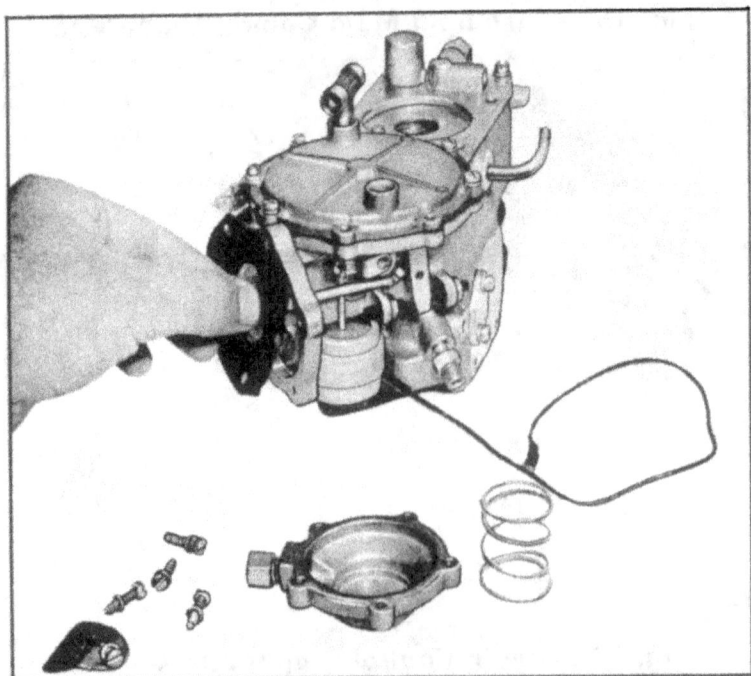

Fig. 153—Installing Power Enrichment Diaphragm

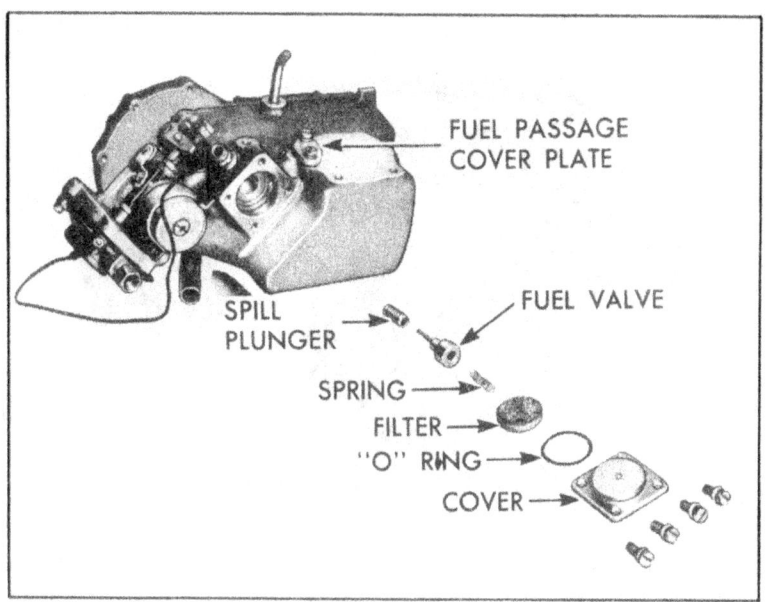

Fig. 154—Fuel Valve Components—Exploded

at 9" Hg or below and arrive at the power stop at 3" Hg or above. At 6" Hg, the lever must not be touching either stop. Adjust rod length by removing the enrichment diaphragm cover and lengthening or shortening the rod length as necessary to meet the above requirements.

16. Position shield on main control diaphragm cover and secure with two screws.
17. If the bowl vent screen and cover were not cleaned and immediately installed during "Disassembly", they should be reinstalled at this time.
18. Using a new gasket, install fuel passage cover plate (fig. 154) on side of fuel bowl with two screws and lockwashers.
19. With the fuel meter upside down, install the spill plunger, fuel valve, spring, and filter (fig. 154). If the original filter is being reused, it must be reinstalled with the same side toward the spill plunger to prevent any back-wash effect. This can be checked by touch as the filter side which was toward the cover will have a noticeable depression at the center. Install a new "O" ring on the spill plunger cover and lubricate with light engine oil — not grease. The addition of oil is important to prevent cutting the "O" ring during installation. Carefully push the cover into place until it is fully seated, then install the four screws and lockwashers in a criss-cross pattern.

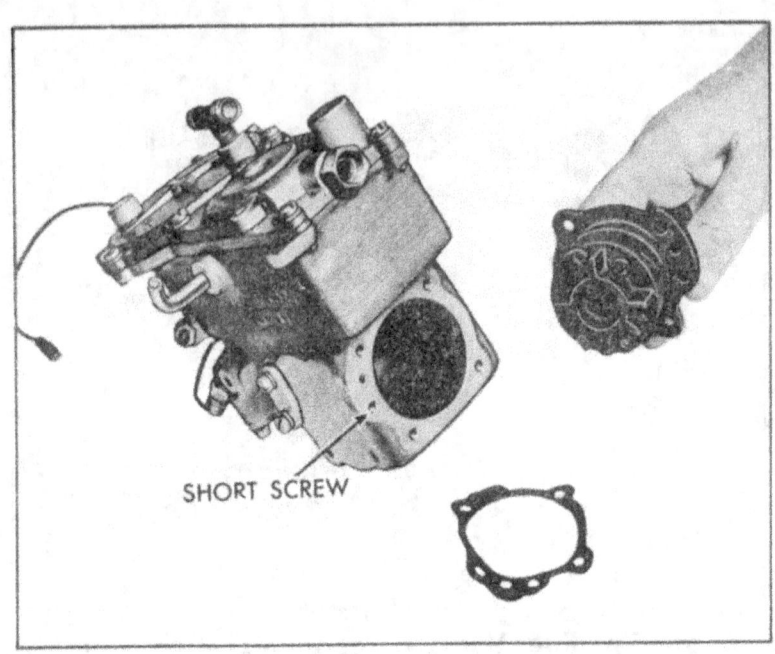

Fig. 155—Installing Fuel Valve Fuel Pump

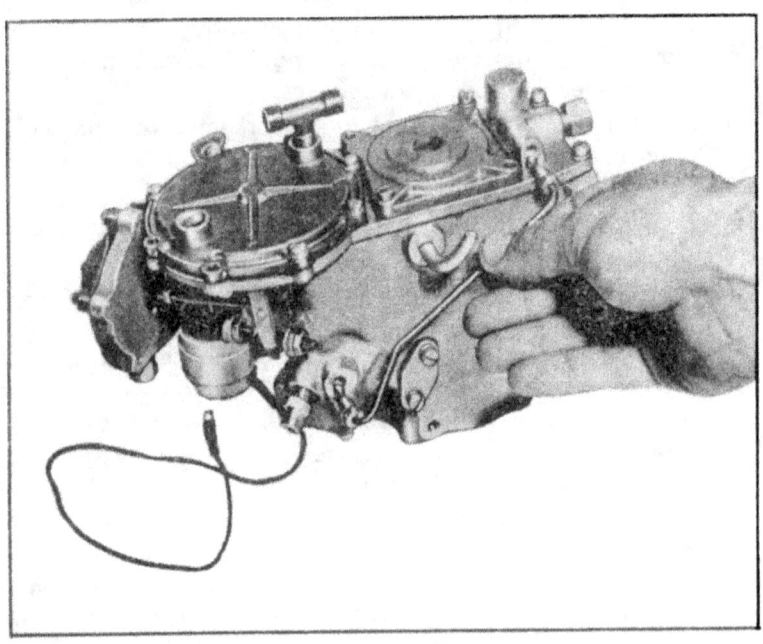

Fig. 156—Installing Starting By-pass Fuel Line

20. To check adjustment of the solenoid, fully depress the solenoid plunger and blow smoke through the starting bypass fuel line port at the spill plunger area. Smoke should come out the fuel distributor line hole in the fuel meter. Repeat this check without depressing the solenoid plunger; smoke should not come out of the fuel distributor line hole. These checks simulate the operation of the fuel valve components during starting. It is necessary that the solenoid provide sufficient throw to unseat the fuel valve when the solenoid plunger is depressed and yet allow the fuel valve to seat when the solenoid is released. Solenoid plunger travel is adjusted by inserting a screwdriver in the plunger slot and turning clockwise to decrease travel or counter-clockwise to increase travel.
21. Using a new gasket held in place with light engine oil, carefully position the high pressure fuel pump into the fuel meter and secure with five screws and lockwashers (figure 155).
NOTE: One screw is shorter and must be installed in hole at 9 o'clock position (fig. 155).
22. Reinstall starting by-pass fuel line (fig. 156).
23. Position two spacers on bowl vent cover, position mounting bracket (fig. 157) and cover plate on spacers, and secure with two screws and lockwashers. Attach bracket to side of fuel

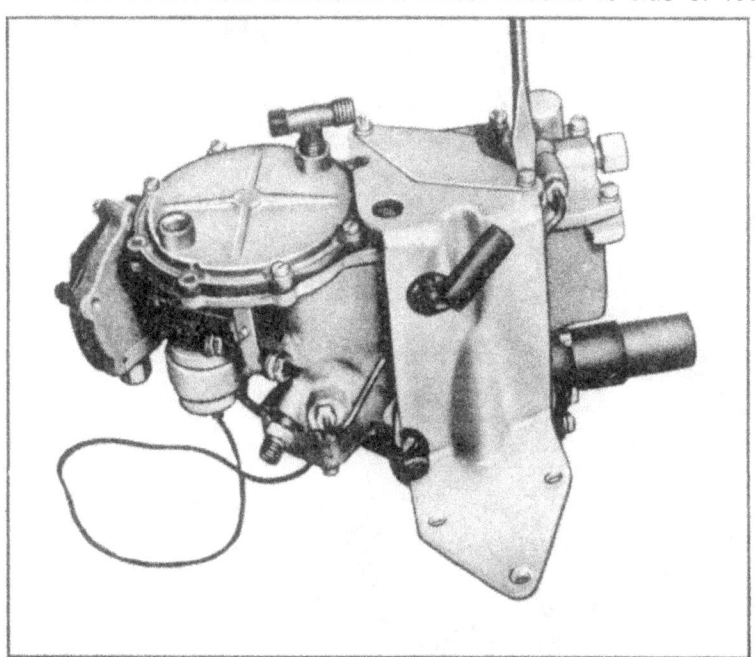

Fig. 157—Installing Fuel Meter Mounting Bracket

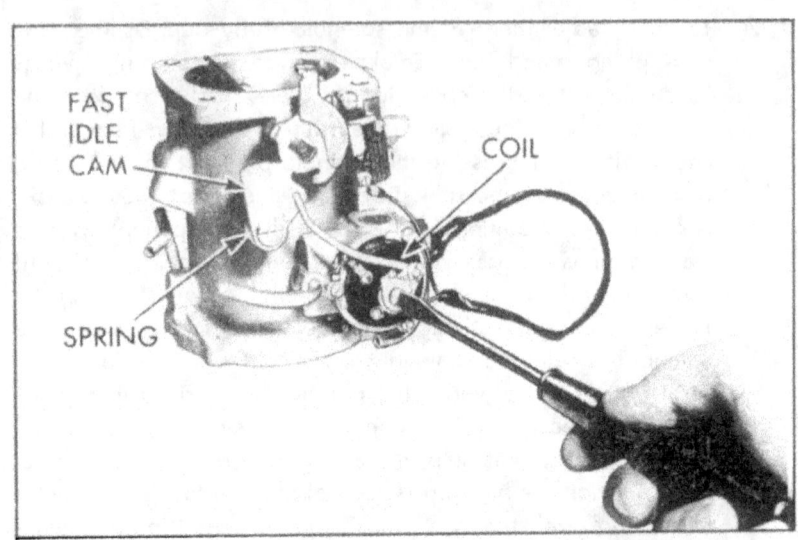

Fig. 158—Installing Cold Enrichment Coil

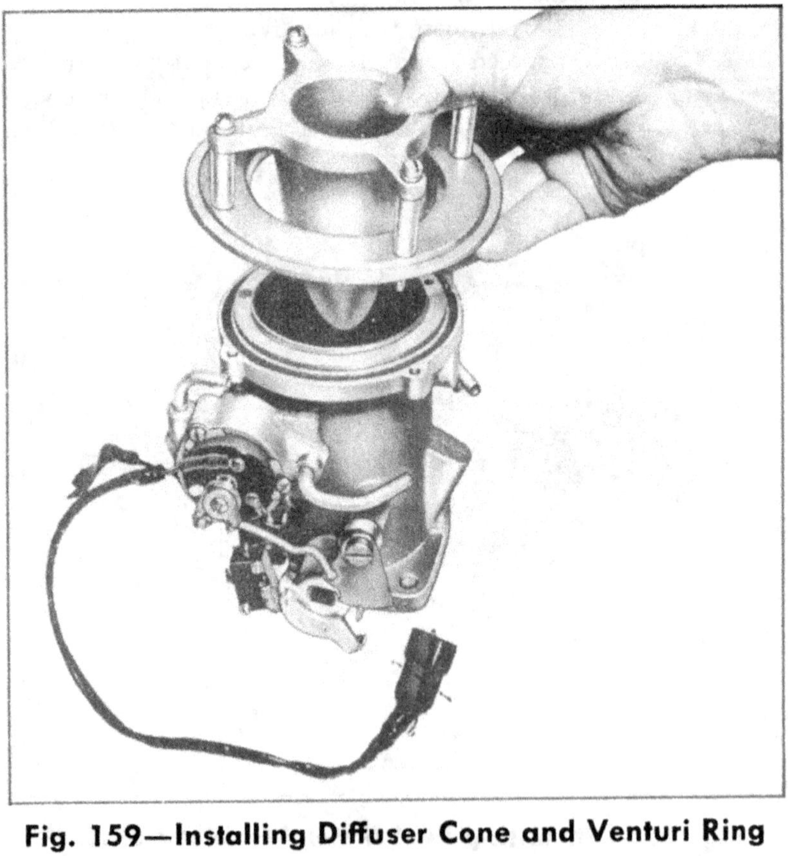

Fig. 159—Installing Diffuser Cone and Venturi Ring

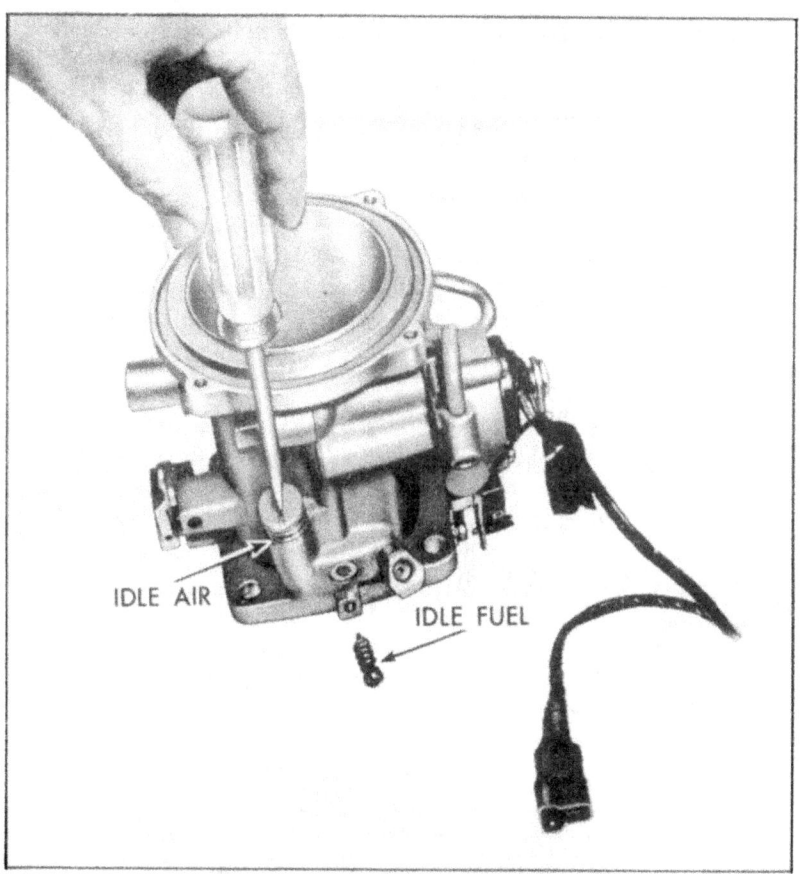

Fig. 160—Installing Idle Fuel and Idle Air Adjusting Screws

meter with two large screws and lockwashers to complete assembly of fuel meter.

Air Meter
1. Position the starting cut-off switch on its boss on the air meter casting and secure with two screws and lockwashers.
2. Using a new gasket, position the cold enrichment housing on the air meter and secure with attaching screws.
3. Insert the cold enrichment coil (fig. 158) into the cold enrichment housing so its operating lever is between the enrichment and signal boost valves. Loosely install three screws and retainers, position cover so scribed index is set 1½ marks rich, and tighten three screws securely. Be sure coil ground wire is fastened by one of the screws.
4. Place fast idle cam return spring on air meter boss with the

spring leg away from the cold enrichment housing (fig. 158). Hook spring tang against the cold enrichment side of the fast idle cam, center cam on boss, and secure with attaching screw. Properly installed, the spring tension should be forcing the fast idle cam away from the cold enrichment housing when the throttle is open.

5. Install new gasket on the venturi ring, then preassemble and install venturi ring and diffuser cone as follows:
    a. Insert the four screws and lockwashers through the diffuser cone, then place a spacer on each of the four screws.
    b. Place venturi ring on screws and spacers as shown in Figure 159.
    c. Holding the diffuser cone and venturi ring, position against air meter casting and tighten the four attaching screws.
6. Install idle air and idle fuel adjusting screws and springs (fig. 160), and back-off two turns as an initial adjustment. This completes assembly of air meter.

INSTALLATION OF ASSEMBLIES
Fuel Meter

To install fuel meter, place manifold casting on end, position mounting bracket over holes in underside of manifold, and install

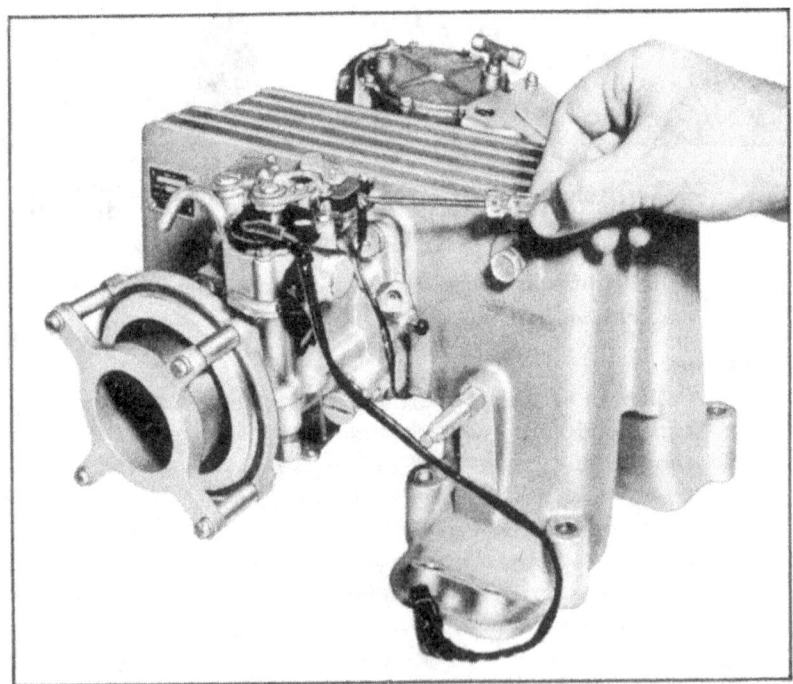

Fig. 161—Connecting Starting Cut-Off Switch

two cap-screws and lockwashers. The third, or center bolt, should not be installed at this time as it is also used to secure the fuel distributor mounting bracket. Complete assembly by sliding fuel bowl vent rubber tube onto tube in intake manifold.

Air Meter

Using a new air meter-to-intake manifold gasket, position air meter on intake manifold studs and secure with four nuts and lockwashers. Wire from solenoid on fuel meter should be run beneath the intake manifold to the starting cut-off switch and attached with small screw and external tooth lockwasher (fig. 161).

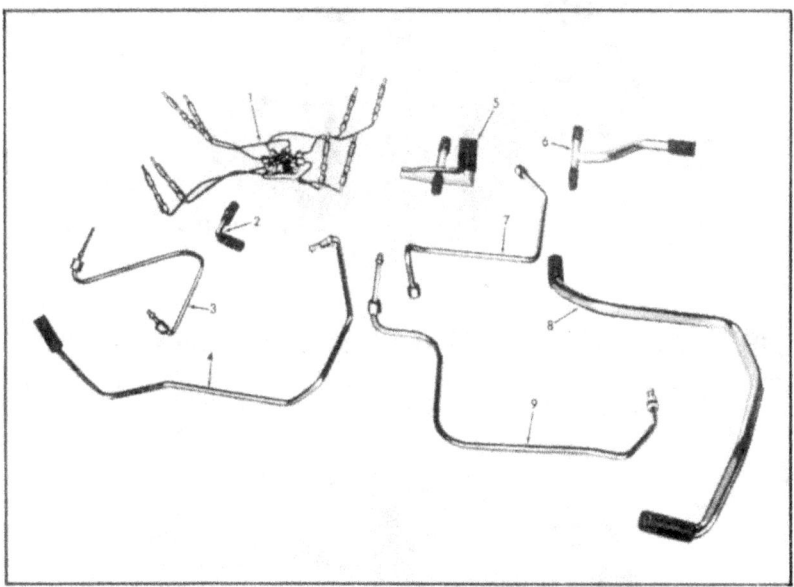

Fig. 162—Identification of Fuel, Signal, and Vent Lines

1. Fuel Distributor with Lines and Nozzles
2. Signal Boost Line
3. Fuel Meter to Distributor Fuel Line
4. Enrichment Vacuum Signal Line (Enrichment Housing to Enrichment Diaphragm)
5. Nozzle Block Vent Tube (Air Meter Side)
6. Nozzle Block Vent Tube (Fuel Meter Side)
7. Venturi Vacuum Signal Line (Venturi Cone Ring to Main Control Diaphragm)
8. Main Control Diaphragm Vent Tube (to Air Cleaner)
9. Idle Signal Vacuum Line (Air Meter to Main Control Diaphragm)

Signal, Fuel and Vent Lines

Refer to Figures 162, 163 and 164.

1. Install venturi vacuum signal line to the front side of the restriction tee in the main control diaphragm cover. Complete

installation by connecting signal line to pipe pressed into air meter with rubber sleeve.

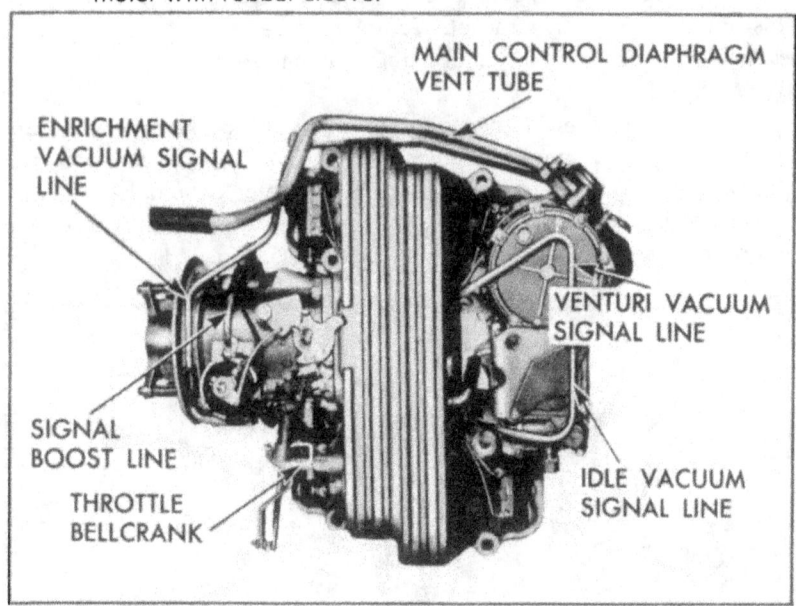

Fig. 163—Signal and Fuel Meter Vent Lines—Top View

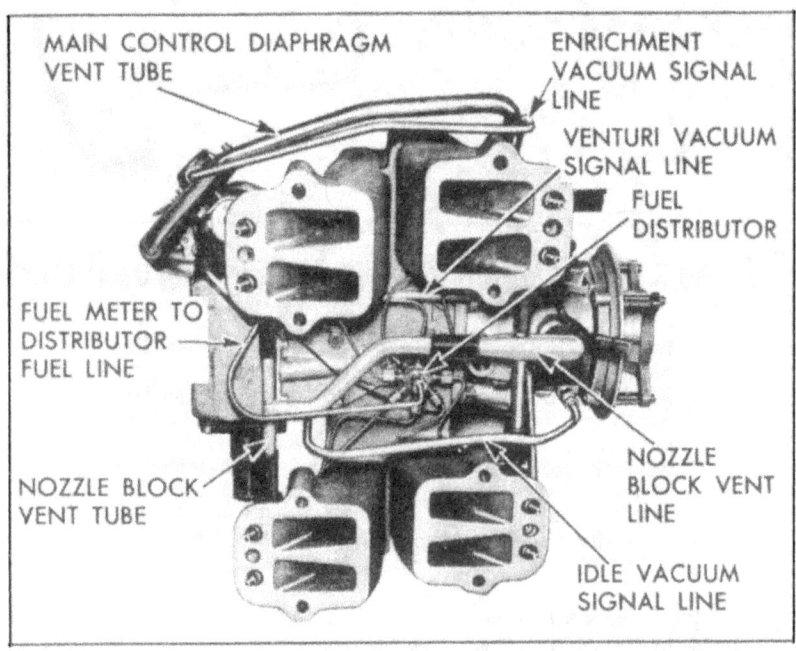

Fig. 164—Fuel, Signal, and Nozzle Vent Lines (Bottom View)

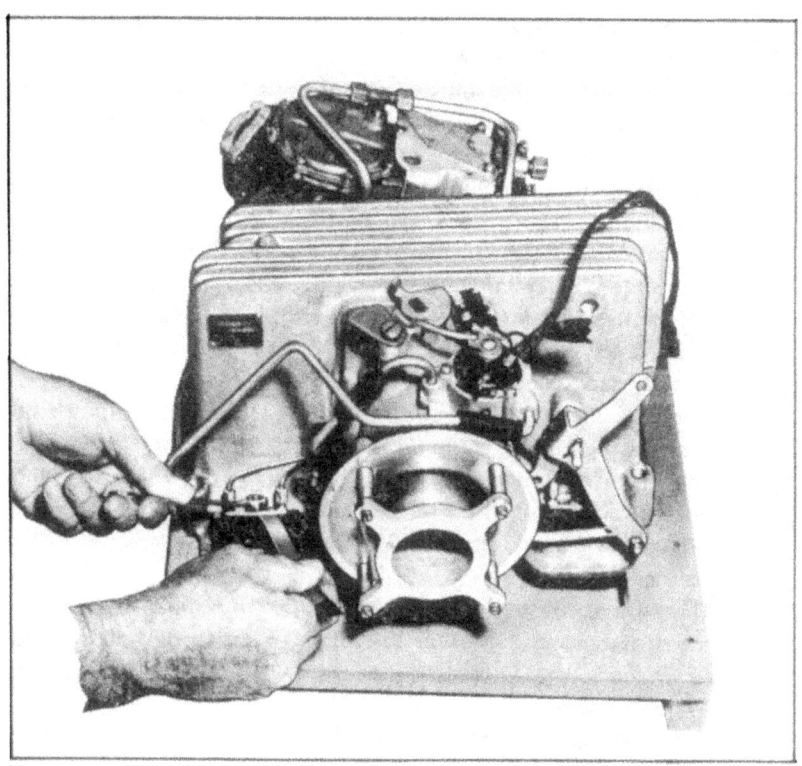

Fig. 165—Tightening Nozzle Retainer

2. Attach fuel distributor mounting bracket to base of intake manifold and secure with capscrew and lockwasher. Push fuel distributor into mounting bracket being careful not to kink nozzle fuel lines. Adjust fuel lines to their approximate positions.
3. Install fuel meter-to-distributor fuel line. Line must extend through brass fitting.
4. Install nozzles and nozzle blocks as follows:
    a. Install new nozzle gaskets on nozzles using light engine oil to hold in place.
    b. Slip two nozzles into slots of nozzle block retainer and install nozzles and retainer in nozzle block as an assembly. It is best to insert the nozzles while holding the nozzle block upside down to insure that the nozzle gaskets form a perfect seal.
    c. Install assembled nozzles and nozzle block on intake manifold using a new nozzle block gasket. Insert bolt into nozzle block, then slip a .002" feeler gauge between the nozzle block and retainer adjacent to the bolt location

(fig. 165). Tighten bolt until .002" feeler gauge can just be removed. Properly installed, the nozzle block will be retained by the tension against the nozzles; the retainer should not touch the nozzle block. Over-tightening will probably cause nozzle block cracking.
- d. Install three remaining sets of nozzles in the same manner.
5. Connect fuel lines to nozzles. Do not over tighten. After line to nozzle connections are completed, check that fuel lines do not contact intake manifold at any point. If necessary, pry lines away from manifold with a small screwdriver.
6. Install nozzle block vent tubes.
7. Connect idle signal vacuum line to the air meter and to the rear (restriction side) of the restriction tee on the fuel meter. With the fuel meter inverted, the line should pass over the nozzle block vent tube on the air meter side, then up alongside of intake manifold casting on the fuel meter side to the restriction tee.
8. Thread enrichment vacuum line into fitting on the enrichment diaphragm housing, then connect opposite end of line to the enrichment tube on the cold enrichment housing using a rubber sleeve.
9. Connect main control diaphragm vent tube to fuel meter, using rubber sleeve. The other end of this tube attaches to the air cleaner, when installed.
10. Connect signal boost line from venturi line to cold enrichment housing making certain restriction is in lower hose of boost line. This completes installation of the signal, fuel and vent lines.

Throttle Control Linkage
1. Position throttle bellcrank on intake manifold post and secure with hairpin retainer.
2. Insert bellcrank rod swivel into throttle valve shaft lever and secure with nut and external tooth lockwasher.
3. Hook throttle return spring onto throttle valve shaft lever and throttle valve crank mounting post to complete assembly.

INSTALLATION OF FUEL INJECTION UNIT ON ENGINE

Prior to reinstalling the Fuel Injection unit on the engine, it is good practice to perform the fuel flow check described earlier and illustrated in Figure 120 to check that fuel lines have been properly reinstalled.
1. Remove masking tape sealing intake ports in adapter plate, position Fuel Injection and adapter gasket on adapter plate, and secure with eight nuts and lockwashers. Tighten nuts evenly in a criss-cross pattern to 15 ft.-lbs.

2. Connect distributor spark control pipe (fig. 166) into 45-degree fitting in air meter, then tighten fitting at distributor end of pipe.
3. Attach electrical connector for starting cut-off switch and cold enrichment coil into wiring harness connector on dash.

Install accelerator and transmission TV rod swivels into throttle bellcrank on intake manifold. If necessary, adjust swivel position to permit free entry into holes in bellcrank levers. Check for full throttle and TV travel by holding the accelerator in the "wide-open" position. Readjust rod swivel positions as required.

5. Install air cleaner as described under "Maintenance and Adjustments."
6. Install fuel line into fitting on fuel meter.
7. Install fuel injection pump drive cable as follows:
   a. Carefully pull the fuel pump drive shaft from its housing being careful not to lose the small fiber washer located at the distributor end of the shaft between the thrust bearing and the shaft housing. Examine the thrust bearing to insure that it is held securely on the shaft and the dimension from the end of the shaft to nearest face of the bearing is 17/32" as shown earlier in Figure 142.
   b. Prealign the fuel injection pump and distributor driveline members by inserting one end of the shaft into the fuel pump, then rotate the shaft to engage the other end in the distributor drive socket.

Fig. 166—Fuel Injection Installed on Engine

    c. Carefully disengage shaft from both distributor and pump without rotating shaft. Reinstall fiber washer in distributor end of shaft housing and install shaft in housing.
    d. Slide drive shaft assembly into position at fuel pump and carefully engage shaft in fuel pump driven member. Do not rotate shaft once it is engaged.
    e. Engage shaft at distributor end and hold shaft housing firmly while tightening retaining nut to secure installation. This nut should be tightened to approximately 10 ft.-lbs.
8. Adjust idle speed and mixture as described previously in "Maintenance and Adjustments." This completes the installation of fuel injection.

7014900-7014900R Fuel Injection

7014900 fuel injection units incorporate design revisions for metering signal and fuel delivery during starting and warm up. Except for the differences outlined here the 7014900 unit (figures 167 and 168) is the same as the 7014800 model injection which was just covered.

The 7014900 design (fig. 169) eliminates the following external parts found on the 7014800 units shown schematically in figure 170.

- Starting Cut-Off Switch (50)
- Starting Solenoid (24)
- Idle Vacuum Signal Tube (42)
- Signal Boost Tube (44)

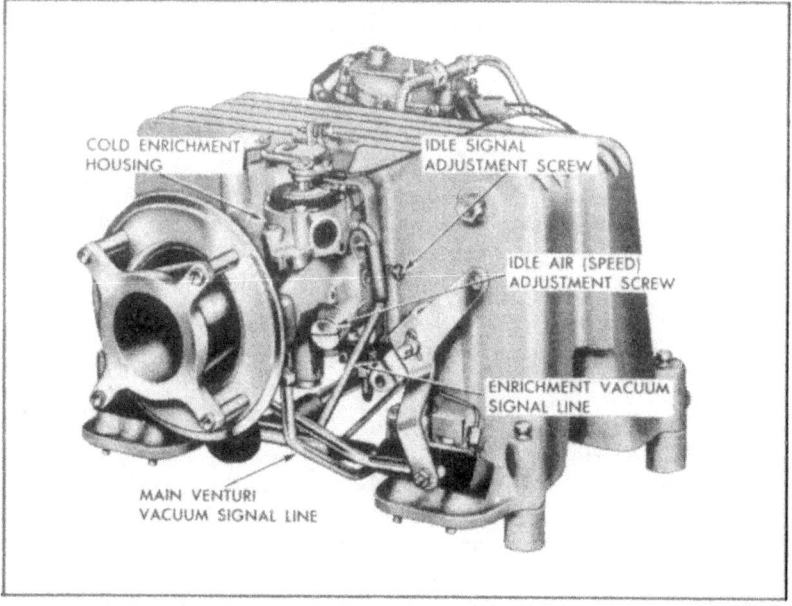

Fig. 167—7014900 Fuel Injection—Left Side View

Through elimination of the separate idle vacuum signal tube and signal boost tube, vacuum signals for fuel control are now transmitted to the main control diaphragm via a single line for all operations except starting. The auxiliary vacuum signals formerly supplied by the separate boost tube and idle vacuum signal tube are added to the main control diaphragm vacuum signal by means of internal air meter passage connections to the main tube pick up point.

Elimination of the starting solenoid, switch, and by-pass fuel line

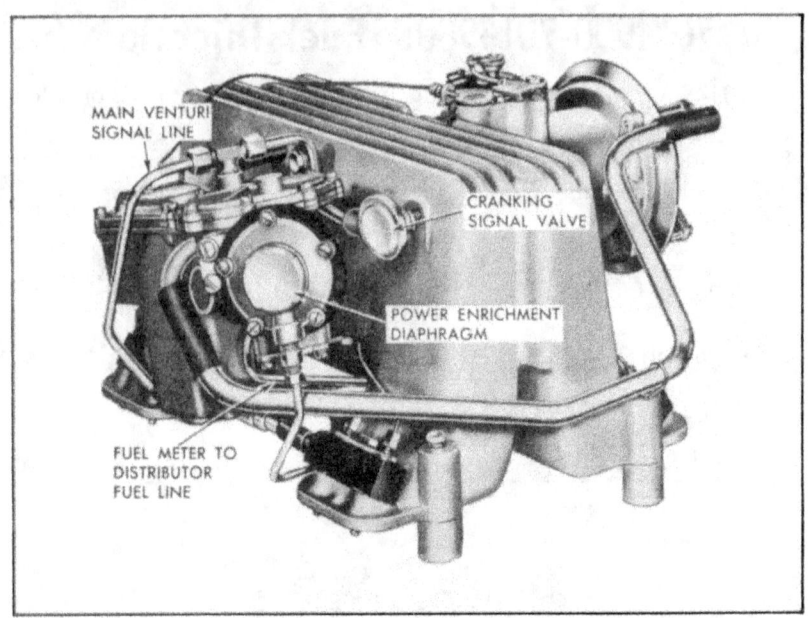

Fig. 168—7014900 Fuel Injection—Right Side View

was made possible by application of manifold vacuum during cranking to provide the necessary enriched fuel delivery (fig. 171). A normally open diaphragm valve is tapped into the injector manifold which transmits manifold vacuum created during cranking through a restriction to the main control diaphragm. This substitute vacuum source is eliminated once the manifold vacuum exceeds 19" water (1.4" mercury) as the manifold vacuum completely overcomes the diaphragm spring tension at that point.

Comparatively, the manifold vacuum applied the main control diaphragm on the 7014900 injection unit positions the spill plunger to provide fuel meter pump fuel delivery to the nozzles during cranking whereas on the 7014800 and earlier fuel injection models, fuel delivery is accomplished mechanically through a solenoid activated by the engine cranking circuit which causes the spill plunger to be fully depressed to allow engine fuel pump pressure to be delivered directly to the nozzles via a starting by-pass fuel line.

As shown (fig. 169), the fuel valve is replaced in the 7014900 by a simple formed wire which acts as a bottoming stop for the spill plunger. With the fuel valve eliminated, fuel delivery from the gear pump, despite its low rate, is of sufficient quantity for starting. This, of course, eliminates the need for the by-pass fuel line and was contributory to the elimination of the solenoid.

Because the fuel valve, solenoid, and cut-off switch are eliminated on 7014900 units, fuel delivery to the nozzles cannot be cut-off when restarting a hot or flooded engine. On this unit, flooding is overcome by the admission of all the air possible by keeping the throttle wide-open during cranking.

Once the engine starts, the operation of the 7014800 and 7014900 units is identical; fuel is delivered only by the fuel meter fuel pump and its rate of flow to the nozzles is regulated by vacuum signals applied to the main control diaphragm.

The cold enrichment units of 7014800 and 4900 fuel injectors operate identically. Their difference is that the 7014800 cold enrichment housing delivers "boost" vacuum via a short external tube to a junction with the main control signal line. Conversely, "boost" signal travels past the boost valve in the 7014900 cold enrichment housing and through a hole in the housing base to an internally drilled passage in the air meter casting which intersects the origination of the main control signal line. Restrictions are used in both boost lines; in 7014800 units a restriction is inserted in the hose

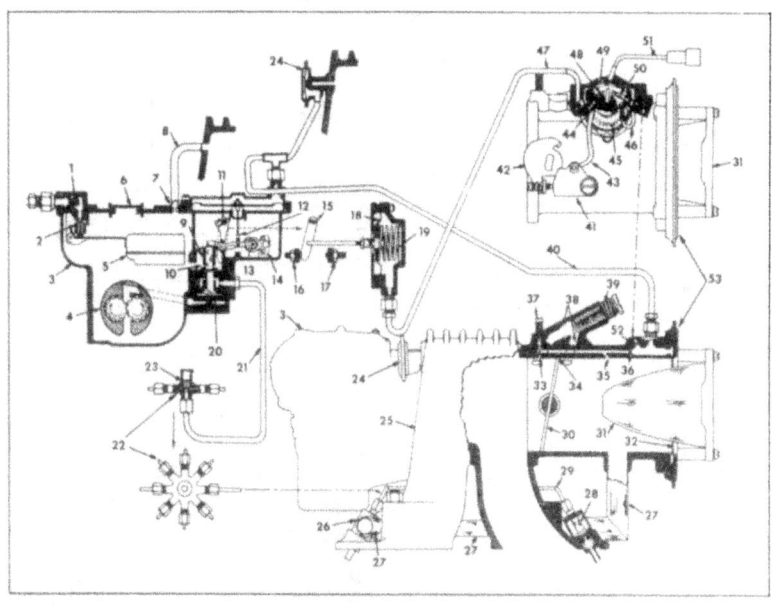

Fig. 169—7014900 Schematic Diagram

1. Fuel Inlet Strainer
2. Float Needle and Seat
3. Fuel Meter Casting
4. Fuel Meter Fuel Pump
5. Float
6. External Bowl Vent Screen
7. Bowl-to-Manifold Vent Restriction
8. Bowl-to-Manifold Vent
9. Spill Plunger
10. Spill Ports
11. Ratio Lever
12. Main Control Diaphragm Link
13. Fuel Control Lever
14. Diaphragm Linkage Counterweight
15. Enrichment Lever
16. Rich (Power) Stop
17. Lean (Economy) Stop
18. Enrichment Diaphragm
19. Enrichment Diaphragm Spring
20. Pump Outlet Strainer
21. Fuel Meter-to-Distributor Fuel Line
22. Fuel Distributor
23. Fuel Distributor Check Valve
24. Cranking Signal Valve
25. Intake Manifold Casting
26. Nozzle Block
27. Nozzle Air Duct
28. Fuel Nozzle
29. Nozzle Fuel Line
30. Throttle Valve
31. Diffuser Cone
32. Venturi
33. Idle Signal Port
34. Off-Idle Signal Port
35. Idle Signal Bleed
36. Idle Signal Restriction
37. Idle Fuel Signal Adjustment Needle
38. Idle Air By Pass
39. Idle Air (Speed) Adjusting Screw
40. Main Control Signal Line
41. Fast Idle Cam
42. Throttle Shaft Cam Lever
43. Cold Enrichment-to-Fast Idle Rod
44. Thermostatic Coil
45. Electric Heat Element
46. Heat Element Ground Wire
47. Enrichment Vacuum Signal Line
48. Enrichment Vacuum Signal Valve
49. Manifold Vacuum Supply to Cold Enrichment Valves
50. Boost Signal Valve
51. Hot Wire to Generator
52. Boost Signal Line Restriction
53. Air Meter

connecting the boost tube to the main signal tube while on 7014900 models, the boost restriction is installed in the drilled boost passage at its intersection with the main control signal in the air meter housing. The signal delivery routes for 7014900 cold enrichment are indicated by dotted lines in figure 172.

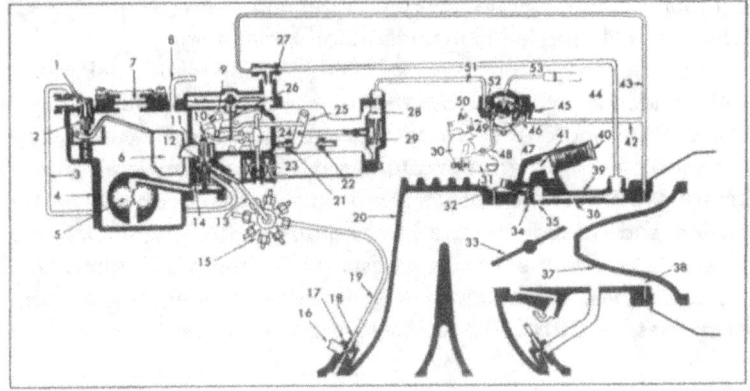

Fig. 170—7014800 Schematic Diagram

1. Fuel Inlet and Strainer
2. Float Needle and Seat
3. Starting By Pass Fuel Line
4. Fuel Meter Casting
5. Fuel Meter Fuel Pump
6. Float
7. External Bowl Vent Screen
8. Bowl-to-Manifold Vent
9. Ratio Lever
10. Fuel Control Lever
11. Spill Plunger
12. Anti-Percolation Valve and Spring
13. Fuel Meter-to-Distributor Fuel Line
14. Pump Outlet Strainer
15. Fuel Distributor
16. Nozzle Air Duct
17. Nozzle Block
18. Fuel Nozzle
19. Nozzle Fuel Line
20. Intake Manifold Casting
21. Rich (Power) Stop
22. Lean (Economy) Stop
23. Starting Solenoid
24. Diaphragm Linkage Counterweight
25. Enrichment Lever
26. Main Control Diaphragm Link
27. Restriction Tee
28. Enrichment Diaphragm
29. Enrichment Diaphragm Spring
30. Throttle Shaft Cam Lever
31. Fast Idle Cam
32. Idle Fuel Signal Adjustment Needle
33. Throttle Valve
34. Idle Signal Port
35. Off-Idle Signal Port
36. Idle Signal Bleed
37. Diffuser Cone
38. Venturi
39. Air Meter Casting
40. Idle Air (Speed) Adjustment Screw
41. Idle Air By Pass
42. Idle Vacuum Signal Line
43. Main Control Signal Line
44. Boost Signal Line
45. Boost Valve
46. Heat Element Ground Wire
47. Electric Heat Element
48. Cold Enrichment-to-Fast Idle Rod
49. Thermostatic Coil
50. Starting Cut-Off Switch
51. Enrichment Vacuum Signal Line
52. Enrichment Vacuum Signal Valve
53. Hot Wire from Battery

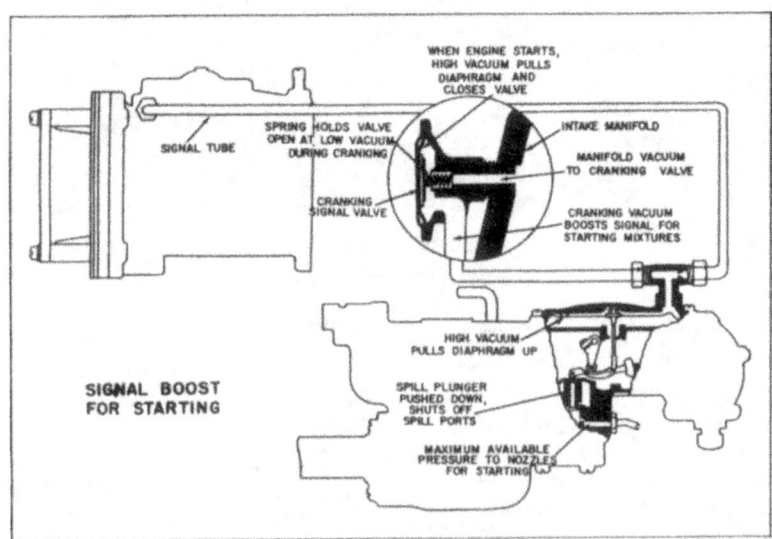

Fig. 171—Cranking Signal Valve Operation

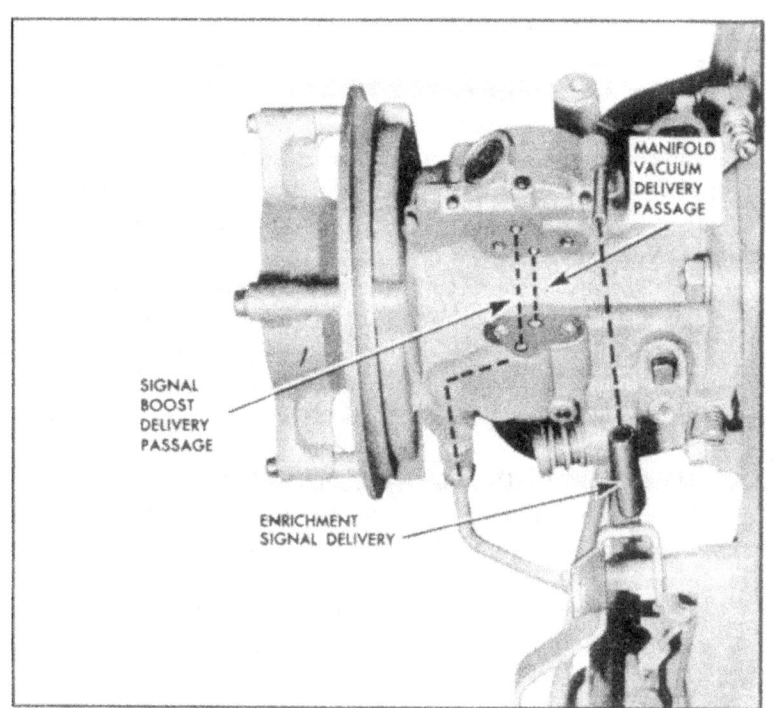

Fig. 172—Cold Enrichment Housing Vacuum Passages—7014900

Idle air and fuel signal circuitry for 7014900 units is shown in figure 94. With the throttle blade closed, air is admitted by two methods; two-thirds of the air bridges the throttle blade via the bypass passage and the remaining one-third enters through the nozzle air ducts. Engine idle speed is controlled by the large adjustment screw in the idle air bypass. Because venturi vacuum signal is practically non-existent during idle due to the small air flow, manifold vacuum is used for idle fuel metering signal to the main control diaphragm. When the engine is warmed up, idle signal is picked up only at the needle controlled idle signal port but when the throttle blade is held open by the fast idle cam during cold operation, the signal is strengthened by additional pickup through the off-idle signal port which is then exposed to manifold vacuum. Since manifold vacuum is far too strong for fuel metering control, it is first weakened by an atmosphere bleed and then further reduced by a line restriction before reaching the main control diaphragm.

As shown (fig. 173), the idle fuel signal operation is basically identical to that in 7014800 units. The major difference is that in 4900 units, the idle signals are delivered to the main control diaphragm through the same line that delivers venturi vacuum signals. Elimination of the separate idle signal line was made possible by relocating the venturi vacuum signal line on the air meter and then extending the idle passage to intersect this connection. The restriction in the idle signal end of the main control diaphragm "tee" is replaced by a pressed in restriction in the idle signal passage of the air meter on 7014900 units.

Service Differences

From a diagnosis standpoint, the addition of the cranking signal valve and the integration of the boost and idle signals into the single venturi signal line constitute the only changes that will alter the adjustments and diagnoses for the 7014900 fuel injection models over those provided for the 7014800 units covered earlier in these pages.

COLD ENRICHMENT ROD LENGTH ADJUSTMENT

To adjust the length of the rod connecting the fast idle cam and counterweight lever on 7014900 units, the following procedure is recommended.

1. Check the thermostatic coil position. Properly installed, the stat housing should be indexed 1½ notches rich (fig. 174).
2. To hold the trip lever and the counter-weight tab together, twist the attaching screw its full limit clockwise. Then note the point where the fast idle screw contacts the cam. If rod length is correct, fast idle screw will touch at the center of the high step of the cam. Otherwise bend rod to lengthen or shorten as required to provide this adjustment.

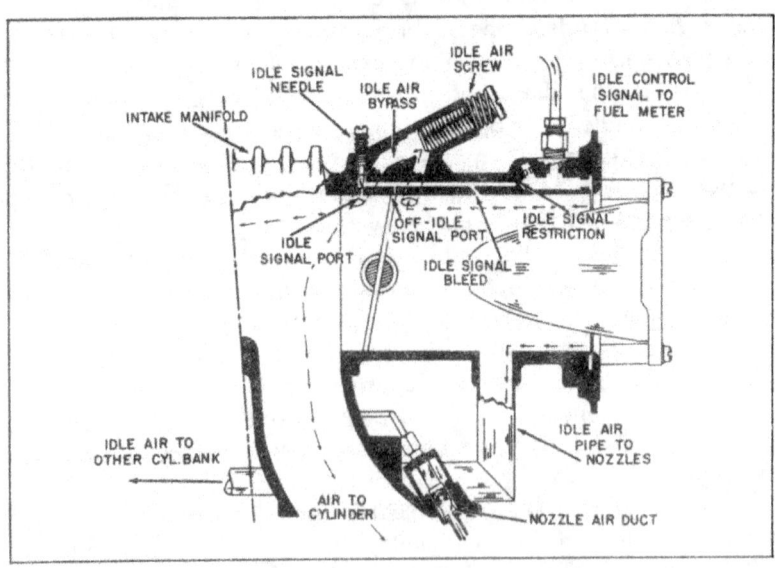

Fig. 173—Idle Air and Fuel Signal Circuits—7014900

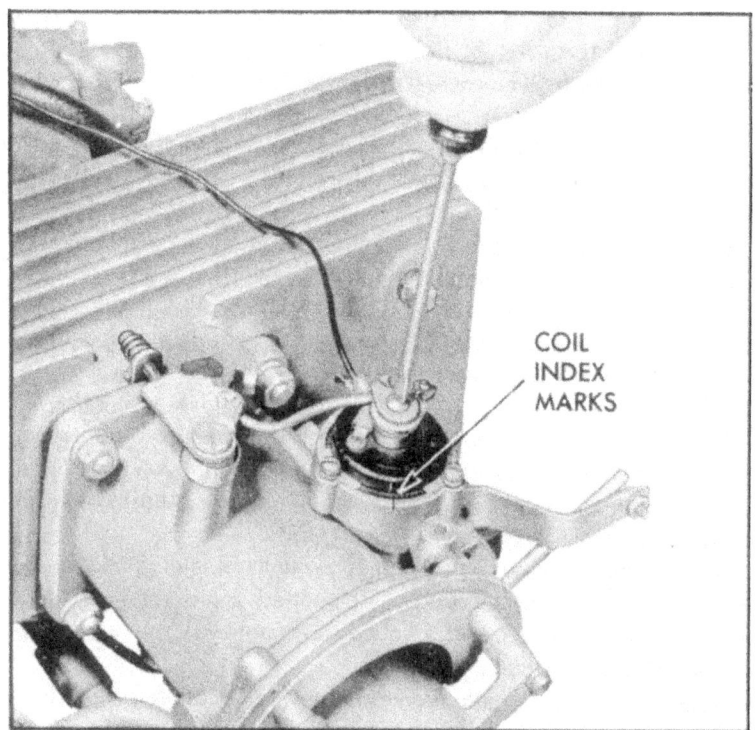

Fig. 174—Adjusting Cold Enrichment Rod Length

TROUBLE SHOOTING
Won't Start
1. Check for correct cold starting procedure. Accelerator should be depressed to the floor and then released to index the fast idle cam. If the driver holds the throttle open by keeping the accelerator depressed, the additional air admitted may be causing the mixture to be too lean for combustion.
2. To check cranking signal valve operation, disconnect the hose connecting the cranking signal valve to the main control diaphragm. Attach a 2 or 3 foot length of windshield wiper hose to the open end of the tube, from the main control diaphragm. Lightly suck on the hose (about as hard as on a cigarette) while cranking the engine. If the engine now starts, it can be assumed that the cranking signal valve is stuck shut and must be replaced.
3. Check for fuel flow during cranking by loosening the fuel meter-to-distributor fuel line at the fuel meter. If fuel flows from the loose connection during cranking, retighten the fuel line connection and check for fuel flow at the nozzles by disconnecting one of the nozzle fuel lines. If fuel flows, the

trouble is probably in the ignition system. However, if fuel flowed from the fuel meter line but does not flow from the nozzle line, the check valve in the 8-way fuel distributor is stuck shut. Free check valve or replace distributor.
4. If fuel flow does not occur after completing the check in step 3, check for a broken fuel meter pump drive cable. Also check for a defective engine fuel pump.
5. When none of the preceding will correct the trouble, it will be necessary to remove the fuel injector from the engine and check for a stuck spill plunger. If the spill plunger is free, either the main control diaphragm is ruptured or the internal linkage in the fuel meter is broken.

Too Rich Operation

This complaint is not shown in the shop manual but could possibly occur with 7014900 units if the cranking signal valve diaphragm would rupture as this would continually apply manifold vacuum to the main control diaphragm.

Any cranking signal valve failure which results in the valve being stuck open should be easily spotted by excessively smoky exhaust. This failure could also cause rough idle, flat spot, and obviously poor fuel economy.

If any cranking signal valve failure is encountered, the later design piece 7017090, which includes back-fire screen should be

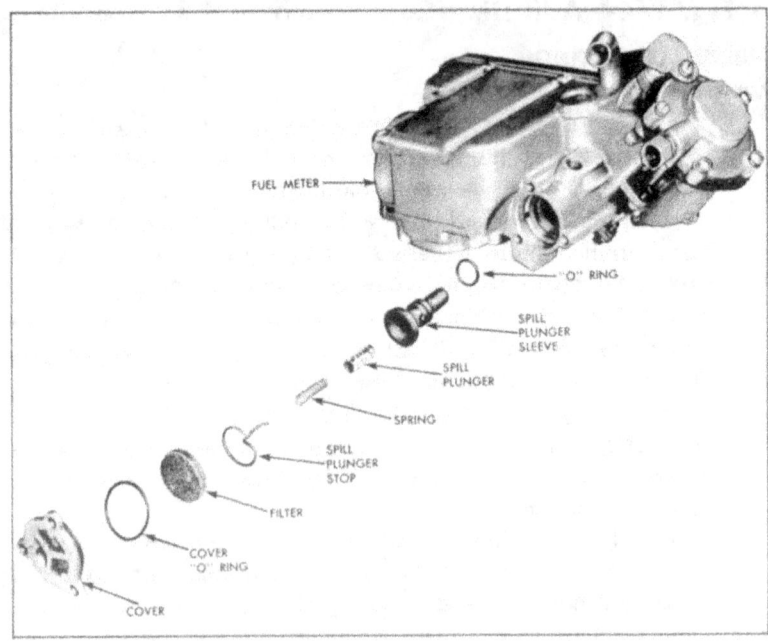

Fig. 175—7014900—Fuel Valve Components—Exploded View

used. These valves are identified by two "C's" stamped back-to-back.

Other Information

Other differences which will be encountered when servicing the 7014900 fuel injection units are the open tee fitting used on the fuel control diaphragm and revision of parts in the spill plunger area.

A comparison of the tee fittings shown in cross section on the 7014800 and 4900 schematic views will show that the 4900 unit tee contains no restriction whereas a restriction is used in the auxiliary idle vacuum signal end of the 7014800 tee. In 4900 units, a comparable restriction is built into auxiliary idle signal passage which is now integral in the air meter casting. The important thing for the serviceman to remember is that the two tee fittings cannot be interchanged.

Because the 7014900 design eliminates the need for by-pass fuel for starting, the fuel valve (fig. 170) used on the 4800 design is replaced by a simple formed wire. A light coil spring (fig. 175) is used between the spill plunger and the wire support to hold the spill plunger up in the maximum spill position when the engine is shut-off. In addition, the 4900 spill plunger is matched to a removable sleeve. Should a spill plunger be lost or damaged, the old pair can be replaced by a new spill plunger and sleeve set whereas formerly this required replacement of the fuel meter.

7014900 fuel injection units which have an "R" suffix on their identification plate are calibrated 6-8% richer on the power stop. These units are used with the 290 hp, 10-to-1 compression ratio engine which incorporates mechanical valve lifters and a special camshaft whereas the 7014900 unit is calibrated for use with the 250 hp, 9½-to-1 compression ratio engine with hydraulic valve lifters. Otherwise the two models, 7014900 and 7014900R, are identical.

Nozzle usage for 7014900 units is identical with those specified for the 7014800 units.

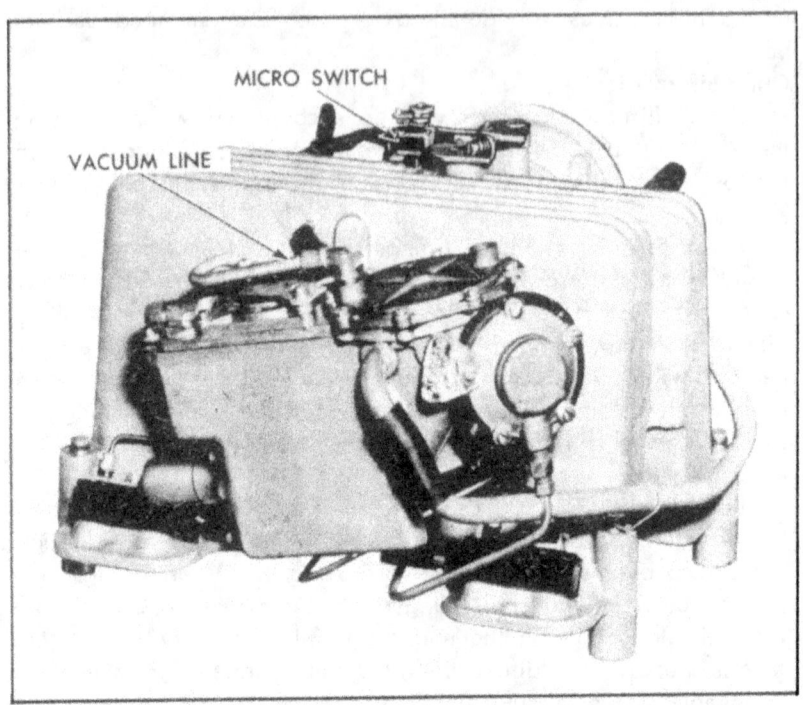

Fig. 176—7017300 Fuel Injection—Right Side View

7017300R-7017300 Fuel Injection

The 7017300 fuel injection units (fig. 176) currently in use on Corvettes first entered production in 1959.

These units are hybrid as the fuel meter and intake manifold are identical to those of 7014800 units whereas the air meter used is idential to that used on 7014900 injectors. Since no cranking signal (manifold vacuum) is needed to enrich the fuel delivery for starting, the usual "Tee" on the main control diaphragm is replaced by a simple "L" which receives the single signal line to deliver venturi vacuum signals. As will be recalled, starting fuel mixtures on 7104800 units are enriched mechanically by means of a starting solenoid which depresses the fuel valve fully for maximum fuel delivery.

Models designated 7017300R are calibrated for hydrauic lifter engines and 7017300 (no suffix) units are calibrated for use with mechanical valve lifter, special camshaft engines.

Obviously, fuel meter service procedures are exactly as prescribed for the 7014800 fuel meter and the air meter procedures are exactly the same as those for the 7014900 models.

Fuel flow recalibration procedures and data are provided at the end of this section for 7017300 and 7017300R units.

7017200-7017250 Fuel Injection

Relative to service procedures and fundamental operation, 7017200 or 7017250 units are identical to 7014900 units with the single exception that a siphon-breaker, which prevents possible hydrostatic lock of the engine, has been integrated into the fuel meter assembly. As there is no servicing relative to the siphon breaker, these injectors are serviced identically to 7014900 units.

7017200 units are calibrated for use with hydrauic lifter engines and 7017250 models are calibrated for use with solid lifter, special camshaft engines.

Fuel flow recalibration procedures and data for these units are provided at the end of this section.

7017310-7017320 Fuel Injection

Like 7017200 and 7017250 units, the 7017310–7017320 model injectors are for practical purposes identical to the 7014900 units except for the inclusion of an integral siphon breaker in the fuel meter casting.

One visible change in these units is that no air fins are cast into the intake manifold above the plenum as on 7014900 units. Actually, the intake manifold used on 7017310-20 units underwent major design revisions to improve performance and efficiency.

The 7017310 model is calibrated for use with hydraulic valve lifters and the 7017320 is calibrated for solid lifters.

Fuel flow recalibration data for these injectors is provided at the end of this section.

Fuel Flow Calibration

Because of the extremely sensitive nature of the fuel flow components, it is necessary to test and readjust the fuel delivery rates at the economy (lean) and power (rich) stops whenever the main control diaphragm cover is removed for any reason. This is necessary because it is practically impossible to remove the cover and then reinstall it without disrupting the position of the main control diaphragm. Any alteration of diaphragm position will greatly effect the fuel delivery from the fuel meter.

While the critical need for such tests may not be readily seen, consider for a moment the minute pressure differences which actuate the main control diaphragm and accordingly, control fuel delivery from the fuel meter. When inhaling a cigarette deeply, the average smoker draws a vacuum of approximately 3" Hg (mercury).

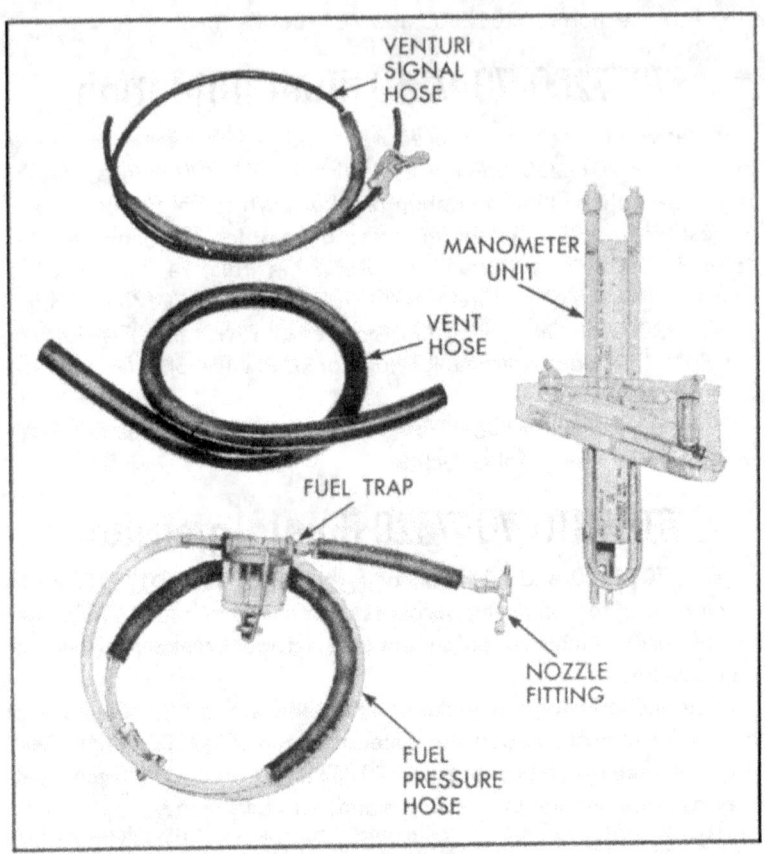

Fig. 177—Fuel Flow Calibration Set J-7090

Comparatively, at approximately 3000 rpm, the venturi vacuum signal reaching the main control diaphragm is ½" water. Since mercury is nominally 13½ times heavier than water, this means that the total "suction" reacting on the main control diaphragm at 3000 rpm is only 1/40th the pressure difference created by inhaling a cigarette. In addition, considering the total engine operating range, the main control diaphragm must accurately react to pressure differences ranging from less than 0.01" H_2O to nearly 30" H_2O in order to accurately control fuel delivery throughout the entire engine operating range.

These facts are covered only to stress the absolute need for recalibration testing whenever the main control diaphragm attachment to the fuel meter is altered in any way. With this in mind, it is easily seen that the slightest change in the reinstallation of the main control diaphragm will change its mobility somewhat and as a result, will change the fuel delivery characteristics of the fuel meter.

Calibration tests are simple to perform and require only a moderate amount of time. Calibration gauge set J-7090 (fig. 177) consists of a mercury and water manometer combined into a single unit, a fuel trap and fittings required for installation to the nozzle and nozzle fuel line, and plastic lines for connections to the mercury and water manometers plus a length of larger hose for attachment to the main control diaphragm vent tube.

Installation of Test Equipment
1. Remove the air cleaner and main control diaphragm vent (balance) tube from the fuel injection unit.
2. Install the large diameter hose on the main control diaphragm vent and lay the open end of the hose out over the side of the fender.
3. Mount the manometer unit on the car. It will be noted that the mounting bracket slot has two angles (fig. 178). The lower portion of the slot is vertical and is used to mount the manometer on 1957 Corvettes and 1957-58 Passenger Cars

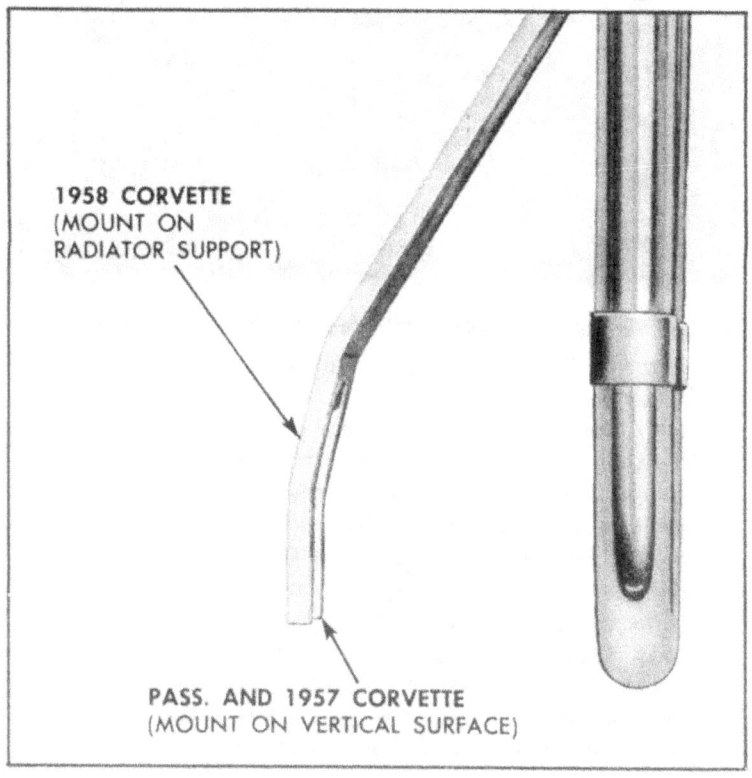

Fig. 178—Manometer Mounting Bracket Angle

Fig. 179—Manometer Mounted on Passenger Cars

whereas the upper angle is used for mounting on 1958 Corvettes.

1957 Corvettes — The instrument can be mounted on one of the screws on the dash panel on the right side of the engine compartment using the **lower angle** of the instrument bracket.

1957-58 Passenger Cars — Loosen the attaching bolt securing the right front fender to the fender skirt directly above the battery and mount the instrument using the **lower angle** in the instrument mounting bracket (fig. 179).

1958 Corvettes — Loosen the upper attaching bolt on the radiator left support and mount the instrument using the **upper angle** of the mounting bracket (fig. 180).

4. Level the manometer unit. A leveling vial is provided in the top of the inclined water manometer (fig. 181).
5. Open the two valves in the top of the water manometer and zero the gauge oil by turning the adjustment screw at the

lower end of the oil column inward to raise the oil level or outward to lower the oil level. If there is insufficient oil in the inclined manometer to zero the instrument, add red gauge oil, specific gravity .826, by completely removing one of the valves. The leveling screw should be almost fully outward when oil is added to provide for subsequent adjustment, but do not overfill.
6. Zero the mercury manometer by sliding the U-tube up or down in its mounting bracket as required. Do not adjust to the meniscus (crown) of the mercury as this is difficult to read and can deflect during the test procedure.
7. Connect the black plastic tube with the clamp attached to the valve at the reservoir end of the water manometer and connect the other end of the hose to venturi vacuum.

On 7014800 and earlier fuel injectors, remove the signal boost line (not shown) on the air meter side of the injection unit and install the hose on the open junction in the main signal line.

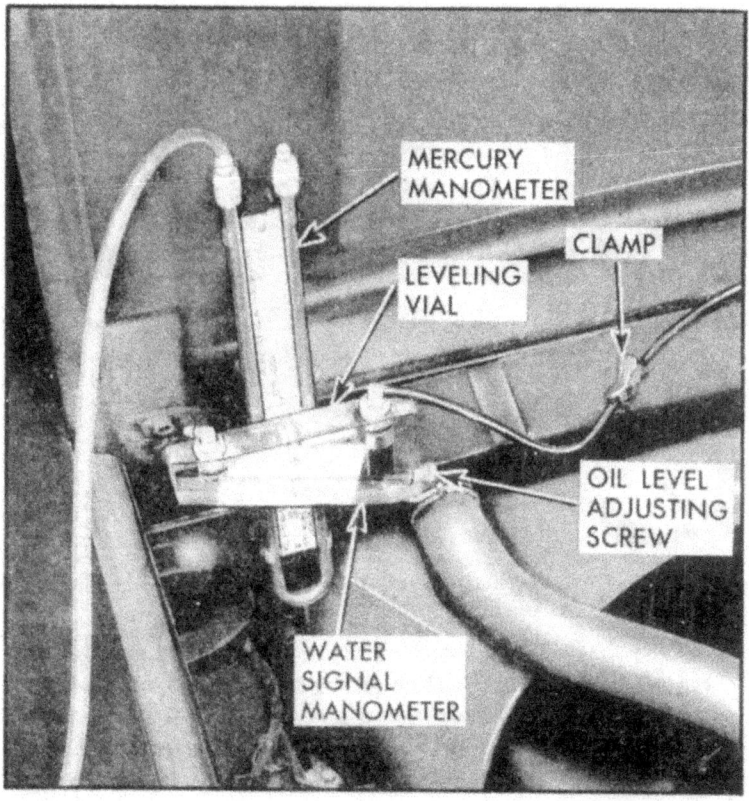

Fig. 180—Manometer Mounted on 1958 Corvette

On 7014900 type units, remove the short line (fig. 181) connecting the cranking signal valve to the main control diaphragm tee and disconnect from the cranking signal valve. Turn the open end of the line upward, reinstall the line, and connect the plastic hose from the water manometer to the tube.

Recheck for zeroing of the water manometer, then shut the clamp (fig. 181) on the hose.

8. To install the fuel trap disconnect the left-front nozzle fuel line and connect it to the male end of the fuel trap tee. Then install the nut-end of the tee to the injector nozzle. Complete the installation by connecting the plastic hose from the fuel trap to the cap on the left (compression) side of the mercury U-tube.

Before starting the test procedure, make sure that the gauge hoses are clear of moving parts. Also, slide the asbestos sleeves on the lines into position so that they will protect the lines from burning on the engine (fig. 182).

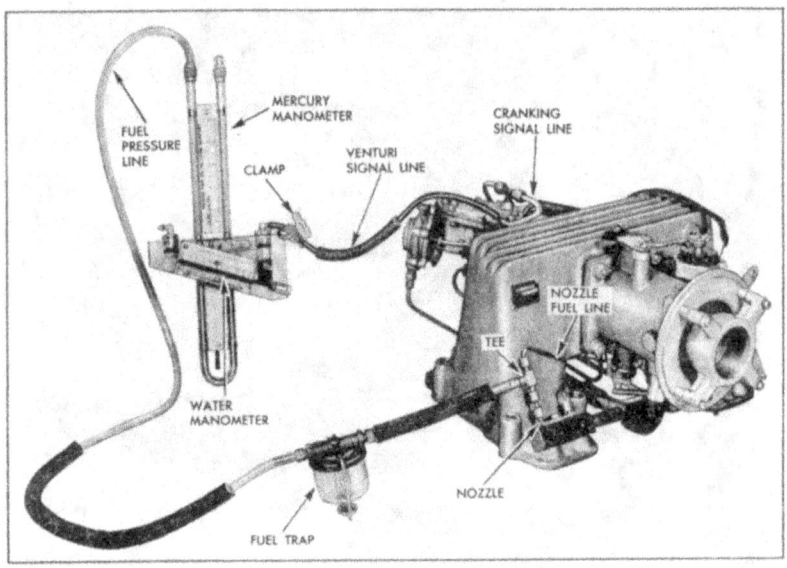

Fig. 181—Typical Manometer Hook-Up

Test Procedure

1. Check that the clip on the hose to the water manometer is closed and start the engine. The hose must be clamped shut or the high vacuum resulting after the engine is "gunned" when starting will pull the oil out of the water manometer.
2. If the ratio stop shield is installed, remove it and reinstall the two attaching screws to prevent any leak at the main control diaphragm.

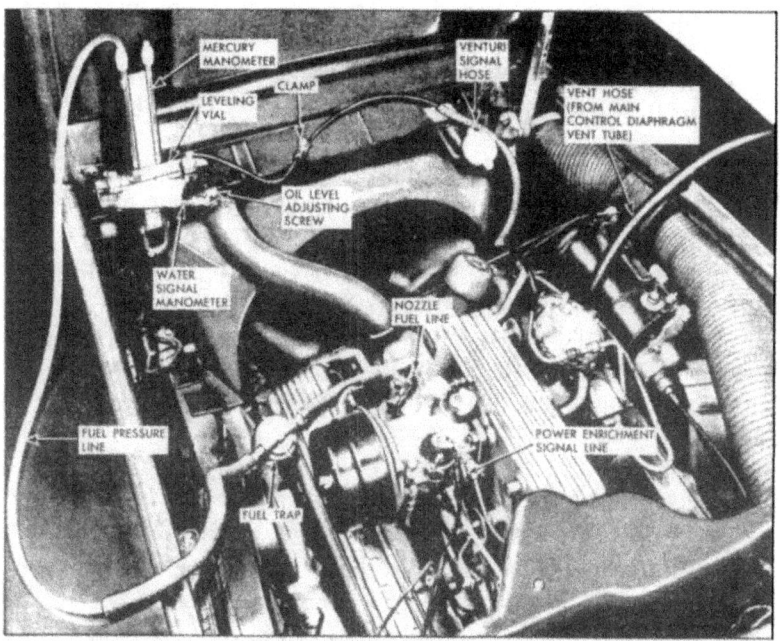

Fig. 182—J-7090 Installed on 1958 Corvette

3. Allow the engine to warm-up at moderate speed to prevent stalling. Warm-up can be considered sufficient when the fast idle cam has rotated clear of the throttle stop and the enrichment lever moves to the economy (lean) stop.
4. Release the clip on the hose to the water manometer and carefully accelerate the engine to hold a steady 0.5" signal on the water manometer. It is suggested that a wedge-shaped block be used between the throttle bellcrank and air meter to hold a steadier throttle.
5. Observe the scale side of the mercury manometer and note the point at which the mercury settles. Record this reading to the nearest 1/10th pound, **e.g.** "Economy" − .9 psi.
6. With the engine speed still creating 0.5" signal on the water manometer, disconnect the line to the power enrichment diaphragm at the cold enrichment housing (fig. 151). This will move the enrichment lever to the power (rich) stop.
7. Observe the mercury manometer and note the point at which the mercury finally settles. Record this reading, **e.g.** "Power" − 2.0 psi.
8. Reconnect the power enrichment line (fig. 182) at the cold enrichment housing and decelerate the engine to 800-1000 rpm approximately to allow the fuel trap to empty and the mercury to fall considerably. Then repeat the tests at the economy and power stops two more times so that at least

three readings will be made for each to insure better accuracy.
9. When the three tests are completed, compare the readings with the specifications listed below for the various fuel injection models:
10. If either the power or economy stop is more than $\pm$ 0.1 psi from the specified pressure, adjust that ratio stop as required. For example, if the pressure at the economy stop was too low, loosen the economy stop screw jam nut and turn the stop screw **toward** the power stop one or two turns and repeat test. Conversely, if settings were too rich, the adjustment would be **away** from the power stop.

When adjustments are complete, retest the fuel pressures at both the economy and power stops.

Test Tips

While there is no need for a tachometer in fuel meter calibration, it can be of definite value for trouble shooting. For example, most engines will deliver ½" H_2O signal @ 3000 rpm $\pm$ 100 rpm. If ½" H_2O signal is obtained at lower engine speeds, the excessive signal may be due to the signal boost valve or cranking signal valve (7014900) type units) leaking manifold vacuum signals to the main control diaphragm.

Be especially watchful for indications of air leaks in the fuel pressure test lines as these invalidate the tests. Leaks are indicated by rapid filling of the fuel pressure trap without comparable displacement of the mercury column. Also, fuel will not purge to the cylinder when engine speed is reduced.

Increasing Power And Performance

As it sits on the Dealer's showroom floor, the Corvette with its 300-plus horsepower engine is as hot a performing automobile as the average man would specify. However, we all feel a competitive urge from time to time and it is recognized that there will be rivalry. For this reason, sometimes the first thing a new Corvette owner does is take his car to be 'hopped up' — or undertakes to modify it himself so that its performance potential is increased. Unless you have some excellent reason for such an action our considered advice is, "forget it".

Under the heading 'excellent reason' of course, would come the desire and knowledge necessary to compete in events where ultimate power and performance are required. (You might only have the desire, at this stage, knowledge will come with experience.) Fine. But be aware of the costs and problems inherent in such motor sports before you begin. Racing and kindred activities are supreme in thrills and pleasure but they are also strictly adult sports for the mature individual. With this in mind, we can discuss competition and Corvettes on the basis of lessons learned over the past five years.

Initially, leaving your car absolutely as it comes from the dealer (with R.P.O.'s) is the wisest course. As you gain know how, you can tinker with it. But the stock Corvette has more performance

The Don Steves "00" Corvette, prepared by co-author Bill Thomas and driven to many West Coast victories by Dave MacDonald.

Driver Jim Peterson in Bill Thomas' Corvette, the first '56 to compete on the West Coast. Jim garnered 3 class victories in as many races.

than the average driver is capable of extracting from it on a road course his first few times.

The owner who is interested in competition should take advantage of all the factory options — in fact they are mandatory. Should your car be not so equipped, your dealer can supply parts to make the conversions, with certain exceptions:

(1) It is inadvisable to try to install a 4-speed gearbox in place of Powerglide. This is complex and expensive. You are better off to trade the car.

(2) The radius rods positioning the rear axle on late models cannot be satisfactorily installed on earlier vintage cars inasmuch as a jig or fixture to maintain relative positions of axle and frame would have to be constructed before welding could be attempted. This improvement is about the only non-interchangeable one which has been introduced.

If too many of the R.P.O.'s have to be added to bring the car up to specs, particularly if it is an older model having seen much service, the owner is much better advised to trade on a newer, fully equipped Corvette. A perusal of the R.P.O. section and checking for local prices will influence this decision.

FOR RACING ONLY

If you are in the market for a new Corvette and are deciding which of the R.P.O.'s to specify, here is a tip: R.P.O. 687, heavy duty brakes and fast steering, should only be ordered if you intend to go road racing. The car is not nearly so pleasant to drive under ordinary circumstances with these modifications and they are not required for anything but competition. Incidentally, the rear stabilizer bar, added as stock production in 1960, and the heavier front sway bar are quite worthwhile installing on earlier models for touring if the driver appreciates improved handling characteristics. With the sway bars the car corners flatter and has less tendency to break loose the inside rear wheel on sharp turns.

Tight turns such as this at the Willow Springs course require a good 'working' relationship between suspension, brakes, and tires.

Under the heading ROAD RACING, we can pass along the following advice:

Use all the options including Positraction and the wide base wheels. Get a ring and pinion gear set above and below the one supplied in the car — depending on the courses you expect to compete on. Normally the Corvette is supplied with a 3.70 rear end. This is a fine all-round ratio, but if you plan to run on track where the longest straightaway is a mile or better, you can use the 3.36 to advantage. If there are some extremely slow corners as well, first gear will take care of you. The 4.11 is handy on short, twisty tracks. The 4.56 is, in our opinion, for drag racing only. Sometimes neither gear seems just right, naturally, and an in-between ratio can be attained by playing with tire sizes. Remember, SCCA requires that the front and rear tires be the same size, so don't get caught short.

COMPUTING PROPER AXLE RATIO

Road Speed Formula:

$$\text{M.P.H.} = \frac{60 \times \text{engine r.p.m.}}{\text{overall gear ratio} \times \text{wheel rev. per mile}}$$

Gear	Transmission Ratio	Overall Gear Ratio		
		3.70:1 axle	4.11:1 axle	4.56:1 axle
Fourth (Top)	1:1	3.70:1	4.11:1	4.56:1
Third	1.31:1	4.85:1	5.38:1	5.97:1
Second	1.66:1	6.14:1	6.82:1	7.57:1
First (Low)	2.20:1	8.14:1	9.04:1	10.03:1

Wheel Revolutions Per Mile
(Disregarding slip and expansion)

Tire/Wheel	Rev. Per Mile	
6.50/6.70 x 15-5K or 15-5.5K	759*	748**
7.10/7.60 x 15-5.5K	738*	727**

*40 lbs. inflation
**55 lbs. inflation

Special tires may vary slightly from these figures. To estimate the wheel revolutions per mile of any tire, mark both tire and floor with chalk, then roll the tire (on fully loaded vehicle) one revolution in a straight line. Make another mark on the floor and measure the distance between marks. Divide this distance in inches into 63,360 (the number of inches per mile) for wheel revolutions per mile. For example, if you very accurately measure 84.7" between marks, you would get 748 revolutions per mile using this formula:

$$\text{Wheel rev. per mile} = \frac{63,360}{\text{Rolling circumference of wheel in inches}}$$

To convert engine r.p.m. from one axle ratio to another:

From	To	Multiply by
3.70	4.11	1.111
3.70	4.56	1.2324
4.11	4.56	1.1095
4.11	3.70	0.9002
4.56	4.11	0.9013
4.56	3.70	0.8114

Properly used, this information can help you select the proper rear axle ratio for a specific course. Here's one example, based on a 1959 Corvette equipped with 6.50/6.70 x 15 tires inflated to a maximum of 55 pounds and 3.70:1 axle ratio, with 4-Speed Synchro-Mesh transmission, lapping a hilly triangular two-mile course with severe reverse bends at either end of a major straightaway less than one-half mile long . . .

Assume you entered the straightaway at 3000 r.p.m. in first gear and accelerated through the gears, reaching 5800 r.p.m. in third immediately before braking down. Through the reverse bends that follow, engine speed dropped to 2000 r.p.m. in first as you entered the short backstretch. Low speed acceleration is too sluggish. What axle ratio will cut lap time?

Using the road speed formula on page 20 compute the road speeds for each condition:

Condition "A" M.P.H. $-\dfrac{60 \times 3000}{8.14 \times 748} = 29.6$ m.p.h. entering the major straightaway

Condition "B" M.P.H. $-\dfrac{60 \times 5800}{4.85 \times 748} = 96.0$ m.p.h. maximum on the straightaway

Condition "C" M.P.H. $-\dfrac{60 \times 2000}{8.14 \times 748} = 19.7$ m.p.h. entering the short backstretch

Assume road speed in Conditions "A" and "C" cannot be increased without losing control of the car on the severe bends. This leaves quicker acceleration or higher top speed as possibilities to reduce lap time. Acceleration out of the bends could be improved through increasing engine speed to nearer 4000 r.p.m. by changing axle ratio to either 4.11 or 4.56. Using Condition "A" as an example, estimate the result to changing from 3.70 to 4.11 ratio by multiplying 3000 engine r.p.m. by factor 1.111, which equals 3333 r.p.m. Similarly, for a change from 3.70 to 4.56 ratio, multiply 3000 r.p.m. by factor 1.2324 which equals 3690 r.p.m. Since the 4.56 ratio permits the higher engine r.p.m., it should produce the quickest acceleration out of the bends. On the major straightaway, the increased acceleration should normally permit a shift to top gear. Use the road speed formula to compute speed at 6000 r.p.m. with 4.56 axle ratio:

$$\text{M.P.H.} = \frac{60 \times 6000}{4.56 \times 748}$$

This indicates a potential speed of more than 108 m.p.h. In addition, the 4.56 ratio should permit improved performance on the hills that predominate this course and total lap time should be reduced.

Photographer Doug Stewart captures Tony Settember as he hydroplanes through Turn #1 on rain-drenched Pomona course. Positraction is a 'must' under such conditions.

In getting the most from the Positraction, stack the clutch plates as outlined under "Optional Clutch Stack Arrangement" for 'off-highway or heavy-duty operation; i.e.: alternately. This results in a oversteer condition which balances the car's tendency to push the front end and delivers a vehicle which has the best neutral steering characteristics. And, never use any lubricant except Hypoid gear lube available under GM part number 3758791 for filling the rear end.

DOLLARS AND CENTS

As in most sports of this type, the amount of performance you can extract within the rules depends on the time and money you want to spend. Inasmuch as the deviations from stock are rigidly defined in club racing, there is no point in discussing the hop-up techniques which can be applied to the Chevrolet V8 engine for unlimited modification. In fact this subject necessitates a book in itself. However, remaining within the rules, and concentrating on tuning and sanitation, the ordinary engine can be bettered consider-

Another view of Chevrolet's CERV-1, co-author Thomas (in white) in background.

ably in performance and reliability.

The serious contender will completely disassemble the engine and put it together as a balanced unit and making sure that all specifications are perfectly adhered to. The Corvette engine is, after all, a mass-produced product and tolerance can be less than ideal. Let us say that it is a remarkable engine as it comes from the factory, but the front runners never leave anything to chance.

You might break it in well and play around modestly before you go this far, but there is no substitute for establishing a situation as close to perfection as possible.

Initially, go through the tune up procedure given in the early part of this book. Power tune it on a dynamometer if possible. Then, if you want to alter the power curve to help acceleration and peak torque where it is generally required in racing, revise the ignition timing so that full advance is achieved at 3,000 r.p.m. (1500 distributor r.p.m.). This is best left to an ignition specialist who has the proper bench equipment to test the distributor. He will adjust the weights and spring to effect this change. The full advance should be 10 distributor degrees. This goes with the recommendation for initial timing as given in the Engine Tuning section of this book.

As noted under tuning, also, bad ignition wiring can cause loss of power which is troublesome to trace. For peak performance from the Chevrolet ignition, it is wise to replace coil and sparkplug leads with Packard 400 cable. Gap plugs to .025". Follow recommendations in tune up section for point gap. 34° exactly, total dwell (29° on each side), using dwell-angle meter.

Champion J-63R or equivalent sparkplugs are recommended for competition. These can be removed and 'soft' plugs substituted for street use.

The expansion tank and aluminum radiator — competition proved — are now standard Corvette equipment.

Skip Hudson, well-known West Coast driver, in his Bill Thomas-prepared Corvette.

AIR-FUEL RATIO

If your engine is equipped with carburetion, a 12.4 to 1 air-fuel ratio at power peak is an ideal. Changing jets to accommodate altitude and weather is, naturally part of the scheme. If you do not have access to an exhaust gas analyzer (which should be used in conjunction with a dyno or a long run under full power) read the sparkplugs and try to attain a **slightly rich** condition, rather than an 'on the nose' reading. You should warm up and run the engine on an old set of plugs, then switch make your power run, for goodly distance, shut off the engine at power, and have a look. Being slightly rich will not cause a power loss and will guard against detonation.

Simultaneous opening of carburetors is the better set up, so adjust the linkage as described earlier. Actually, fuel injection is to be preferred for competition because of its lack of reaction to car attitude.

IMPROVED INJECTION

The injectors, all of which have been detailed in other chapters, are good. They have their limitations and idiosyncracies — and they have been improved by the factory as well as by private individuals including one of the persons responsible for this book.

It is not possible to go into detail as to these modifications, which entail the use of considerable shop equipment, and are beyond the scope of the average owner-tuner, but verified dynamometer readings show a consistent gain of 17 to 24 h.p. It is enough to say that all successful racing Corvettes are using these tricks. If the reader would like further details he is invited to correspond with William P. Thomas, 506 Santa Rosa Road, Arcadia, California.

DUNTOV CAM

There have been many statements (usually by cam grinders) to the effect that the Duntov cam, as supplied with the Corvette (the so-called "special cam") is inferior in several respects to proprietary grinds. As far as road racing is concerned the statements are absolutely in far left field. In the SCCA, where no optional proprietary grind is allowed, there is no choice for the individual anyway, but in California Sports Car Club racing, where modifications are permitted, as long as the part is based on the manufacturer's component, Duntov cams are back in all the winning Corvettes. Don't let anybody sell you a triple-wild-fire-super-zoomer. It is good only for his bank account.

ALL OUT

The winning Corvettes have, needless to say, been completely disassembled, put back together meticulously and loosened up just the right amount.

If you are serious, here is the way to go about it:

Grind the crankshaft to .003 of an inch clearance on the main bearing journals, .0025 of an inch clearance on the rod journals.

At the same time, establish .005 of an inch additional thrust clearance on the rear main, .010 of an inch additional side clearance for rods.

Hone the piston pin holes to .0008 of an inch clearance.

If necessary, surface grind the block for truth in relation to the center line of the crank . . . 90° angle and longitudinally parallel. (This is not necessary with '60 and '61 blocks, but is advisable on

The "XP-700" Corvette in a demonstration tour around the Riverside course.

earlier models) This will also establish a uniform deck height for pistons.

Hone the barrels to establish piston skirt clearance of .005 of an inch.

Check the deck height of the pistons for exactitude. The clearance for the undomed piston is .025 of an inch, measured parallel to the wrist pin, of course.

Measure the capacity of each combustion chamber and establish each at exactly 62.2 ccm for Fuel Injection and 59.7 cc for Dual 4 Barrels ... with sparkplug in place. If they are found to vary, or if one is over, bring all the chambers up to the displacement of the one with the greatest volume (by relieving around the valves — don't sink the valve) then surface grind the head to restore the 62.2 ccm volume.

Grind the valves, grind the stem to exact length as given in the specifications.

Break all sharp edges in the head and block. No need to radius everything, just take off the corners.

The valve opening should be enlarged out to the edge of the valve. Use a 45° stone, then a 70° cutter and conclude with a .040 of an inch intake valve seat width, .050 of an inch on the exhaust valve seats.

Bring the valve springs up to the latest specifications as to length and tension. Use all new springs, keepers.

Match manifold-to-head ports by grinding, using a gasket as a template. Do not enlarge the ports on the 1961 heads.

Balance the engine statically and dynamically.

Remember to check the little things! Here an unlatched trunk lid will cost the leader precious seconds for a pit stop — and probably a victory.

The aluminum radiator and "free wheeling" fan.

Do not balance the flywheel, pressure plate, harmonic balancer and crankshaft as a unit, as is done on some engines. Balance each separately, mark carefully when assembling.

Silver solder the oil pickup tube into the oil pump.

Assemble with proper torque readings on each bolt.

All these operations are within the most rigid enforcement of the rules and are merely designed to establish manufacturer's specifications where mass production may have allowed mis-mated parts. Such an engine also has the best chance of living to a ripe old age, as well as developing its greatest potential power.

If it is necessary to rebore the engine to true the cylinder walls, remember Chevrolet only supplies .030 of an inch oversize pistons.

EARLIER MODELS

The best and least expensive method for bringing 1957-and later models up to equal the 315 hp engine now being installed is to obtain the 1961 fuel injection heads (Part #3788796), and pistons (Part #3769731 and 4-3769732). If your engine is not equipped with the Duntov cam and solid lifters, these should be installed at the same time (Cam: Part #3736097 Lifters: Part #5231585). The baffled oil pan now being offered is also a worthwhile investment. It is part #3769768 and offers added security against loss of oil pressure on long sweeping turns.

We have presumed that your earlier model is already fitted with R.P.O.'s relaying to chassis which were discussed earlier, so these engine changes should give you performance identical to the latest model. But, the newest cars will still have the drop on you inasmuch as they come equipped with an aluminum radiator and "free wheeling" cooling fan. The radiator is expensive, frankly, but obtainable as Part #3150916. If you don't want to sail for the fan (Part #988294) at least arrange your engine front pulleys and belts in this fashion:

This double pulley arrangement — 'borrowed' from the 350 h.p. (348 cu. in.) sedan engine — provides double protection against fan belt failure.

The aluminum bell housing now used on the latest engines saves several pounds of weight, but unless money is no object, forget it. You can probably figure out some other method of losing the weight.

One advantageous change you can make if you are serious is to switch your four speed shift linkage to the new, shorter-throw tower, (1959 and later), which also has the reverse inhibitor. This shift lever definitely feels better and is superior.

RACING PRECAUTIONS

The outer bearing retainer in the rear axle is a press fit as it comes from the factory. This is perfectly satisfactory for any and all road conditions, but under the extreme stresses of high speed cornering, lap after lap, it could conceivably come un-pressed — with the consequent loss of a wheel. To be on the safest side, heliarc weld this retainer in position.

Note: The chamfered side of the ring goes against the bearing.

Check the drive line angle at the universal joint. The differential housing should nose down 3 degrees, plus or minus nothing. These have been discovered to be as much as 12 degrees out, so do not neglect this procedure. In order to effect the necessary change, rotate the axle housing in the spring perches and top radius rod.

BRAKES

It is hard to find brakes superior to the sintered metallic type fitted as R.P.O. 687. In tests conducted by our group at Riverside International Raceway, a deceleration rate of 28 feet per-second-per second was attained before wheel lockup. This is extremely good performance compared with any brake unit in the world. As mentioned previously these brakes do have a higher pedal pressure and are not required for any but all-out competition. The standard brakes are fine for touring and ordinary highway driving. If you indulge in rallies and sporty events of this nature, specify R.P.O. 686 — the sintered metallic shoes and regular drums.

Extreme usage does not produce the drum and lining wear that one might expect from such powerful brakes and this component should be the least of your worries. In our experience one set of brakes was used (on three different cars, incidentally) for a total of 20 races — most of which were won — on both long and short

Who says Corvettes are heavy?

Co-author OCee Ritch points out 4" holes cut to admit cooling air to front brakes.

courses, including Riverside with its 145 mph straight (for Corvettes). At the end of this period the brakes were still silent, there was no appreciable shoe wear and the drums were unscored.

One of the reasons for this kind of performance is good heat dissipation. To assist in cooling the front drums, cut two 4 inch diameter holes in the recess under the headlights (behind bumper strip). Do not merely remove all of this identation in the oval shape, instead of cutting the holes, as some owners have done, the fiberglass will flex and you will soon discover troublesome cracks. The holes do not seem to weaken the structure this much, however.

In preparing for a race, inspect the master cylinder, all lines and fittings, wheel cylinders and retracting springs. These springs get pretty warm during hard use, so it is wise to change them after every three or four race events as a precaution. Use Lubriplate on the backing plates so the shoes will slide easily, adjust the brakes by backing off 22 notches, loosen the handbrake to be sure it is not causing slight drag and you are set. GM Heavy Duty Hydraulic Brake Fluid is our recommendation. It is always available at any General Motors dealership and should not be mixed with any other brand.

SHOCK ABSORBERS

If your car is a 1960 or 61, with options it will be equipped with nitrogen-filled heavy duty shock absorbers. Many owners prefer to leave these unchanged. Experiments have indicated that the 1959 Chevrolet Heavy Duty type is even stiffer and longer-lasting ... up to 15 races. These are part #5543738 front and part #5543738 rear. They will replace the front shocks exactly but a 1½ inch spacer at the top of each and longer rebound control straps will be needed in the rear to make the conversion.

A number of different brands of shocks have been tried but without finding a better unit for this particular car and racing applications.

A small alteration to the rear stabilizer bar bushing makes a noticeable difference, too. The rubber used in these components varies to a certain degree and with the hardness, the stiffening effect. A more consistent but identical component is nominally an Oldsmobile part.

A note for those interested in drag racing: Get the sloppiest, most worn out shocks you can find for the front end and jack the front end up with spring spacers about 1½ inches. Leave the stock shocks on the back. This will increase rear tire adhesion to a considerable degree.

TIRES AND WHEELS

The wide base (5½ inch) rim wheels which are optional are mandatory for racing or high speed rallying. Tires are a matter of choice into which many factors enter. On the West Coast practically

Bill Thomas checks the wide-base wheels on a competition-prepared Corvette.

everybody runs on retreads (recaps, properly), using Firestone Super Sport, Dunlop, Continental or Goodyear Blue Streak carcasses. In the Los Angeles area there are at least three recapping specialists who have devoted a lot of time to experimentation with tread patterns, widths, rubber composition and so on. As a result the drivers in this sector have no excuses for not getting the right tire for their driving styles and the track conditions. In other parts of the country you may or may not be so fortunate.

The proper tread and pressure combination is essential for maximum cornering adhesion.

If you are hung with a stock tire, start with Firestone Super Sports or Goodyear Road Racing. If you are allowed to use it Firestone's Smooth Tread model is a real good thing for the rear. Pirellis seem to deliver good wear but do not have the adhesion of the Firestones. Engleberts are excellent in both departments but their diameter is 1 inch smaller than a recap on the same size carcass and this will throw your gear ratios off — which you may have previously laboriously established. They are good up to the highest speeds you can attain, however.

You will have noted that many cars use different brands on front and back, although they must be the same size. This is the result of experimentation, pure and simple, and often the driver can select the proper combination of tire size, tread and pressure in a hurry. Generally speaking, this fine-tuning ability is an attribute only of the old-timer — driver or mechanic. Get a set of tires that feels good to you, work on the pressure pattern first, then if you are in the game long enough you can go esoteric.

Unless you have a straight where speeds in excess of 120 m.p.h. are attained, start with 30 lbs. pressure all around and watch for understeer or oversteer or general ill-handling and adjust in accordance. (Raise rear pressure to correct understeer.) If pressure is too low the tire rolls under and you lose adhesion. If it is too high the tires tend to react as though the surface was loose. If speeds above 120 are common, start with about 38 lbs.

For drag racing, there are several good tires. The best are, of course, those slicks obtained from the speed shops specializing in this equipment. Speaking of E.T. — which is generally the object in eliminations). Get the recaps that put the most rubber surface on the pavement, if you are not allowed to run slicks. "Stock" (no capped) tires found excellent for dragstrip adhesion are Firestone Butyl-Air and Atlas Bucron. To attain the highest terminal speed without so much regard for E.T., Vogue tires have been found to be exceptional. Start with about 30 lbs. pressure.

All the above references are, it almost goes without saying, to the rear tires. Front tires are quite unimportant. Just be sure they are in good condition and will stand about 60 lbs. of pressure — to which point they should be inflated.

CHASSIS

The chassis requires maintenance in exactly the same fashion as any other portion of the car. Do not neglect regular lubrication and inspection. After every race check to see that there are no bent or loose parts. Pay particular attention to the air scoops, blow out the brakes with compressed air, tighten up the motor mounts, go over the steering from wheel to wheel.

In setting up the front end, go toward the negative end of the specifications on camber . . . generally 0 to ¼ degree positive. A setting of ⅛" toe-in and 2 degrees positive caster is recommended.

Co-author Thomas admires a well-made racing screen . . . tinted, to minimize glare.

A leather strap buckled through these eyelets insures a secure hood under competition stresses.

Beautifully chromed — and well braced — roll bar exemplifies attention to detail on a well-prepared competition car.

GETTING READY

If you are going to be a serious competitor, the first pre-race preparation is the removal of the windshield and substitution of a plexiglas windscreen. A nice full-width type can be made from ¼ inch lucite as shown in the photo. This same type of screen has been advertised in enthusiasts magazines recently, ready to bolt on, if you do not want to go through the heating and bending process. 1960-61 Corvettes have a good hood clamp. Earlier models should be revised so that the hood will not fly up while in action.

Take off the bumpers and mounting brackets. They are heavy and useless. You will have to perform this chore first if you are going to cut the vents described in the bit on brakes.

Take out the inner fender panel (lower rear) in the engine compartment for better ventilation.

It is presumed that you know the rollbar requirements of the SCCA or other sanctioning organizations. They are spelled out in the rules. By all means lean toward the hell-for-strong end of the spectrum when installing one of these good things. The full-cockpit width bar with a brace to the floor is the easiest type to install and yet remain removable. If the car is to be used for nothing but racing you can install the hoop type and brace it to the rear.

Another almost mandatory installation is that of a towbar — unless you have access to a trailer. It is the height of optimism to drive a car to the races — although, one of the premises of amateur sports car racing is that it can be done. Without going into the obvious drawbacks, the driver should arrive at the course in as

The towbar mounting bracket. (A friendly reminder: don't forget to safety-wire that wing nut!)

relaxed a mental state as possible and with as little to do before the race as possible. If he (or the crew) has to worry about converting the automobile from street to racing use in the pits, needless handicap is imposed. And, if luck is against you and some incident makes the car inoperable on the highway, you are stuck. Have a strong set of brackets welded to the front bumper supports (as pointed out in the photo) and buy or build a towbar which fits a standard trailer hitch. If you plan to tow the car for a considerable distance, disconnect the drive shaft at the universal joint or remove it. This will prevent needless wear and tear on the transmission.

IN CONCLUSION

We trust that the tips presented here will serve you in any attempt to further your enjoyment of your Corvette. They are given solely on the basis of personal experience and are not intended to be the final word. Perhaps you will discover additional or varied tricks which will supplant or supplement them. This is also a part of the pleasure of owning and maintaining a fine sports car.

Good motoring and good luck!

AUTOBOOKS WORKSHOP MANUALS

ALFA ROMEO GIULIA 1300, 1600, 1750, 2000 1962-1978 WSM
BMW 1600 1966-1973 WSM
BMW 2000 & 2002 1966-1976 WSM
BMW 2500, 2800, 3.0 & 3.3 1968-1977 WSM
BMW 316, 320, 320i 1975-1977 WSM
BMW 518, 520, 520i 1973-1981 WSM
FIAT 1100, 1100D, 1100R & 1200 1957-1969 WSM
FIAT 124 1966-1974 WSM
FIAT 124 SPORT 1966-1975 WSM
FIAT 125 & 125 SPECIAL 1967-1973 WSM
FIAT 126, 126L, 126 DV, 126/650 & 126/650 DV 1972-1982 WSM
FIAT 127 SALOON, SPECIAL & SPORT, 900, 1050 1971-1981 WSM
FIAT 128 1969-1982 WSM
FIAT 1300, 1500 1961-1967 WSM
FIAT 131 MIRAFIORI 1975-1982 WSM
FIAT 132 1972-1982 WSM
FIAT 500 1957-1973 WSM
FIAT 600, 600D & MULTIPLA 1955-1969 WSM
FIAT 850 1964-1972 WSM
JAGUAR E-TYPE 1961-1972 WSM
JAGUAR MK 1, 2 1955-1969 WSM
JAGUAR S TYPE, 420 1963-1968 WSM
JAGUAR XK 120, 140, 150 MK 7, 8, 9 1948-1961 WSM
LAND ROVER 1, 2 1948-1961 WSM
MERCEDES-BENZ 190 1959-1968 WSM
MERCEDES-BENZ 220/8 1968-1972 WSM
MERCEDES-BENZ 220B 1959-1965 WSM
MERCEDES-BENZ 230 1963-1968 WSM
MERCEDES-BENZ 250 1968-1972 WSM
MERCEDES-BENZ 280 1968-1972 WSM
MG MIDGET TA-TF 1936-1955 WSM
MINI 1959-1980 WSM
MORRIS MINOR 1952-1971 WSM
PEUGEOT 404 1960-1975 WSM
PORSCHE 911 1964-1973 WSM
PORSCHE 911 1970-1977 WSM
RENAULT 16 1965-1979 WSM
RENAULT 8, 10, 1100 1962-1971 WSM
ROVER 3500, 3500S 1968-1976 WSM
SUNBEAM RAPIER, ALPINE 1955-1965 WSM
TRIUMPH SPITFIRE, GT6, VITESSE 1962-1968 WSM
TRIUMPH TR2, TR3, TR3A 1952-1962 WSM
TRIUMPH TR4, TR4A 1961-1967 WSM
VOLKSWAGEN BEETLE 1968-1977 WSM

VELOCEPRESS AUTOMOBILE BOOKS & MANUALS

ABARTH BUYERS GUIDE
AUSTIN-HEALEY 6-CYLINDER WSM
AUSTIN-HEALEY SPRITE & MG MIDGET 1958-1971 WSM
BMW 600 LIMOUSINE FACTORY WSM
BMW 600 LIMOUSINE OWNERS HAND BOOK & SERVICE MANUAL
BMW ISETTA FACTORY WSM
BOOK OF THE CARRERA PANAMERICANA - MEXICAN ROAD RACE
COMPLETE CATALOG OF JAPANESE MOTOR VEHICLES
CORVETTE V8 1955-1962 OWNERS WORKSHOP MANUAL
DIALED IN - THE JAN OPPERMAN STORY
FERRARI 250/GT SERVICE AND MAINTENANCE
FERRARI 308 SERIES BUYER'S AND OWNER'S GUIDE
FERRARI BERLINETTA LUSSO
FERRARI BROCHURES AND SALES LITERATURE 1946-1967
FERRARI BROCHURES AND SALES LITERATURE 1968-1989
FERRARI GUIDE TO PERFORMANCE
FERRARI OPP, MAINTENANCE & SERVICE H/BOOKS 1948-1963
FERRARI OWNER'S HANDBOOK
FERRARI SERIAL NUMBERS PART I - ODD NUMBERS TO 21399
FERRARI SERIAL NUMBERS PART II - EVEN NUMBERS TO 1050
FERRARI SPYDER CALIFORNIA
FERRARI TUNING TIPS & MAINTENANCE TECHNIQUES
HENRY'S FABULOUS MODEL "A" FORD
HOW TO BUILD A FIBERGLASS CAR
HOW TO BUILD A RACING CAR
HOW TO RESTORE THE MODEL 'A' FORD
IF HEMINGWAY HAD WRITTEN A RACING NOVEL
JAGUAR E-TYPE 3.8 & 4.2 WSM
LE MANS 24 (THE BOOK THAT THE FILM WAS BASED ON)
MASERATI BROCHURES AND SALES LITERATURE
MASERATI OWNER'S HANDBOOK
METROPOLITAN FACTORY WSM
MGA & MGB OWNERS HANDBOOK & WSM
OBERT'S FIAT GUIDE
PERFORMANCE TUNING THE SUNBEAM TIGER
PORSCHE 356 1948-1965 WSM
PORSCHE 912 WSM
SOUPING THE VOLKSWAGEN
TRIUMPH TR2, TR3, TR4 1953-1965 WSM
TUNING FOR SPEED (P.E. IRVING)
VEDA ORR'S NEW REVISED HOT ROD PICTORIAL
VOLKSWAGEN TRANSPORTER, TRUCKS, STATION WAGONS WSM
VOLVO 1944-1968 ALL MODELS WSM

BROOKLANDS BOOKS & ROAD TEST PORTFOLIOS (RTP)

AC CARS 1904-2009
ALFA ROMEO 1920-1933 ROAD TEST PORTFOLIO
ALFA ROMEO 1934-1940 ROAD TEST PORTFOLIO
BRABHAM RALT HONDA THE RON TAURANAC STORY
BUGATTI TYPE 10 TO TYPE 40 ROAD TEST PORTFOLIO
BUGATTI TYPE 10 TO TYPE 251 ROAD TEST PORTFOLIO
BUGATTI TYPE 41 TO TYPE 55 ROAD TEST PORTFOLIO
BUGATTI TYPE 57 TO TYPE 251 ROAD TEST PORTFOLIO
DELAHAYE ROAD TEST PORTFOLIO
FERRARI ROAD CARS 1946-1956 ROAD TEST PORTFOLIO
FIAT 500 1936-1972 ROAD TEST PORTFOLIO
FIAT DINO ROAD TEST PORTFOLIO
HISPANO SUIZA ROAD TEST PORTFOLIO
HONDA ST1100/ST1300 PAN EUROPEAN 1990-2002 RTP
JAGUAR MK1 & MK2 ROAD TEST PORTFOLIO
LOTUS CORTINA ROAD TEST PORTFOLIO
MV AGUSTA F4 750 & 1000 1997-2007 ROAD TEST PORTFOLIO
TATRA CARS ROAD TEST PORTFOLIO

VELOCEPRESS MOTORCYCLE BOOKS & MANUALS

AJS SINGLES & TWINS 250cc THRU 1000cc 1932-1948 (BOOK OF)
AJS SINGLES 1955-65 350cc & 500cc (BOOK OF)
AJS SINGLES 1945-60 350cc & 500cc MODELS 16 & 18 (BOOK OF)
ARIEL 1939-1960 4 STROKE SINGLES (BOOK OF)
ARIEL LEADER & ARROW 1958-1964 (BOOK OF)
ARIEL MOTORCYCLES 1933-1951 WSM
ARIEL PREWAR MODELS 1932-1939 (BOOK OF)
BMW M/CYCLES R26 R27 (1956-1967) FACTORY WSM
BMW M/CYCLES R50 R50S R60 R69S (1955-1969) FACTORY WSM
BSA BANTAM (BOOK OF)
BSA ALL FOUR-STROKE SINGLES & V-TWINS 1936-1952 (BOOK OF)
BSA OHV & SV SINGLES - 250cc 1954-1970 (BOOK OF)
BSA OHV & SV SINGLES 1945-54 250-600cc (BOOK OF)
BSA OHV SINGLES 350 & 500cc 1955-1967 (BOOK OF)
BSA PRE-WAR MODELS TO 1939 (BOOK OF)
BSA TWINS 1948-1962 (BOOK OF)
BSA TWINS 1962-1969 (SECOND BOOK OF)
CATALOG OF BRITISH MOTORCYCLES (1951 MODELS)
DOUGLAS PRE-WAR ALL MODELS 1929-1939 (BOOK OF)
DOUGLAS POST-WAR ALL MODELS 1948-1957 FACTORY WSM
DUCATI 160cc, 250cc & 350cc OHC MODELS FACTORY WSM
HONDA 50 ALL MODELS UP TO 1977 INC MONKEY & TRAIL (BOOK OF)
HONDA 90 ALL MODELS UP TO 1966 (BOOK OF)
HONDA MOTORCYCLES 125-150 TWINS C/CS/CB/CA WSM
HONDA MOTORCYCLES 250-305 TWINS C/CS/CB WSM
HONDA MOTORCYCLES C100 SUPER CUB WSM
HONDA MOTORCYCLES C110 SPORT CUB 1962-1969 WSM
HONDA TWINS & SINGLES 50cc THRU 305cc 1960-1966 (BOOK OF)
HONDA TWINS ALL MODELS 125cc THRU 450cc UP TO 1968 (BOOK OF)
INDIAN PONYBIKE, BOY RACER & PAPOOSE ILL PARTS LIST & SALES LIT
LAMBRETTA ALL 125 & 150cc MODELS 1947-1957 (BOOK OF)
LAMBRETTA LI & TV MODELS 1957-1970 (SECOND BOOK OF)
MATCHLESS 350 & 500cc SINGLES 1945-1956 (BOOK OF)
MATCHLESS 350 & 500cc SINGLES 1955-1966 (BOOK OF)
NORTON 1932-1947 (BOOK OF)
NORTON 1938-1956 (BOOK OF)
NORTON DOMINATOR TWINS 1955-1965 (BOOK OF)
NORTON MODELS 19, 50 & ES2 1955-1963 (BOOK OF)
NORTON PREWAR MODELS 1932-1939 (BOOK OF)
NSU QUICKLY ALL MODELS 1953-1963 (BOOK OF)
ROYAL ENFIELD SINGLES & V TWINS 1937-1953 (BOOK OF)
ROYAL ENFIELD SINGLES 1946-1962 (BOOK OF)
ROYAL ENFIELD 736cc INTERCEPTOR FACTORY WSM
ROYAL ENFIELD 250cc & 350cc SINGLES 1958-1966 (SECOND BOOK OF)
SUZUKI 50cc & 80cc UP TO 1966 (BOOK OF)
SUZUKI T10 1963-1967 FACTORY WSM
SUZUKI T20 & T200 1965-1969 FACTORY WSM
TRIUMPH PRE-WAR MOTORCYCLE 1935-1939 (BOOK OF)
TRIUMPH MOTORCYCLES 1937-1951 WSM
TRIUMPH MOTORCYCLES 1945-1955 FACTORY WSM
TRIUMPH TWINS 1956-1969 (BOOK OF)
VELOCETTE ALL SINGLES & TWINS 1925-1970 (BOOK OF)
VESPA 1951-1961 (BOOK OF)
VESPA 125 & 150cc & GS MODELS 1955-1963 (SECOND BOOK OF)
VESPA 90, 125 & 150cc 1963-1972 (THIRD BOOK OF)
VESPA GS & SS 1955-1968 (BOOK OF)
VINCENT MOTORCYCLES 1935-1955 WSM

PLEASE VISIT OUR WEBSITE
www.VelocePress.com
FOR A DETAILED DESCRIPTION
OF ANY OF THESE TITLES

www.VelocePress.com

Please check our website:

www.VelocePress.com

for a complete up-to-date list of available titles

www.ingramcontent.com/pod-product-compliance
Lightning Source LLC
Chambersburg PA
CBHW071953220426
43662CB00009B/1119